HISTORY OF THE PEOPLE
OF THE
UNITED STATES

MATERIALS OF AMERICAN HISTORY SERIES

Editorial Board

Farrar, Straus & Company is preparing a new series of historical materials, primary materials which illustrate the history of every large geographical section and every important historical period in the history of the United States. The series will ultimately include reprints of important historical studies, collections of documents and memoirs, anthologies of classical sources on various historical, economic, and philosophical topics, and important biographies and autobiographies.

John Bach McMaster

HISTORY OF THE PEOPLE

OF THE

UNITED STATES

From the Revolution to the Civil War

Selected and Edited

with an Introduction by

Louis Filler

NOONDAY PRESS

FARRAR, STRAUS & COMPANY   NEW YORK

TABLE OF CONTENTS

McMaster's History:
A People's Heritage

1

It is impressive to realize how wide and deep has been the influence of John Bach McMaster on our visions and views of the American past. Not only was his monumental *History of the People of the United States* generously purchased and attentively read by the public. Not only was it liberally used by history professors and writers on the higher levels of instruction and communication. McMaster went on to prepare, in his striking and original prose, textbooks for the use of primary, grammar, and high school students. These were purchased for schools to the number of two and a half million copies. They informed a generation. Many of the impressions we have—of the disturbed Confederacy following the Revolutionary War, of the quarrels between Federalists and Jeffersonians, of the turmoil attending the War of 1812, and of the Jackson Administrations—many of them come directly out of McMaster's accounts of these eras, or were carried on by his readers and disciples. McMaster's energy and inimitable grasp of detail created portraits and events which historians following him could not resist. So we see the States following the Revolution as McMaster saw them, moving through chaos toward the famous Annapolis Convention which gave birth to the even more famous Constitutional Convention. With McMaster, we see a new government, enigmatically called the Federal Government—to distinguish it from the preceding Confederation—set under way. McMaster carries us on the gaudy quarrels of the 1790's to and through the election of Thomas Jefferson in 1800 and deep into the Nineteenth Century. . . .

How true were McMaster's accounts? This must always be a matter of judgment, of materials, and of philosophy. There have been conscientious studies which "prove" that the United States, under the Articles of Confederation, were by no means in a state of anarchy. Americans, according to this interpretation, *desired* a loose confederation; they feared centralized authority; they preferred states-rights. A majority of them—or, at least, those who had won the war—had just fought it to rid themselves of centralized authority. Historians have "proved" that Aaron Burr was no traitor, that Jefferson was anything they pleased, that the United States Supreme Court had indeed been a danger to democratic institutions, that Andrew Jackson was kind, gentle, just, and very much like Franklin D. Roosevelt.

And so with many other controversial and partisan issues. McMaster's judgments—always sharp and unequivocal and suffused with relevant facts—are all open to debate. What is not debatable is his enthusiasm, and the vivid prose it engenders. McMaster rivets attention, persuades us of the importance of his situations and protagonists, wins us with varied, novel, and story-bearing exposition. The last was not accidental. McMaster often noted in historians he admired—Macaulay, especially—that they were entertaining as well as informative and perceptive. He labored to attain their power of phrase-making and picture-drawing.

2

Behind McMaster's *History* lies one of the great sagas of the American historical profession. It tells how a young, obscure engineering instructor at first from City College in New York, later from what became Princeton University, conceived a project of writing a many-volumed work which would reflect the spirit of a growing, destiny-starred America. The story goes on to tell how he worked through library collections on his own time, without subsidies, without encouragement, poring through old newspapers and other ephemera to learn how the American people themselves, rather than merely their great men, had lived, and struggled, and aspired. McMaster's 622-page Volume One of what became his

History, written entirely in his own hand out of his mountain of notes and his phenomenal memory, was accepted without much enthusiasm by D. Appleton and Company in 1883, but it was resoundingly successful. In the next thirty years, McMaster, now a professor at the University of Pennsylvania, produced seven more volumes to set beside the multi-volumed works of George Bancroft, Francis Parkman, William Hickling Prescott, Henry Adams, James Ford Rhodes, and a few others whose writings are at the base of our knowledge of the American past. Nevertheless, McMaster stands apart from the others on one vital score. Bancroft, Adams, and their peers illuminate our earlier eras and draw us into their ways and concerns, if we will let them. McMaster makes the past seem like the present. His unmistakable creation was a social history which penetrated beyond politics and wars to the constant qualities of family and community. It is these qualities which show McMaster at his best, and which are mainly illustrated in the abstracts from his *History* which follow.

It will be noted that the abstracts describe life in the United States during eras of peace. McMaster found our wars exciting and devoted many pages to them. But, whether he realized it or not, peacetime seemed to him the norm, and it was for such periods that he marshaled his research to give accounts of the growth of American populations and industries, American fads and enthusiasms, inventions, reform movements, social crises and debates, cultural pursuits, travels, geographical sections, and other themes. McMaster was a great nationalist, and tended to believe that America could do no wrong. But it is perhaps significant that his most characteristic chapters should have required tranquil times for richest treatment.

What needs to be noted is that McMaster's social history is not confined to such chapters as are here reproduced; and if these are well received, it might be possible to offer the reader another selection from McMaster's *History,* emphasizing this time not so much the diverting detail of normal—or, at least, peaceful—times, but rather those times of crisis and change.

As a sample, let us examine a page from a momentous day, to indicate that social history was McMaster's instinct, whatever the occasion. It is 1789. There have been warm debates on every aspect of the new government. A new President has been elected.

There is wrangling on the choice of a permanent seat of government: Yorktown, Harrisburg, the town of Peach Bottom. . . . There are public arguments respecting a proper title for the President. Should he be called His Highness, or perhaps His Excellency? Sarcastic critics suggest such titles as High Mightiness, and argue for a "more humble appellation":

> While the House was busy debating by what name the President should be called, Washington was troubled to know in what manner he should behave. He was the first of our long line of Presidents. He had therefore no precedents to guide him in private and public treatment of men. The place was one of great dignity. But just how much dignity was consistent with that republican simplicity which was the boast of the time he did not know. The city was gay. The people affected fashion, and many among them who had enjoyed opulence in the colonial days looked back with some regret on the fine clothes, the hosts of servants, the equipage, and the ceremonial of the royal governors. They would gladly have seen the modest, sad-looking gentleman in black, whom they had raised to the chief place in the land, have a guard at his door, ride out followed by a train of menials, and would have gone, on reception-days, with some pride, through lines of liveried servants to bow at the foot of a very low throne. But the extreme Antifederalists, the men who every election-day denounced aristocracy and the well-born, begrudged him even the fine house and the fine furniture already given him by Congress, and cursed the vandals who were levelling the ramparts of the old fort to make way for a new mansion, yet more costly and spacious than the old. Neither party was to be offended. He did not wish by a too great simplicity to lay himself open to the jibes and sarcasms of that influential class whose after-dinner talk was, as Jefferson complained, monarchical to a shocking degree. He did not wish, by a too great exclusiveness, to call forth the reproaches of those who bitterly bemoaned what they termed the decline of republican spirit. In 1775 they were accustomed, they said, to hear the phrase, *"vox populi, vox dei."* Now they were daily told that democracies were a volcano. Then it was, "the natural equality of mankind"; now it was, "the well-born." Then it was, "sons of liberty"; now it was, "State demagogues." Then it was, "our excellent State constitutions"; now it was, "the monster with thirteen heads." Fifteen years before, the expression was, "the free and United States of America"; now it was, "the national Government."

So the new national government got underway. It moved among stormy crises which make ridiculous John Fiske's famous old notion that the period of the Confederacy had been uniquely a "Critical Period." The early national period continued critical throughout Washington's, and then Adams', Jefferson's and Madison's administrations. There were plots to separate New England from the United States, possibly taking New York into a new New England Confederation. The country dragged on into its unhappy war with Great Britain, in 1812. Let McMaster's inexhaustible researches take us, for a moment, into one locale which responded to the burning of the Capitol in 1814:

> The example thus set by New York was closely followed in Philadelphia. There, when it was known that Washington had been captured, the people met in the State Yard, chose a committee, organized for defence, formed a military association, and, under such names as the Philadelphia Volunteers, the Hamilton Guards, the Washington Guards, the Yankee Guards, the Rifle Corps, began active drilling. Calls were made for shipwrights and boat-builders to make gun-carriages; for draymen to form a company of artillery; for guns, blankets, clothing, and stores; and for volunteers to aid in throwing up works of defence on the hills bordering the west bank of the Schuylkill. There, too, the response was prompt, and in a few days the artists, the cordwainers, the cabinet-makers, the brick-makers, the printers, and the patriotic young men under twenty were applying to the committee to assign them a day. The people of color were reminded of what Pennsylvania had done to promote the abolition of slavery, and were summoned to defend her. The physicians were asked to be ready in the event of a battle to hurry to the field. "Pious men, whose conscientious views would deter them from joining other corps" made up of irreligious men, were urged to form one of their own kind. As fast as the citizens responded, the committee would form them into companies, each in charge of a captain, name some place of rendezvous, and select a day upon which the teachers or the Sons of Erin, the friendly aliens or the victuallers, or whoever they might be, would assemble at five in the morning with lunch in a knapsack or a handkerchief, march out to Fairmount or Grey's Ferry, and fall to work. At ten, by order of the quartermaster, the drum would beat for grog, when each captain would hurry to the tent and receive the liquor for his company. At noon the drum would beat for

dinner, and the captains attend a second time for grog. At five o'clock all work stopped, and at that hour "it is hoped," said the quartermaster in his rules, that "for the honor of the cause we are engaged in, every man will retire sober." Before the works were finished fifteen thousand men had labored on them one day each.

3

From time to time, McMaster took stock of where his studies were leading him. His faith in American democracy enabled him to view its less inspiring episodes with serenity. Americans, he felt, were bound to emerge from shabby circumstances stronger than ever. The "riotous" career of the Know-Nothings, the political connivings of the Founding Fathers, the hectic adventures of Americans in finance, all left him with a strong conviction that "all questions of great importance are finally settled . . . by the hard common sense of the people. . . ." * But it was in his *History* that the gusty nature of his research had largest fulfillment. He needed its scope, its outpouring of famous leaders and pretenders, of quaint and extraordinary incidents, of enterprises and programs, to develop, illustrating in his own way a manifest destiny which he sensed in his country. McMaster, close examination reveals, was, besides a great patriot, a racist, as were many of his contemporaries: McKinley, Theodore Roosevelt, Woodrow Wilson. They saw America as the proud creation of a breed of people headed by the Anglo-Saxon pioneers: individualistic, courageous, aggressive, indomitable. McMaster opposed pensions for professors. He was, in his own time, opposed to the social welfare program of the Populists. Though slight of frame and almost meek in outward appearance, there was a lion of militant personality hidden in him. His achievement was that his personal preferences and attitudes did not significantly influence the truth-seeking direction of his history. He wrote with ruthless regard for the facts; his errors were errors of detail and interpretation which were inevitable in a man who had assumed a giant's taks. The little men could criticize this detail or that detail; they could add little more, for the most part, than footnotes to the master's work.

* See his *The Political Depravity of the Founding Fathers, and Other Essays* (Noonday Press, 1964), p. 252.

The *History* was his major achievement. His essays help us in appraising its purposes and dimensions. Other of his large-scale writings were too little digested, or (as with his history of American participation in World War I) too rudely partisan to be enlightening. But his overall accomplishment offers unique runways into American life and tendencies. It is inspiring in reminding us of what one individual can accomplish, automation or no automation. In his own times, social philosophers complained that Darwinism had demeaned man, and that the industrial revolution had robbed him of his creativity.

We need more than McMaster, today; we need a world view that his own view of life simply did not comprehend. The French, the English, the Spanish, and other Europeans were, to him, somewhere far off beyond American ramparts. Other continents were all but abstractions to him, especially in modern times. McMaster is not enough. But in an educational world which has dignified "Outlines of American History," creating chaos in student minds, offering them dessicated trifles as reality, with the goal no more than worthless grades on imperceptive examinations, we very much need McMaster. He teaches us that history is, indeed, life; and having understood our lives and ourselves better, we can go on to understand our neighbors. Historical insight is indivisible. Social history is not gossip, it is not the random data of "Believe It or Not": it is the base of society. On it we can build our own vital social and political structures. This McMaster once taught us. It is time to relearn this fact.

Antioch College   —LOUIS FILLER
June, 1964

JOHN BACH McMASTER: A BRIEF CHRONOLOGY

1852—Born June 29, Brooklyn, New York.

1872—Graduated City College in New York, and served the year following as an instructor in engineering.

1873—Made a survey of the battlefield of Winchester for General Philip H. Sheridan, who was writing his memoirs.

1874—Practiced engineering in New York.

1875—Published *Bridge and Tunnel Centres*.

1876—Published *High Masonry Dams*. He completed a ms., "The Struggle of Man with Nature," which he later destroyed.

1877-1883—Taught engineering at the College of New Jersey.

1878—Headed a Princeton scientific expedition to the Bad Lands of Wyoming, on the trail of fossil remains. His trip excited his desire to capture the American spirit on paper.

1881—Volume One of *A History of the People of the United States*.

1883—Accepted professorship at the University of Pennsylvania.

1885—Published *The Life, Memoirs, Military Career and Death of General U. S. Grant. With War Anecdotes and Freely Drawn Extracts from His Autobiography*.

1887—Married. Published *Benjamin Franklin as a Man of Letters*.

1896—Published *With the Fathers: Studies in the History of the United States*, a major selection of his essays. (Pirated) *The Origin, Meaning and Application of the Monroe Doctrine*, one of many reprints of his lengthy *New York Times* article which defended American foreign policy.

1902—Published *Daniel Webster*.

1903—Published lectures at Western Reserve University under title of *The Acquisition of Political, Social and Industrial Rights of Man in America*.

1913—Volume Eight of the *History* published.

1918—Published *The Life and Times of Stephen Girard*. . . .

1918-1920—Published *The United States in the World War*.

1920—Retired as Emeritus Professor.

1927—Published *A History of the People of the United States during Lincoln's Administration*.

1932—Died, May 24, Darien, Connecticut.

1

1784: The New Nation

THE subject of my narrative is the history of the people of the United States of America from the close of the war for independence down to the opening of the war between the States. In the course of this narrative much, indeed, must be written of wars, conspiracies, and rebellions; of presidents, of congresses, of embassies, of treaties, of the ambition of political leaders in the senate-house, and of the rise of great parties in the nation. Yet the history of the people shall be the chief theme. At every stage of the splendid progress which separates the America of Washington and Adams from the America in which we live, it shall be my purpose to describe the dress, the occupations, the amusements, the literary canons of the times; to note the changes of manners and morals; to trace the growth of that humane spirit which abolished punishment for debt, which reformed the discipline of prisons and of jails, and which has, in our own time, destroyed slavery and lessened the miseries of dumb brutes. Nor shall it be less my aim to recount the manifold improvements which, in a thousand ways, have multiplied the conveniences of life and ministered to the happiness of our race; to describe the rise and progress of that long series of mechanical inventions and discoveries which is now the admiration of the world, and our just pride and boast; to tell how, under the benign influence of liberty and peace, there sprang up, in the course of a single century, a prosperity unparalleled in

the annals of human affairs; how, from a state of great poverty and feebleness, our country grew rapidly to one of opu-
lence and power; how her agriculture and her manufactures
flourished together; how, by a wise system of free education
and a free press, knowledge was disseminated, and the arts
and sciences advanced; how the ingenuity of her people became fruitful of wonders far more astonishing than any of
which the alchemists had ever dreamed.

Such a mingling of social with political history is necessary to a correct understanding of the peculiar circumstances
under which our nation was formed and grew up. Other
people in other times have become weary of their rulers, have
thrown off the yoke, have come out of the house of bondage
and set up that form of government which has always been
thought the freest and most perfect. But our ancestors were
indeed a highly favored people. They were descended from
the most persevering, the most energetic, the most thrifty of
races. They enjoyed the highest form of civilization; their
climate was salubrious; their soil rich; their country boundless; they were hampered by no traditions; they were surrounded by no nations of whom they stood in fear. Almost
alone, in a new land, they were free to work out their own
form of government in accordance with their own will. The
consequence has been such a moral and social advancement
as the world has never seen before. The Americans who,
toward the close of 1783, celebrated with bonfires, with
cannon, and with bell-ringing, the acknowledgment of independence and the return of peace, lived in a very different
country from that with which their descendants are familiar.
Indeed, could we, under the potent influence of some magician's drugs, be carried back through one hundred years, we
should find ourselves in a country utterly new to us. Rip
Van Winkle, who fell asleep when his townsmen were throwing up their hats and drinking their bumpers to good King
George, and awoke when a generation that knew him not
was shouting the names of men and parties unknown to him,
did not find himself in a land more strange. The area of the
republic would shrink to less than half its present extent.
The number of the States would diminish to thirteen, nor

would many of them be contained in their present limits or exhibit their present appearance. Vast stretches of upland, which are now an endless succession of wheat-fields and corn-fields and orchards, would appear overgrown with dense for-ests abandoned to savage beasts and yet more savage men. The hamlets of a few fishermen would mark the sites of wealthy havens now bristling with innumerable masts, and the great cities themselves would dwindle to dimensions scarce exceeding those of some rude settlement far to the west of the Colorado river. Of the inventions and discoveries which abridge distance, which annihilate time, which extend com-merce, which aid agriculture, which save labor, which trans-mit speech, which turn the darkness of the night into the brilliancy of the day, which alleviate pain, which destroy dis-ease, which lighten even the infirmities of age, not one ex-isted. Fulton was still a portrait-painter, Fitch and Rumsey had not yet begun to study the steam-engine, Whitney had not yet gone up to college. Howe and Morse, M'Cormick and Fairbanks, Goodyear and Colt, Dr. Morton and Dr. Bell, were yet to be born.

By the treaty which secured the independence of the colonies, the boundaries of the region given up by the mother country were clearly defined. The territory ceded stretched from the Atlantic Ocean westward to the banks of the Missis-sippi, and from a line running along the great lakes on the north it spread southward to the thirty-first parallel and the southern border of Georgia. This vast tract was parcelled out among the thirteen original States. Of the thirteen, seven had well-defined boundaries; of the remaining six, some laid claim to lands since given to other States, while a few would content themselves with no limits short of the waters of the Mississippi river.

But, though the Fourth of July orators then boasted that their country extended over fifteen hundred miles in length, and spread westward across plains of marvellous fertility into regions yet unexplored by man, they had but to look about them to see that the States were indeed but little better than a great wilderness. A narrow line of towns and hamlets ex-tended, with many breaks, along the coast from the province

of Maine to Georgia. Maine was still owned by Massachusetts, and did not contain one hundred thousand souls. Portland existed, then Falmouth, and along the shore were a few
fishers' cots, built of rough-hewn logs, and thatched with sea-
weed. But an almost unbroken solitude lay between Portland and the St. Lawrence. In New Hampshire a few hardy
adventurers had marked out the sites of villages in the White
Mountains. In New York, Albany was settled, and Schenectady ; but the rich valleys through which the Mohawk and the
Genesee flow down to join the Hudson and the lake, were the
hunting-grounds of the Oneidas, the Mohawks, the Cayugas.
In Pennsylvania, dense forests and impassable morasses covered that region where rich deposits of iron and of coal have
since produced the Birmingham of America. In Virginia,
a straggling village or two was to be found about the head-
waters of the Potomac and the James. Beyond the Blue
Ridge, Daniel Boone was fighting the Cherokees in the canebrakes of Kentucky. Some villages of log huts surrounded
by stockades were rising on the fertile plains of western
Tennessee. A handful of pioneers had settled at Natchez.
Pittsburgh was a military post. St. Louis was begun, but the
very name of the village was unknown to nine tenths of the
Americans. So late as 1795, Cincinnati consisted of ninety-
five log cabins and five hundred souls. In truth, that splendid section of our country drained by the Ohio and the Tennessee was one vast solitude. Buffaloes wandered in herds
over the rich plains now the granaries of Europe. Forests
of oak and sycamore grew thick on the site of many great
and opulent cities whose population now exceeds that of Virginia during the revolution, and whose names are spoken
in the remotest corner of the civilized world. No white
man had yet beheld the source of the Mississippi river.
Of the country beyond the Mississippi little more was
known than of the heart of Africa. Now and then some
weather-beaten trapper came from it to the frontiers of
the States with stories of great plains as level as the floor,
where the grass grew higher than the waist, where the
flowers were more beautiful than in the best kept garden,
where trees were never seen, and where the Indians still

looked upon the white man as a god. But this country lay
far to the west of the frontier, and the frontier was wilder
then than Wyoming is now. There the white man lived in
an unending war with the red man.

The opinion which many careful and just-minded persons
of our time have formed touching the Indians of whom the
settlers in the border-land then stood in constant dread, is a
singular mixture of truth and romance. Time and absence
have softened all that is vile and repulsive in his character,
and left in full relief all that is good and alluring. We are
in no danger of being tomahawked. We are not terrified by
his war-whoop. An Indian in his paint and feathers is now a
much rarer show than a Bengal tiger or a white bear from the
Polar sea. Of the fifty millions of human beings scattered
over the land, not five millions have ever in their lives looked
upon an Indian. We are therefore much more disposed to
pity than to hate. But, one hundred years ago, there were to
be found, from Cape Ann to Georgia, few men who had not
many times in their lives seen numbers of Indians, while thousands could be found scattered through every State, whose
cattle had been driven off, and whose homes had been laid
in ashes by the braves of the Six Nations, who had fought
with them from behind trees and rocks, and carried the scars
of wounds received in hand-to-hand encounters. In every
city were to be seen women who had fled at the dead of
night from their burning cabins; who had, perhaps, witnessed the destruction of Schenectady; or were by a merciful
Providence spared in the massacre of the Minisink; whose hus-
bands had gone down in the universal slaughter of Wyoming;
or whose children had, on that terrible day when Brant came
into Orange county, stood in the door of the school-house when
the master was dragged out, when their playmates were scalped,
when their aprons were marked with the black mark which,
like the blood upon the door-posts, a second time staid the hand
of the Angel of Death. The opinion which such men and
women held of the noble red man was, we may be sure, very
different from those current among the present generation, and
formed on no better authority than the novels of Cooper, and
the lives of such warriors as Red Jacket and Brant.

Of the true character of the Indian it is difficult to give any notion to those who are acquainted with it only as it appears exalted or debased in the pages of fiction. In him were united in a most singular manner all the vices and all the arts which form the weapons, offensive and defensive, of the weak, with many of those high qualities which are always found associated with courage and strength. He was, essentially, a child of Nature, and his character was precisely such as circumstances made it. His life was one long struggle for food. His daily food depended not on the fertility of the soil or the abundance of the crops, but on the skill with which he used his bow; on the courage with which he fought, single-handed, the largest and fiercest of beasts; on the quickness with which he tracked, and the cunning with which he outwitted the most timid and keen-scented of creatures. His knowledge of the habits of animals surpassed that of Audubon. The shrewd devices with which he snared them would have elicited the applause of Ulysses; the clearness of his vision excelled that of the oldest sailor; the sharpness of his hearing was not equalled by that of the deer. Men of a less-gifted race were astounded at the rapidity with which he followed the most obscure trail over the most difficult ground; at the perfection with which he imitated the bark of the wolf, the hoot of the owl, the whistle of the whippoorwill; at the cat-like tread with which, over beds of autumn-leaves and heaps of dried twigs, he walked to the very side of the grazing deer. Nor was his success in the hunt without its effect. Many of the qualities of the creatures he hunted were, as he believed, imbibed with their blood. Courage, such as enables a man to go through a campaign or a battle with credit, such as makes him first in the breach and last in the retreat, and sends him, with a measured step and cool head, to the cannon's mouth, the brave possessed in the highest degree. Nor did he lack a more exalted fortitude. While he underwent the most excruciating torture the ingenuity of his enemies could devise, while his ears were being lopped off, while his nose was being slit, while slices of flesh were being cut from his body and the bleeding wounds smeared with hot ashes, while his feet were roasting, while his limbs were being torn with not splinters, while the flames leaped high about him, he shouted his death-song with a steady voice till his tormentors plucked out his tongue or brained him with a tomahawk.

Yet this man whose courage was unquestionable, was given to the dark and crooked ways which are the resort of the cowardly and the weak. Much as he loved war, the fair and open fight had no charms for him. To his mind it was madness to take the scalp of an enemy at the risk of his own, when he might waylay him in an ambuscade, or shoot him with a gun or an arrow from behind a tree. He was never so happy as when, at the dead of night, he roused his sleeping enemies with an unearthly yell, and massacred them by the light of their burning homes. Cool and brave men who have heard that whoop, have left us a striking testimony of its nature; how that no number of repetitions could strip it of its terrors; how that, to the very last, at the sound of it the blood curdled, the heart ceased to beat, and a strange paralysis seized upon the body. The contrast between the savage on the war-path and the savage in his wigwam was indeed striking. When the hatchet was dug up, when the war-paint was put on, when the peace-pipe was broken, the idle, shiftless savage was all activity. Patient of hunger, patient of cold, he would march all day through the snow with the thermometer far below zero; and at night, rolled in buffalo robes, go hungry to sleep. But when the chase was over, when the war was done, and the peace-pipe smoked out, he abandoned himself to debauchery and idleness. To sleep all day in a wigwam of painted skins, filthy and blackened with smoke, adorned with scalps, and hung with tomahawks and arrows, to dance in the shine of the new moon to music made from the skin of snakes, to tell stories of witches and evil spirits, to gamble, to sing, to jest, to boast of his achievements in war, and to sit with a solemn gravity at the councils of his chief, constituted his most serious employment. His squaw was his slave. With no more affection than a coyote feels for its mate, he brought her to his wigwam that she might gratify the basest of his passions and administer to his wants. It was Starlight or Cooing Dove that brought the wood for his fire and the water for his drink, that ploughed the field and

sowed the maize. The bead-work which adorned his mocca
sins, the porcupine quills which set off his cloak, were ar
ranged by her hands. When he travelled she trudged along
with the pappoose on her back beside the led-horse that carried the wigwam and the few pots and jars of sun-baked clay.

The mental attainments of the Indian were quite of a piece
with his character. His imagination was singularly strong,
his reason singularly weak. He was as superstitious as a Hot-
tentot negro and as unreasonable as a child. When a long
succession of fasts and gorgings, when bad food and fire-
water had done their worst, he awoke screaming from his
dreams to assert that a wolf had sat upon his breast, that he
had been in the clutches of Pauguk. Every twig that fell
upon him in the forest was an omen. The simplest occurrences of life were full of significance. If he were sick some
enemy had brought it on him. If misfortune overtook him
it was the work of a medicine man or a witch whose anger
he had excited. Then it was that, in his hour of need, he
betook himself to the magic of his medicine bag and the skill
of the medicine man, and, during incantations and strange
mutterings and exorcisms, was beaten and bruised from head
to foot and finally made to believe that a toad or a bright
stone had been taken out of him, and was the cause of his
ills. Gay colors pleased him beyond expression. Over a red
blanket or a patchwork quilt the sedate and dignified savage
would go into raptures of delight. To possess it he would
gladly part with a bundle of skins which exceeded it many
times in value, or with a hundred bushels of Indian corn.

Thus hemmed in on the east by the waters of the ocean,
and on the west by a crafty and ever vigilant foe, were scattered the inhabitants of the thirteen States. Unfortunately
the precise number of the population cannot now be ascertained
with any high degree of certainty. But from such information as we have, it is safe to say that, in 1784, the number
could not have been far from three millions and a quarter. It
has been estimated that at the opening of the war there were
in the country, both white and black, 2,750,000 souls.* Five

---

* This estimate is given by De Bow, as made from reliable sources. Vol. iii,
p. 404.

years later these, in spite of the ravages of war, had increased, it is thought, to 2,945,000.* The first periodical counting of the people was made in 1790, and, from the returns then sent in, it appears that the population was 3,929,214 human beings † —less than are now to be found in the single State of New York, but a little over three times the number crowded within the city of New York, and not many more than a third of the number of the men who every four years cast their votes for a president.‡ We may, therefore, with confidence declare that when peace was announced the population of the country did not vary far from three and a quarter millions.

Nor were these by any means equally distributed. More were in the southern than in the northern States. Virginia alone contained a fifth, Pennsylvania a ninth, while the five states of Maryland, Virginia, the two Carolinas, and Georgia, counted as citizens almost one half of all the English-speaking people in America.# The reason is obvious. The southern colonies had long before the revolution become renowned as the seat of a lucrative agriculture. Nowhere else could such tobacco be raised as was annually grown on the banks of the Rappahannock, the Potomac, and the James. The best rice in the English market came from the swamps of the Carolinas. Georgia was already famous for pitch, for indigo, for tar. New England, on the other hand, produced scarce enough corn and rye for the needs of her citizens. Beyond a few stately trees,

---

* An estimate of the white population of the States made in 1783, for purposes of assessment, gives the number as 2,389,300. American Remembrancer, Part ii, 1783, p. 64.

† See United States Census for 1870.

‡ The popular vote in the presidential election in the fall of 1880 was, all told, 9,192,595.

The population of the States in 1790, soon increased to fifteen by the admission of Kentucky and of Vermont, was—

Connecticut	= 237,946.	New Jersey	= 184,139.
Delaware	= 59,094.	New York	= 340,120.
Georgia	= 82,548.	North Carolina	= 393,751.
Kentucky	= 73,677.	Rhode Island	= 68,825.
Maryland	= 319,728.	South Carolina	= 240,073.
Massachusetts	= 378,787.	Vermont	= 85,425.
Maine	= 96,540.	Virginia	= 747,610.
New Hampshire	= 141,885.	Pennsylvania	= 434,373.

suitable for masts for his Majesty's ships of war, the eastern
States grew nothing the mother country wished to buy.*
There men built ships, sailed the ocean, caught fish, extracted
oil from the blubber of whales, put up great warehouses, and
kept great shops; but found the climate of a country where
snow lay deep on the ground for five months out of twelve too
rigorous for profitable farming. That gigantic system of manufactures which has since made every stream and every river of
Massachusetts and Connecticut an endless succession of mills,
and covered the land with factory towns, had not begun to
exist. Every housewife spun her own flax and made her own
linen. Boston and New York were, indeed, the great centres
of commerce; but the packets that entered the Narrows, or
drew up at the long dock heavy laden, went back to Liverpool
freighted with skins which the traders of the new world had
purchased from the Indians for bushels of periwinkle shells
or strings of wampum. Thus, under the favoring circumstances of climate and soil, agriculture flourished, and wealth
and population rapidly increased in all the States south of
Virginia, but especially in the Old Dominion. Nor is it to
be forgotten that probably one seventh of the population was
in slavery.

Diverse as the inhabitants of the States thus were in occupations, they were not less diverse in opinions, in customs, and
habits. Though lately united in a common league against a
common foe, though now living, nominally, under a common
government, many causes conspired to keep them anything
but a united people. Differences of race, differences of na-
tionality, of religious opinions, of manners, of tastes, even of

---

* New England pine-trees were famous, and were guarded with great care.
Foresters were appointed by the Crown to range the woods, pick out such lofty
pines as were suitable for masts for men-of-war, and mark them with a royal
brand. Many years after the present century had come in, loggers in the forests
of Maine continued to find, here and there, magnificent trees, which had been set
apart for the use of King George's navy, and which still bore upon their trunks
the marks of the royal axemen. James Allen, a noted poet of ante-revolutionary
days, writing of the supplies England drew from America, says:

"E'en the tall mast, that bears your flag on high,
    Grew in our soil, and ripened in our sky."

To cut any tree that was to be so used was a trespass. Bancroft, Hist. of U. S.,
vol. iii, p. 391.

speech, were still distinctly marked. New England had been settled by the Puritans, and there the levelling spirit, the stern theology, the rigid and straitlaced morality were as unyielding as ever. Virginia had been settled by the cavaliers, and was still the stronghold of aristocracy, of social refinement and episcopacy. In New York the Dutch element prevailed and the language of Holland was very generally spoken. Maryland was the home of the English Catholics; Pennsylvania of the Germans and the Quakers. Along the Delaware river were flourishing settlements of Swedes. In the Carolinas might be found many villages where the inhabitants were all Highlanders, or all Huguenots.*

In truth, the traveller who at that day, prompted by curiosity to see the youngest republic, had the hardihood to endure the discomforts and dangers of a journey over the bad roads and through the almost desolate lands of the States, saw nothing more noticeable to put down in his journal than the marked difference of manners, of customs, of taste and refinement which prevailed in the country. Such a traveller usually landed in Boston after a seven weeks' voyage in a packet, and found himself in a city which then ranked third in importance, but would now be thought mean and poor. Indeed, carried back to the close of the revolution Boston would present a strange contrast to its present appearance. But for a few time-worn landmarks yet remaining a Bostonian of to-day would seek in vain to recognise the provincial town of 1784 in the great city of 1882. He would not be able to find his own office, his own house, the street in which he lives. Cows were pastured where the houses of a dense population now crowd each other for room. Boys played ball in streets now noisy with the rush of traffic. Faneuil Hall, the Old South, the Old State-House, and a few other relics of ancient times still exist; but so many houses of that time are gone, or to go, that, before another generation has passed away, Old Boston will be known in tradition only. The city in 1784 stood on the three hills which gave to it the second name of Trimoun-

---

* The Highlanders came over in ship-loads after the suppression of the rebellions of 1715 and 1745. Ramsay's History of South Carolina, vol. i, p. 11. The Huguenots, Ramsay says, came over after the revocation of the edict of Nantes.

tain and contained, all told, fifteen thousand souls. There
was then no bridge over Charles river, and, when the tides
were up, the neck being entirely submerged, it often happened that the town was cut off from all connection with the
mainland.* The importance of a bridge was quite manifest,
and the matter was carefully discussed in the taverns and
coffee-houses by all classes, till three opinions prevailed. Many
of the better educated who had travelled far for that day,
and whose knowledge of the applied sciences was, therefore,
above question, held that it was quite impossible to build a
bridge because of the great depth of the water in the channel
of Charles river. Others of a bolder turn of mind asserted
that the depth of the water could offer no insurmountable obstacle, but that the ice of the first winter would surely carry
away the bridge however stout. But the merchants depre-
cated the idea, and proved from statistics drawn from the
customs that such a structure would be highly injurious to
navigation. It was not till 1786 that the river was spanned
by a bridge.† In the mean time a rude ferry-boat plied between the North End and Charlestown.‡

The streets of the city were laid out with no regularity,
and were given names which, either from their English associations or the coarseness of the times they recalled, were, by
a more refined generation, gradually changed. George street
has thus become Hancock street; King has been changed to

---

* The neck seems to have been quite a barrier to the daily travel between
Boston and Roxbury. Thomas, who had often been over it, says: "There was
no bridge then, and at very high tides the neck by which the peninsula on which
the town is built is connected with the main-land, was sometimes overflowed."
Reminiscences of the Last Sixty-five Years, S. E. Thomas, p. 14. "Within the
recollection of persons now living, the water has been known to stand up to
the knees of horses in the season of full tides at some places on the road on the
neck." Drake, Landmarks of Boston, p. 419.

† The building of the bridge was looked upon as a great feat of engineering.
Indeed, Cox, the mechanic who built it, made such a reputation by his work that
he was called over to Ireland to build the bridge at Londonderry. He was loudly
praised for using on the Irish structure American timber and workmen. For a
description of the Charlestown bridge, see Boston Gazette, June 6, 1786. For
the ceremonies of the opening of the bridge, see Boston Gazette, or the New
York Gazette, June 6, 1786. An ode written for the occasion, June 17, 1786,
is printed in American Museum, February, 1787.

‡ Thomas's Reminiscences of the Last Sixty-five Years, p. 14.

State ; Queen to Court ; Marlborough to Washington. What was once Black Horse lane is now Prince street; Cow lane is now High street ; Frog lane is now Orange street; Hog alley is Avery street; Longacre has become Tremont street; Love lane has been changed to Tileston; Pond to Bedford; Paddy's alley to North Centre; Flounder lane is now merged in the south end of Broad street.*

The carriage-way along these narrow lanes and alleys was unpaved. The sidewalks or footways were unflagged. Each was, in the language of the time, pitched with large pebbles, and the footway was marked off from the carriage-way by a line of posts and a gutter, after the manner of many old English towns. The roads were such as would now excite the indignation of a country newspaper. The pebbles were ill-laid and ill-kept. Yet travellers admitted the road was as good as could then be found in many parts of London, and the horseman who galloped over it was fined to the amount of three shillings and fourpence. As to the houses which lined the streets on either side, they were, in the older portion of the city, mean and squalid. Built entirely of wood, with unpainted weatherboard sides and shingle roofs surmounted by ugly wooden railings, within which, every washing-day, shirts and petticoats flapped in the wind, they contrasted strongly with the better class of dwellings on the west side of town.† There the streets were neater. There the houses of brick with Corinthian pilasters up the front, and columns of the same order supporting the porch, and handsome entrances to which led up a long flight of sandstone steps, stood back in little gardens dense with English elms and shrubs. Honeysuckles twined round the porch and high damask roses grew under the windows.

The furniture in these dwellings was often imported from England. The side-boards were heavy with articles of porce-

---

* An interesting account of the Boston of the revolution may be read in Drake's Landmarks of Boston. So, also, in the Memoirs of Josiah Quincy; Life of Dr. John Warren ; Henry Wansey's Excursion in the United States of North America in the Summer of 1794 ; and in A Description of Boston : With a View of the Town of Boston, finely engraved. Columbian Magazine, December, 1787.

† Henry Wansey's Excursion to the United States of North America in the Summer of 1794, p. 39.

lain and china, many of them of the celebrated Wedgwood
ware, whereon blue lovers walked by the side of blue waters
and blue deer lay down to rest in the shade of blue trees.
The crockery that adorned the table gave evidence of the
good taste of the lady of the house, and not seldom was mingled with silver plate and cut-glass articles such as the épergne
Josiah Quincy saw broken at a dinner in Governor Hancock's
banqueting room.* In the corners of the rooms, or on the
landing of the stairs, stood the high clocks of English make,
many of which yet remain to attest the excellence of the
manufacture. Some were surmounted by an allegorical representation of Time. Others had a moving disk to illustrate
the phases of the moon and show when it was crescent, when
in the second quarter, and when full. Still others at the
final stroke of every hour chimed forth a tune which, when
the Sabbath came round, was such a one as our grandfathers
sang to their hymns in meeting. There were high cande-
labra to be drawn about the room on rollers, and huge fireplaces adorned with scripture tiles whose rudeness excited the
disgust of Franklin, and brass andirons that shone like gold.
On the walls were pictures by the brush of Copley or West,
or engravings such as Trumbull copied in the library at Cambridge.†

The library was a strange assortment of good books and
books so gone out of fashion that no second-hand dealer will
buy them. Huge volumes, long since out of print, and now
to be found, covered with dust, on the back shelves of public libraries, were then high in favor. Among the sober
and sedate readers of Boston the puritanical taste was yet
strong. The delightful novels of Richardson, of Fielding, of
Smollett, and of Sterne found no place on their shelves.

---

* One of the best descriptions of the interiors of the Boston houses of that
day is in the Life of Dr. John Warren. See, also, Life of Josiah Quincy.

† Colored engravings vilely executed were then the fashion. Among the most
popular were "Joseph Interpreting," "Pharaoh's Cup Found," and "Apollo and
the Muses on Mount Parnassus." Two others, often to be seen in the parlors of
the well-to-do, were "African Slave Trade" and "African Hospitality." Each
represented a scene on the African coast. In the one a band of negroes were
being torn from their families and dragged to a ship. In the other, a band of
negroes were struggling to save shipwrecked mariners. See Life of Warren.

Reading was a more serious business. "The Lives of the Martyrs; or, The Dreadful Effects of Popery," stood side by side with Vattel's "Law of Nations" and Watts's "Improvement of the Mind." There might have been seen Young's "Night Thoughts," Anson's "Voyages," Lucas on "Happiness," Rollin's "Ancient History," "The Pilgrim's Progress," "The Letters of Junius," "The Spectator," but not the works of the hated author of "Taxation no Tyranny." If the owner had a taste for politics, and there were few who had not, no small space on the shelves was taken up with lampoons, with caricatures, with poems such as that in which Hopkinson celebrated the Battle of the Kegs, and pamphlets such as those in which Otis defended so ably the cause of the colonies, and Hamilton silenced the Westchester Farmer.

Uninviting as such a collection would now be thought, their contents were familiar not only to the master, but also to the lady of the house who, despite her many household cares, found much time for reading. The young woman of that day generally received her early education at home, or at the school taught by the minister of the parish and his wife, passed thence to some school kept in Boston, and came back to practice the more homely duties of a housewife. She learned embroidery and could draw and paint; knew less of novels and more of receipt-books than her descendants; knew little of French, nothing of German, and never went to a play in her life. Many a young damsel passed from girlhood to womanhood without ever having looked within the covers of Shakespeare or Sheridan, without ever having attended a dance, and could not tell whether the ace of spades was black or white, or if the king outranked the knave. Her musical acquirements were not such as her granddaughters would consider deserving of more than a smile. Her favorite instruments were the spinet and the harpsichord, instruments which, with the sombre and plaintive melodies once sung to their music, have long ago gone out of fashion.

The less austere, however, indulged in a round of festivities such as excited the horror of their more rigid neighbors. Their time was spent in dispensing hospitality to strangers, in paying and receiving calls, in attending quilting parties and spinning-matches, and, once a fortnight, in going to the public assemblies in Concert Hall where the minuet and country dance still held the floor. But the most fashionable of entertainments were the dinners after the English fashion, where the fun and jollity were prolonged till the candles had long been lighted, and where, after the ladies had withdrawn, discussions were held on politics, on religion, on the topics of the day, over rare vintages of Madeira whose excellence was acknowledged by all.

The mean appearance of the houses in Old Boston was, to some extent, relieved by the rich display of painted and sculptured signs which adorned the front of the taverns and stores. The numbering of shops and houses had not come into fashion, and every business street was an endless succession of golden balls, of blue gloves, of crowns and sceptres, dogs and rainbows, elephants and horseshoes. They served sometimes as advertisements of the business, sometimes merely as designations of the shops which were indicated popularly and in the newspapers by their signs. The custom still lingers among opticians, glove-makers, boot-makers, furriers, and barbers. But we are now accustomed to regard the sign as bearing a direct relation to the character of the business it advertises. We should never seek for eye-glasses in a shop over whose entrance hangs a gilt boot, nor inquire for gloves in a shop before whose door stands an Indian in war-paint and feathers. One hundred years ago no such relation was understood to exist, and it was not thought remarkable that Philip Freeman should keep his famous book-store at the " Blue Glove," on Union street. From the notices given in the newspapers of the time we may justly conclude that the goods offered for sale in the shops, and designated often as " men's stuffs " or " women's stuffs," did not differ greatly in kind from those to be had in similar shops at present. Many of them, however, passed by names unknown to this generation. This is especially true of the articles sold at the counters of the haberdashers. There were to be found plushes, lawns, and fine dyed jeans ; galloons and silk-ferrets, crimson velvets from Genoa, silks from China, linens from Ireland, ich damasks and cambrics from England, Bellandine sewing

silk and Prussian flowered silk bonnets, then in the height of
fashion, swords, garterings, vest patterns, and figured silk
cloaks. On the stalls on a market-day we would miss, again,
many of the fruits and vegetables now considered not as luxuries but as essentials. The tomato was not only uncultivated,
but almost unknown.* Apples and pears were to be had in
abundance, but none of those exquisite varieties, the result of
long and assiduous nursing, grafting, and transplanting, which
are now to be had of every green-grocer. The raspberries
and strawberries were such as grew wild on the hills, and
the best of them could bear comparison neither in flavor nor
in size with the poorest that are often to be seen at county
fairs. Oranges and bananas were the luxury of the rich, and
were, with all the tropical fruits, rarely seen; for few packets could then make the voyage from the West Indies under
several weeks. Since that day our dinner-tables have been
enriched by the cauliflower and the egg-plant. No great companies existed as yet for the distribution of ice. This article, since come to be regarded as much a necessity of life as
meat and bread, and which, in ten thousand ways, administers to our comfort and promotes our health, was almost, if
not quite, unused. The coolest water the tavern could afford
came from the town pump. Every thunder-storm curdled
the milk. The butter was kept in the dampest and coolest
nook of the cellar, or hung in pails down the well.

With the exception of such vegetables and fruits as grew
among the rose-bushes and tulip-beds of their gardens, the
citizens of Boston depended for their daily food on the produce of the farms without the town. We should indeed be
much mistaken if we pictured to ourselves the farms such as
Warren and Webster were reared upon, as the pleasant places
we know so well. The lands were ill-fenced, the barns were
small and mean, nor could there be seen in the barn-yard, or
under the cow-shed, one of those implements of agriculture
with which American ingenuity has revolutionized a great
branch of human labor, has cheapened food, and brought

---

* The seed of the tomato was brought over by emigrants from France. For
many years after the present century came in the plant was used for ornament.
The fruit was thought to be poisonous, and called the love-apple.

millions of acres into a high state of cultivation. The first thrashing-machine was not invented till 1786; the cast-iron wheeled plough, the drill, the potato-digger, the reaper and binder, the hay-raker, the corn-cutter, are not fifty years old. The Massachusetts farmer who witnessed the revolution ploughed his land with the wooden bull-plough, sowed his grain broadcast, and, when it was ripe, cut it with a scythe, and thrashed it on his barn-floor with a flail. His house was without paint; his floors were without carpet. When darkness came on his light was derived from a few candles of home manufacture. The place of furnaces and stoves was supplied by huge cavernous fireplaces which took up one side of the room, and, sending half the smoke into the apartment, sent half the heat up the chimney. His food was of the simplest kind, was served in the coarsest of dishes, and eaten with the coarsest of implements. Beef and pork, salt fish, dried apples and vegetables, made up the daily fare from one year's end to another. Josiah Quincy has left us a pleasing picture of such a home.* There was then little, or indeed no communication with the South; and the bread, he tells us, was, therefore, of rye or Indian meal and not always well baked. The minister alone had white bread, for brown bread gave him the heart-burn and he could not preach upon it. Of this simple fare we may, perhaps, with justice, recognise some trace in the world-famous brown bread and baked beans which, on a Sunday morning, are now to be found on half the breakfast-tables of New England.

If the food of such a man was plain, so were his clothes. Indeed, his wardrobe would, by his descendants, be thought scanty in the extreme. For meeting on a Sabbath and state occasions during the week he had a suit of broadcloth or corduroy which lasted him a lifetime, and was at length bequeathed, little the worse for wear, with his cattle and his farm, to his son. The suit in which his neighbors commonly saw him, the suit in which he followed the plough, tended the cattle, and dozed in the chimney corner while Abigail or Comfort read to him from Edwards's sermons, was of homespun or linsey-woolsey. The entire sum annually laid out, in

* Life of Josiah Quincy.

those days, by a New England farmer on clothes for himself,
his wife, and his eleven or thirteen children, was ridiculously
small; nor is it too much to say that many a well-to-do father
of to-day, with a less numerous family, expends each year on
coats and frocks and finery a sum sufficient, one hundred
years since, to have defrayed the public expenses of a flourishing village, school-master, constable, and highways included.*

It must not, however, be supposed that because the New
England farmer of 1784 was not in possession of a well-
stocked and highly-cultivated farm, that because he ate plain
food and wore plain clothes, he was by any means an insig-
nificant personage. His education, though not as profound as
is within the reach of men of his class at present, was far
from contemptible. His reading was not extended and was,
in general, confined to such books as found their way into
pedlers' packs. The newspaper he rarely saw unless it came
wrapped about a bundle; but his inquisitiveness amply supplied its place. There is, undoubtedly, much exaggeration
in the stories that have come down to us regarding this singular characteristic. Yet it is impossible to doubt in the
presence of such a mass of evidence, that he was the most
shrewd, the most talkative, the most inquisitive of mortals.
The horseman who stopped at his door to inquire the road
was astounded at the eagerness with which he sought for
news. The jaded traveller at an inn, or, as the phrase went,
a tavern, sat hungry at the board while the landlord plied
him with question after question and gave him the latest bit
of town scandal, or the last action of the committee men.†

---

* In a paper, called Cause of and Cure for Hard Times, published in 1787,
an honest old farmer is made to say: "At this time my farm gave me and my
whole family a good living on the produce of it, and left me, one year with another, one hundred and fifty silver dollars, for I never spent more than ten dollars
a year, which was for salt, nails, and the like. Nothing to wear, eat, or drink,
was purchased, as my farm provided all." American Museum, January, 1787.
Connecticut Courant, August 18, 1788. Had his case been an uncommon one, the
force and value of the paper would have been lost.

† It is almost impossible to take up a diary, written at that time by a foreigner, without finding some story or some comment on Yankee inquisitiveness.
Anburey, who was a lieutenant in Burgoyne's army, narrates an amusing anecdote
of the inquisitiveness of New England inn-keepers, told him by an officer of Virginia line. Anburey's Travels through the Interior Parts of America. Smyth, in

In politics he was a stanch patriot; in religion he was a Congregationalist. Neither his views on politics, nor his opinions on matters touching original sin, were the result of long and patient reflection. He was zealous in the cause of the States not because he considered taxation without representation as unjust, or the stamp act as tyrannical, but because the men he looked up to were patriots, and because he believed the King had serious intentions of making the Church of England the established church of America. He was a Congregationalist because his father and his grandfather had held such a belief before him. Yet he seemed not to know that his religious belief and his religious practices were very different from those of his ancestors, and that the changes then begun were to go silently on into our own time. Compared with his grandfather and his grandson, his opinions are as far removed from those of the one as from those of the other. To his grandson they seem to belong to a straitlaced, bigoted and narrow-minded man; to his grandfather they would have seemed such as became a man on the high road to episcopacy. He held it an abomination to read a novel, to see a play, to go to a dance, to make a jest, to sing a comic song, to eat a dinner cooked on a Sunday, or to give a present on Christmasday.* Yet he would, at times, so far forget his austerity as

---

his Tour through the United States of America, in 1784, has some remarks on this characteristic, vol. ii, p. 346. Riedesel calls them "inquisitive and credulous." Riedesel Memoirs.

* The strictness of the New England Sabbath was the subject of considerable mirth and satire elsewhere. In an old poem it said that God had thought one day in seven sufficient for rest, but in New England men had improved on this, and set apart a day and a half:

> "And let it be enacted further still,
> That all our people strict observe our will;
> Five days and half shall men and women, too,
> Attend their bus'ness and their mirth pursue.
> But after that, no man without a fine
> Shall walk the streets or at a tavern dine.
> One day and half 'tis requisite to rest
> From toilsome labor and a tempting feast.
> Henceforth let none, on peril of their lives,
> Attempt a journey, or embrace their wives;
> No barber, foreign or domestic bred,
> Shall e'er presume to dress a lady's head;

to play a game of draughts with his wife, or spend an hour at fox and geese with his children. His conscience did not smite him when he drank palm-tea at a quilting, or listened to the achievements of his better half at the spinning match. He drank ale and cider at the apple-paring bees, and laughed as loudly as any one when, at the corn-husking, the lucky finder of the red ear kissed his favorite daughter. But the moment the fiddles were produced he went home to his pipe and sermons, or to a long talk with the school-master.

In few things is the great advance made in this country during the past one hundred years more strikingly apparent than in the change which has taken place in the social and intellectual condition of the school-master. The education of the young has now become a lucrative profession by itself, and numbers among its followers many of the choicest minds of the age. The school-master is specially prepared for his work, and is in receipt of a sum sufficient to maintain him in comfort, to enable him to procure books, and, if he be so inclined, to travel. Booksellers and publishers make a liberal discount in his behalf. The government allows him to import the text-books and apparatus used in his work duty free. He is everywhere regarded as an eminently useful member of society. But the lot of the school-master who taught in the district school-house three generations since fell in a very different time and among a very different people.* School was then held in the little red school-houses for two months in the winter by a man, and for two months in the summer by a woman. The boys went in the winter, the girls in the sum-

---

No shop shall spare (half the preceding day)
A yard of riband or an ounce of tea."

The Connecticut Sabbath. See American Museum for February, 1787.

A few of the laws of the Vermont Blue Book, which were copied from the laws of Massachusetts, are given in Acts and Laws of Vermont, 1779; Slade's State Papers, pp. 313, 315; Hall's History of Eastern Vermont, vol. ii, p. 579. Whoever was guilty of any rude, profane, or unlawful conduct on the Lord's-day, in words or action, by clamorous discourses, shouting, hallooing, screaming, running, riding, dancing, jumping, was to be fined forty shillings, and whipped upon the naked back, not to exceed ten stripes.

* In many parts of New England it must be owned the condition of the school-master has improved but little since 1784.

mer. The master was generally a divinity student who had graduated at one of the academies, who had scarcely passed out of his teens, and who sought by the scanty profits derived from a winter's teaching to defray the expenses of his study at Harvard or at Yale. His pay was small, yet he was never called upon to lay out any portion of it for his keep. If the district were populous and wealthy a little sum was annually set apart for his board, and he was placed with the farmer who would, for that amount, board and lodge him the longest time. But this was a far too expensive method for many of the districts and the master was, therefore, expected to live with the parents of his pupils, regulating the length of his stay by the number of the boys in the family attending his school. Thus it happened that in the course of his teaching he became an inmate of all the houses of the district, and was not seldom forced to walk five miles, in the worst of weather over the worst of roads, to his school. Yet, mendicant though he was, it would be a great mistake to suppose that he was not always a welcome guest. He slept in the best room, sat in the warmest nook by the fire, and had the best food set before him at the table. In the long winter evenings he helped the boys with their lessons, held yarn for the daughters, or escorted them to spinning matches and quiltings. In return for his miserable pittance and his board the young student taught what would now be considered as the rudiments of an education. His daily labors were confined to teaching his scholars to read with a moderate degree of fluency, to write legibly, to spell with some regard for the rules of orthography, and to know as much of arithmetic as would enable them to calculate the interest on a debt, to keep the family accounts, and to make change in a shop.

Nor was making change a simple matter. We who are accustomed to but one unit of value and purchase with dollars and cents can form but a faint conception of the difficulties which beset our ancestors in their money payments. The Constitution had not yet been framed. There was, therefore, no supreme authority, and no national currency based upon a universally recognized unit. In every State there were at least two units of value; the State pound and the

Spanish milled dollar, which had been adopted by Congress in
the early years of the revolution. But the values of these stand-
ards were by no means common ones. The pound in Georgia
contained fifteen hundred and forty-seven silver grains; in Virginia it fell to twelve hundred and eighty-nine grains, which
was also recognised as the pound in Massachusetts, Rhode
Island, Connecticut, and New Hampshire. In New Jersey,
Delaware, Pennsylvania, and Maryland, it fell to ten hundred
and thirty-one and a quarter grains, while in New York and
North Carolina it reached the minimum of nine hundred and
sixty-six. The pound being divided into shillings, and the
shillings into pence, made the value of the penny far from
equal in the different States. These local or State pounds had
no existence off the books of the merchants, nor out of the
mouths of the people. They were used in keeping accounts
and expressing debts; but when the debts were to be settled
the pounds were translated into johannes, doubloons, moidores,
dollars, or some other coin, and in such coin paid. Chief of
the silver pieces was the Spanish milled dollar, then in general circulation, and divided into a half, a quarter, an eighth,
and a sixteenth, each represented by a silver coin, and each
containing more or less shillings or pence according to the
section of the country into which it was taken. Thus, in
New England and Virginia, six shillings, or seventy-two pence,
were accounted a dollar. In New Jersey, Pennsylvania, Delaware, and Maryland, seven shillings and sixpence made a dollar; in New York and North Carolina, eight shillings, or
ninety-six pence; in South Carolina and Georgia, four shillings and eight pence. The school-boy, therefore, was expected to convert, with some readiness, the local pounds and
shillings of his State into dollars and joes, and to know the
rules for turning York money into Pennsylvania money, and
be able to tell how many shillings and pence a pistole contained in the various sections of the country.

As to geography, such books and maps as could then
be procured were not of a kind likely to convey much
knowledge to a lad of an inquiring mind. Monteith, and
Olney, and Guyot had not yet appeared. That splendid
series of school-books which now stands unrivalled had but

just found a beginning in the spelling-book of Noah Webster.*

With the district school the education of half the lads in the country ended. A few, however, more fortunate, passed thence to a seminary kept by some minister, or to one of the famous academies which were regarded as the feeders of Harvard and of Yale. But those were still days of Puritan austerity, and the boy who quitted his home for school left behind him, too often, peace and happiness. Little Paul at the Blimbers, Smike at Dotheboys Hall, did not have a much harder fate. Indeed, the pedagogue who, in our day, should subject his pupils to the rigid discipline, to the hard fare, to the sermons, the prayers, and the flogging which then fell to the lot of the school-boy, would be held up by the press to universal execration, and might count himself fortunate if he escaped without a prosecution by a society for the prevention of cruelty to children. Masters knew no way of imparting knowledge but by the rod. To sit eight hours a day on the hardest of benches poring over Cheever's Accidence; to puzzle over long words in Dilworth's speller; to commit to memory pages of words in Webster's American Institute; to read long chapters in the Bible; to learn by heart Dr. Watts's hymns for children; to be drilled in the Assembly Catechism; to go to bed at sundown, to get up at sunrise, and to live on brown bread and pork, porridge and beans, made up, with morning and evening prayer, the every-day life of the lads at most of the academies and schools of New England. When Sunday, or, as the boys would say, the Sabbath, came round, they found it anything but a day of rest. There were long prayers in the morning by the master, there were commentaries on some scripture text to be got by rote before meeting, to which, dressed in their best, they marched off with ink-pot and paper to take down the heads of the sermon, and give what account of it they could at evening prayers. Between morning and afternoon meeting they were indulged with a cold dinner.

The system of instruction was crude in the extreme. The

---

* Webster published his American Spelling-Book or First Part of a Grammatical Institute of the English Language, in 1784.

appliances of the modern teacher were wholly wanting. The
maps and charts, the globes and models that enable the eye to
make clear to the mind what might otherwise be confused,
found no place in the school-room. To explain away the
difficulties of the task, to elucidate the obscurities of pedants,
to make smooth the rough path of knowledge, formed no part
of the duty of the master. His business was to stand, rod in
hand, while his pupils pondered hopelessly over lessons which
ten words would have sufficed to make clear. Thus, Trumbull, the artist, spent three weeks in the vain endeavor to
solve an example in long division. Josiah Quincy went over
his Accidence " twenty times." *

From the academy the lad passed to Harvard or to Yale.
Were it not for the old buildings which still remain, surrounded by the splendid memorials of later days, it would be
impossible to recognize in the great university of our time
any trace of the humble college which boasted of Adams, and
whose students turned out in full force to welcome Lafayette.
The faculty then would be outnumbered by the instructors in
a single department now. Subjects of which Dr. Willard
knew nothing are at present taught by the most distinguished
men of the time, and illustrated by museums filled with collections far exceeding in value all the property the college then
possessed. So little was understood of palæontology that the
bones of a mastodon dug up at Claverack, on the Hudson,
seventy two years before, were still believed to be those of a
giant. So little was known of geology that the drift and
erratic bowlders of the Glacial Age were cited in the sermons
of the time as evidence of the flood so conclusive as to silence
all doubters. Of political economy nothing was heard. The
same year which witnessed the publication of the Declaration
of Independence had, indeed, also witnessed the publication
of the Wealth of Nations. But it may well be questioned
whether, in 1784, there could be found from Boston to Savannah one hundred copies of the book.

The four years of residence at college were spent in the

* For an account of school-life, see Life of Josiah Quincy, pp. 24, 25; Personal Memoirs of J. T. Buckingham, vol. i, pp. 17–19; Life of J. K. Paulding;
Memoirs of Roger B. Taney.

acquisition of Latin and Greek, a smattering of mathematics, enough of logic to distinguish barbara from celarent, enough of rhetoric to know climax from metonymy, and as much of metaphysics as would enable one to talk learnedly about a subject he did not understand. The students lodged in the dormitories and ate at the commons. The food then partaken of with thankfulness would now be looked upon as prison fare. At breakfast, which was served at sunrise in summer and at daybreak in winter, there were doled out to each student a small can of unsettled coffee, a size of biscuit, and a size of butter weighing generally about an ounce. Dinner was the staple meal, and at this each student was regaled with a pound of meat. Two days in the week, Monday and Thursday, the meat was boiled, and, in college language, these were known as boiling days. On the five remaining days the meat was roasted, and to them the nickname of roasting days was fastened. With the flesh went always two potatoes. When boiling days came round, pudding and cabbage, wild peas and dandelions were added. The only delicacy to which no stint was applied was the cider, a beverage then fast supplanting the small beer of the colonial days. This was brought to the mess in pewter cans which were passed from mouth to mouth, and, when emptied, were again replenished. For supper there was a bowl of milk and a size of bread. The hungry Oliver who wished for more was forced to order, or, as the phrase went, "size it," from the kitchen.*

Rude as was the school system of New England, it was incomparably better than could be found in any other section of the country. In New York and Pennsylvania a schoolhouse was never seen outside of a village or a town. In other places, children attending school walked for miles through regions infested with wolves and bears.† In the

---

* A description of college life at Harvard at this time is given in the Harvard Book, vol. ii. See, also, Hall's Coll. Words and Customs, ed. 1856, pp. 115–117; New England Mag., iii, p. 239; Willard's Memories of Youth and Manhood, vol. ii, pp. 192, 193.

† "I was compelled to walk three miles through a deep and tangled forest, infested with wolves, wildcats, snakes, and other animals." Autobiography of Chas. Caldwell, p. 64. See, also, for scarcity of schools in Virginia, Life of Archibald Alexander, pp. 11, 12.

southern States education was almost wholly neglected, but
nowhere to such an extent as in South Carolina. In that
colony, prior to 1730, no such thing as a grammar-school
existed. Between 1731 and 1776 there were five. During
the revolution there were none.* Indeed, if the number of
newspapers printed in any community may be taken as a
gauge of the education of the people, the condition of the
southern States as compared with the eastern and middle was
most deplorable. In 1775, there were, in the entire country,
thirty-seven papers in circulation. Fourteen of them were in
New England, four were in New York, and nine in Pennsylvania. In Virginia and North Carolina there were two each,
in Georgia one, in South Carolina three.† The same is true
to-day. In 1870, the population of Georgia was, in round
numbers, twelve hundred thousand souls, and the circulation
of the newspapers less than fourteen and a half millions of
copies. The population of Massachusetts was, at the same
time, fifteen hundred thousand, but the newspaper circulation
was far in excess of one hundred and seven and a half millions
of copies.‡

Not less important than the school-master, in the opinion
of his townsmen, was the doctor. With the exception of the
minister and the judge, he was the most important personage in the district. His professional education would now be
thought insufficient to admit him to practice ; for there were
then but two medical schools in the country, nor were they,
by reason of the expense and dangers of travelling, by any
means well attended. In general, the medical education of a
doctor was such as he could pick up while serving an apprenticeship to some noted practitioner in Boston or New York,
during which he combined the duties of a student with many
of the menial offices of a servant. He ground the powders,
mixed the pills, rode with the doctor on his rounds, held the
basin when the patient was bled, helped to adjust plasters, to
sew wounds, and ran with vials of medicine from one end of
the town to the other. In the moments snatched from duties

* Ramsay's History of South Carolina.
† Hudson's History of Journalism in the U. S.
‡ Ninth United States Census.

such as these he swept out the office, cleaned the bottles and jars, wired skeletons, tended the night-bell, and, when a feast was given, stood in the hall to announce the guests.*

It was a white day with such a young man when he enjoyed the rare good fortune of dissecting a half-putrid arm, or examining a human heart and lungs. So great, indeed, was the difficulty of procuring anatomical subjects,† that even at the medical school which had just been started at Harvard College, a single body was made to do duty for a whole year's course of lectures.‡ It was only by filching from grave-yards or begging the dead bodies of criminals from the Governor that subjects could be obtained.#

Under such circumstances, the doctor's knowledge was derived from personal experience rather than from books, and the amount so obtained bore a direct relation to the sharpness of his powers of observation and the strength of his memory. If he were gifted with a keen observation, a logical mind, and a retentive memory, such a system of education was of the utmost value. For in medicine, as in mechanics, as in engineering, as in every science, in short, where experience and practical skill are of the highest importance, a practical education is most essential. The surgeon who has studied anatomy from a book without ever having dissected a human body, the physician who learns the names and symptoms of diseases from a work on pathology, and the remedies from the materia medica, without ever having seen the maladies in active operation and the remedies actually applied, is in a fair way

---

* Life of Dr. John Warren, p. 314.

† On the difficulty of procuring subjects for dissection, see Life of Dr. John Warren, pp. 228-231. Sometimes students were permitted to view the bodies of men and women who had died of an extraordinary disease. Life of Dr. John Warren, p. 226.

‡ Harvard Book, vol. i, pp. 240, 241. The school was started in 1783.

A very innocent exposure of a limb from a window of a hospital in New York led, one Sunday in April, 1788, to a most serious riot, in which John Jay, Baron Steuben, and a number of prominent citizens, were hurt. The affray has come down to us under the name of The Doctors' Mob. The common practice was to rob the graves of negroes and strangers, but on this occasion the bodies of "respectable persons had been removed." See New York Packet, April 25, 1788; Pennsylvania Gazette, April 23, 1788; Life of John Jay; Life of Baron Steuben.

to kill far more patients than he will ever cure. But the value of knowledge obtainable from books alone is on that account not the less useful, and by no means to be despised. The student who has read much in his profession is in possession of the results of many centuries of experience derived from the labors of many thousands of men. He is saved from innumerable blunders. He is enabled to begin his career with a knowledge of things which, if left to his own experience to find out, would cost him years of patient waiting and careful observation. The advantages of such a system of study were, however, but sparingly enjoyed by the medical students of the last century when but few physicians boasted a medical library of fifty volumes.*

His apprenticeship ended, the half-educated lad returned to his native town to assume the practice and to follow in the footsteps of his father. There as years went by he grew in popularity and wealth. His genial face, his engaging manners, his hearty laugh, the twinkle with which he inquired of the blacksmith when the next boy was expected, the sincerity with which he asked after the health of the carpenter's daughter, the interest he took in the family of the poorest laborer, the good-nature with which he stopped to chat with the farm-hands about the prospect of the corn-crop and the turnip-crop, made him the favorite of the county for miles around. When he rode out he knew the names and personal history of the occupants of every house he passed. The farmers' lads pulled off their hats, and the girls dropped courtesies to him. Sunshine and rain, daylight and darkness, were alike to him. He would ride ten miles on the darkest night, over the worst of roads, in a pelting storm, to administer a dose of calomel to an old woman, or to attend a child in a fit. He was present at every birth; he attended every burial; he sat with the minister at every death-bed, and put his name with the lawyer to every will.

But a few of the simplest drugs were then to be found

---

* Dr. Hubbard, first president of the New Haven County Medical Society, organized in 1784, was, perhaps, the most wealthy practitioner in the county. Yet, when he died, his books were valued at $82. See Papers of the New Haven Colony Historical Society, vol. ii, pp. 260–262.

stowed away on the shelves of the village store, among heaps
of shoes, Rohan hats, balls of twine, packages of seed, and
flitches of bacon.   The physician was, therefore, compelled to
combine the duties both of the doctor and the apothecary
He pounded his own drugs, made his own tinctures, prepared
his own infusions, and put up his own prescriptions.   His
saddle-bag was the only drug-store within forty miles, and
there, beside his horn balances and his china mortar, were
medicines now gone quite out of fashion, or at most but rarely
used.   Homœopathy, with its tasteless mixtures and diminutive doses, was unknown, and it is not too much to say that
more medicine was then taken every year by the well than is
now taken in the same space of time by the sick.   Each
spring the blood must be purified, the bowels must be purged,
the kidneys must be excited, the bile must be moved, and
large doses of senna and manna, and loathsome concoctions of
rhubarb and molasses, were taken daily.   In a thousand ways
the practice of medicine has changed since that day, and
changed for the better.   Remedies now in the medicine-box
of every farmer were then utterly unknown.   Water was denied the patient tormented with fever, and in its stead he was
given small quantities of clam-juice.   Mercurial compounds
were taken till the lips turned blue and the gums fell away
from the teeth.   The damsel who fainted was bled pro-
fusely.   Cupping and leeching were freely prescribed.   The
alkaloid quinia was unknown till 1820.   The only cure
for malarial diseases was powdered cinchona bark ; but the
amount required to restore the patient was so great, and the
supply so small, that the remedy was all but useless.   Vacci-
nation was not made known by Jenner till 1798.   Inoculation
was still held by many to be attended by divine punishment.
Small-pox was almost as prevalent as pneumonia now is.   The
discovery of anæsthesia by the inhalation of ether or chloro-
form was not given to the world by Morton till 1846.   Not
one of the many remedies which assuage pain, which destroy
disease, which hold in check the most loathsome maladies and
the most violent epidemics, was in use.   Every few years dur
ing the dog-days the yellow fever raged with more violence
in the northern cities than it has ever done in this generation

in the cities of the far South. Whole streets were depopulated
Every night the dead-cart shot its scores of corpses into the
pits of the Potters' Field. Better surgery is now generously
given to every laborer injured by the fall of a scaffold than
could then have been purchased at any price.

High as the doctors stood in the good graces of their fellow-men, the ministers formed a yet more respected class of
New England society. In no other section of the country
had religion so firm a hold on the affections of the people.
Nowhere else were men so truly devout, and the minister
held in such high esteem. It had, indeed, from the days of
the founders of the colony been the fashion among New Englanders to look to the pastor with a profound reverence, not
unmingled with awe. He was not to them as other men
were. He was the just man made perfect; the oracle of
divine will; the sure guide to truth. The heedless one who
absented himself from the preaching on a Sabbath was hunted
up by the tithing-man, was admonished severely, and, if he
still persisted in his evil ways, was fined, exposed in the
stocks, or imprisoned in the cage. To sit patiently on the
rough board seats while the preacher turned the hour-glass
for the third time, and, with his voice husky from shouting,
and the sweat pouring in streams down his face, went on for
an hour more, was a delectable privilege. In such a community the authority of the reverend man was almost supreme. To speak disrespectfully concerning him, to jeer at
his sermons, or to laugh at his odd ways, was sure to bring
down on the offender a heavy fine. His advice was often
sought on matters of state, nor did he hesitate to give, un-
asked, his opinion on what he considered the arbitrary acts of
the high functionaries of the province. In the years immediately preceding the war the power of the minister in matters of government and politics, had been greatly impaired
by the rise of that class of laymen in the foremost rank of
which stood Otis and Hancock and Samuel Adams. Yet
his spiritual influence was as great as ever. He was still a
member of the most learned and respected class in a community by no means ignorant. He was a divine, and came
of a family of divines. Not a few of the preachers who

witnessed the revolution could trace descent through an unbroken line of ministers, stretching back from son to father
for three generations, to some canting, psalm-singing Puritan
who bore arms with distinction on the great day at Naseby,
or had prayed at the head of Oliver's troops, and had, at the
restoration, when the old soldiers of the Protector were turning their swords into reaping-hooks and their pikes into prun-
ing-knives, come over to New England to seek that liberty of
worship not to be found at home.   Such a man had usually
received a learned education at Harvard or at Yale, and
would, in these days, be thought a scholar of high attainments.   Of the men who Sunday after Sunday preached to
the farmers and blacksmiths of the petty villages, one had
explored the treasures of Hebrew literature, another was an
authority on matters of Greek grammar, while a third added
to his classical acquirements a knowledge of metaphysics
and philosophy.   His narrow-mindedness and sectarianism,
his proneness to see in the commonest events of daily life
manifestations of Divine wrath, his absurd pedantry, his
fondness for scraps of Latin, may well seem laughable.   Yet,
bigoted as he was, the views he held and the doctrines he
preached would by his great-grandfather have been despised
as latitudinarian.   Compared with Cotton or Hooker, a
New England minister of 1784 had indeed made vast strides
toward toleration.   He was a very different man from the
fanatics who burned Catholics at the stake, who drove out the
Quakers, who sent Roger Williams to find an asylum among
the Indians of Rhode Island, and sat in judgment on the
witches of Salem and Andover.   In the general advance of
society from ignorance toward knowledge, the whole line was
going forward.   The tail was constantly coming up to where
the head had been.   Errors beaten down by the front rank
were in turn trampled on by those that followed, and truths,
once dimly discernible only to the far-sighted men who
marched foremost in the van, were becoming plainly visible
to the most short-sighted bigots who dragged along far in the
rear.   Yet the distance between the head and the tail was as
great as ever, and the New England preacher seems liberal
only by contrast with men of an earlier time.   Long after

Jefferson had secured complete religious toleration among the
Episcopalians of Virginia, the Massachusetts divines were still
denouncing that sect, were still cautioning their flocks never to
suffer the wicked heresy to take root in the commonwealth,*
and heard, with uplifted hands, that a parcel of nonjuring
Bishops at Aberdeen had ordained a Bishop for Connecticut.†

Such doctrine, however, was confined to the sermons which
he preached on Sabbaths, and to the papers which he contributed to the press. In the election sermon which he
delivered on the return of every election-day, he taught a
very different lesson, exerted his eloquence to set forth the
equality of all men and the beauties of a pure democracy,
and taxed his learning to defend his politics with passages
from scripture and quotations from the writers of Greece.

Hatred of Kings and Princes had, indeed, always been a
marked characteristic of his sect, and in the pre-revolutionary
days he was among the most eager in the patriot cause. It
cannot be denied that this show of patriotism was, in most
cases, the result of personal interest rather than of a deeply
rooted conviction of the necessity of resisting the oppression
of England. If there was one sect of Christians which he
detested above another, that sect was the Episcopalian. He
firmly believed that the stupid King, who cared as little for the
Church of England as for the Church of Scotland, was fully
determined to make Episcopacy the established religion of the
colonies. He was sure that His Majesty had even matured
a plan for the establishment of the Church, and that, before
many months had gone by, laws as odious as the Conventicle
Act and the Five-Mile Act would be in full operation; that
hundreds of dissenting divines would be ejected from their
churches, stripped of their livings, and sent to starve among
the Indians on the frontier.‡ While, therefore, the rectors

---

* A warm discussion on the propriety of admitting bishops into Massachusetts
was carried on in one of the Boston papers early in 1785. Boston Gazette, January 3, 10, 17, 1785.

† When the news came of the ordination, which took place November 14,
1784, the Gazette exclaimed: "Two Wonders of the World—a stamp act in Boston and a Bishop in Connecticut." Boston Gazette, May 30, 1785.

‡ Fear of the Church of England "contributed as much as any other cause,"
says John Adams, "to arouse the attention, not only of the inquiring mind, but

of Virginia and the Carolinas were ranging themselves on the Tory side, the ministers of the eastern colonies were all active on the side of the Whigs.

When at last the independence the minister so much wished was achieved, he found himself, with all his neighbors, in the depths of poverty. His stipend, which had once been paid with punctuality to the last pistareen, was now delayed till long after the day of payment, and often consisted of barrels of turnips, bushels of corn, sacks of beans, and flitches of bacon.* Patches appeared on his homespun suit, and, in extreme need, he betook himself in his moments of leisure to teaching school. His home was turned into a seminary for a half dozen boys, whom he undertook, for a miserable pittance, to board, lodge, and fit for college. Yet his dignity and self-complacency were never for a moment laid aside. He had grown up among his flock. He had succeeded his father in the pastorship of the little white meeting-house, and he never left his charge till he was carried out to be laid away in the shade of the elm and chestnut trees in the bury-ing-ground beside the church. His sermon was the one event of the week. There were no concerts, no plays, no lectures, none of the amusements which, in the great towns like Boston, drew away the thoughts of men from religion. On a Sabbath the whole village turned out in force with note-book and pencil to take down the text and so much of the discussion as they could, and, when the services were over,

---

of the common people, and urge them to close thinking on the constitutional authority of parliament over the colonies." Works of John Adams, vol. x, p. 185. "The establishment of a Protestant episcopate in America is very zealously contended for, . . . and we desire you would strenuously oppose it," was the instruction given by the Massachusetts Assembly to its agent in London in 1768. Thompson, Church and State in the United States, pp. 42, 43.

* The salary of a minister a century ago was, unless he preached in a great town, but a pittance; was never the same two years in succession, and was rarely paid in money. Few preachers stood higher than Joseph Buckminster. Yet "his settlement was upon the value of wheat and Indian corn, and varied extremely in different years; but never did the amount, I think, exceed six or seven hundred dollars." Memoir of Joseph Buckminster, D. D., p. 69. In more favored places the preacher was allowed "£130 with glebe lands and parsonage, and the donation from strangers;" that is, the money laid upon the plate, which in those early times was placed in some conspicuous part of the meeting-house. Memoir of Buckminster, p. 39.

drew up along the aisle to let the great man and his family pass out first.

Nor were his discourses altogether undeserving such marks of distinction. The theology of New England was strongly tinged with philosophy, and every Sabbath there went forth from half the pulpits of the eastern States elaborate discussions of the most obscure points of the most obscure of all sciences. Not a few of the sermons which have come down to our time are vigorous and logical arguments in behalf of the freedom of the will, and the presence of God in conscience. In truth, of the writers who, up to the peace, and for many years after, put forth treatises, arguments, and expositions on metaphysical themes, scarcely one can be named who was not a native of New England, and a pastor of a New England church. Each minister, therefore, felt in duty bound to discuss his text in a philosophical way, and, however crude his attempt, the reasons he advanced, the analogies he drew, the hints and suggestions he threw out, furnished each week many new topics for an evening's talk. And such topics were needed, for of news the dearth was great. Almost every means of collecting and distributing it familiar to this generation was unknown to our great-grandfathers. There were, indeed, newspapers. Forty-three had come safely through the long revolutionary struggle to publish the joyful tidings of peace. But, with a few exceptions, all were printed in the large towns, and news which depended on them for circulation was in much danger of never going fifty miles from the editor's door.

An interchange of papers did go on among the printers; and some copies of the "Spy" and the "Columbian Centinel" found their way to subscribers at New York. But the papers were not received by the post-office, and it was only by rewarding the post-riders that a place was made for a dozen copies in the portmanteaus containing the letters. Even then, on reaching New York, they were almost a week old, and had they been carried on to Charleston would have entered that city twenty days after the date of publication. Had the time been less it would have mattered little, for the news to be derived from them was usually of small value, and

likely to convey only the most general information. Even
the Connecticut "Courant," the Boston "Gazette," and the
Pennsylvania "Packet," the three best, rarely had much news,
and were badly printed with old-fashioned type on coarse paper,
which, under the influence of time and dust, has grown brown
and brittle. Few came out oftener than thrice in a week, or
numbered more than four small pages. The amount of reading matter which the whole forty-three contained each week
would not be sufficient to fill ten pages of ten daily issues of
the New York "Herald." Nothing in the nature of an editorial page existed. Its place was given up to long essays on
politics or morals by some unknown writer who subscribed
himself "Seneca" or "Tully." The printer and the editor
were generally one, and it was "to the printer" that correspondents addressed their notes. It was seldom that he felt
himself called on to do more than make appeals, sometimes
serious, sometimes humorous, to his delinquent subscribers,
begging them to pay their bills, if not in money, in quarters
of wheat, in pounds of cheese, or the flesh of hogs.* The rest
of the paper was filled up with advertisements for runaway
slaves or stray horses, with scraps taken from other papers,
with letters written from distant places to friends of the editor,
a summary of the news brought by the last packet from Lisbon
or London, a proclamation by Congress, a note to the editor
posting some enemy as a coward in the most abusive and
scurrilous language, a long notice setting forth that a new
assortment of calamancoes and durants, colored tammies, shal-
loons, and rattinels were offered for sale at the shop of a
leading merchant, and, now and then, a proposal for the
reprinting of an old book. The columns devoted to such
advertisements were commonly adorned with rude wood-
cuts. A stage-coach, or a pair of top-boots, a prancing
horse, or a ship under full sail, a house, a plough, or a man
running away with a bundle and a stick in his hand, meet

---

* "In order to accommodate subscribers, any kind of grain will be taken in
payment at market rates." New Jersey Gazette, July 16, 1783. This consideration on the part of the editor was not appreciated, and in a little while the
Gazette ceased to come out. "Those who cannot pay cash or country produce,
it is expected will have no objection to acknowledge their accounts by notes."
New Jersey Journal, January 10, 1787.

the eye on almost every page. Occasionally odes, ballads, and bits of poetry made their appearance in the poet's corner. Now and then a paper of enterprise and spirit undertook to enlighten its readers and to fill its columns by the publication in instalments of works of considerable length and high literary merit. Robertson's "History of America" was reprinted in the "Weekly Advertiser" of Boston,* and ran through more than one hundred and fifty numbers. A "History of the American Revolution" came out in the "Spy," "Cook's Voyages" were published in the Pennsylvania "Packet," † while other papers of lesser note found room among essays and lampoons, epigrams, anecdotes, coarse "bon-mots," and town resolutions to discourage extravagance, for short treatises on geography and morals. But everything which now gives to the daily paper its peculiar value, and passes under the general name of news, was wanting. The student of history who seeks in the Packets and Advertisers of that day for information on matters which it concerns him to know, will, in all likelihood, search long and find but little. He will read much about the sins of idleness, about the value of economy, about the wretchedness of the wicked woman whose feet take hold on hell. But he will meet with nothing, or next to nothing, on many of the most exciting topics and important events of the time. He will, for instance, look in vain for any extensive information on the abhorrence which the people felt for the Cincinnati, on the proceedings of the Middletown convention, on the action against the Mayor's Court for its decision in the case of Rutgers against Waddington; he will see scarce a word about the formation of the State of Franklin, or the rupture of the Committee of the States whereby the country was left without a government for many weeks. The reason is plain. What took place in Boston or New Haven, what was going on among the flat-boatmen on the Ohio, or among the settlers on the Holston; what prospect there was of a war with the Shawanese and Twightwees, what prospect there was of the people of Vir-

---

* See also Continental Journal for 1784, 1785.

† Pennsylvania Packets for the closing months of the year 1784 and opening of 1785.

ginia granting the impost, were matters concerning which an editor two hundred miles away had no direct means of knowing. To tell the readers of the New York Packet what they already knew, that they hated Tories, and were indignant at the Commutation Act, would, to him, have seemed absurd. To keep them posted as to what was doing elsewhere he found a most difficult task. He had not in every city and town a well-paid correspondent, whose duty it was to collect the freshest bits of scandal, to interview the latest public character, and to send accounts of the course of popular opinion. For all this he was indebted to a source now rarely, if ever, used even in a backwoods village or a prairie town. Any gentleman who was so fortunate as to receive a letter from a distant part of the country was expected to display his public spirit by sending to the printer such portions of it as were likely to be of interest to the community. Scarce a week, therefore, went by but the Gazettes contained many scraps of valuable information under such headings as, " A Letter from a Gentleman at the Falls of the Ohio to his Friend in New England," " A Letter from a Gentleman resident in Virginia to his Friend in this City." Sometimes these communications would fill a column, and were almost always well worth a careful perusal.

In truth, the marvellous mechanical inventions that have compressed the whole world to the limits of a single town, and have made the collection and distribution of news so easy and so quick, have brought about a great change in the art of writing letters. Men who were, a century since, separated by three hundred miles, were, to all intents and purposes, much farther away, and saw much less of each other, than men who in our time are parted by three thousand miles. It was no uncommon thing for one who went on business or on pleasure from Charleston to Boston or New York, if he were a prudent and a cautious man, to consult the almanac before setting out, to make his will, to give a dinner or a supper to his friends at the tavern, and there bid them a formal good-by. Many incentives, therefore, to letter-writing then existed which the railroad, the steamboat and the telegraph have quite destroyed. Men who were of the same family, who had grown up in the

same village, who had known each other at school, or had fought
side by side under Washington or Gates, were constantly exchanging epistles or notes. The number who, at present, have
the disposition and the time for a like correspondence is very
small indeed; nor do they write of the same class of subjects.
No merchant in New York would now think of acquainting
his friends in Chicago with the result of a late election, with
the last action of the Legislature, with the price of commodities, with opinions held on matters of state or national importance, with what took place on 'change or on the street, with
anything in short, which can be read in the newspapers
under the head of general news. Yet all this our ancestors
thought worthy to be communicated to distant friends. No
city in 1784 had its public library, no tavern its reading-room
where papers from every State in the Union could be seen,
and where even a busy man could, with a little pains, make
himself as familiar with what went on a thousand miles away
as with what went on at his very door. For such information
he was dependent on his correspondents, and on his correspondents alone. He therefore wrote, and received in return, letters in which, among much that is of no concern to us, assur-
ances of friendship and esteem, thanks for small favors conferred, are mingled many items full of interest to the historian of the times. It is from this source alone that a just and
accurate knowledge is to be obtained of many great events
and many stirring times; of the troubles in New England, of
Shay's rebellion in Massachusetts, of the indignation felt at
the conduct of Rhode Island, of the fears and anxiety of the
people during the long secret session of the Federal Convention. It is therefore much to be deplored that so few have
been saved from *autos-da-fé* more sweeping than that performed by the curate, the barber, and the house-keeper on
the little library at La Mancha. Nor should it be forgotten
that such missives were much prized by the recipient; for the
difficulties of transmitting letters were many, and the rate of
postage high.

In the early colonial times no such thing as a post existed.
Indeed, two hundred years have not gone by since the first
royal patent was issued to Thomas Neals creating him Postmas-

ter-General of "Virginia and other parts of North America." The population, however, was at that time so scattered that nothing ever came of the royal patent, and the postmaster appears to have found little to do. Three years later matters had so much improved that in the course of a twelvemonth eight mails passed from the banks of the Potomac northward as far as Philadelphia. The end of the first decade of the eighteenth century had come before a line of posts ran from Philadelphia to the Piscataqua. This enterprise met with such success that, a few years later, the service was extended to Williamsburg, then an important town in Virginia. But the post-rider was not to leave the city till enough letters had been lodged to pay all expenses of the trip. At last, in 1753, the post-office passed to the hands of Franklin, and long before he was put out of office, in 1774, had become a source of revenue to the Crown. It was his boast that this branch of the public service, which, till he assumed its charge, had never paid one penny to the King, yielded in his day more than three times the income of the Irish post-office. When Franklin retired, Goddard, a brother printer of Baltimore, proposed a plan for a "Constitutional American Post-office." But the war broke out, and the duty of transmitting letters was again given to Franklin, with authority to establish a line of posts from Falmouth, in New England, to Savannah, in Georgia, with as many cross-posts as should, in his judgment, be thought necessary. In the mean time Massachusetts had, at her own charge, set up fourteen offices within her boundaries, and New Hampshire one. The mail routes thus established ran out from Cambridge, already renowned as the seat of Harvard College, and went as far north as Georgetown, in Maine, and as far south as Falmouth, then a flourishing hamlet, whose busy population were deeply concerned in the whale-fishery. From Cambridge mails also went out to Haverhill, to Providence, to Woodstock by way of Worcester, and from Worcester by way of Springfield, to Great Barrington. At Falmouth the bags were taken in charge by riders who travelled at the expense of Congress. The average day's journey of the postman was from thirty to fifty miles in summer, and considerably less in winter. Nor was it till Jefferson had been some years Secretary of State that the possibility of sending letters one hundred miles a day was seriously considered.* Not long after the opening of the war two packets were chartered by Congress, one to ply between the ports of Georgia, and one between the ports of North Carolina and such harbor as should at any time be most convenient to the seat of government.

Such was the humble beginning of that branch of the public service, which, more than any other, has aided the growth of trade and the prosperity of the nation. The sums now annually expended on the carriage of letters and newspapers exceed one half the amount of the domestic debt at which our ancestors stood appalled at the close of the revolution.† The number of letters carried from place to place in a twelvemonth exceeds six hundred millions; the distance traversed by these letters, over one hundred millions of miles. More mails are now each day sent out and received in New York than in Washington's time went from the same city to all parts of the country in the course of half a year. More letters are delivered in that city every four-and-twenty hours than, when Franklin held office, were distributed in the thirteen States in a whole year.‡ When the British evacuated New York, letters were sent to Boston thrice in a week during the summer months, and twice in a week during the winter. Six days were passed on the road. But at New Year's time, when the snow lay deep, the post-riders between these great cities rarely saw the church-spires of Boston till toward the close of the ninth day. Many years elapsed before the bulk and weight of the mails attained such proportions as to exceed the capacity of a pair of saddle-bags. That from New York to

---

* Jefferson's letter to Colonel Pickering, March 28, 1792. See Life of Pickering, vol. iii. Jefferson's Works, vol. iii, p. 158. Ed. 1830.

† In 1879, the amount expended in mail service was $20,012,872; the number of post-offices, 40,855; and the length of mail routes, 316,711 miles.

‡ The daily average of mail matter distributed at New York for 1882 was 2,400,000 pieces. In Barber and Howe's Historical Collections of New Jersey it is stated that, so late as 1791, there were but six post-offices in New Jersey. These were at Newark, Elizabeth, Bridgeton (now Rahway), New Brunswick, Princeton, and Trenton. The gross receipts were for the year ending October 15, 1791, $530. Of this the six postmasters received $108.20, leaving for net revenue $421.80.

Philadelphia went out five times in a week, and was for many years carried by boys on horseback.

It was, however, in the small country towns far removed from the great post-roads that the slowness and irregularity of the mails were greatest. In the mountains of New Hampshire, in the hill-country of Pennsylvania, in the rice-swamps of Georgia and the Carolinas, letters were longer in going to their destination than they now are in reaching Pekin. Letters sent out from Philadelphia spent five weeks in winter going a distance now passed over in a single afternoon.* In more favored places they were received and dispatched once a week, and that was an occasion of no small importance. On the day when the post-rider was due, a day which was known not by its name, as set down in the weekly calendar, but as "post day," half the village assembled to be present at the distribution of the mail, which, in good weather and in bad alike, took place at the inn. The package for the whole village was generally made up of a roll of newspapers a week old, and a few bundles of drugs for the doctor. It was a great day whereon, in addition to the usual post, a half dozen letters were given out. Then, as the townsmen pressed around the inn-door to make arrangement for borrowing the "newsprint," or to hear the contents of it read aloud by the minister or the landlord, the postman was carried home by one of the throng to share the next repast, at which, as the listeners preserved an admiring silence, he dispensed the news and the gossip collected along the way. In some regions remote from the travelled highways, it often happened that the post-rider was a man stricken in years, who, as his beast jogged slowly along, whiled the hours away by knitting woollen mittens and stockings.† At other places the letters lay for months in the

---

* "The letter which you did me the honor to write to me on the 20th of last month only came to my hands by the post preceding the date of this." Washington to R. H. Lee, December 14, 1784; Washington to Sir J. Jay, January 25, 1785; to L. W. Otto, December 5, 1785. "The bad weather, and the great care which the post-riders take of themselves, prevented your letters of the 3d and 9th of last month from getting to my hands till the 10th of this." Washington to Knox, February 20, 1784; to Knox, March 20, 1784; to General Lincoln, February 6, 1786.

† Memoirs of the Life of Eliza S. M. Quincy, p. 29.

office, there being no money wherewith to pay their transportation.

For the security of mails carried over long distances there was no protection whatever. It was well known and loudly complained of that letters and packages were opened and their contents read and examined by the riders. That most salutary law which extends a sure protection to letters, and even to telegraphic messages, had no existence. Nor was it till many years later, when the bulk and number of the mails had greatly increased, and the carriers found no time to read the notes they bore, that this flagrant evil ceased to exist. For a long time after the revolution business men, and men holding high places in the state, were accustomed to correspond in cipher. Such was the practice of Madison, of Jefferson, of Monroe, and of Aaron Burr, against whom it has often been foolishly cited as a sure indication of a crafty and a cunning disposition.* As stage-wagons and coaches became more and more common between the large towns, letters were often intrusted to a friend, or even to a stranger, to be left at the Red Dragon, or some other inn frequented by the person to whom they were addressed.†

These precautions might insure a safe but not a speedy delivery, for a journey of any length was beset with innumerable difficulties and delays. Towns and cities between which we pass in an hour were a day's journey apart. For all purposes of trade and commerce two hundred and fifty miles was a greater distance then than twenty-five hundred miles now. A voyage across the ocean to London or Liverpool, a trip across the prairies to the Pacific coast, is at present performed with more ease and comfort, and with quite

---

* A few instances will suffice. " My two last, neither of which were in cipher, were written, as will be all future ones in the same situation, in expectation of their being read by the postmasters." Madison to Jefferson, October 17, 1784. " Your favor without date was brought by Thursday's post. It enclosed a cipher, for which I thank you, and which I shall make use of as occasion may require it." Madison to Monroe, November, 1784. See, also, Madison to Jefferson, September 7, 1784 ; Washington to Lafayette, September 1, 1785 ; Hamilton to G. Morris, June 22, 1792.

† Frequent references to this custom may be found in the letters of Washington, Franklin, Ames, Madison, Burr, indeed, in any collection of letters written a century ago.

as much expedition as, a hundred years since, a journey from
Boston to New York was made. It was commonly by stages
that both travellers and goods passed from city to city. In
sufferably slow as such a mode of conveyance would seem to
an American of this generation, it had, in 1784, but lately
come in, and was hailed as a mark of wonderful progress.
The first coach and four in New England began its trips in
1744. The first stage between New York and Philadelphia,
then the two most populous cities in the colonies, was not set
up till 1756, and made the run in three days.* The same year
that the stamp act was passed a second stage was started.
This was advertised as a luxurious conveyance, " being a covered Jersey wagon," and was promised to make the trip in
three days, the charge being two pence the mile.† The success which attended this venture moved others, and in the
year following it was announced that a conveyance, described
as the Flying Machine, " being a good wagon, with seats on
springs," would perform the whole journey in the surprisingly
short time of two days. This increase of speed was, however,
accompanied by an increase of fare, the charge being twenty
shillings for the through trip and three pence per mile for
way passengers.

When the revolution came most of these vehicles ceased
to ply between the distant cities ; horseback travelling was resumed, and a journey of any length became a matter of grave
consideration. On the day of departure the friends of the
traveller gathered at the inn, took a solemn leave of him,
drank his health in bumpers of punch, and wished him God-
speed on his way. The Quaker preacher, Hicks, setting out in
1779 for yearly meeting, remarks : " We took a solemn leave
of our families, they feeling much anxiety at parting with us
on account of the many dangers we were exposed to, having
to pass, not only through the lines of the armies, but the deserted and almost uninhabited country that lay between them."‡

---

* Watson, Historical Tales of the Olden Times in N. Y. City and State.

† Some account of the stage-coaches in New Jersey may be had in Historical
Collections of New Jersey, by Barber and Howe, pp. 43, 44. Rude cuts of the
stage-coaches may be seen in almost any number of the N. Y. Packet for 1784,
or after.

‡ Journal of the Life and Religious Labors of Elias Hicks, p. 18.

With the return of peace the stages again took the road; but many years elapsed before traffic over the highways became at all considerable. While Washington was serving his first term, two stages and twelve horses sufficed to carry all the travellers and goods passing between New York and Boston, then the two great commercial centres of the country. The conveyances were old and shackling; the harness made mostly of rope; the beasts were ill-fed and worn to skeletons. On summer days the stages usually made forty miles; but in winter, when the snow was deep and the darkness came on early in the afternoon, rarely more than twenty-five. In the hot months the traveller was oppressed by the heat and half choked by the dust. When cold weather came he could scarce keep from freezing.* One pair of horses usually dragged the stage some eighteen miles, when fresh ones were put on, and, if no accident occurred, the traveller was put down at the inn about ten at night. Cramped and weary he ate a frugal supper and betook himself to bed, with a notice from the landlord that he would be called at three the next morning. Then, whether it rained or snowed, he was forced to rise and make ready, by the light of a horn-lantern or a farthing candle, for another ride of eighteen hours. After a series of mishaps and accidents such as would suffice for an emigrant train crossing the plains, the stage rolled into New York at the end of the sixth day.† The discomforts and

* See, on the discomforts of stage-coaches, a letter from Fisher Ames to Dwight, October 30, 1791.

† Many gentlemen who lived through this period, and saw railroads and steamboats introduced, have left us amusing accounts of the difficulties of travel. Breck relates how on one occasion he set sail on the regular ferry-boat at Elizabethport for New York. The distance between the two places is fifteen miles; but, after waiting all day for a breeze to spring up, he was forced to hire a fisherman to put him ashore in his canoe. Recollections of Samuel Breck, p. 102. In another place he describes how, by getting up at three or four o'clock in the morning and prolonging the journey until late at night, he used to make the trip from New York to Boston in six days. Id., p. 90; see, also, pp. 99, 100, 103, 271-273. Josiah Quincy says that during such journeys travellers were called at three in the morning, made ready by the light of a horn-lantern and a farthing candle, and went on their way over the worst of roads till ten at night. Often they were forced to get down and lift the coach out of a quagmire or a rut, and when New York was reached, after a week's travelling, they used to wonder at the ease as well as the speed with which the journey was made. Life of Josiah

trials of such a trip, combined with the accidents by no means
uncommon, the great distance from help in the solitary places
through which the road ran, and the terrors of ferry-boats on
the rivers, made a journey of any distance an event to be remembered to the end of one's days. Such was the crude state
of the science of engineering that no bridge of any considerable length had been undertaken in the States. No large river
had yet been spanned. While going from Boston to Philadelphia, in 1789, Breck crossed the Connecticut at Springfield,
the Housatonic at Stratford, the Hudson at New York, the
Hackensack and Passaic between Paulus Hook (now Jersey
City) and Newark, the Raritan at New Brunswick, the
Delaware at Trenton, and the Neshamung at Bristol on what
were then known as ferry-boats.*   The crossing of any of
these streams was attended by much discomfort and danger ;
but the wide stretch of water which flowed between Paulus
Hook and the city of New York was especially the dread of
travellers. There, from December till late in March, great
blocks of ice filled the river from either bank far out to the
channel. On windy days the waves were high, and when
the tide ran counter to the wind, covered with white-caps.
Horse-boats had not yet come in ; the hardy traveller was,
therefore, rowed across in boats such as would now be thought
scarcely better than scows. In one of her most touching letters to her husband, Mrs. Burr describes to him the alarm
occasioned by his making the dangerous crossing.† How she
had anxiously waited for his return, hoping that the dangers

Quincy, by Edmund Quincy, pp. 47, 48.   On one occasion Quincy spent a month
in his own coach, going from Boston to Washington. Id., p. 72 ; see, also, pp. 37,
56.   For some of the difficulties that beset travellers between New York and
Philadelphia, and New York and Albany, see the Letters of Aaron Burr to his
wife ; also, some curious Directions to Mrs. Arnold on her way to West Point,
in Arnold's Life of Benedict Arnold, p. 235.

  * Breck, p. 103.

  † See a letter from Mrs. Burr to her husband, dated March 22, 1784. Though
the letters of Theodosia Burr exhibit an unnecessary amount of apprehension for
the safety of a worthless man, the letter is worth quoting as illustrative of the
terrors of the river. "Every breath of wind whistled terror ; every noise at the
door was mingled with hope of thy return, and fear of thy perseverance, when
Brown arrived with the word *embarked*, the wind high, the water rough. . . . A
tedious hour elapsed when our son was the joyful messenger of thy safe landing
at Paulus Hook."

of the passage would deter him; how, when she heard tha
he was really embarked, she gave herself up to an agony of
fear as she thought of him exposed in the little boat to the
rough waters and the boisterous winds, and what thankfulness
she felt when her son brought word of his safe arrival at
Paulus Hook.*

Even a trip from Brooklyn to New York, across a river
scarce half as wide as that separating the city from New Jersey, was attended with risks and delays that would now be
thought intolerable. Then, and indeed till the day thirty
years later, when the rude steamboats of Fulton made their
appearance on the ferry, the only means of transportation for
man and beast were clumsy row-boats, flat-bottomed square-
ended scows with sprit-sails, and two-masted boats called peri-
aguas.† In one of these, if the day were fine, if the tide
were slack, if the watermen were sober, and if the boat did
not put back several times to take in belated passengers who
were seen running down the hill, the crossing might be made
with some degree of speed and comfort, and a landing effected
at the foot of the steps at the pier which, much enlarged,
still forms part of the Brooklyn slip of the Fulton Ferry.
But when the wind blew with the tide, when a strong flood
or an angry ebb was on, the boatmen made little headway,
and counted themselves happy if, at the end of an hour's hard
pulling, the passengers were put ashore opposite Governor's
island, or on the marshes around Wallabout bay.

In summer these delays, which happened almost daily,
were merely annoying and did no more harm than to bring

---

* Mrs. Quincy, on her way to the Commencement of Princeton College in 1790,
met with the following adventure on the Elizabethtown ferry: "We had a stormy
passage across the bay, and I was excessively frightened. Having arrived at the
ferry-house, we were shown into a room where a venerable old man was waiting
to go over to the city. The moment I entered he took off his great-coat, and
said to his wife: ' My dear, I do not go to New York to-day; the looks of that
young lady are enough to deter me.' This was the celebrated General Gates."
Memoirs of Eliza S. M. Quincy, p. 55. For the dangers of the ferry, see New
York Packet, June 17, 1788.

† Much information concerning the Brooklyn ferries is given in Stiles's His-
tory of the City of Brooklyn, vol. iii, pp. 504–540. Another reliable source is
An Historical Sketch of Fulton Ferry and its Associate Ferries, by a Director.
(H. E. Pierrepont.)

down some hearty curses on the boatmen and the tide.   But when winter came, and the river began to fill with huge blocks of ice, crossing the ferry was hazardous enough to deter the most daring.   Sometimes a row-boat would get in an ice-jam and be held there in the wind and cold for many hours.   At others a periagua would go to pieces in the crush, and the passengers, forced to clamber on the ice, would drift up and down the harbor at the mercy of the tide.   It is not improbable that the solicitude of Mrs. Burr for the safety of her husband was heightened by the recollection of such an occurrence which took place but a few months before.*

Nor were the scows, in the best of weather, less liable to accidents than the row-boats.   It was on these that horses, wagons, and cattle were brought over from city to city, for the butchers of the Fly market drew their supplies of beef and mutton from the farms that lay on the hills toward Flatbush and what is now Williamsburg.   Every week small herds of steers and flocks of sheep were driven to the ferry, shut up in pens, and brought over the river, a few at a time, on the scows.   The calmest days, the smoothest water, and a slack tide, were, if possible, chosen for such trips.   Yet even then whoever went upon a cattle-boat took his life in his hands.

If a sudden gust of wind struck the sails, or if one of the half dozen bullocks became restless, the scow was sure to upset.†   No one, therefore, who was so fortunate as to own a fine horse or a handsome carriage would trust it on the boats if the wind and sea were high, or much ice in the river, but

---

* In January, 1784, a row-boat coming from Brooklyn was caught in the ice, crushed, and sunk within a few feet of the New York shore.   Eight persons were on board.   One was drowned, but the seven climbing upon the ice were swept into the East river, then back into the Hudson, and were finally carried down the bay to the Narrows, where some soldiers overtook them with a boat.   New York Packet, January 22, 1784.   Pennsylvania Packet, January 22, 1784.

† The newspapers of the times contain many accounts of such disasters.   One Saturday, in 1784, as a ferry-boat with five horses on board was crossing the river, one of the horses became unmanageable, and so disturbed the rest that they all shifted to one side of the scow which immediately filled and went down. Independent Journal, 1784.   Like accidents continued to be noticed till paddle-wheel boats came into use in 1814.   See New York Journal and Post-Rider, December 17, 1795; New York Journal, April 3, 1798; American Citizen, May 27. 1801.

would wait two or three days for a gentle breeze and smooth
water.

But it was not solely by coaches and ferry-boats that our
ancestors travelled from place to place. Packet sloops plied
between important points along the coast, and such of the
inland cities as stood upon the banks of navigable rivers.
The trip from New York to Philadelphia was thus often
made by packet to South Amboy, thence by coach to Burlington, in New Jersey, where a packet was once more taken to
the Quaker city. A similar line of vessels ran between
New York and Providence, where coaches were in waiting to
convey travellers to Boston. This mode of conveyance was
thought to be far more comfortable than by stage-wagon, but
it was, at the same time, far more uncertain. Nobody knew
precisely when the sloops would set sail, nor, when once
started, how soon they would reach their haven. The wind
being favorable and the waters of the sound quite smooth,
the run to Providence was often made in three days. But it
was not seldom that nine days or two weeks were spent in the
trip.* On the Hudson were many such sloops, bringing
down grain, timber, and skins from Albany, to be exchanged
for broadcloth, half-thicks, and tammies, at New York. They
ceased to run, however, when the ice began to form in the
river, trade was suspended, and the few travellers who went
from one city to the other made the journey on horseback or
in the coach. In summer, when the winds were light, two
weeks were sometimes spent in sailing the one hundred and
fifty miles. The difficulties, indeed, which beset the English
traveller John Maude on his way to Albany, would now be
rarely met with in a canoe voyage on the rivers of the Northwest.† Burr, on his way to Albany to attend court, changed
from sloop to wagon, from wagon to canoe, and from canoe
back to wagon ere his journey was ended.‡ Travellers by
these packets often took boat as the vessel floated slowly down
the river, rowed ashore and purchased eggs and milk at

---

* "I have myself," says Breck, "been that length of time (nine days) going
from New York to Boston." Recollections of Samuel Breck, p. 90.

† Watson's Historical Tales of Olden Times in New York City and State.

‡ Letter of Burr to his wife, October 26, 1788.

the farm-houses near the bank, and overtook their vessel with
ease.

The present century had long passed its first decade before any material improvement in locomotion became known.
Our ancestors were not wholly unacquainted with the great
motive-power which has within the life-time of a generation revolutionized every branch of human industry, and enabled great ships of iron to advance in the face of wind and
waves, and long trains of cars to traverse the earth at a speed
exceeding the pace of the fleetest horse.   Before the close of
1787, Fitch at Philadelphia, and Rumsey at Shepherdstown,
Virginia, had both moved vessels by steam. Before 1790, a
steamboat company had been organized at Philadelphia, and a
little craft built by Fitch had steamed up and down the Delaware to Burlington, to Bristol, to Bordentown, and Trenton.
Before 1800, Samuel Morey had gone up the Connecticut
river in a steamer of his own construction and design, and
Elijah Ormsbee, a Rhode Island mechanic, had astonished the
farmers along the banks of the Seekonk river with the sight
of a boat driven by paddles.*   Early in this century, Stevens
placed upon the waters of the Hudson a boat moved by a
Watt engine. The same year Oliver Evans ran a paddle-
wheel vessel on the waters of the Delaware and the Schuylkill.   Fulton, in 1807, made his trip to Albany in the famous
Clermont, and used it as a passenger-boat till the end of the
year.   But he met with the same opposition which in our
time we have seen expended on the telegraph and the sewing-
machine, and which, some time far in the future, will be en-
countered by inventions and discoveries of which we have
not now the smallest conception.   No man in his senses, it
was asserted, would risk his life in such a fire-boat as the
Clermont when the river was full of good packets. Before
the year 1820 came, the first boat had steamed down the Mississippi to New Orleans ; the first steamboat had appeared
upon the lakes, and the Atlantic had been crossed by the
steamship Savannah.   But such amazing innovations as these
found little favor with men accustomed from boyhood to the
stage-coach and the sail-boat.   In 1810, nine days were spent

---

* Westcott's Life of John Fitch.   Thurston's Growth of the Steam-Engine.

in going from Boston to Philadelphia. At the outbreak of
the second war with England, a light coach and three horses
went from Baltimore to Washington in a day and a half.
The mail-wagon, then thought to make the journey with surprising speed, left Pennsylvania avenue at five in the morning
and drew up at the post-office in Baltimore at eleven at night.*
Ocean travel was scarcely known. Nothing short of the most
pressing business, or an intense longing to see the wonders of
the Old World, could induce a gentleman of 1784 to leave his
comfortable home and his pleasant fields, shut himself up in
a packet, and breathe the foul air of the close and dingy cabin
for the month or seven weeks spent in crossing the Atlantic.
A passage in such a space of time would, moreover, have been
thought a short one, for it was no very uncommon occurrence
when a vessel was nine, ten, eleven weeks, or even three
months, on a voyage from Havre or L'Orient to New York.†
So formidable was this tedious sail, and the bad food and
loathsome water it entailed, that fewer men went over each
summer to London than now go every month to South America. In fact, an emigrant steamer brings out each passage
from Queenstown more human beings than, a hundred years
ago, crossed the ocean in both directions in the space of a
twelvemonth. So late as 1795, a gentleman who had been
abroad was pointed out in the streets even of the large cities
with the remark, " There goes a man who has been to
Europe." ‡

---

* S. E. Thomas's Reminiscences, vol. ii, p. 126.

† The letters of Jefferson, when Secretary of State, to William Short, *chargé* at
the French court, and William Carmichael, *chargé* at that of Madrid, are full of
evidence on this point. " I will state to you the dates of all your letters received by me, . . . and length of their passage. . . . You will perceive that they
average eleven weeks and a half; that the quickest are of nine weeks, and the
longest are of near eighteen weeks' coming. Our information through the English papers is of about five or six weeks. . . . " Jefferson to W. Short, July 26,
1790. Again he writes: ". . . I have received Nos. 45 and 50; the former in
three months and seven days, the latter in two months and seventeen days, by
the English packet, which had an uncommonly long passage." Jefferson to W.
Short, March 15, 1791. See also letters to Short, March 19, 1791, and to Carmichael, April 11, 1791.

‡ "At that time (1795), and for a number of years after, a man, not a seaman,
who had made a voyage to Europe, was pointed at in the streets as a curiosity,
with some such a remark as this : ' There goes a man who has been to London.' "

Much of the delay in land travelling was caused by the wretched condition of the highways. On the best lines of communication the ruts were deep, the descents precipitous. Travellers by coach were often compelled to alight and assist the driver to tug the vehicle out of the slough. Nor were such accidents limited to the desolate tracks of country. Near the great cities the state of the roads was so bad as to render all approach difficult and dangerous. Out of Philadelphia a quagmire of black mud covered a long stretch of road near the village of Rising Sun. There horses were often seen floundering in mud up to their bellies. On the York road long lines of wagons were every day to be met with, drawn up near Logan's hill, while the wagoners unhitched their teams, to assist each other in pulling through the mire. At some places stakes were set up to warn teams out of the quicksand pits; at others, the fences were pulled down, and a new road made through the fields.*

With such obstacles to communication between the different parts of the country, it is far from surprising that each city was broadly distinguished from every other by the habits and customs of its citizens. A Bostonian who found himself in New York, could spend an hour or two no more profitably than in strolling about the streets and noting the superiority of his own native city to the Dutch town at the mouth of the Hudson; and, indeed, his opinion was not an erroneous one, for the condition of the city after the war was very different from its condition before. Prior to the revolution the commerce of New York was surpassed by that of Boston alone. The number of the population rolled up to three-and-twenty thousand. In her streets were heard the languages of all the civilized nations of the world. But, after seven years of warfare, the city was almost ruined. On the day the last of the British soldiers sailed down the Narrows, her commerce was gone, her treasury was empty, her citizens starving in the wilds of New Jersey. The city, as the term was then understood, ended at Anthony street

---

S. E. Thomas, Reminiscences of the Last Sixty-five Years, p. 29. At Philadelphia, foreigners were stared at. American Daily Advertiser, August 19, 1791.

* Watson's Annals of Philadelphia and Pennsylvania in the Olden Time.

on the north; Harrison street was the last toward the Hudson river, as Rutgers was toward the East river. This region, which now consists for the most part of immense warehouses and counting-houses and public buildings, crowded by traders and their clerks during the day, and left almost in total solitude at night, was then the place not only of business, but of residence. Yet, even within these narrow limits, the houses were scattered and surrounded by large gardens, not a few of which ran down to the shores of the rivers, and were thick with hedges and trees. Innumerable creeks and kills flowed through broad meadows, or lost themselves in swamps and pools, where are now the sites of great mercantile houses; dwellings stand crowded together on land then covered with orchards and fields of buckwheat; farms spread out where is now the fashionable part of the city; men fished and snared fowl in ponds and in marshes long since given up to the wants of trade. So late as 1787, the seine was regularly drawn on the beach where Greenwich street now is; ducks were often shot in Beekman's swamp; wild pigeons were plentiful in Berkley's woods.

More than a third part of the old town lay in ashes; in the very week wherein Howe entered the city in triumph, a terrible fire destroyed five hundred houses on the west side of the city near the present Washington market. Again, three years later, a second fire consumed three hundred houses on the east side. But little building had been done, and, in 1784, the two sites were still covered with heaps of blackened plaster and fragments of burned brick. Between these sites lay the Common. Originally, this stretch of land had been rectangular, but the post-road ran through it, cutting off a large triangle. The present City Hall park occupies the piece of common known as the "Flat" or "Vlackte." What Faneuil Hall was to Boston, what Independence Hall was to Philadelphia, that was the Common to New York. There the Sons of Liberty, led by Seares and Scott and Lamb, met to denounce the stamp act; there they fought for their liberty-pole; there they ended the battle of Golden Hill.

North of the Common was the fresh-water pond, called, also, the Collect. In this sheet of sparkling water many a belated

traveller and unwary fisherman had found an untimely grave;
and around it many traditions and myths had gathered. The
pond was reported, and the story was believed by the educated, to have no bottom; it was confidently affirmed by the
ignorant to be the abode of strange sea-monsters. Every one
knew it to be full of most excellent roach and sunfish. Below the Common, to the east, lay Beekman's swamp, a patch
of low, flat land, overgrown with coarse grass and tangled
briers, and, when the tides were unusually high, covered with
water. There, fifty years before, Jacobus Roosevelt laid out
his tanneries, and so began that branch of industry of which
the Swamp is, to this day, the centre. Along the Bowery
lane lay a succession of orchards and gardens; near Gram-
ercy park was Crummashie hill; the Zant Berg hill lay
above it, with the Minetta brook winding its way through a
marshy valley to the river; Broadway disappeared in the
meadows above Anthony street; to the west of Canal street
the Lispenard meadows, a great resort of sportsmen, stretched
away to the North river.

Three roads then ran out of town: the Kingsbridge road,
a continuation of the Bowery lane, joined with the South-
ampton road, and went out by McGowan's pass to Kingsbridge, and along the river to Albany; the old Boston post-
road started from the neighborhood of Madison square, and,
winding its way to Harlem, crossed the river, and turned eastward toward Boston; the Middle road ran direct to Harlem.

Scattered here and there along these were the homes of
many wealthy citizens. Not a few of them had been the
scenes of revolutionary incidents. Thus, at Inclenbergh was
the home of Robert Murray, father of the famous gramma-
rian, and husband of the fair Quakeress who, when the American army was in full retreat, detained the British officers till
the last man of Silliman's brigade was well on toward Harlem; higher up, on the Bloomingdale road, was Apthorpe
mansion, where, on the same day, Washington waited for his
scattered troops till the British came in sight, and barely
escaped capture by a hasty flight; on the shore of the East
river, hard by Turtle bay, was the Beekman mansion, beneath
whose roof Nathan Hale, the martyr spy, was tried and sen-

tenced to execution; while high up, on the banks that over-
look the waters of the Harlem, stood the home of Colonel
Roger Morris, afterward the home of the famous Madame
Jumel.

In the city scarce a street was paved, and these few were
so illy done that Franklin observed that a New Yorker could
be told by his walk as he shuffled over the smooth pavements
of Philadelphia. Street-lamps, which came into fashion ten
years before, were few in number, and rarely lighted on wet
nights.* Nor was there indeed much need of them, for the
fashion of keeping late hours had not then come in. The
city was famous among all the colonial towns for routs and
riots, the luxury and display of its citizens, and for gayety and
festivity. But the rout was over, and the guests safe at home,
long before the watchman was heard crying in the streets,
"Nine o'clock and all's well."

Many of the old Dutch customs were still kept up. New
England could boast of no such day as New Year's day. Boston and Philadelphia saw no such scenes as on every Christmas and every Easter day were enacted in New York. For,
despite the boast that men speaking the tongue of every civilized people were to be found in the city, the Dutch element
was still strong, and the language and religion of Holland were
most prevalent. Half the signs on William street were in
Dutch. At the Hudson market, and along the slips of the
Hudson river, a knowledge of Dutch was absolutely indispen-
sable. Until twenty years before, no sermon in the English
language had ever been preached in either of the three Dutch
churches, and, even after the revolution, prayers were still
made, and sermons still preached, at times, in the language
of the Stuyvesants and Van Dams. But a change in church
language had been attended by no change in church ceremo-
nial. The dominie in his black silk gown still preached in
in the high pulpit. The hour-glass yet stood at his right hand,
and the huge sounding-board over his head. The first psalm
was still announced by movable numbers hung on three sides
of the pulpit; the clerk still sat in the deacon's pew, and when

---

* The papers of that and a later day contain many notices of gangs of ruffians
who frequented the streets at night, and waylaid and robbed passers-by.

the congregation were in their seats, when the preacher was in the pulpit, the psalm sung and the prayer made, prefaced the sermon with a chapter from the Bible at morning service, and by chanting the Apostles' Creed at evening service. To him were intrusted the notices to be read, which he fastened to the end of a long pole and passed up to the minister. When the last grain of sand had run out of the glass, his three raps brought the sermon to a close. Then the deacons rose in their pew, listened to a short address from the minister, and, with velvet bags and bells hung to long rods, went among the congregation collecting alms for the poor.*

Hard by the Dutch church stood a smaller and less pretentious chapel, on whose worshippers Episcopalians and Dissenters alike looked down with horror not unmingled with contempt. The building had been put up some sixteen years before. Yet the congregation was not numerous, and was made up chiefly of shopkeepers and negroes, for the Methodists were still a new sect. Indeed, the society at New York, though it dated no further back than 1766, could have boasted, with justice, of being the oldest Methodist society, and of worshipping in the oldest Methodist church in America.† The first of the sect to come to our shores was undoubtedly Whitfield, who preached and exhorted through the southern provinces in 1737. But the man who may well be called the father of American Methodism, the man who watched and tended it in its early years, who shaped its course, who found it weak and left it strong, was Francis Asbury. He was an Englishman of hard sense and strong religious feeling, and sprang from the great middle class, which has, in every generation, furnished numbers of men whose names are held in grateful remembrance. When he landed in America, in 1772,

---

* My description of the city of New York is made up of materials taken chiefly from M. L. Booth's History of the City of New York; Watson's Historical Tales of the Olden Times in New York City and State; Duer's New York as it was during the latter part of the Last Century; Valentine's History of the City of New York; Denton's Brief Description of New York; Dunlap's History of New Netherlands, and the history by the loyalist Jones.

† An Appendix to the Methodist Memorial, containing a Concise History of the Introduction of Methodism on the Continent of America, etc. Charles Atmore, Manchester, 1802.

there were scattered from New York to Georgia six preachers and a thousand members of the sect.* But such was the excitement of the time, the energy and force of the preacher, that, when Burgoyne surrendered, the membership had increased to seven thousand souls, and the ministers to forty.† This growth is the more remarkable as every English preacher except Asbury deserted his flock and went back to England when the war broke out.‡ When peace came, eighty-one men were spreading the Methodist worship through the States. Then, it seemed to Wesley, the time had come when the Methodist church in America should be separated from the Methodist church in England. Coke, therefore, was ordained, and a letter dispatched directing the American brethren to receive him and Asbury as joint superintendents of the flock. A few days later Coke was on the sea. A few weeks later he landed at New York, and went with all speed toward Baltimore. On Sunday, the fourteenth of November, 1784, the very day on which the first Protestant Episcopal Bishop for America was ordained at Aberdeen, he preached to a great crowd in a little meeting-house in the woods. When he was done, a rough-clad man came out of the crowd and kissed him. The man was Asbury, who, the next Christmas eve, at Baltimore, was raised to the dignity of Bishop.

It was long, however, before the Methodists made proselytes and built churches in the towns along the great river that flowed by New York. Chief among them was Albany.‖ The city, indeed, was next in importance to New York in the State, and sixth in rank in the country. The place had been laid out early in the seventeenth century, and, after an existence of over a hundred years, had grown to be a flourishing Dutch town of five hundred houses and thirty-eight hundred souls.△ It could not, indeed, be said to have a rival on the river unless it was Poughkeepsie, then a village large enough

---

* Atmore's Appendix to the Methodist Memorial.
† Ibid.   ‡ Ibid.
‖ For an account of Albany, see Morse's American Geography, edition 1784, a most curious book; Mrs. Grant's Diary of an American Lady; Watson's Historical Tales; and the Scammel Letters, Historical Magazine, September, 1870.
△ New York Gazette, August 17, 1786.

and prosperous enough to support a weekly journal. Troy was not much more than a collection of the houses and barns of a half-dozen Van Rensselaers. The site of Hudson was a farm. Tarrytown was a pretty village. At Newburg a few buildings clustered about an inn. Albany was, therefore, in the estimation of the inhabitants, a great city. The prosperity of her merchants was the envy of far larger places. Her steadily growing trade was the boast of her citizens. The time, they said, was surely coming, nay, was almost at hand, when she would rival Boston and Philadelphia in magnificence, and become the emporium of northern trade. Did she not stand at the very head of the navigable waters of the Hudson? It was plain, therefore, that she need fear no northern rival. Was she not surrounded by boundless forests of fir and pine? Was she not on the only open route to Canada? Did she not command the Indian trade of the North and North-west? Was she not at the foot of that rich and splendid valley already famous for its wheat-fields and corn-fields and rye? Did not her commerce employ upward of ninety shallops? It was simply a question of time then how soon her docks would be crowded with sloops from the four quarters of the earth, bringing the spices and rich fabrics of the South to be exchanged for the rare furs of the North; when her warehouses would be filled with skins from Canada and Oswego; when her yards would be stocked high with lumber from the mountains; when her streets would be blocked with long trains of wagons laden with the products of the western farms; when, after every harvest, her granaries would run over with wheat and corn and rye from the fertile lands along the borders of the Mohawk and the Genesee.

But with boasts of the citizens were mingled the invectives and sarcasms of strangers. Travellers of every rank complained bitterly of the inhospitality of the Albanians, and the avarice and close-fistedness of the merchants. The fertility of American soil, the salubrity of an American climate, had not, they said, modified one jot the cold, taciturn, stingy Dutchman. They admitted that Albany was a place where a man with a modest competence could, in time, acquire riches; where a man with money could, in a short space of time, amass a fortune. But nobody would ever go to Albany who could by any possibility stay away, nor, being there, would tarry one moment longer than necessary. There, Dutch names and families, Dutch habits and customs, survived for the longest time. Albanians continued to keep Kerstydt and Nieuw Jar, Paas, Pinxter, and San Claas, in the old Dutch fashion many years after they had been greatly modified at New York. It was remarked by an humble topographer that so late as 1784 they knew nothing of the plays and social amusements common in New York. The few who affected a life of ease and pleasure spent their time in walking and "sitting in mead-houses," went regularly to their favorite tavern at eleven o'clock, played cards, billiards, and chess, staid till dinner, and came home in the evening. The town water was so bad as to be undrinkable by a stranger, and was but sparingly indulged in by the inhabitants. Its place was therefore largely supplied by punch, schnapps, and Madeira. The principal streets ran parallel to the river, were wide, unpaved, and in many months of the year heavy with mud. Six or eight lanes crossing these almost at right angles completed the town. The shops, seventy in number, clustered along Pearl and Water streets. In them were offered for sale, among heaps of wampum and strings of glass beads, goods whose names are wholly unintelligible to the shopkeepers of this generation.* There were to be found tammies, half-thicks, persians and pelongs, blue sagatha and red bunts, ticklen-burghs and black everlastings, and handkerchiefs known under the names of bandanoe, lungee, romals, culgee, putti-cal, and silk setetersoy.† The houses, scarce one of which can now be found in the city, were built after the Dutch Gothic style; three sides were of boards, or roughly squared

---

* Wampum, or white money, was originally made from the periwinkle; suck-hannock, or black money, from the inside of the shell of the hard clam. The most valued money of the Indians—their gold, in fact—was a black glass bead about a third of an inch long, highly polished, and bored lengthways. Three pieces of black, and six of white money, made a penny, or a Dutch stuyver. Among the fur-traders at this time was the father of Gerrit Smith. See Life of Gerrit Smith, by O. B. Frothingham, p. 6. John Jacob Astor had but just landed at New York with his stock of violins.

† See the newspaper advertisements of the time.

timbers. The fourth, always a gable end facing the street, was of yellow Holland brick, with a high pediment roof stepped off on each side like a flight of stairs, and surmounted by an iron horse as a weather-vane. In the middle of the brick gable was the door, with a stoop flanked on each side by seats, where, in the long summer evenings, the whole family gathered.

But one other appendage to the house must be noticed, as it greatly excited the derision of travellers familiar with the neater streets of Boston and New York. Tin gutters projected from the roofs far out over the foot-paths, and in rainy weather discharged torrents of water into the unpaved streets, drenching the horsemen and splashing the foot-traveller with mud from head to foot.*

Beyond the city, to the north and west, the country was an unbroken wilderness. That beautiful region renowned for the majesty of its scenery, whose wilds are now the sites of watering-places famous from one end of the country to the other, whose mountains and forests are every summer the resort of artists and tourists, fishermen and hunters, was rarely explored by trappers. The fertility of the valley of the Mohawk was indeed well known, but the power of the Six Nations was far from broken, and the jealousy with which the Indians beheld the slightest encroachment on their hunting ground made every attempt at opening up the country an undertaking full of danger. As if the vengeance of the savage were not enough, there came up from the newly ploughed land a terrible malaria, known as the Genesee fever, which, unchecked by the rude medical knowledge of the time, swept off whole families of settlers. It was not till 1789 that the tide of immigration began to set in strongly,

* A traveller who saw Albany in 1776 has left us a pleasing description of the place. "I was not a little surprized to find Albany to be so durty a city the houses in the Dutch Taste, the Inside clean to a fault even their Cyder Barrels are kept scour'd as clean as their Dishes, their women are continually employ'd in scouring the floors, one drop of Ink In a house will breed a Riot, till it is erazed by Soap and sand, and Dishclouts, whilst their Streets are excessive durty, and the outside of the Houses resemble welchmans Breeches, void of all form and Comliness." A letter to Miss Nabby Bishop, June 2, 1776. In the Scammel Letters. Historical Magazine, September, 1870.

and that thousands of ox-sleighs annually went out from Albany.

When Washington, in the summer of 1783, went through the central part of New York State with Clinton, Oswego was a military post on the extreme frontier, where a few enterprising traders carried on a flourishing commerce with the Cayugas, the Senecas, and the Tuscaroras, who brought thither skins of the buffalo, the bear, the otter, and the lynx, to exchange for strings of wampum, hundreds of periwinkle shells, and bits of colored glass. Deer browsed and black bears roamed at will over the plain where Rochester now stands. Foxes and wolves were plentiful on the site of Syracuse. At Saratoga, since renowned over the whole earth for its mineral-waters, a single spring, long known to the Indians for its medicinal properties, bubbled up through a barrel sunk in the ground.

It would indeed be tedious to enumerate the many towns now great and opulent which were then wretched hamlets, or whose streets had not yet been laid out. No manufacturing villages were to be found in all New England. Beavers built their dams unmolested along the banks of streams since crowded with mills and factories, each one of which finds work for more men and women than, to the end of the eighteenth century, made up the population of the largest country town of America. At Springfield a few houses were strung along the post-road; Lawrence was a squalid hamlet; Manchester was no better. When, in 1820, the fourth census was taken, the country around Lowell was a wilderness where sportsmen shot game. The splendid falls which now furnish power to innumerable looms were all unused, and the two hundred needy beings who comprised the whole population of the town found their sole support in the sturgeon and alewives taken from the waters of the Concord and the Merrimack.* Indeed, the condition of the manufactures at that time was most deplorable. With the exception of a few mills for the manufacture of paper, scarce so good in quality as that grocers are now accustomed to wrap around pounds of sugar and tea; a foundry or two, where iron was melted into rude pigs, or beaten into bars or nails; a factory where cocked hats

---

* Miles's Lowell as it Was and as it Is, p. 10.

and felts were made, no manufactures could be said to exist.
Cotton was never seen growing but in gardens among the
rose-bushes and honeysuckle-vines. A little had indeed been
sent to Liverpool five years before the fight at Lexington.
Eight bags were again sent out in 1784, but when the ship
sailed into that port the officers of the customs seized them,
as it was well known that so much cotton could never have
come from America.* The Constitution had been framed and
adopted before the first Arkwright spinning-machine was set
up in this country, before the first bounty was offered, or the
first cotton-mill erected in Pawtucket. The place now held
by cotton fabrics was filled by linen spun at every farmer's
hearth, but nowhere so extensively as in New England. To
spin well was then esteemed an accomplishment of which any
damsel might well be proud. Nor were any means of encouragement left untried. To the poor, bounties were offered.
The rich brought into fashion the "spinning bee," which
continued in vogue in many country towns when the ladies of
the great cities had long deserted the wheel for the harpsichord and the spinet. The bee was generally held in the
town-hall; but if the village were not prosperous enough to
own such a building, the house of some minister was chosen.
Thither the women went with their spinning-wheels and flax,
and, as they spun, were brought cake and wine and tea by the
fine gentlemen of the town.

Though the inland towns were thus mean and squalid,
those scattered along the sea-coast from Portsmouth to New
London were thriving and populous. Their proximity to the
water had made them great trading and fishing ports. Indeed,
before the revolution, scarcely one could be found among
them whose citizens had not some venture on the sea, either
of a regular or irregular kind. The harsh restrictions laid by
the mother country on the commerce of her colonies had led
to smuggling, and smuggling had proved a sure road to wealth.
In every town prominent characters could be pointed out
who, when the States were under British rule, had constantly
stowed away in their cellars and attics goods they would have

* Smithers' History of Liverpool, p. 129; De Bow's Industrial Resources of
the United States, vol. i, pp. 119, 120.

been loath to have the officers of the customs see. To these harbors came vessels built for speed and laden with contraband ware gathered in the colonies of France and Spain. Of this trade Boston was long the centre, and many a merchant of high repute did not disdain to engage in it. Thus, on the very day when the farmers and ploughmen of Middlesex drove the British out of Lexington, John Hancock was to have stood trial for defrauding the customs.

The war changed all this. Smuggling almost ceased, and the crews once engaged in it found occupation at the Grand Banks or on the whaling fleets that went out each year. Spermaceti whales, now almost driven from the sea, were then most plentiful, came some seasons as far south as Cape Ann and Montauk Point, had been seen by old whalers in schools off the coast of Rhode Island and Connecticut, and were at times found stranded on the shores of Long Island sound.*

The oil obtained from these creatures commanded a ready sale and a high price. The whale-fishery became, accordingly, in spite of its hardships and dangers, a favorite occupation of the fishermen of New England. Falmouth and Barnstable, Martha's Vineyard and Cape Ann, were noted whaling ports; but foremost among them all was Nantucket. The town stood on a little strip of sand scarce four miles wide and fifteen

---

* The fishermen of Cape Cod were the first to begin whale-fishing, and it was from them that the Nantucket fishers learned the use of the harpoon. Spermaceti whales had from time to time been found dead on the Massachusetts and Rhode Island shore; but it was not till 1712 that the first living one was captured by Christopher Hassey. Hassey was a Nantucket fisherman, and had gone out in search of right whales, was caught in a storm, blown off shore and into a school of spermaceti whales. One of them he killed and towed to land. From that time forth great numbers were taken every year. In 1726, as many as eighty-six were killed off the Nantucket coast. In 1784, the favorite cruising-ground was the gulf of St. Lawrence, banks of Newfoundland, Davis's strait, straits of Belle Isle, and even so far away as Cape Desolation. The crude oil then brought £24 per ton, and paid a duty of £18 per ton at the port of Liverpool. It may be interesting to state that the first vessel that ever entered a British port bearing the stars and stripes was a Nantucket whaler laden with oil. A good history of the New England whale-fishery has yet to be written, but some facts regarding it may be had from Hunt's Merchant's Magazine, vol. iii; North American Review, vol. xxxviii; and Obed Marcy's History of Nantucket. See, also, Brown's Whaling Cruise, and History of the Whale-Fishery.

long, that rose from the ocean, and was, before the war, a
busy hive of seafaring men, where ships were built, where
cordage and rigging were made, and whence set sail each year
to the whaling grounds one hundred and fifty ships.   When
the war closed, all this prosperity and greatness had ended.
The rope-walks were deserted.   The docks and wharfs had
fallen into decay.   A few old hulks were all that remained of
the once gallant little navy.   The population had sadly decreased.   Grass grew in the streets of the town.   Of the
whalemen, a few were serving in the crews of privateers,
but the larger number, enticed by the liberal offers of England, had settled at Halifax to take part in the whaling ventures that went out from thence.*

To the south of New York no place of importance was to
be met with till Philadelphia was reached.   The city was
then the greatest in the country.   No other could boast of so
many streets, so many houses, so many people, so much re-
nown.†   There had been made the discoveries which carried the name of Franklin to the remotest spots of the civilized world.   There had been put forth the Declaration of
Independence.   There had long been held the deliberations
of Congress.   No other city was so rich, so extravagant, so
fashionable.   Seven years before, Lee had described the place
as an attractive scene of amusement and debauch.‡   Lovel [#]
had called it a place of crucifying expenses.   And this reputation it still maintained.   But the features that most impressed travellers from distant lands were the fineness of the
houses, the goodness of the pavement, the filthiness of the
carriage-ways,‖ the regular arrangement of the streets, and the

---

* See Obed Marcy's History of Nantucket Island; Letters from an American
Farmer, by Hector St. John Crèvecœur.

† In 1786, the number of houses in Philadelphia was 4,600; in New York,
3,500; in Boston, 2,100.   The population of Philadelphia was 32,205; of New
York, 24,500; of Boston, 14,640.   See New York Gazette, August 17, 1786.

‡ R. H. Lee to Washington.   Sparks's Correspondence of the Revolution,
vol. i.

[#] James Lovel to Washington.   Sparks's Correspondence of the Revolution,
vol. i.

‖ The streets of the city finally became so full of filth, dead cats and dead
dogs, that their condition was made the subject of a satire by Francis Hopkinson,
better known as the author of the Battle of the Kegs.   In a piece which he

singular custom of numbering some and giving to others the names of forest-trees.*

One of these. Chestnut, long since given up to the demands of commerce, and lined with banks, with warehouses, and with shops, was the fashionable walk. There every fine day, when business was over, when the bank was closed, when the exchange was deserted, crowds of pleasure-seekers gathered to enjoy the air and display their rich clothes. If the dress that has displaced the garb of that period be less tasteful, it must be owned it is at least more convenient. A gentleman of the last century, if he were a man of fashion or of means, wore a three-cornered cocked hat heavily laced. His hair was done up in a cue, and its natural shade concealed by a profusion of powder. His coat was light-colored, with diminutive cape, marvellously long back, and silver buttons engraved with the letters of his name. His small clothes came scarce to his knees; his stockings were striped; his shoes pointed, and adorned with huge buckles; his vest had flap-pockets; his cuffs were loaded with lead. If he were so happy as to have seen some service during the war, he affected a military bearing, and had much to say of campaigns. When he bowed to the damsels that passed him, he took half the sidewalk as he flourished his cane and scraped his foot. Nor does the dress of the lady, as she gravely returned his salutation and courtesied almost to the earth, seem less strange to us. Those were the days of gorgeous brocades and taffetas, luxuriantly displayed over cumbrous hoops, which, flattened before and behind, stood out for two feet on each side; of tower-built hats, adorned with tall feathers; of calash and muskmelon-bonnets; of high wooden heels, fancifully cut; of gowns without fronts; of fine satin petticoats; and of implanted teeth. This singular custom had but lately been brought in by one La Mayeur, and had rapidly become fashionable. La Mayeur called himself a doctor, advertised his business ex-

---

called Dialogues of the Dead, a conversation is made to take place between the carcasses of a cat and dog lying in one of the streets. The dialogue is without wit, but is said to have aroused the street commissioners to a sense of duty. It was afterward republished in the American Museum for March, 1787.

* Smyth, in his Tour through the United States of America in 1784, comments on these singular appellations of the streets.

tensively, was largely patronized by the ladies, and, at the end of a few months, went off, it was believed, with a small fortune. One of his advertisements is yet extant. In it he announces to the people of Philadelphia that his business is to transplant teeth; that he has, within the six months just passed, successfully transplanted one hundred and twenty-three, and assures those having front teeth for sale that he will give two guineas for every sound one brought him.

The dreariness of winter evenings was broken by dancing assemblies and plays. The assemblies were of fortnightly occurrence, and very select.* The price of a season ticket was three pounds fifteen shillings. But it was thought highly improper that divertisements of this kind should be attended by young men under twenty, or by young women under eighteen. They were, therefore, rigorously excluded. Nor did such damsels as found admittance reap any benefit from beauty, from wit, or from the possession of any of those charms now so highly prized. The plainest and the fairest were treated alike. For partners were chosen by lot, and were partners for the evening.† They danced, walked, and flirted with no one else, and, when the dancing was over, partook together of rusks and tea. The next evening the gentleman came to sup with the parents of the young woman who had fallen to his lot at the assembly, an event which was made the occasion for a great display of plate, of china, and of ceremony.‡ Many of the table manners then in vogue have fallen into disuse and been utterly forgotten, but one has been preserved to us by

---

* In many of the old advertisements it is announced that these assemblies will open with a Passe-Pie and end with the Sarabund à l'Espagnole. See New York Packet, January 5, 1784.

† On the Ohio such matters were differently managed. One who was no mean observer has left us an amusing account of the routs and balls of Louisville: "The Manager who distributed the numbers, call'd Gent No. 1. He takes his stand.—Lady No. 1. she rises from her seat, the Manager leader to the floor & introduces the Gentⁿ No. 1— & so on 'till the floor is ful. . . . At the refreshments, the Gentⁿ will, by instinct, without Chesterfieldian monition, see that his better half (for the time being) has a quantum sufficit, of all the nice delicacies, & that without his cramming his *jaws* full untill he has reconducted her to the ball-room —then he is at liberty to absent himself a while." Autobiography of Major Samuel S. Forman. See Historical Magazine for December, 1869.

‡ Scharf's Chronicles of Baltimore, p. 229.

an anecdote that is worth citing. It would, it seems, have been thought as rude for the guest to refuse to partake of a dish a fourth or fifth time, if asked so to do, as it would have been thought negligent in the hostess to omit to press him. There seemed, therefore, to be no limit to the number of times the lady of the house was constrained to ask, and the number of times the visitor was constrained to accept. But, happily, there was in use a kind of freemasonry signals by which he conveyed, by the position of his plate, by the arrangement of his knife and fork, by the way in which he disposed of his spoon, his wish not to be invited to be helped again to slices of chicken and saucers of jam. This custom sorely puzzled the uninitiated, and gave rise to many amusing incidents, one of which happened to the Prince de Broglie. The prince, who travelled in our country in 1782, relates, in one of his letters, that he was invited to dine with the lady of Robert Morris; that he went; that he was repeatedly asked to have his cup refilled; that he consented; and that, when he had swallowed the twelfth cup of tea, his neighbor whispered in his ear and told him when he had had enough of the water diet he should place his spoon across his cup, else the hostess would go on urging him to drink tea till the crack of doom.*

From Philadelphia ran out the road to what was then the far West. Its course after leaving the city lay through the counties of Chester and Lancaster, then sparsely settled, now thick with towns and cities and penetrated with innumerable railways, and went over the Blue Ridge mountains to Shippensburg and the little town of Bedford. Thence it wound through the beautiful hills of western Pennsylvania, and crossed the Alleghany mountains to the head-waters of the Ohio. It was known to travellers as the northern route, and was declared to be execrable. In reality it was merely a passable road, broad and level in the lowlands, narrow and dangerous in the passes of the mountains, and beset with steep declivities. Yet it was the chief highway between the Mississippi valley and the East, and was constantly travelled in the summer months by thousands of emigrants to the western country, and by long trains

* Pennsylvania Magazine of History and Biography, 1878, vol. ii, No. 2, pp. 166, 167.

of wagons bringing the produce of the little farms on the banks of the Ohio to the markets of Philadelphia and Baltimore. In any other section of the country a road so frequented would have been considered as eminently pleasant and safe. But some years later the traveller who was forced to make the journey from Philadelphia to Pittsburg in his carriage and four, beheld with dread the cloud of dust which marked the slow approach of a train of wagons. For nothing excited the anger of the sturdy teamsters more than the sight of a carriage. To them it was the unmistakable mark of aristocracy, and they were indeed in a particularly good humor when they suffered the despised vehicle to draw up by the road-side without breaking the shaft, or taking off the wheels, or tumbling it over into the ditch.* His troubles over, the traveller found himself at a small hamlet then known as Pittsburg. The place bore no likeness to the great and wealthy city now standing on the same spot and bearing the same name, whose streets are bordered with stately dwellings and stores, whose population numbers more than one hundred and fifty thousand, and whose air is thick with the smoke and soot of a hundred foundries, machine-shops, and factories.† Yet, small as was the town, many historical associations gathered about it. At that very point, where the Alleghany sweeping from the north, and the Monongahela from the south, mingle their waters to form the Ohio, had stood, years before,

---

* Such mishaps were, in 1784, quite unknown, for no carriages then found their way to so remote a spot as Pittsburg. But in a few years they became of common occurrence, and continued to be when Madison was President.

† A good description of Pittsburg at that time was published in the Pittsburg Gazette of July 29, 1786, the first number of the first newspaper ever printed west of the Alleghanies. H. H. Brackenridge, whose famous novel, Modern Chivalry, is still to be found on the shelves of circulating libraries, wrote it. See, also, Diary of Arthur Lee, 1784, and An Early Record of Pittsburg, in Historical Magazine, vol. ii. "The Towne," says one who saw it in 1789, "The Towne at that time was the muddiest place that I ever was in; and by reason of using so much Coal, being a great manufacturing place & kept in so much smoke & dust, as to effect the skin of the inhabitants." Autobiography of Major Samuel Forman, Historical Magazine, December, 1869. In 1795, the place is described as "a thriving Town containing at present about two hundred Houses, fifty of wch are brick and framed, & the remainder Log." Journal of Thomas Chapman, Historical Magazine, June, 1869. See, also, Craig's History of Pittsburg.

Fort Duquesne, one of the long chain of posts the French erected from the St. Lawrence to the Mississippi. Not far away was "Braddock's Fields," a little patch of land whereon the English general had sustained his memorable defeat, and whence the young Virginia captain had led the remnant of his troops. Just back of the town, and hard by the banks of the Monongahela, rose "Grant's Hill," on whose summit a detachment of Highlanders were surprised and massacred by the French and Indians. So late as 1784, the top was strewn with their whitened bones, and with arrow-heads and toma-hawks used in the battle. Near by, on the same hill, was a mound thrown up by that prehistoric race whose tumuli are found on the crests of half the hills from the Mohawk to the Rio Grande.

On the destruction of Fort Duquesne, the place passed into the hands of the British, who built Fort Pitt. In 1764, at the end of the Indian war, Colonel Campbell laid out the town in four squares just without the walls of the fort, and named it Pittsburg, in honor of the great commoner. When Wash-ington saw it in 1770, the town numbered twenty log huts along the Monongahela; but in the course of fourteen years many new settlers had come in, many new houses had been put up, till, in 1784, Pittsburg numbered one hundred dwell-ings and almost one thousand inhabitants. It was the cen-tring point of emigrants to the West, and from it the travel-lers were carried in keel-boats, in Kentucky flat-boats, and Indian pirogues down the waters of the Ohio, past the beau-tiful island where long afterward Blennerhasset built his palace, to the filthy and squalid settlement at the falls of the Ohio, or on to the shores of the Mississippi, where La Clede, twenty years earlier, had laid the foundations of St. Louis. Two dangers constantly beset the voyager. The boat was at every moment likely to become entangled in the branches of the trees that skirted the river, or be fired into by the Indians who lurked in the woods. The cabin was therefore low, that it might safely glide under the limbs of the overhanging sycamores, and lined with blankets and with beds to guard the inmates from Indian bullets.* From St. Louis rude boats and

* For a description of one of these boats, and the trouble they had when

rafts floated down the river to Natchez and New Orleans.
But of the many that went down the river scarce one ever
came back, for the current was so rapid that it seemed hopeless to attempt a return.   The boats were therefore hastily put
together and sold at New Orleans as lumber.

Some settlements had been attempted in the region now
portioned out between the States of Indiana and Illinois, but
the most thickly settled portion of the valley lay along the banks
of the Kentucky river, and the tributaries of the Licking.
In all, upward of twelve thousand souls were there, most of
them having come across the Blue Ridge mountains from the
neighboring States of Georgia and Carolina.   For in the three
States of Georgia, North Carolina, and South Carolina were
then living near one fifth of the population of the country.
They could, therefore, well spare the restless colonists who
yearly went out from them to dwell in the canebrakes and
wilds of Kentucky.   One cause of this emigration was,
beyond a doubt, the extreme difficulty which the most help-
less and dependent class of society, whose province it was to
follow the plough, to tend the cattle, and to toil in the swamps,
found in eking out even a miserable existence.   Almost
every acre of land close to the sea-ports was portioned out
into plantations and held by the great landed proprietors.
The labor was largely slave labor.   The immense yield of
the rice-fields and the indigo-fields, of pitch and rosin, had
brought wealth, and with wealth had come in all the blessings
and all the evils which flourish best in opulent societies.
Nowhere else was good blood and noble descent held in such
high esteem.   Nowhere else was social rank so clearly defined.
Toil was the only thing from which the rich planter abstained.

---

passing under trees, see Autobiography of Major Forman, Historical Magazine,
December, 1869, pp. 325, 326.

All travellers down the Ohio comment on the great size of the trees.   General
Parsons measured a black-walnut near the Muskingum, and found the circumference, five feet from the ground, to be twenty-two feet.   A sycamore near the
same spot measured forty-four feet in circumference, five feet from the ground.
See a pamphlet by Cutler, called An Explanation of the Map which delineates
that part of the Federal Lands, etc., Salem, 1787, p. 10.   This statement is
copied by Morse in his Geography, edition 1789, p. 461.   Connecticut Courant,
September 1, 1788.

Horse-racing by day and deer-hunting by night, duelling and gambling, made up, with the social festivities of the class to which he belonged, his sole occupation and pleasure.*

The country lying to the south of the Potomac was therefore, to a New Englander or a Pennsylvanian, a land almost as strange as if it had been in the tropics. There he sat in the shade of trees whose foliage bore no resemblance to that of the elms and chestnuts that grew along the streets of his native village. He rode for days through an endless succession of tobacco-fields. The rank vegetation of the Dismal Swamp; the rice-fields covered with water; the sugar-cane growing higher than he could reach; the great forests of pine yielding an inexhaustible supply of pitch and tar; the indigo-plant, the fruits, the very birds, filled him with astonishment; nor did the people seem less strange to him than the country. He admired, indeed, their open hospitality, but their appreciation of good blood excited only his derision. Their pride, their arrogance, their keen sense of what they were pleased to term personal honor, inspired him with disgust. He could not understand why men of sense and courage should be ever ready to seek each other's lives in revenge for slights and insults so trivial that they would, among his friends, scarcely have elicited a hearty curse. The appearance of the towns and cities, the social customs and festivities of the people, were unlike anything he had ever seen in Boston or Philadelphia. The language seemed scarcely to be English. Nor was he in turn less an object of wonder to his host. His walk, his dress, the eagerness with which he plied his new friends with questions, and the strange language in which he conveyed his feelings of surprise and pleasure, marked him out at once as an object of interest. The way he compacted his vowel sounds and clipped his words; the long sound which he gave to *a;* the broad sound with which he pronounced *e;*

---

* An account of the social life of Georgians and Carolinians before the revolution may be found in Ramsay's History of South Carolina, 1809. See, also, the American Museum for 1790. It did not change much after the war. In 1791, the grand jury for the district of Charleston, S. C., presented duelling "as a grievance of a very serious and alarming nature." Gazette of the United States, July 6, 1791.

the boldness with which he substituted that letter fo⟍ *⟍*, and *u*
for *o*—excited many a good-natured laugh at his expense.
Odd phrases, delightful in vigor and made up of words long
gone out of use in the mother country, and to be found only
in the pages of Dryden, of Chapman, of Ben Jonson, were
constantly in his mouth.

Strange as this section of the country seemed to men from
the Eastern States, it never failed to impress visitors from the
continent with the many resemblances it bore to England.
Especially was this true of Virginia.   There the traveller
journeying through the tide-water region may still meet,
along the banks of the Rappahannock and the James, with
the crumbling ruins and dilapidated remains of what, one
hundred years ago, were the spacious mansions of the rich
planters.   Like the opulent families that once dwelt in them,
by far the larger number have long since fallen into decay,
while the few that still withstand the ravages of time bear
but feeble testimony to the ancient grandeur of their former
owners.   Yet it is not impossible to form from them even
now some conception of what they were a century ago.   The
house was usually of wood, one story and a half or two stories
high, for it dated back to a time when the country did not
yet furnish permanent building materials, except at vast expense, nor provided skilled architects to make use of them.
But the spacious gardens, laid out in the prim style, with the
terraces, the arbors, the box-borders, and the geometrically
shaped parterres so fashionable a century since; the cupola;
the broad veranda, supported on massive columns; the high
chimney of sun-baked bricks; the ample dimensions of the
structure, and the broad entrance, gave to it an aspect of state-
liness by no means diminished by the lack of architectural
adornments, and the windows full of diminutive panes of ill-
pressed glass.   It was, however, in the internal arrangements
that the good taste and wealth of the owner were most
apparent.   The spacious rooms were decorated with carved
oaken wainscoting, reaching above the mantel-piece in an
unbroken expanse of flowers, and grinning faces and armorial
devices in the corners.   There were Chelsea figures, and
Japanese cabinets, and Kidderminster carpets; sideboards

full of plate; and huge tiled fireplaces, whose brass andirons shone like gold; nor were the stairways and landings wanting in grandeur.

In such abodes the heads of the great families, whose estates stretched far inland from the banks of the Rappahannock, lived splendidly and hospitably. Numerous slaves and white servants attended them in every capacity that use or ostentation could suggest. On their tables were to be found the luxuries of the Old World and the New, and chief among these stood Madeira wine and rum. That the men of that generation drank more deeply than the men of this, is not to be doubted. Then, and for many years after, whenever a public character was to be entertained, or a day famous in revolutionary history to be celebrated, a dinner was gotten up and toasts drunk. The number of regular toasts was always equal to the number of States in the Union. But when they were disposed of, "volunteers" were in order, and to these there was no fixed limit. Sometimes as many as ten would be offered and drunk to. Indeed, on more than one occasion thirty toasts were responded to, and the bumpers by which they were followed were strong Jamaica rum.

In the moments snatched from pleasures such as these, the rich Virginian devoted himself to the care of his estate and the performance of his public duties. He followed the judges on their circuits; he voted bills and addresses in the House of Deputies, and, if he were a military man, was present at the muster of the militia. No law had yet been passed by Congress for the formation of a national militia. Each State governed its own troops in its own way. Yet it would be unjust to suppose that the military was not an efficient body of men. Among the officers were to be found men with records of which any soldier might well be proud. Not a few of the captains and majors who stood before the ranks were veterans of a former war. Some had shared in the victory of the Great Meadows; had defended to the last Fort Necessity, and, when no longer tenable, marched out with all the honors of war; had followed Washington and Braddock to the fatal field of Monongahela, and, by their coolness and skill, covered the disorderly retreat of the more disciplined soldiers

of England. Others, too young to have shared in such ex-
ploits, had hastened, when independence was declared, to join
the army commanded by the illustrious Virginian, had stood
by him in his retreat through the Jerseys, marched with him
through the ice and snow of that glorious December morning
when he charged the Hessian camp at Trenton, took part in
the fight at Princeton, shared in the defeats at Brandywine
and Germantown, and beat back the troops of Cornwallis
when they sallied from the works at Yorktown.

The son of a great landed proprietor usually grew up to
manhood on his father's plantation, rode every morning, attended by his servant, to the school kept in the neighboring
parish by a clergyman of the English Church, passed thence
to William and Mary's college, spent a winter at Richmond,
and came back to the old hall an aspirant for a seat in the
House of Deputies.   His opinions respecting forms of government and forms of creed were not the result of long study or
of deep meditation, but were inherited with his estate, which
passed from father to son by the strictest laws of entail.
Whether Catholicism or Protestantism embraced the purer
creed or the more divine form of worship, whether nations
were wiser, better governed, more prosperous, under hereditary monarchs, electoral princes, or presidents, were matters
on which it would have puzzled him to give an opinion; he
was devotedly attached to the ritual and polity of the Angli-
can Church because his father and grandfather had been so
before him, and because he believed them to be a necessary
badge of what he considered his patrician descent; he was
a non-imposter, not because his reading had taught him that
imposts were bad things, but because the men on whom he
looked down with contempt were strongly in favor of the
measure.   The few deductions, indeed, which he derived
from reading had much of a foreign character, for his books,
like the lace for his hat and the frill for his shirt, his silver
shoe-buckles and his sword, came from over the sea.

That he should import his books is far from strange, for,
with few exceptions, all books came from beyond the Atlantic.
Fully three fourths of every library were volumes written by
English men of letters, and published by English printers,

No American writer had yet appeared whose compositions possessed more than an ephemeral interest, or were deemed worthy to be ranked with those of Goldsmith and Johnson, of Swift and Gibbon. It is true, indeed, that a few productions had come out during the revolutionary war, which had gained much notoriety for their authors, and had been widely read. It is true that Trumbull's "McFingal" went through as many editions when the population of the country was three millions, as did "Evangeline" when the numbers of the people had swollen to thirty millions. But the cause of the popularity of "McFingal" and the cause of the popularity of "Evangeline" are very different indeed. So long as the war lasted, phrases, expressions, whole pages of "McFingal," were on every tongue; but of the thousands who laughed over the first canto in 1775, not one in ten read the third canto in 1780, and not one in a hundred read the poem in 1784. Paine's "Crisis," it is true, had enjoyed an equal share of popularity, and was still reprinted and read. It is true, also, that Paine's little pamphlet, "Common Sense," had gained for him national reputation and national gratitude; but the circumstances which called it forth had passed away, and men were already beginning to forget the great services he had rendered to the cause of liberty.* Ramsay had not commenced his history; Gordon's was soon to come out. One author had indeed appeared, an author whose name has since become familiar to three genera-

---

* Toward the middle of the year 1784, a bill was brought in by some members of the Virginia house of deputies to reward the patriotism and public services of the now famous author of "Common Sense" by a grant of land known as the Secretary's land, on the eastern shore, equal to four thousand pounds sterling. The bill was known to have the approval of Washington, and was warmly supported by Madison; yet it was, on the third reading, thrown out. His friends again rallied, and proposed that the tract should be sold, and two thousand pounds of the money applied to the purchase of an estate for Mr. Paine. Even to this many of the deputies would not listen, and, after a sharp fight, the bill was again rejected by a single vote. See the letter of Washington to Madison, June 12, 1784, and that of Madison, in reply, July 2, 1784. The bill had passed two readings, when Arthur Lee made some statement which produced a sudden change in many votes. In New York he fared much better. The legislature, on the 19th of April, presented him with a farm in Westchester. Packet, May 29, 1784.

tions of school-boys, and whose works have, in our time, greatly changed our written language.   Noah Webster, then a youth of four-and-twenty, had lately put forth his "American Institute," the first of a splendid series of spelling-books, and the forerunner of his dictionary, and had seen it introduced into many New England schools, and rapidly displacing the ancient Dilworth.   But, with these few exceptions, and perhaps as many more in the domain of theology, no work had been produced which was, seventy-five years later, read by any but the curious.*

There is, in fact, no portion of our literary annals which presents a spectacle of so much dreariness as the one hundred and sixty years which followed the landing of the Pilgrims. In all that time scarcely any work of the imagination was produced which posterity has not willingly let die.   It would be a hard task to the most assiduous compiler to glean from the literature of that period material enough to make what would now be thought a readable book.   A few poems of the " Tenth Muse," an odd chapter from the " Magnalia Christi," a page or two from the essay on " The Freedom of the Will," some lyrics of Hopkinson, a satire by Trumbull, a pamphlet by Paine, would almost complete the book, and, when completed, it would not be a very large volume, nor one of a very high order of merit.   It would not be worth fifty lines of " Evangeline," nor the half of " Thanatopsis."   The men whose writings now form our national literature, the men we are accustomed to revere as intellectual patriarchs, all whose works have become classics, belong, without exception, to the generation which followed the revolution.   Irving was not a year old when peace was declared.   Cooper was born in the same year that Washington went into office.   Halleck, one year later. Prescott, in the year Washington came out of office.   The Constitution was five years old when Bryant was born.   The first year of the present century witnessed the birth of Bancroft, and, before another decade had come and gone, Emerson

---

* In the list of text-books that came out in 1784, Morse's American Geography must not be omitted.   It was full of errors, and received a scorching criticism in a pamphlet called Remarks on the American Universal Geography, by J. F., 1793.

was born, and Willis, and Longfellow, and Whittier, and Holmes, and Hawthorne, and Poe. Before the year 1825 was reached, "Thanatopsis" was published, Motley was born, the "Spy," the "Pioneer," and the "Pilot" were written, and Drake, after a short and splendid career, carried with honor to the grave. Scarcely a twelvemonth went by unmarked by the birth of a man long since renowned in the domain of letters—1783, 1789, 1790, 1791, 1794, 1795, 1796, 1800, 1803, 1806, 1807, 1808, 1809, 1811, 1814, such is the almost unbroken succession.

It may, at first sight, seem strange that, after so many years of intellectual weakness, of feeble tottering, and of blind gropings, there should suddenly have appeared so great a crowd of poets and novelists, historians and essayists, following hard upon the war for independence. But the fact is merely another illustration of a great truth with which the history of every people is replete with examples, the truth that periods of national commotion, disorder, and contention are invariably followed by periods of intellectual activity. Whatever can turn the minds of men from the channels in which they have long been running, and stir them to their inmost depths, has never yet failed to produce most salutary and lasting results.

The age of Pericles, of Augustus, of Leo and Elizabeth, of Louis Quatorze, and the splendors of the reign of Ferdinand, are but so many instances in point. The same is true of our own land. For the first time since white men began to inhabit America, the colonists were united in a common league against a common foe. For seven years the strife continued. When it ended, yet another seven years followed, during which the fury of war gave way to the rage of faction. There was never a moment of rest. No sooner was one storm over than another appeared on the horizon. Yet here again years of national commotion were followed by years of great mental activity the like of which our country had never witnessed before. Yet again were the evils of war succeeded by the fruits of genius.

Our ancestors were, therefore, in 1784, shut out from the only native authors whose writings are by this generation

thought worthy to be read.   They possessed no poets better
than Philip Freneau and Timothy Dwight.   No novelist, no
dramatist, no really great historian, had yet arisen.   Among
the living statesmen none had as yet produced anything more
enduring than a political pamphlet or a squib.   Hamilton and
Madison and Jay had not begun that noble series of essays
which finds no parallel in the English language save in the
"Letters of Junius."   A knowledge of German, of Italian, and
of Spanish was not considered a necessary part of the education of a gentleman.   Men of parts and refinement listened in
astonishment to the uncouth gutturals in which the officers of
the Hessian troops commanded their men to "carry arms"
and to "right wheel."   All, therefore, who did not understand
French, and they made up the majority of readers, were of
necessity compelled to peruse the works of English authors, or
read nothing, or what was worse than nothing.   They filled
their library-shelves, as a consequence, with volumes which are
at this day much more admired than studied.   The incom-
parable letters of Philip Francis to Woodfall were imitated by
numberless pamphleteers, who, over the signature of Cassius
or Brutus, reviled the Cincinnati, or set forth most urgent
reasons why no Tory refugee should ever again be allowed to
find a footing on American soil.   Damsels envious of distinction as correspondents made themselves familiar with the polished diction and pure English of the "Spectators" and the
"Tatlers."   Nor were they ignorant of many books which no
woman would now, without a blush, own to having read.   The
adventures of Peregrine Pickle and Roderic Random were
as well known to the women of that generation as were
those of Leatherstocking to the women of the succeeding.
It would, however, be a great mistake to suppose that they
read no novels of a less objectionable character than "Tom
Jones" and "Tristram Shandy." *   The lighter literature of

---

* The favorite novels of the young women of that age were Victoria, Lady Julia Mandeville, and Malvern Dale.   A critic who confessed to being a great novel-
reader has said of Lady Julia Mandeville: "The stile is beautiful, but the tale is
horrid."   Malvern Dale was, she thought, "something like Evelina, though not
so pretty."   Journal of a Young Lady of Virginia, pp. 12, 17, 25.   Edited by E.
V. Mason.   The Sylph also stood high.   Many others are advertised in the Pennsylvania Packet, January 28, 1785.

England had long been growing purer and purer. The re-proach which from the time of Fielding and Smollett had lain on the novel was rapidly passing away. Even among grave and reflecting people the feeling against all works of fiction was far less strong that it had been when, a few years before, Sir Anthony Absolute pronounced the circulating library to be an evergreen-tree of diabolical knowledge. "Evelina" and "Camilla" had appeared, had been read with admiration, and had shown that a popular novel might be written without an amour or a debauch. From letters and journals still extant, it should seem that, with the exception of the few novels named, the staple reading was of a serious character. After years of patient toil, Gibbon had lately put forth the third volume of his majestic work; Robertson had published the first readable history of America.

The cost of such books was then much in excess of what it now is, yet the price, though high, was very considerably less than they could have been published for at home.* Paper was both scarce and expensive. Some few mills had recently been put up in Pennsylvania, but the machinery was rude, the workmen unskilled, the number of reams turned out each month by no means equal to the demand, and the quality of the paper not much better than that at present used for printing hand-bills and posters. Bristol-board seems not to have been made in the country, and so little of it was brought in from abroad that the lack of it was severely felt. A hundred uses to which it is now put were unknown. No trades-man notified his patrons, by a generous distribution of neatly printed and ornamented cards, of the arrival of a new stock of tammies and everlastings; the fine gentleman gave his name,

---

* In the advertisement of Ramsay's History of the Revolution in South Caro-lina, edition of 1786, it is stated: "The author has taken on himself the risk and expense of the whole edition, amounting to more than four thousand nine hundred dollars." An abridgment of the Lives of the Poets, in twenty-five num-bers, paper covers, sold for thirty-seven shillings and sixpence, a sum that would not now be equalled by fifteen dollars; Claypole's History of Ireland brought half a guinea. Pennsylvania Packet, January 8, 1784. Moore's Travels sold at a dollar for each of the four volumes. Packet, March 27, 1784. It may be ob-served that the sale of Ramsay's History was prohibited in England. See a poem on the subject in the American Museum for February, 1787.

not his card, to the servant who courtesied before him at the
open door; the fine lady sent out no richly engraved invitations to her routs and her feasts; for such a purpose playing-
cards were made to do duty, for of these, as the taste for
whist, for ombre, and quadrille was universal, there was no
stint. The custom, indeed, lingered till the present century
had come in, and the descendants of many of the fashionable families of those days preserve, among the stately love-
letters of their grandmothers, queens of hearts and aces of
spades on the back of which are printed invitations to dancing assemblies and to balls.

Low as was the state of letters, that of the fine arts was
lower still; they were wholly neglected. There did not then
exist in the country a single piece of architecture which, when
tried even by the standard of that day, can be called respectable. Not a church, not a public building, not a hall has been
preserved to us that is not a deformity; here and there, in the
great towns, some merchant prince had put up a costly pile,
which was believed by his townsmen to rival in magnificence
the palace-like homes of the English aristocracy. Such an
one was the Walton house, at New York, whose spacious rooms
were long since turned into emigrants' lodgings and stores.
The home of Robert Morris, at Philadelphia, was another. It
was by far the most magnificent in the city; had called forth
the admiration of a distinguished foreigner accustomed to the
splendors of Paris and Versailles, and led him to comment on
the huge doors of solid mahogany, on the hinges of glittering
brass, and on the rich display of porcelain. But these were
the exception. The houses which made up the towns and
cities were of the low-brow, hip-roofed order, strung along the
streets in disorderly array; some had their gable-ends toward
the road, others stood back in small gardens full of sunflowers and hollyhocks. If of brick, they were commonly
smeared with stucco and defaced with pilasters; had great
wastes of wall between the stories, and windows which resembled nothing so much as a checker-board. Their beauty
consisted solely in spacious rooms, in costly furniture and
rich hangings; but among the hangings a landscape, a battle-
piece, or an interior, indeed, an oil-painting of any kind other

than a portrait by Smybert or a head by Copley, was never
to be seen. A vague rumor of a gallery of pictures that
once existed in New Jersey has come down to us. We
are told how one Watson, a Scotchman, settled at Perth
Amboy; how he loaned money, how he painted portraits,
how he kept in a barn, which he dignified by the name of
a gallery, a few pictures done in oil; how, at his death,
they passed to his nephew, how the nephew took sides with
the Tories, how he fled for his life, and how the militia so
effectually scattered these works of art that not a trace of one
of them can now be found. But with that exception, no
extensive collection was made for more than twenty years.
In truth, at the close of the revolution the country could
boast neither of artists nor of paintings.* Of the men who,
in after years, reached a questionable distinction as painters,
some were busy with their tops and marbles, some were in
long clothes, and some had not been born. Peale was at that
time six years old, Allston was five, Sully was one. Of the
three Americans who had already reached distinction in the
fine arts, not one was in the country. West was in England
daubing canvas with representations of Cupid, of Death on
the Pale Horse, and with scenes drawn from the writings of
Shakespeare, of Homer, and the Apostles. Gilbert Stuart,
who first saw the light of day in the dingy garret of a Rhode
Island snuff-mill, went abroad two years before the fight at
Lexington, and did not return till Washington had been four
years president. Copley, too, departed at the opening of
the war, leaving behind him many excellent portraits of the
beauties and fine gentlemen of colonial days. The place of

*In a paper, entitled Thoughts on American Genius, published in the Ameri-
can Museum, for March, 1787, some names and works are cited to "explode
the European creed that we are infantine in our acquisitions and savage in
our manners, because we are inhabitants of a new world, lately occupied by a race
of savages." Among artists, the men of genius are West, Copley, and John
Trumbull; Mr. Taylor, of Philadelphia, in landscape; Mr. Stuart, of Rhode Island,
and Mr. Brown, of Boston, in portrait-painting. The best prose writer is Dr.
Ramsay, of South Carolina. The finest poet is Barlow, whose Vision of Columbus is as far below the epics of Blackburn as the epics of Blackburn are beneath
the epics of Homer. Some idea of the style of painting popular at that day may
be had by reading the list of paintings that were drawn as prizes in Mrs. Pine's
lottery at Philadelphia, in 1789. Pennsylvania Gazette, November 25, 1789.

these men was filled by foreigners. Smybert had long been
busy in Boston. Pine, now chiefly remembered for his fine
portrait of Washington, had just come over. He brought
with him the first plaster cast of the " Venus de Medici" ever
seen in the United States. But the women of Philadelphia
were prudes ; the statue was a nude one, and the cry of
shame that went up was so strong that Pine was forced to
show it to his friends in private. Nor did this unwholesome
morality soon disappear. Twenty-two years later, when a
new generation had grown up, the exhibition of the Philadelphia Academy of Fine Arts was held in the Rotunda. Among
the pictures then shown were fifty casts of famous statues in
the Louvre ; but many of these were naked, were pronounced
indecent, and the managers compelled to set apart one day in
each week for women, and, on such days, to keep the naked
figures carefully covered up. Nay, more : in our own time,
when the " Greek Slave," one of the few works of art of which
our country has reason to be proud, was shown at Cincinnati,
the world was edified by the sight of a delegation of distinguished clergymen sent to view it, that Christian people might
know if they could with safety behold it. Trumbull, himself an artist, spoke the truth when he assured a young friend
that it would be better for him to learn to make shoes or
to dig potatoes than to paint pictures in America. Thirty-
six years later, a famous writer in the Edinburgh Review
tauntingly asked, and his taunts were none the less galling
because they were true : Who, in the four quarters of the
globe, reads an American book, or goes to an American play,
or looks at an American painting or statue ? What does
the world owe to American physicians or surgeons ? What
new substances have their chemists discovered ? What new
constellations have their astronomers discerned ? Who drinks
out of American glasses ? Who eats from American plates ?
Who wears an American coat, or lies down to sleep in an
American blanket ? * The first quarter of the present cen-

---

* Edinburgh Review, 1820.
    The feelings aroused by this performance were quite as bitter as any Mr.
Dickens awakened by the American Notes, and everywhere editors and writers
hastened to hurl foul scorn at the Review. Nor did the resentment soon die

tury passed away before a single painting or a single piece of statuary was produced which will, one hundred and fifty years from now, be examined by our descendants with pride.

There was, however, one art, an art which is half a fine art, not wholly neglected. It is true that in many parts of the community the theatre was still proscribed. In Massachusetts it was held in abhorrence, and the sharp laws of earlier times were in 1784 re-enacted. In New York and Philadelphia the stage was frowned upon, and plays and players pronounced immoral. But there remained many towns of lesser note where the actors were made welcome and rich. Such an one was Baltimore, for the city, small as it then was, had already achieved a high reputation for jollity.* Market street was the fashionable quarter, and ran out from the crowd of shops and taverns, far into the green fields and orchards of what was then the country, but is now covered with blocks of houses. The street was lined on either side by an endless succession of low, rambling houses, and was the particular pride of the citizens. They boasted that neither Philadelphia nor New York could show a street so long, so beautiful, and so gay. Nor was their pride altogether unfounded. The houses, brightly colored, some blue, some white and blue, others yellow, lighted up the deep shade of the locust-trees, while here and there loomed up the brick mansions of the rich merchants, with quaint entrances and great patches of wall between the windows. Along this highway, too, in the cool of the summer evening, sauntered a great throng of young men and damsels dressed in their best clothes, flirting, jesting, and enjoying the air. The spectacle, unimposing as it would seem to a generation accustomed to much finer ones, was still attractive to strangers, and led not a few of them to put down in their journals comments on the beauty of the women, on the gallantry of the men, and the rich display of brocades, of taffetas, and of hoops.

---

out, for, many years later, there appeared in the North American Review a vigorous reply, entitled, Who reads an American Book ? North American Review, No. lv.

*See a lecture on Baltimore Long Ago, by J. P. Kennedy ; also, Scharf's Chronicles of Baltimore for a good account of Baltimore at the revolution. Mr. Kennedy's lecture is quoted by Scharf, p. 231.

The favorite amusements of the Baltimoreans were balls, routs, and dancing assemblies. But in the intervals between assembly nights the theatre was the place of resort. The theatres to which the town then went to weep and applaud were wanting in the luxury, the richness and display of the rooms wherein we are accustomed to witness the impersonations of Salvini and of Booth. In the best of them the stage was narrow and contracted, the scenery wretched daubs, which produced little illusion in the dim light of a multitude of oil-lamps and candles. That portion of the house at present believed to contain the best seats was then known as the pit, was looked upon as the least desirable, and nightly filled with a rabble more noisy and obstreperous than is now to be found in the top gallery on the night of a benefit. In the boxes and stalls above the pit were the seats of the better class and the aristocracy of the town. The gallery was taken up by the lower classes. As the fashion of reserving seats had not yet come in, it was customary to send servants to occupy places as soon as the doors were thrown open, and hold them till their masters and mistresses arrived. It was, however, announced among the notices at the foot of the play-bills that the curtain would rise promptly at a quarter after six o'clock, and that all servants were then expected to leave. Other notices informed the audience that they were not to call upon the musicians to play their favorite airs, that if they did not bring exact change they could purchase no tickets, and that the managers would be greatly obliged, and the public much diverted, by the loan of any plays fit to be brought on the stage.* Among the plays considered as fit to be performed were one or two of Sheridan's, as many more of Shakespeare's, and some of O'Keefe's. But the taste of the public was not critical, and

---

* On some of the play-bills of 1784, and earlier, are notices as follows: "Any Gentlemen possessed of good Farces, and will lend or dispose of them to the Managers, will greatly oblige them." "Some Tunes having been called for by Persons in the Gallery which have given Offence to others, the Managers have resolved that no Music will be played but such as they shall order the Day before the Representation." "Children in Laps will not be admitted." Scharf's Chronicles of Baltimore. See, also, the play-bills printed in the Philadelphia papers of 1790–1796.

none called forth such rounds of applause as "Love in a Village" and "Miss in her Teens." The price of admission to the boxes was commonly one dollar, to the pit five shillings, to the gallery ninepence. This sum placed the luxury of a night at the theatre within the means of the poorest classes. Every night the playhouse was open, which rarely was more than thrice in a week, the gallery was crowded with apprentices, with shopkeepers, and with tradesmen. But on no occasion was the press so great, and the audience so jolly, as on an evening when it was expected that Harlequin would bound through hogsheads of fire and chests of drawers. Then the mob was wild with delight. They would call upon the fiddlers to play their favorite tunes, not always the most select, would sing snatches of lewd songs, would make coarse jokes, would shout to the people in the boxes, jeer one actor and applaud another, and, when Columbine was hard pressed, call upon Harlequin to come to her relief.

From such spectacles as these, however, a large part of the community kept aloof. Some pronounced them to be immoral, others denounced them as a piece of foolish and wicked extravagance. The country, they declared, was surely going to be ruined by the taste for expensive luxuries that was coming in. The times were full of signs. Coaches were becoming more and more common in the great towns. Shops were springing up filled with all manner of finery brought from beyond the sea. Damsels whose mothers had been content to wear homespun were quite unhappy unless they were tricked out in brocades, in taffetas, in Rohan hats. Young men now thought it becoming to scoff at sacred things, and frequented the playhouse much more than they did the church. A stop should be put to this, and as the theatre was the newest evil, it was quite fitting to begin the attack there. Some earnest moralists accordingly took up the matter. The discussion grew warmer and warmer, till in a little while the community was divided between the defenders and the detractors of the stage. All kinds of grounds were taken, and all manner of arguments advanced. Indeed, the whole range of history, ancient and modern, was ransacked for instances to prove that plays and shows had

been made use of by tyrants as engines to destroy liberty;
that they had been employed by virtuous rulers to promote
liberty; that they were purely monarchical institutions; that
they were eminently republican institutions; that they fos-
tered vice; that they taught morality.

The dispute began at Philadelphia, and for several months
the good points and the bad points of the theatre were sharply
debated by several individuals under the names of Janus,
Thespis, and Philo-Thespis.* Nothing came of the dispute,
however, till in the following year it broke out in New York.
Some champion of the good cause published, about the middle of September, 1785, an address to the citizens of New
York. A new species of luxury and dissipation had, he said,
lately come among them, and was making ground so rapidly
as to give much cause for alarm. It was really true then that
the measure of folly, of extravagance, and of pride was not
yet full; and to fill it to overflowing the theatre must needs be
set up in their midst. It was well, in such matters, to listen
with attention to the warning voice of great moralists who
knew whereof they spoke. Montesquieu had truly said that
morality was the principle of republican government, and on
this it would be an easy matter to prove that the playhouses
were, in a political view, a pest. They would, beyond anything
else, undermine the glorious fabric the sons of America had
been rearing, and prepare the way for anarchy and monarchy.
But the political was not the only view. Looking at the
matter from a financial point, dramas were equally ruinous
to the good of the community. There was a time for everything, and this was no time for gayety, for jollity, and for
plays. Think for a moment on the situation. They were
just emerging from the horrors of a protracted war. They
were beginning as a new people. They were too poor to support an army, though the enemy was still on the frontier; or a
navy, though they stood exposed to the depredations of the
whole world. It was stark madness in such a situation to
waste their money on a set of British players with their Harlequin trumpery. Yet a little while and these men would

---

* See The Freeman's Journal for February 11, 18, 25, and March 3, 10, 24,
1784.

squeeze a rich spoil in hard cash out of their dupes. Nay, more: they would perchance, if suffered to go on, soon teach their hearers to laugh at the exertions of those hardy spirits to whose efforts, under God, it was due that every American had a house to sit in without a British bayonet at his throat. Why did they seek to hide the true character of their performances under innocent names? The paltry titles of Moral Lecture, Serious Lecture, and the like, were at best but a trifling preface to the theatre. It was time the magistrates took up the matter; but if they did not, a party could easily be got together to lay the playhouse in the dust.*

Attacks like this were not suffered to pass unnoticed. They found so much approval, and seemed so important, that grave answers were put forth, in which all the merits of a good play were illustrated and defended by scraps of Latin from the early philosophers, and such bits of history as were familiar to men fresh from the high-schools and colleges. Plays, it was said, were by no means new and untried things. All well-regulated states had, in earlier times, thought it fitting, both in a political and moral sense, to have some kind of show for the amusement of the people. And what kind of show had been so much a favorite as well-acted dramas? Every man who knew anything of the history of Greece knew at what enormous expense the men of Athens kept up their theatre, what pains they were at to secure the finest actors, how often they made their favorite poets guardians of their liberties, or sent them forth to govern provinces and command armies. And was there ever a people so jealous of their liberties as the Athenians? Was there ever a people who knew so well that corruption and debauchery are the greatest foes of liberty, and that the freedom of the theatre is, next to the freedom of the senate, its best and safest foundation? Socrates, whose teachings seemed almost Christian, delighted to assist Euripides in his compositions. Solon, the wise legislator, whose laws had been the admiration of seventy generations of men, was, even in the decline of life, a frequenter of plays. Plutarch held the belief that plays were useful in polishing manners. Brutus, the virtuous, the moral Brutus,

* New York Packet, September 15, 1785.

thought his time well spent in journeying from Rome to Naples to see a play, and that, too, at a time when the imperial city was all tumult and confusion over Cæsar's death. Could anybody doubt that Mr. Addison had done great things as a moralist? Yet Mr. Addison wrote "Cato." Was there anything which breathed a more exalted piety than the "Night Thoughts"? Yet Doctor Young wrote "Busiris" and "The Revenge." *

To the arguments about the high regard the people of old held for the theatre, the reply was made that he who read Greek history in such wise read it ill. It was quite true that the stage had its birth at Athens. But even there both tragedy and comedy were soon abolished by public will. The Romans, also, were not adverse to plays. But so cautious were that people that they did not suffer a theatre when once put up to stand many days. How long was it before the theatre of Scaurus, which cost upward of a million sterling, came down? As for the opinions of Socrates and Solon, they were set off, and more than set off, by the opinions of Seneca and Tertullian, whose writings abounded in passages condemning such amusements. Who was it that wrote "Nihil est tam damnosum bonis moribus, quam in alioquo spectaculo desidere. Tunc enim per voluptatam facilius vitia surrepunt"? † Much was said about the advantages that would flow from a well-regulated theatre. What were they? Would the merchant choose to have his apprentice learn exactness and frugality of the stage? Was it a fact that men whose generosity had been strengthened by weeping over virtue in distress made the best paymasters? ‡ There were, on the other hand, a few evils which would perhaps flow from the boasted well-regulated theatre. It would promote discontent, it would create a taste for show. How contemptible and mean did the affairs of a family seem to the wife and daughter of a mechanic after the gaudy scenes of the stage! But, aside from all this, the theatre was improper because it tended to effeminate manners and corrupt that virtue which was the living principle of all good republican government. Let the intruders then be driven out!

---

* New York Packet, October 20, 1785.   † Ibid., January 23, 1786.
‡ Ibid., October 20, 1785.

And now the papers began to abound in addresses to the inhabitants of New York, in "Thoughts for the Rulers of the Free," * and the coffee-houses with petitions and memorials. One wit went so far as to assert, facetiously, that the name drama was derived from the custom of always having a dram-shop near the theatre.† Another besought all good men not to put their hands to the petition, then going the rounds, for the suppression of virtue and morality, as a counter one would shortly be offered them wherein the fallacy of every argument in favor of the theatre would be shown, and the impropriety of the drama clearly set forth.‡ A third remarked that, while he had no fault to find with the theatre, he had much to find with the plays. It was a shame that while the English language afforded so many energetic tragedies abounding in excellent morals, and so many comedies replete with the justest satire, they were made to listen to such trash as the "Genii of the Rock," "The Witches," "Harlequin in the Moon," and a thousand other pantomimic mummeries at which common-sense stood aghast. The paltry farces in two acts which preceded the dumb show were nothing. The hornpipe might perhaps have some meaning to one who had studied the laws of motion. Let the actors bring out good pieces, and the clap of approval would be heard from men who had emancipated half the world.#

In the midst of this discussion no small merriment was afforded by the news which came down the river from Albany. A party of strolling players had lately made their appearance in that staid city, had obtained permission of the Mayor to perform their parts, and, to the horror of the more sober inhabitants, drew large crowds. A petition was soon written, and presented with many signatures to the Mayor. His Honor was assured that, although the inhabitants were suspected of rusticity and a want of politeness, they had, it was hoped, enough common-sense to judge and declare that they stood in no need of plays and play-actors to instruct them in their duty and good manners. The pressing necessities of many families, after a long and distressing war, and the debts still due to the

* New York Packet, January 23, 1786.   † Ibid., January 23, 1786.
‡ Ibid., January 16, 1786.   # Ibid., October 10, 1785.

public, called upon them to ask for an impartial reconsideration of the late resolution granting a license to the players. They would assuredly drain the people of much money, and instil into the minds of the giddy principles inconsistent with that virtue which is the true basis of republican liberty and happiness.*

The inhospitality, the rude manners, and the parsimony of the men at the head of the river, had long been a source of ill will to the men at the mouth of the river. The news, therefore, that the Albanians were really spending their money on theatrical shows excited much amusement. Many persons, it was said, had supposed the friends of the theatre to be confined to New York. But the delirium had spread far and wide. And, strange to relate, the honest, sober Dutchmen of Albany, who were once distinguished by industry and laudable parsimony, were now wasting their substance on shows.

Meanwhile a like discussion was going on in Philadelphia. The city had long been justly renowned for the extravagance of its people, and for the favor with which they looked on every kind of amusement. Yet there was in Philadelphia a respectable party, composed largely of Quakers, which held that the country had much more to fear from the theatre than from the weakness of Congress, the navigation act, and the quarrelsome disposition of the States put together. When, therefore, the bill for the suppression of vice and immorality was undergoing discussion in the Assembly, these men were much elated to hear that an attempt was being made to tack on to it a clause providing that whoever should put up a theatre, playhouse, stage or scaffold for tragedy, comedy, tragi-comedy, farce, prelude or interlude, should be heavily fined. It was proposed by a member named Whitehill, and boldly attacked by that General Wayne whose reckless, eccentric character had earned for him the title of Mad Anthony. He told the members that he for one hoped they would not think of introducing into the bill a clause for the suppression of the theatre; for a well-regulated theatre was everywhere acknowledged to improve morals, to polish manners, and to teach virtue. Should one be

---

* New York Packet, December 26, 1785.

set up in their midst, this would undoubtedly be the result.
For an illustration they had but to look to Paris. To this
Dr. Logan objected. The government under which it was
their happiness to live was a republican government. France
was an absolute monarchy, and no argument drawn from an
absolute monarchy could apply to a republic. Nobody liked
to see a well-acted tragedy better than he did. Yet he was
clearly of the opinion that theatres were suited to monarchies
and despotic governments. Look at the Genevese. They
abolished theatres; and immediately the King of France and
Sardinia, who had long sought to enslave them, attempted to
set up one in their midst. In this he failed; but he did succeed in building a playhouse within two or three miles of
their very gates. Look at Paris. Did they not have soldiers
with fixed bayonets in the theatres to keep down riot and
tumult? When the doctor had finished, General Wayne reminded the House that the whole city was desirous to have
Congress return, and told them that he was fully borne out in
saying that a theatre would be a great inducement for that
body to come back, as there were in it a number of young
fellows who did not intend to be debarred so innocent an
amusement. This was replied to by Mr. Smiley. The argument made by the gentleman from Chester was, he thought,
no argument at all. A theatre would bring back Congress
because some young fellows in that body were fond of plays!
Of all arguments this surely was the strongest against the
theatre. Had the gentleman said the drama would be an
inducement to the grave, the sober, and the wise, his reason-
ing would have had some weight. But the Legislature of
Pennsylvania did not intend to hold out inducements to the
dissolute, the thoughtless, and the giddy. Mr. Findley declared that he did not know what was meant by a well-regulated theatre. What should regulate it? Government? Then it
became indeed a dangerous tool. The stage, it was true, could
be made the source of most rational amusement. But it was
undeniable that it was frequently subservient to licentiousness
and immorality. Let any man read over a catalogue of plays.
Let him look into the plot of each narrowly. Ten to one he
would find the *dénoûment* in general to be the running away

with an only daughter, violating the chastity of a friend's
wife, separating a married pair, or putting matrimony out of
countenance, to say nothing of *doubles ententes*, which, as suc
cedaneums for wit, were interspersed through the scenes.   In
England, to be sure, the dramatic taste was contradictory.
Indelicacies were rigidly excluded from the new plays.   Yet
the indecent pieces written during the Augustan age of that
nation, the age of Queen Anne, were played without any
opposition, and a Farquhar, a Congreve, a Vanbrugh, held
possession of the stage.   "At present play-writers are at
liberty, when they wish to throw their audiences into fits
of laughter, to make a smutty joke, throw the ladies into confusion, and give the jessamies a chance of tittering to show
their teeth."   As a consequence not one of the many plays
written during ten years past had done more than, by dint of
puffing in the newspapers, eke out for the writer a miserable
pittance from a third night's performance.   Sensible of this,
a Mr. O'Keefe, who had of late written several farces, "filled
them with the most rank nonsense, which, from its very absurd-
ity, forced even the stoic to grin."   Mr. Findley then repeated, amid roars of laughter, several selections from the
pieces of O'Keefe.*   As to American plays, he was adverse to
censorship.   The manners and morals of his countrymen were
too chaste to leave any reason to think that an improper comedy would be written by one of them for perhaps a century to
come.   Robert Morris replied to this, and when the question

---

* A couple of selections from the works of O'Keefe may perhaps serve to
illustrate the "rank nonsense" to which Mr. Findley referred.   The first is from
the Castle of Andalusia :

> "A master I have, and I am his man,
>   Galloping dreary dun.
> And he will get married as fast as he can,
>   With my haily, gaily gambolarity,
>   Giggling, niggling, galloping,
>   Galloway dreary dun."

The chorus of another song is :

> "Ditherum doodle, adgety,
>   Nadgety, tragedy rum,
> Goosterum foodle, fidgety,
>   Nidgety, nagety mum,
>   Goosterum foodle."

to postpone was called, the noes were twenty-nine, the ayes were thirty-four.*

In Boston the old Puritanic hatred of players, and play-houses, though much weakened, was still strong. Indeed it was not till the close of Washington's first administration that a company of players dared to show themselves in the town. An attempt, it is true, was made in June, 1790, to break down the ancient prejudice against the stage, and a petition was sent in by one of the famous American Company of play-ers for leave to open a theatre under proper regulations. But permission was flatly refused. The town was much disap-pointed, and a year later thirty-eight gentlemen signed a like petition to the select-men, begging them to take the sense of the people in town-meeting. This prayer was heard. A great meeting was held in Faneuil Hall, the morality of come-dies and tragedies discussed in the usual way, and when the question, "Theatre or no Theatre," was put, the number in favor of the theatre was thought to be at least three to one.† Such an expression of town feeling soon had its result. The matter was carried to the General Court, and a bill brought in to regulate the expense and prevent the excess of theatrical shows. Gardiner was the champion of the showmen, and on the twenty-sixth of January, 1792, made a long and exhaustive speech.‡ Yet the best argument he could adduce was the profit such things would bring to tradesmen. The emolument, said he, that the masons, the carpenters, the white-smiths, the wood-carvers, and the painters must derive from building and repairing the playhouse will be very great. The milliners, too, would not be forgotten. They would furnish the silks, the laces, and the ducks, while the rope-walkers would be called on to supply rope to ring the bells and gibbet the vil-lains and traitors. As to morality, he was as well acquainted

---

* Quite a full report of the debate in the Pennsylvania Assembly is given in New York Packets for December 5, 1785, and February 6 and 9, 1786. Also, in the Pennsylvania Packet, from which the New York report is copied. For other remarks on the theatre, see Carlisle Gazette, February 15, 1786; New York Packet, December 5 and 27, 1785; Ibid., April 6 and 10, 1786.

† See the Columbian Centinel, October 22, November 2, 12, 1791.

‡ See a pamphlet entitled A Speech in the Massachusetts House of Repre-tatives, January 26, 1792.

with the scriptures as any man who heard him speak. Yet he
could recall nothing reflecting on actors. Nay, there were
many things in the Holy Book that partook of dramatic poetry
and action. Had not Saint Paul borrowed whole passages
from the Greek poets? The bill ultimately passed the House
and the Senate, and was signed by the Governor.*

Meanwhile a company of comedians, encouraged by the
townsfolk, began their season in an old stable that had been
hastily fitted up for the purpose in Broad Alley. To evade
the law against such performances, they called the theatre the
New Exhibition Room, and the plays Moral Lectures. On the
sixteenth of August the room was opened with tight-rope
dancing, tumbling, hornpipes, minuets, and a gallery of portraits.† No interference took place. The actors grew more
daring, and when September came, announced that on the
twenty-sixth of the month "Douglas and the Poor Soldier," a
moral lecture in five parts, would be presented. But Hancock
was Governor, and not a man to be deceived by a name or to
tolerate so bold an evasion of the law. One night in December,
therefore, while the company were playing the moral lecture
of "School for Scandal," and the play had gone as far as the
end of the second act, the sheriff suddenly rushed upon the
stage and carried off Sir Peter to the jail. The house in a fit
of fury denounced the Governor, damned liberty, and pulled
down and trampled under foot a painting of the Governor's
Arms that hung before the stage-box.‡ The next number of
the Centinel was full of cards. One expressed the thanks of
Harper, the arrested comedian, for the sympathy manifested by

---

* For the discussion over the theatre in Boston see the Independent Chronicle,
November 3, 18, and December 1, 8, 15, 1791. Also a pamphlet by W. Hali-
burton, called, Effects of the Stage on the Manners of a People and the Propriety of encouraging and establishing a Virtuous Theatre, Boston, 1792.

† Independent Chronicle, August 16, 1792.

‡ Some account of the disturbance is given in the Columbian Centinel, December 8, 1792. After the arrest of December 5th, threats were made of tar
and feathers and rotten eggs. See New York Journal, December 19, 1792,
and January 2, 1793. See, also, the slightly conflicting accounts given in Dunlap's History of the American Theatre, vol. i, pp. 244-252, and Thomas's Reminiscences of the last Sixty-five Years, vol. i, p. 28. Thomas says it was a portrait
of Hancock the mob pulled down. The newspapers say it was a painting of the
"Governor's Arms."

the audience on the evening of his arrest. A second informed
the public that, at the request of the select-men, the performance
would be discontinued for a while.* A third, it was pretended,
came from the tavern-keepers, and stated, amid a profusion of
thanks, that since the theatre had been stopped the tap-rooms
had been crowded, that the tapsters no longer slept over the
empty pots, and that the cry of "Coming, sirs, coming, sirs,"
was nightly heard on every side.†

The desire of the select-men to have the plays cease for a
while was the result of well-founded alarm. On the Friday
after the arrest an angry discussion took place in the Apollo,
and threats of tearing down the theatre were made openly.
This so impressed a few sailors who were present, that they
collected a mob and went that night to Hancock's house and
asked for leave to pull the building to the ground. The
Governor forbade it, scolded them mildly, and sent the crowd
home.‡ But the papers flatly accused him of having gathered
the mob himself.#

When the trial of Harper came on the arrest was declared
illegal, for, by a strange oversight, the complaint had not been
sworn to, and the warrant was, therefore, void by the four
teenth article of the Declaration of Rights. Nothing more
was heard of the matter.‖ The plays were soon resumed,
and a year later the first theatre was put up. A stock com·
pany built it. The shares were one hundred and twenty
in number, and fifty pounds sterling apiece. Yet when the
books were opened for subscription all were taken in a few
minutes.ᐃ

To know something of that great class of the community
whose republican principles and good morals could not, it was
feared, withstand the corrupting influence of the playhouse,
would indeed be most interesting. Yet it is, unfortunately,
precisely the class concerning which our information is most

---

  * Columbian Centinel, December 8, 1792.   † Ibid., December 15, 1792.

  ‡ Boston Gazette, December 24, 1792.

  # Columbian Centinel, December 22, 1792.

  ‖ A town meeting was held on the matter of the theatre, December 21, 1792,
and instructions to the delegates in General Court adopted, December 27, 1792
See Independent Chronicle, December 27, 1792.

  ᐃ Gazette of the United States, April 24, 1793.

imperfect.   There can, however, be no doubt that a wonderful
amelioration has taken place since that day in the condition of
the poor.   Their houses were meaner, their food was coarser,
their clothing was of commoner stuff, their wages were, despite the depreciation that has gone on in the value of money,
lower by one half than at present.   A man who performed
what would now be called unskilled labor, who sawed wood,
who dug ditches, who mended the roads, who mixed mortar,
who carried boards to the carpenter and bricks to the mason,
or helped to cut hay in the harvest-time, usually received as
the fruit of his daily toil two shillings.   Sometimes when the
laborers were few he was paid more, and became the envy of
his fellows if, at the end of a week, he took home to his family fifteen shillings, a sum now greatly exceeded by four dollars.   Yet all authorities agree that in 1784 the hire of workmen was twice as great as in 1774.*

On such a pittance it was only by the strictest economy
that a mechanic kept his children from starvation and himself
from jail.   In the low and dingy rooms which he called his
home were wanting many articles of adornment and of use now
to be found in the dwellings of the poorest of his class.   Sand
sprinkled on the floor did duty as a carpet.   There was no
glass on his table, there was no china in his cupboard, there
were no prints on his wall.   What a stove was he did not
know, coal he had never seen, matches he had never heard of.
Over a fire of fragments of boxes and barrels, which he lit
with the sparks struck from a flint, or with live coals brought
from a neighbor's hearth, his wife cooked up a rude meal and
served it in pewter dishes.   He rarely tasted fresh meat as
often as once in a week, and paid for it a much higher price
than his posterity.   Everything, indeed, which ranked as a
staple of life was very costly.   Corn stood at three shillings
the bushel, wheat at eight and sixpence, an assize of bread
was fourpence, a pound of salt pork was tenpence.   Many

---

* "On an average forty to fifty per cent. more can now be obtained for labour
and country produce than their current price was in 1774." A Seventh Essay
on Free Trade and Finance, January 10, 1785, Pelatiah Webster.   Jay also complains of the "wages of mechanics and labourers, which are very extravagant."
Jay to B. Vaughan, September 2, 1784.

other commodities now to be seen on the tables of the poor were either quite unknown, or far beyond the reach of his scanty means. Unenviable is the lot of that man who cannot, in the height of the season, when the wharfs and markets are heaped with baskets and crates of fruit, spare three cents for a pound of grapes or five cents for as many peaches, or, when Sunday comes round, indulge his family with watermelons or cantaloupes.* One hundred years ago the wretched fox-grape was the only kind that found its way to market, and was the luxury of the rich. Among the fruits and vegetables of which no one had then even heard are cantaloupes, many varieties of peaches and pears, tomatoes and rhubarb, sweet corn, the cauliflower, the egg-plant, head lettuce, and okra. On the window-benches of every tenement-house may be seen growing geraniums and verbenas, flowers not known a century ago. In truth, the best-kept gardens were then rank with hollyhocks and sunflowers, roses and snowballs, lilacs, pinks, tulips, and, above all, the Jerusalem cherry, a plant once much admired, but now scarcely seen.

If the food of an artisan would now be thought coarse, his clothes would be thought abominable. A pair of yellow buckskin or leathern breeches, a checked shirt, a red flannel jacket, a rusty felt hat cocked up at the corners, shoes of neat's-skin set off with huge buckles of brass, and a leathern apron, comprised his scanty wardrobe. The leather he smeared with grease to keep it soft and flexible. His sons followed in his footsteps, or were apprenticed to neighboring tradesmen. His daughter went out to service. She performed, indeed, all the duties at present exacted from women of her class; but with them were coupled many others rendered useless by the great improvement that has since taken place in the conveniences of life. She mended the clothes, she did up the ruffs, she ran on errands from one end of the town to the other, she milked the cows, made the butter, walked ten blocks for a pail of water, spun flax for the family linen, and, w̶ ̶n the year was up, received ten pounds for her wages. Ye̶ , small as was her pay, she had, before bestowing herself

---

* Cantaloupe-seed was first brought over from Tripoli by Colonel James Barron. To the French immigrants we owe the artichoke and okra.

in marriage on the footman or the gardener, laid away in her stocking enough guineas and joes to buy a few chairs, a table, and a bed.

But there is one other change which has, it must be admitted, done far more to increase the physical comforts of the poorest class than better food, higher wages, finer clothes. Men are no longer imprisoned for debt. No crime known to the law brought so many to the jails and prisons as the crime of debt, and the class most likely to get into debt was the most defenceless and dependent, the great body of servants, of artisans, and of laborers, those, in short, who depended on their daily wages for their daily bread. One hundred years ago the laborer who fell from a scaffold or lay sick of a fever was sure to be seized by the sheriff the moment he recovered, and be carried to jail for the bill of a few dollars which had been run up during his illness at the huckster's or the tavern.

It is pleasing to reflect that while our countrymen have been making such astonishing progress in all that administers to the comforts and conveniences of life, they have at the same time grown charitable and humane. There is indeed scarce a scrap of information bearing upon the subject extant which does not go to prove beyond question that the generation which witnessed the revolution was less merciful and tender-hearted than the generation which witnessed the civil war. Our ancestors, it is true, put up a just cry of horror at the brutal treatment of their captive countrymen in the prison ships and hulks. So great and bitter was their indignation, that money was to be stamped with representations of the atrocities of which they complained, that their descendants to the remotest generation might hold in remembrance the cruelty of the British and the suffering of the patriots. Yet even then the face of the land was dotted with prisons where deeds of cruelty were done, in comparison with which the foulest acts committed in the hulks sink to a contemptible insignificance. For more than fifty years after the peace there was in Connecticut an underground prison which surpassed in horrors the Black Hole of Calcutta. This den, known as the Newgate prison, was in an old worked-out copper-mine in the hills near

Granby.* The only entrance to it was by means of a ladder down a shaft which led to the caverns under ground. There, in little pens of wood, from thirty to one hundred culprits were immured, their feet made fast to iron bars, and their necks chained to beams in the roof. The darkness was intense; the caves reeked with filth; vermin abounded; water trickled from the roof and oozed from the sides of the caverns; huge masses of earth were perpetually falling off. In the dampness and the filth the clothing of the prisoners grew mouldy and rotted away, and their limbs became stiff with rheumatism. The Newgate prison was perhaps the worst in the country,† yet in every county were jails such as would now be thought unfit places of habitation for the vilest and most loathsome of beasts. At Northampton the cells were scarce four feet high, and filled with the noxious gases of the privy-vaults through which they were supposed to be ventilated. Light came in from two chinks in the wall. At the Worcester prison were a number of like cells, four feet high by eleven long, without a window or a chimney, or even a hole in the wall. Not a ray of light ever penetrated them. In other jails in Massachusetts the cells were so small that the prisoners were lodged in hammocks swung one over the other. In Philadelphia the keeps were eighteen feet by twenty feet, and so crowded that at night each prisoner had a space six feet by two to lie down in.

Into such pits and dungeons all classes of offenders of both sexes were indiscriminately thrust. It is therefore not at all surprising that they became seminaries of every conceivable form of vice, and centres of the most disgusting diseases. Prostitutes plied their calling openly in the presence of men and women of decent station, and guilty of no crime but an inability to pay their debts.‡ Men confined as wit-

---

* The mines were known as the Sinsbury, and the company that worked them, chartered in 1709, was the first incorporated mining company of any kind in the United States.

† An interesting account of the Newgate prison is to be found in a little tract entitled A History of the Newgate Prison, R. H. Phelps, 1844.

‡ "The grand jury on Monday last presented as a nuisance the general intercourse between the criminals of the different sexes in the jail, and likewise the indiscriminate mixture of debtors and criminals in the hall originally intended

nesses were compelled to mingle with the forger besmeared
with the filth of the pillory, and the fornicator streaming with
blood from the whipping-post, while here and there among
the throng were culprits whose ears had just been cropped, or
whose arms, fresh from the branding-iron, emitted the stench
of scorched flesh.   The entire system of punishment was such
as cannot be contemplated without mingled feelings of pity
and disgust.   Offences to which a more merciful generation
has attached no higher penalty than imprisonment and fine
stood upon the statute-books as capital crimes.   Modes of punishment long since driven from the prisons with execrations
as worthy of an African kraal were looked upon by society
with a profound indifference.   The tread-mill was always going.
The pillory and the stocks were never empty.   The shears,
the branding-iron, and the lash were never idle for a day.
In Philadelphia the wheel-barrow men still went about the
streets in gangs, or appeared with huge clogs and chains hung
to their necks.*   In Delaware, which to this hour treats her
citizens with the degrading scenes of the whipping-post, twenty
crimes were punished with a loss of life.   Burglary and rape,
sodomy and witchcraft, were among them.   In Massachusetts
ten crimes were declared by the General Court to be punishable
with death.   There the man who, in a fit of anger or in a fit
of drunkenness, was heard cursing and swearing, or spreading
evil reports of his neighbor, was first set in the stocks, and
then carried off to the whipping-post and soundly flogged.
If, however, he was so unfortunate as to be caught in the arms
of a prostitute, he was suffered to escape with a fine.   In
Rhode Island, a perpetual mark of shame was for many offences

---

for debtors only."   Philadelphia, September 22, 1787.   This report declares that
"the prison seems to them to be open as to a general intercourse between the criminals of the different sexes; and that there is not even the appearance of decency
with respect to the scenes of debauchery that naturally arise from such a situation; insomuch that it appears to the jury, from undoubted information, that the
gaol has become a desirable place for the more wicked and polluted of both
sexes."   Grand Jury of the County of Philadelphia to the Court of Oyer and Terminer.   Pennsylvania Gazette, September 26, 1787.

* A great reform in the Penal Code of Pennsylvania was effected in 1790,
when many crimes ceased to be capital, and the wheel-barrow punishment was
abolished.   See Journal of Prison Discipline, vol. i, p. 4.

judged to be a most fitting punishment. There a counterfeiter was punished with the loss of a piece of his ear, and distinguished from all other criminals by a large C deeply branded on his forehead. A wretch so hardened as to be recommitted was branded on the arm. Keepers knew no other mode of silencing the ravings of a madman than tying him up by the thumbs and flogging him till he was too exhausted to utter a groan.*

The misery of the unfortunate creatures cooped up in the cells, even of the most humanely kept prisons, surpasses in horror anything ever recorded in fiction. No attendance was provided for the sick. No clothes were distributed to the naked. Such a thing as a bed was rarely seen, and this soon became so foul with insects that the owner dispensed with it gladly. Many of the inmates of the prisons passed years without so much as washing themselves. Their hair grew long. Their bodies were covered with scabs and lice, and emitted a horrible stench. Their clothing rotted from their backs and exposed their bodies tormented with all manner of skin diseases and a yellow flesh cracking open with filth. The death-rate often stood as high as sixty in the thousand. As if such torments were not hard enough to bear, others were added by the half-maddened prisoners. No sooner did a new-comer enter the door of a cell than a rush was made for him by the inmates, who stripped him of his clothing and let him stand stark naked till it was redeemed by what in the peculiar jargon of the place was known as drink-money. It sometimes happened that the prisoners were in possession of a carefully preserved blanket. Then this ceremony, called garnishing,† was passed over for the yet more brutal one of blanketing. In spite of prayers and entreaties, the miserable stranger was bound, thrown into the blanket, and tossed till he was half dead and ready to give his tormentors every superfluous garment to sell for money. With the tolls thus exacted, liquor was bought, a fiendish revel was held, and, when bad rum and bad

---

* In Vermont the adulteress still wore the scarlet letter.

† For a definition of garnish, see a virulent pamphlet called Pigott's Political Dictionary, London, 1795.

tobacco had done their work, the few sober inmates of the
cell witnessed such scenes as would be thought shocking in
the dance-houses which cluster along the wharfs of our great
sea-board towns.*

To a generation which has beheld great reforms in the
statutes of criminal law and in the discipline of prisons and
jails; to a generation which knows but two crimes worthy of
death, that against the life of the individual, and that against
the life of the State; which has expended fabulous sums in
the erection of reformatories, asylums and penitentiaries,
houses of correction, houses of refuge, and houses of deten-
tion, all over the land; which has furnished every State prison
with a library, with a hospital, with workshops, and with
schools, the brutal scenes on which our ancestors looked with
indifference seem scarcely a reality. Yet it is well to recall
them, for we cannot but turn from the contemplation of so
much misery and so much suffering with a deep sense of
thankfulness that our lot has fallen in a pitiful age, in an age
when more compassion is felt for a galled horse or a dog run
over at a street-crossing than our great-grandfathers felt for a
woman beaten for cursing or a man imprisoned for debt.

---

* Some account of the state of the prisons may be found in Defence of the
System of Solitary Confinement, G. W. Smith; also, North American Review,
July, 1839.

Confederation and Constitution

Our cultural beginnings look better to us than they did to Mc-Master, even though he was a biographer of the great Ben: Franklin, of the *Autobiography* and numerous other writings which were witty and intelligent and well-turned. . . . McMaster should have enjoyed much else of colonial and Federalist prose and verse, and probably did. . . . Believing in Progress, he took principled stands on behalf of his own times, as contrasted with the past. . . . He took, I think, some satisfaction in the weaknesses of the Confederation, and displayed them at length. . . . He ignored John Hanson's claim to the first Presidency of the United States as head of the Confederate Congress, though George Washington had himself congratulated the Maryland statesman on having received the honor. . . . From early beginnings, there had been a movement west, and the movement continues. . . . Quaint pages of the *History* suggest absurd schemes for naming western territories which seem ripe for settlement: Cherronesus, Assenisipia, Metropotamia, among others. . . . McMaster made much of the Order of the Cincinnati, an elite organization of Revolutionary War officers, with ominous suggestions of anti-democratic political opinion: ridiculed and sharply repudiated by the people. . . . McMaster described a time in which "there was no national treasury, no banks, and when the old stockings of the people were full of coins bearing the stamps of many foreign mints, called by all manner of names, and expressing different values in different places." . . . Some four hundred counterfeiters and clippers operated to such good purpose that "a good half-penny or a full-weight pistareen could seldom be found in the States." . . . Our "Low State of Trade and Commerce" created wranglings with the British and such feelings as were expressed in *A Few Salutary Hints pointing out the Policy and Consequences of admitting British Subjects to engross our Trade and become our Citizens* (Charleston, S.C., 1786). . . . Quarrels broke out between and within our states, notoriously in Rhode Island, but also in New Hampshire, Vermont, and elsewhere. . . . McMaster vividly recounts the classic tale of Shays's Rebellion in western Massachusetts. . . . The nation grows, steamboats and spelling reforms challenge attention. . . . Noah Webster fights doubt and conservatism in the interests of simplified spelling and grammar. . . . Determined Constitution-makers overthrow the Articles of Confederation, despite the suspicion and protest, for example, of Peter Prejudice in the *American Museum;* he complained ingeniously that his tailor had thrown away old clothes that he had given him for repair, "and made a new pair of small clothes out of the stuff sent for the mending." . . . The new New Nation, under President George Washington, began operations in New York, following what were sometimes elaborate celebrations. . . . Soon Congress was engaged in ill-natured debates, and the President was finding his dignity affronted by popular demonstrations in opposition to his conservative attitudes and policies. . . .

2

Southern Ways and People

THE State that sent James Jackson to Congress was the youngest of the thirteen. Indeed, six years had not gone by since the founder died. Old men still lived at Savannah who could distinctly recall how on a January morning, in 1733, the galley Ann sailed into Rebellion Roads and dropped anchor off the bar; how her deck was crowded by broken farmers and debtors fresh from the English jails; how the people of Charleston welcomed them, and fed them, and gave them lodgings in the barracks; and how their leader hastened southward to choose the site of the first settlement in Georgia.

Of all the men who brought out colonists and founded settlements on our shores, James Oglethorpe is the most interesting. He was no ordinary man, and his name has come down to us associated with no common personages and with no common events. In his youth he served under Marlborough in the Low Countries. He was with the eccentric Peterborough in Italy. He gained under Eugene, while fighting Turks in the Old World, that military skill which he displayed when he came to fight the Spaniards in the New. He was the friend of Atterbury and Johnson. Whitefield and the Wesleys owed him much. Pope gave him a couplet. Walpole did him honor by calling him a bully. He is described in the letters of Hannah More. He is mentioned by Boswell in the greatest of all biographies, and by Samuel Rogers in one of the most readable of all diaries. A polished gentleman, a brave soldier, a kind-

hearted and an upright man, Oglethorpe appears in our own
history as the promoter of a noble charity. The plan failed.
But, long before he died, the little colony for which he had done
so much had grown to be a prosperous State, and had become
a member of a prosperous confederation of States. Jews and
Scotchmen, Salzburgers and Moravians, Quakers, and settlers
from New England had come n. and had raised the population of Georgia, in days before the war, to fifty thousand souls.
Many perished in the war. Yet the number went on increasing, and, when the first census was taken, was nearly thirteen
thousand greater than in Rhode Island. The State, however,
could boast of no such collection of streets and houses as the
traveller beheld when he stood on the long wharf at Newport,
or walked along the streets of the busy city on Providence
Bay. The towns were few and small, and lay along the sea-
coast or on the banks of the Savannah and the Medway rivers.
On a bluff overlooking the Savannah stood the city of the same
name. It was at that day but little more than a pretty village,
with houses of wood, surrounded by gardens and broad veran-
das and trees. Not one of the highways was paved. In wet
weather the sandy soil kept them dry. But when the days
were hot and sultry, the streets became, as strangers said, like
the great Sahara desert.* The glare was intolerable. Half
the inhabitants wore " goggles." † At every step the foot-
passenger sank to the shoe-top in sand. ‡ Every gust of wind
drove clouds of dust through the open windows and doors.#
Commercially, Savannah had now no rival in the State. Sunbury had once seemed likely to surpass it. Twelve miles, indeed, separated that town from the sea. But the waters of the
Medway river were deep; the inhabitants of Sunbury were
from New England, and the place grew rapidly to a port of
note. There were ship-yards, and stores, and fine docks faced
with palmetto-logs and filled in with oyster-shells and sand.
The fees of the port are known to have amounted to ninety

---

* Travels of Four Years and a half in the United States of America, during
1798-'99, 1800, 1801, and 1802, etc. John Davis, p. 100.

† Ibid., p. 100.

‡ A New and Complete American Encyclopædia; or, Universal Dictionary of
Arts and Sciences, on an Improved Plan. J. Low. New York, 1805, p. 210.

Washington's Diary. Sunday, May 15, 1789.

pounds sterling in one year. Fifty-six ships did, in a twelve-month, go out from the docks. Indeed, it was recorded with pride that seven square-rigged vessels had been seen to sail up the Medway in the light of a single day. Much of the lumber, the indigo, the rice, put down in the returns as the export of Georgia in colonial times, was loaded at the Sunbury wharves. When the war began, this prosperity ended. When the Constitution was adopted the town had fallen into decay. Part of it lay in ashes. The docks were rotting. The fort was in ruins. Few ships were seen in the river. Farms once under high cultivation were overgrown with myrtle and Bermuda-grass.*

Nor was the condition of Frederica much better. Oglethorpe had founded the town, fifty years before, on the island of St. Simon, and had there put up the quadrangular rampart and the fort of "tappy," which so long kept the Spaniards in awe. The climate was delightful. The people were thrifty Scotch, and Frederica soon grew to be the chief settlement of southern Georgia. The salubrity of the air, the broad streets shaded by orange-trees, the houses overlooking the waters on which Oglethorpe won his famous victory, made the town the resort of the rich planters who each summer left their plantations and came down to the coast. But, when the place ceased to be a frontier post, the energy which danger had in-spired grew languid. Frederica, in 1790, was a ruined town. Augusta was a thriving village where the Indians came to barter skins for powder and rum. The site of Old Ebenezer was a cow-pen. Of New Ebenezer little more than the name remained. The Salzburgers had laid it out, and brought thither a love of learning and a knowledge of the culture of silk. In the library were books written in thirteen tongues. Nowhere else in the country could be seen so fine a collection of works in Coptic, in Arabic, in Hebrew, in Chaldaic. In 1772 four hundred and eighty-five pounds of raw silk went out from Ebenezer to the English mills. A few years later the British took the town. When they left it the church had been dese-

---

* For an account of Sunbury and Frederica, see Jones's Dead Towns of Georgia. Bartram's Travels through North Carolina, South Carolina, Georgia, etc., p. 60.

crated, the inhabitants abused, the books scattered, and the prosperity of the town too deeply injured ever to be repaired.*

It was hard indeed for the most favored village to grow and thrive in Georgia. There the town life of New England was unknown. Spots which, had they been in Massachusetts, would have been the sites of prosperous hamlets, were in Georgia parts of great plantations, where small families lived in indolence and ease. On such estates the chief products were negroes, rice, and tobacco. The silk industry was neglected. Indigo was fast ceasing to be profitable. Cotton was just beginning to be extensively grown.† The staple was tobacco, and this was cultivated in the simplest manner with the rudest of tools. Agriculture as we now know it can scarcely be said to have existed. The plough was little used. The hoe was the implement of husbandry. Made at the plantation smithy, the blade was ill-formed and clumsy; the handle was a sapling with the bark left on. After a succession of crops had exhausted the soil, the cow-pen was passed over it. Few roads were ever marked by the tires of a four-wheel wagon or a tumbrel. When the tobacco was ready for the inspector's mark, stout hogsheads were procured, the leaves packed, the heads fastened in, a shaft and a rude axle attached, and, one by one they were rolled along the roads for miles to the tobacco-house nearest by. ‡ There the merchants bought them, sometimes with money, sometimes with such goods as the planters wanted from over the sea. The list was a long one, for not so much as a broom was made in the State. The books and the furniture, the harpsichord and the spinet, the wine, the linen,

---

* Jones's Dead Towns of Georgia; also, History of the Salzburgers.

† "The planters of South Carolina are making experiments in the culture of cotton, and they have proved hitherto very satisfactory, promising great profit. We hope to see their cotton-bags, before long, the wool-packs of America. We learn that they have got the gin, or machine for cleaning it, by which the profit of raising it must be much increased. . . . The large towns in the middle and northern States will probably become the scenes of considerable cotton manufactures. . . ." American Museum, April, 1788, p. 391. Anburey describes the cotton-gin of Virginia in 1779. Travels, etc., vol. ii, p. 377.

‡ See a good description in Richmond in By-gone Days, pp. 270–272. See, also, Jones's Dead Towns of Georgia, p. 325, Bolles's Industrial History of the United States, and a paper by Mr. Trenholm, in South Carolina, a book published by the State Board of Agriculture, 1883.

the china, and the shoes, all came in from abroad. The cards with which they gambled, the coach in which the fine lady took her airing or went to church, the saddle on which the fine gentleman went to the hunt, were each of foreign make. Nor was there any stint of French and English goods. Separated by miles from each other, the prosperous planters spent their money in the adornment of their homes, and their time in the exercise of a noble hospitality and the enjoyment of the roughest of sports.* Bees and huskings, plays and assemblies, barn-raisings and tea-parties, were indeed not in vogue. No pastime could flourish among them that did not partake of danger or risk. They formed hunting clubs, and met once a fortnight. They gambled, they bet, they gathered in crowds to see cocks cut each other to pieces with spurs made of steel. They came from all parts to enter their horses for quarter races or contest for a purse in three-mile heats.† At such times the men of a lower caste played E. O. and faro, wrestled, and seldom went home without a quarrel, or perhaps a brutal fight. We are told by those who beheld these scenes that the fighting was rarely in hot blood ; that the preliminaries were coolly arranged, and that each combatant agreed before he began whether it would be fair to bite off an ear, to gouge an eye, or maim his opponent in a yet more terrible way. ‡ Gouging was always permissible. Every bully grew a long thumb-nail or finger-nail for that very purpose, and when he had his opponent down would surely use it, unless the unfortunate man cried out " Kings' cruse," or enough. If the gouger took out the eye of but one man, his punishment might be a few hours in the pillory and a few lashes of the whip. When he repeated the offence, he might, the law declared, be put to death. Yet the practice was long a favorite one, and common as far north as the Maryland border.⁎

* A Georgia Planter's Method of spending Time. American Museum, November, 1790.

† At the great towns the quarter-races took place on the course. But, in the country districts, the quarter racing was done on two broad, straight paths near some tavern in the woods. The paths were one quarter of a mile long, parallel, and eight or ten yards apart. Anburey's Travels, etc., vol. ii, p. 349.

‡ Travels through the States of North America. Weld, vol. ii, p. 144. Anburey, Travels, etc., vol. ii, p. 333. Anburey calls it " Abelarding each other."

⁎ Rochefoucauld, vol. i, p. 64. Memoirs of Elkanah Watson, pp. 47, 60.

South of that border the greatest of cities was Charles
ton. The place stood upon a low tongue of land which nowhere rose more than ten feet above the high spring tides
in the Ashley and Cooper rivers.* Men who still felt
young could recall the time when the site of the State-
House was a pond where sportsmen shot ducks; when a
creek ran up to where the French church stood; when boys
swam over a spot of ground which in 1791 was covered with
shade-trees and shrubs, and they looked forward to the time
when the marshes should be diked, when the bogs should
be dried, when the streets should be paved and provided with
covered drains.† Already the city was a great commercial
centre. At the wharves might have been seen, almost any
day, scores of vessels laden with every article of luxury or
use Great Britain could supply. In the hands of her subjects was all the trade and all the commerce of the State. To
own a ship, to keep a shop, to do any of those things done
by merchants and traders, was, in the opinion of a Carolina
planter, degrading. The one serious occupation for such a
man was the care of his negroes and his land. If his estate
lay far from the coast, he saw it but seldom. The overseer
ruled the slaves. The master spent his time in the enjoyment of such festivities as Charleston could afford. There he
lived in a fine house, gave fine dinners, went to the theatre to
see Mrs. Rawson, or to the circus to see Mr. Ricketts, subscribed to the assembly, joined the Hell-Fire Club or the Ugly

---

Travels through the States of North America. Isaac Weld, Jr., vol. ii, p. 143.
Travels through the Interior Parts of America. Anburey, vol. ii, pp. 309–311. See,
also, an allusion to the custom in The Echo, No. xviii. Connecticut Courant,
August 24, 1795. At a later period Nolte mentions the practice of gouging as
common in the western States, and declares that in the Legislature of Kentucky
he heard a speaker exclaim: " We must have war with Great Britain. War will
ruin her commerce. Commerce is the apple of Britain's eye. There we must
gouge her." Fifty Years in both Hemispheres; or Reminiscences of the Life of
a former Merchant. Vincent Nolte. Gouging has also been made the subject of
what is, undoubtedly, one of the very best told of anecdotes. It occurs in the
opening pages of Georgia Scenes, Characters, Incidents, etc., in the First Half
Century of the Republic, by a native Georgian.

* A Sketch of the Soil, Climate, Weather, and Diseases of South Carolina.
Charleston, 1796. David Ramsay, p. 11.

† A Sketch, etc. Ramsay, pp. 25, 26.

Club, the Jockey Club, or the Mount Zion Society, and rode his favorite horse at the races.*

No other sports were so popular and so fine. They took place in February, continued four days, and made the event of the year. One who often attended them declares that for hours before the sport began the roads to the course were choked with horses and coaches and men; that the shops were closed, that the streets were deserted, that a dead stillness fell upon the town. On the night of the third day the Jockey Club gave a ball; gentlemen hastened to settle their bets, and large sums of money changed hands.† Betting and gambling were, with drunkenness and a passion for duelling and running in debt, the chief sins of the Carolina gentleman. ‡ Before the revolution, duels had been few in number and the sword the only weapon used. Since the war they had become a crying evil,# and the pistol had taken the place of the sword.‖ To punish offenders was impossible. The juries, indeed, would convict them of manslaughter, and for this the penalty was burning in the hand; but the penalty was never enforced.△

On such plantations as lay within an easy journey of the city, the owners passed many months of each year. ◊ There the houses of wood, surrounded by rice-fields and corn-fields, and negro huts, stood back several miles from the travelled road. ‡ Men who had journeyed far and seen much were amazed to come suddenly before such buildings in the midst of what seemed a wilderness. The handsome gardens and the

---

* "Man zahlet bei 20 verschiedene Clubbs, und die meisten Einwohner sind Glieder von mehr, als einem. Diese gesellschaftlichen Verbindungen geben sich zum Theil wunderliche Namen, als, Mount Zion Society, Hell-Fire Clubb, Marine Anti-Britannic Society, Smoking Society, u. dgl." Reise. J. D. Schoepf, vol. ii, p. 266.

† Ramsay, History of South Carolina, vol. ii, pp. 403, 404.

‡ "Drunkenness may be called an endemic vice of Carolina." Ramsay, History of South Carolina, vol. ii, p. 391. "A disposition to contract debts is one of the vices of Carolinians." Ibid., p. 395. "These (duels) take place oftener in Carolina than in all the nine States north of Maryland." Ibid., pp. 387, 388.

Ibid., p. 389.   ‖ Ibid., p. 389.   △ Ibid., p. 389.

◊ Life and Correspondence of the Rev. William Smith, D.D., vol. i, p. 469.

‡ Travels of Four Years and a half in the U. S. of America. John Davis, p. 68. See, also, Anburey, p. 114; Memoirs of Elkanah Watson, p. 54; Smyth's Tour, vol. i, pp. 15, 16 ; Travels through the States of North America. Weld.

broad paths, the fine paintings that hung on the walls, the
books that made up the library, all bore evidence of the refinement and good sense of the owner.   Educated in England, he
had come back to his native State with a lively appreciation of
good blood and a fondness for ceremony and display.   At his
home strangers were heartily welcome and nobly entertained.
Some bade their slaves ask in any traveller that might be seen
passing by.*   Some kept servants on the watch to give notice
of every approaching horseman or of the distant rumble of a
coming coach-and-four.   Then in a moment a transformation
began.   Shirts and jackets were hastily thrown aside, and, ere
the visitors arrived, a band of idle blacks had become a dozen
liveried slaves.†

Were it not for such hospitality, the lot of the traveller
would have been a hard one indeed.   The roads that led north
and south were good and well cared for; but the inns throughout the whole South were execrable. ‡   Travellers of all sorts
have agreed that the condition of the buildings, the coarseness
of the fare, the badness of the beds, and the exorbitance of the
reckoning,# could not be equalled elsewhere.   Not one of
them displayed a sign, and, save for the number of handbills
posted up beside the door, the inn was like every other house
along the way. ‖   The windows had often no sashes, the
roofs let in the rain.   Mattresses were unknown, and on
the hottest night in summer the weary lodger was compelled
to lie down upon a feather bed.   Breakfast cost six shillings; dinner cost a dollar.   A night's lodging was half as
much; but if clean sheets were demanded, the price was sixpence more.   Supper was rarely eaten.   Innkeepers attributed these evils to the customs of the land, and declared that,
while wayfarers found entertainment at the houses of the
great, the condition of the taverns could never be improved.ᴬ
There were, of course, exceptions. Here and there in the large
towns were to be seen ordinaries with which the most fastidious

* Travels of Four Years and a half in the U. S. of America.   John Davis.
† Travels of Four Years and a half in the U. S. of America.   John Davis.
‡ Smyth's Tour, vol. i, p. 50.   Memoirs of Elkanah Watson, p. 47.   Travels
through the States of North America.   Weld, p. 137.
New Travels in the U. S. of America.   De Warville, p. 374.
‖ Weld's Travels, p. 41,   ᴬ Ramsay, History of South Carolina, vol. ii, p. 886

could find little fault. No better specimen of a good southern inn existed than the Eagle Tavern at Richmond. The building was large, was of brick, and provided with a long veranda in front. For a shilling and sixpence, Virginia currency, the traveller was shown to a neat bed in a well-furnished room up one flight of stairs. On the wall was fastened a printed table of rates. From this he learned that breakfast cost two shillings, and dinner, with grog or toddy, was three; that a quart of toddy was one and six, that a bottle of porter was two and six, and that the best Madeira wine sold for six shillings a quart. When he rose in the morning he washed his face, not in his room, but on the piazza, and ate his breakfast, in the coolest of dining-rooms, at a table adorned with pewter spoons and china plates. Off at one side was a tub full of water wherein melons and cucumbers, pitchers of milk and bottles of wine, were placed to cool. Near by was a water-case which held two decanters. If he called for water, a wench brought it fresh from the spring, and he drank from a glass which had long been cooling in a barrel which stood in one corner of the room. For his lodging and his board, if he ate a cold supper and was content with one quart of toddy, he paid to the landlord of the Eagle ten shillings, Virginia currency, or one dollar and sixty-six cents, Federal money, each day.* The tavern was indeed a famous one. In it, during race week, the ball was held, and of all balls this was the finest. Gentlemen would have found no admittance had they come in boots and pantaloons. Silk stockings and small clothes, pumps set off with huge buckles, and heavily powdered hair, was then the dress. The ball began soon after sundown, and the opening dance was always a minuet de la cour. The music was as solemn as that of a hymn. When the company had assembled, the managers, each with a huge cocked hat beneath his arm, would lead some favored lady, at arm's length, by the tips of her fingers, to the floor. The bowing and scraping, the courtesying, the tiptoeing, the solemn advancing and turning of the minuet once through, a contra-dance or a reel would begin. Then the fine gentlemen showed their skill at cutting pigeon-wings. A hornpipe

---

* See an extract from the Journal of Rev. Henry Toulmin descriptive of Richmond in 1793. Richmond Standard, August 14, 1880.

or a congo followed, and, when the old people had retired, a jig.*

Taverns of the poorer kind derived their support from loungers and tipplers, and from the crowd which gathered in the tap-room during the sitting of the court, on election days, on holidays, and when a neighbor's goods were to be disposed of in a public way. Vendue was almost unknown. When a collection of household furniture was to be sold, the whole village assembled, gun in hand. A mark was set up, the distance measured, a table or a chair made the prize, and, when all who wished it had paid down a few pence, the shooting began. The best marksman won the article.† Sometimes a bullock was the prize. Then the best shot had the first choice of parts. When he made it, more shooting and more choosing followed till the whole carcass was sold.

Still more wretched were the inns of North Carolina. ‡ The traveller who at that day quitted Charleston and journeyed northward went commonly along a good road, which led by plantations, and over swamps, and through pine-barrens to Beaufort and Georgetown and Wilmington, and on to the little village of Duckinfield on Albemarle Sound. There, if the wind were high and the Sound rough, he might be forced to wait two days before the ferryman would carry him over the eight miles of water that lay between him and the Edenton shore.# Once in Edenton, the road ran along the edge of the great Alligator Dismal Swamp to the Carolina border, and thence to Suffolk in Virginia. Beaufort was a straggling village. ‖ Georgetown numbered one hundred houses.△ Wilmington had twice as many more. ◊ In these towns rude accommodations were to be had. But if hunger or night compelled the traveller to stop at a roadside tavern or an ordinary in the woods, he found poor cheer awaiting him. The house was of clapboards or logs. Without was an oven of clay. Within was a single room. The roof and the walls were neither ceiled

---

* Richmond in By-gone Days, pp. 179, 180.

† Ramsay, History of South Carolina, vol. ii, p. 408.

‡ Description of a North Carolina Ordinary. American Museum, December 1790, pp. 278, 279.   # Smyth's Tour, vol. ii, p. 91.

‖ Smyth's Tour, vol. ii, p. 85.   △ Ibid.   ◊ Ibid.

nor plastered. Some benches, a bed, a table, and a chest or
two were all the furniture to be seen. In winter he might sleep
by the fire. In summer he lay out of doors under a blanket
made fast to four small stakes to keep off flies and the dew.
Whether he asked for breakfast or dinner gave little concern
to his host. One meal was like another, and they all consisted
of bacon, eggs, hominy, coarse bread, and New England rum.
When at last Suffolk was reached, two roads were before him.
One skirted the Dismal Swamp and led to Norfolk. The other
passed through Smithfield and Williamsburg in Virginia.

Williamsburg had, in colonial times, been the capital of the
province. There had been the Governor's palace, long since
reduced to ashes, and there every winter, when the House of
Burgesses was sitting, had gathered all the wealth and all the
fashion of Virginia. No such handsome women, no such assemblies, no such dinners, no such liveries, it was thought, could
be seen anywhere else in America. The rich planters who
sauntered into the House of Burgesses to hear Patrick Henry
speak, or went, on reception-days, to pay their respects to the
Governor, and rode up and down the great street at the proper
time of day, bowing to the fine ladies in their coaches, followed
by slaves in rich liveries, were, in the opinion of every Virginian, the most polished and refined of gentlemen. With the
departure of the Government had gone much of the ancient
splendor of the town. Yet the place was still an attractive
one to foreigners and travellers. Scarce one of them failed to
note in his journal that, in the new part of the town, the
by-ways were laid out as a W,* and that in the old the main
street was a mile long, very broad, very sandy, and unpaved.
Across one end of this street stood the capitol.† At the other
the College of William and Mary closed the way, ‡ a college
that boasted of being among the oldest in America, and
dated its origin from the days when no such thing as a
printing-press existed in Virginia. The faculty at one time

---

* Einige Nebenstrassen, welche nach Süden und Osten liegen, sind in der
Gestalt des Buchstaben W angelegt. Reise. J. D. Schoepf, vol. ii, p. 121; also
Smyth's Tour, vol. ii, p. 19.

† Smyth's Tour, vol. ii., p. 19. "Die gerade und breite Hauptstrasse ist
beynahe einer Meile lang." Reise. J. D. Schoepf, vol. ii, p. 121.

‡ Reise. J. D. Schoepf, vol. ii, pp. 121, 122. Smyth's Tour, vol. ii, p. 19.

numbered six professors and a president. On the library
shelves three thousand volumes were gathering dust. For
a hundred years divinity and mathematics, Greek and Latin,
philosophy and metaphysics, had been taught to lads whose
fathers could not afford to send them to the great universi-
ties of England. Nor was the number of such men small.
The Virginia gentlemen were far from rich. Their estates
indeed were noble. Their hospitality was profuse. They
kept studs and raised fine horses. They owned coaches and
chariots, and filled their houses with richly liveried slaves.
But much of this splendor was deceptive. As a community
they were bankrupt and steeped in debt. That financial integ-
rity which flourishes best among merchants and traders was
unknown to the landed gentry of Virginia. While the trades-
man was clamoring for the price of his goods, while the
doctor called again and again for his fees, the great planter
was ready to bet a slave at a horse-race, or squander at a cock-
fight hundreds of pounds borrowed at high rates of interest.
Tobacco notes made no inconsiderable part of the currency of
the State.* Coppers did not exist. In place of small change
were silver dollars cut into quarters and halves,† a kind of
currency long known in Richmond as "sharp-shins." The
merchants held what ready money there was. If any were
wanted to improve a highway, to build a school-house, to make
some repairs on a country church, a lottery was the only means
by which the sum could be collected. Many of the parish
churches had been put up by the great families on whose
estate they stood. But the days of Episcopal supremacy
were gone. The Church had been disestablished. Toleration
had been secured. The clergy had fallen into disrepute, and,
even in the large towns, the buildings were given over to vermin and decay. In such as were kept open, much of the ancient ceremony was maintained. There were seats without
cushions, to which the poor hurried and sat down. There were

---

* New Travels in the U. S. of America. De Warville, pp. 437, 438.

† Richmond in By-gone Days, pp. 213, 214. "This scarcity of small money
subjects the people to great inconveniences, and has given rise to a pernicious
habit of cutting pieces of silver coin into halves and quarters." New Travels in
the U. S. of America. De Warville, pp. 438, 439, London Edition, 1792.

high box-pews, to which the great ladies and their families gravely walked, followed by slaves, who bore the prayer-books and shut the pew-doors with a bang. The bans were still cried. The minister still climbed to the lofty pulpit by a spiral stair. On the walls were hanging pews ; and tablets of stone sacred to the memory of the dead who slept without. Distinguished.parishioners were still put to rest in the vault under the communion-table or the broad aisle. The congregation was still summoned by the bell that hung from the branches of some sturdy tree near the church-door.* Service ended, the old men discussed the last election, or the last hunt. The young men, hat in hand, escorted the women to the coaches, and, mounting their horses, rode home after them to partake of a heavy dinner, and, perchance, go under the table in a drunken sleep.

The daily life of such men was a strange mixture of activity and sloth. When they were not scouring the country in search of a fox, when they were not riding twenty miles to a cock-fight or a barbecue, they seem to have indulged in all the idleness of an Eastern pasha. Travellers from a colder climate were amazed to see a man in the best of health rise at nine, breakfast at ten, and then lie down on the coolest pallet in the house to drink toddy, bombo, or sangaree, while a couple of slaves fanned him and kept off the flies. At two he ate his dinner; supper he rarely touched. At ten he went to bed.†

Nor did men of a lower rank act any better. Their manners, indeed, were coarser; their education was poorer; their plantations were smaller; their pedigrees could not be traced back even to the third son of an English baron. Yet they were as idle and hospitable, indulged in the same excesses, and took part in the same sports as the great proprietors, who affected to look down upon them with contempt. Beneath them, and far beneath them, were the poor whites. Made up in great part of indentured servants whose time had run out, they were the most lazy, the most idle, the most shiftless, the

---

* Travels of Four Years and a half in the U. S. of America. John Davis, p. 305.
† For a description of the life of a Virginia planter of that day, see Smyth's Tour, etc., vol. i, pp. 41, 42, and Burnaby's Travels, p. 156. Anburey's Travels through the Interior Parts of America, vol. ii, pp. 293, 2**.

most worthless of men. Their huts were scarce better than
negro cabins. The chimneys were of logs with the chinks
stuffed with clay; the walls had no plaster; the windows had
no glass; the furniture was such as they had themselves made.
Their grain was thrashed by driving horses over it in the open
field. When they ground it they used a rude pestle and mortar, or, placed in the hollow of one stone, they beat it with another. Work of every kind they abhorred. Some among
them might, with proper encouragement, have become artisans
and mechanics. No class of laborers was more needed. Beyond the limits of the great towns or the seaboard villages, a
carpenter or a smith, a mason or a wheelwright, was seldom to
be seen. Now and then some half-starved mechanic would
earn a precarious livelihood by wandering from plantation to
plantation repairing harpsichords, mending clocks, or perform-
ing such services as were beyond the skill of the slaves. But
for these men the poor whites felt contempt. Their days were
passed in lounging about the taverns, quarrelling and gambling, and creating disturbances at elections.

The fights and brawls which took place at such times in
Virginia were worthy of an Irish fair. The manner of con-
ducting elections throughout the entire South was bad. A
southern representative well described it on the floor of the
House as "a nursery of mischief." * In place of bringing men
together in small bodies, the electors of an entire county were
gathered at one court-house, and in the presence of the sheriff
were polled. The rival candidates would appear with bands
of followers, and whichever was the stronger would drive the
other away. Such a scene was described to the House of Representatives by a committee on a contested election, and was
declared by the southern members of the House to be quite
common. The place was Montgomery Court-House, in Virginia. The occasion was the choosing of a representative to
Congress. One of the contestants was so fortunate as to have
a brother who, in command of sixty or seventy Federal troops,
was camped near by. On the morning of election-day the
soldiers were paraded, marched to town, led thrice around
the court-house, drawn up before the door, and polled for the

---

* Annals of Congress, April, 1794.

brother of their chief. They then threatened to beat any one who wished to vote against their man, knocked down a drunken magistrate, mounted guard at the court-house door, and stopped the voting till the countrymen stoned them back to camp. The committee, shocked at such proceedings, reported that the sitting member should lose his seat; but the southern representatives supported him. One who came from Maryland declared that he never knew of an election in the southern States where so little mischief was done. He could name one at which a chancellor of a court of justice bred a riot in his own court to help his own party. Much had been said about a man coming to Montgomery Court-House with a club under his coat. That was nothing. At his own election five hundred of his constituents had clubs under their coats. If such a matter were to unseat a member, the House had better begin by unseating him. How were elections conducted in the South? A man of influence came to the polls at the head of two or three hundred of his friends, and, naturally, would not suffer any one of the other party to give a vote if he could help it. The custom might be a bad one; yet it was the custom. A gentleman from South Carolina affected to be much surprised at this; but was promptly reminded that at his own election a riot had occurred, that it had occurred in a church, and that a magistrate began it by knocking down a voter and dragging him into the road. The speaker who made this statement declared he was present and saw the affray.*

Beneath the poor whites were the negro slaves. If the infamy of holding slaves belongs to the South, the greater infamy of supplying slaves must be shared by England and the North. While the States were yet colonies, to buy negroes and sell them into slavery had become a source of profit to the inhabitants of many New England towns. Scarce a year passed by but numbers of slavers went out from Boston, from Medford, from Salem, from Providence, from Newport, from Bristol, in Rhode Island. The trade was of a threefold kind. Molasses brought from Jamaica was turned to rum; the rum dispatched to Africa bought negroes; the negroes, carried to Jamaica or the southern ports, were ex-

* Annals of Congress, April 29, 1794.

changed for molasses, which in turn, taken back to New Eng‑
land, was quickly made into rum.* The ships were light
of draught and built for speed. The captain and the crew
were men little troubled with scruples touching the work they
had to do. Once off the coast of Mozambique or Guinea, the
cargo was rapidly made up. If a band of blacks, moved by
curiosity, came round the vessel in a skiff, they were sure to be
lured on board, ironed, and hurried into the hold. If a boat's
crew went on shore, they came back dragging some wretched
man between them. For rum the native princes gladly sold the
prisoners that their subjects made in war. When every avail‑
able inch of space in the hold had been filled, the slaver turned
westward and made for some southern port. The coast-line
had scarcely disappeared from view when the hatches were
taken off and the terrors of the voyage began. Every fine
day at sunrise the slaves were driven on deck. Such as were
noisy had the thumb-screws put on. Such as were hard to
manage were chained in pairs by the arms, or the ankles, or
the necks. At the first signs of insurrection the leaders were
shot down and cast into the sea. Their food was salt pork
and beans. Their sole exercise was dancing and capering
about the deck. This they were made to do. If any refused,
the cat-o'-nine-tails or the rope's end was vigorously applied.
When the sun set, the whole band went below. There the space

* The transactions of one slaver may be cited as illustrative of those of many
others. The cargo of the Cæsar, out-bound, was: 82 barrels, 6 hogsheads, and
6 tierces of New England rum; 33 barrels of best Jamaica spirits; 33 barrels of
Barbadoes rum; 25 pairs of pistols; 2 casks of musket-balls; 1 chest of hand-
arms; 25 cutlasses. The return cargo was: "In the hold on board of the scow
Cæsar, 153 adult slaves and 2 children." Brooks's History of Medford, pp. 436,
437. The books of another give a more detailed account:

Dr. THE NATIVES OF ANNAMBOE.		PER CONTRA.	*Cr.*
1770.	Gals.	1770.	Gals.
April 22. To 1 hogshead of rum...	110	April 22. By 1 woman slave......	110
May 1 " rum..............	130	May 1. " 1 prime woman slave.	130
" 2. " 1 hogshead rum......	105	" 2. " 1 boy slave, 4 ft. 1 in.	105
" 7. " " "	108	" 7. " " " 4 ft. 3 in.	108
" 5. " cash in gold.......	5 oz. 2	" 5. " 1 prime man slave.	5 oz. 2
" 5. " " " ..2 oz. }	3 oz. 0	" 5. " 1 old man for a }	3 oz. 0
" 5. " 2 doz. of snuff.1 oz. }		Lingister....}	

History of Medford, pp. 436, 437.

assigned each to lie down in was six feet by sixteen inches. The bare boards were their beds. To make them lie close, the lash was used. For one to turn from his right side to his left was impossible, unless the long line of cramped and stiffened sufferers turned with him.* But the misery of a night was as nothing to the misery of a stormy day. Then the hatches were fastened down, tarpaulins were drawn over the gratings, and ventilation ceased; the air grew thick and stifling; the floor became wet with perspiration; the groaning and panting of the pent-up negroes could be heard on deck; their mouths became parched, their tongues swollen. When the storm was over, the hatches opened and the tarpaulin drawn away, the air that would come from the hold was like that from an oven. The hardiest in the crew could not inhale it without growing faint. The stench was terrible. It was not uncommon for as many as five dead bodies to be brought up and flung over the ship's side. On a slaver making the middle passage a mortality of thirty per cent was not rare. As the voyage drew to a close the treatment of the slaves improved. The sick were cared for; those in chains were set free; whip-

---

* The arrangement of the negroes in a slave-ship is illustrated by a folding cut in American Museum, May, 1789. The cut was prepared at the expense of the Philadelphia Society for Promoting the Abolition of Slavery, and is a copy of a plate accompanying the report of a committee who investigated the slave-trade of Plymouth, England. The plate is rarely found in such copies of the Museum as can now be purchased, but is common in the antislavery documents of a later day. By the Plymouth Pamphlet we are assured that " In the men's apartment the space allowed to each is six feet in length by sixteen inches in breadth. The boys are each allowed five feet by fourteen inches, the women five feet ten inches by sixteen inches, and the girls four feet by one foot each." Many facts regarding the terrors of the slave-ships are given in " The Substance of the Evidence of Sundry Persons on the Slave-Trade. Collected in the course of a Tour made in the Autumn of 1788." London.

The Plymouth Pamphlet describes the manner of packing away the slaves on a vessel which carried six hundred and nine of them. " Platforms, or wide shelves, were erected between the decks, extending so far from the side toward the middle of the vessel as to be capable of containing four additional rows of slaves, by which means the perpendicular height between each tier was, after allowing for the beams and platforms, reduced to two feet six inches, so that they could not even sit in an erect posture; besides which, in the men's apartment, instead of four rows, five were stowed by putting the head of one between the thighs of another." For letters of instruction to captains of slavers, see Felt's History of Salem, vol. ii, pp. 289, 290. Brooks's History of Medford, pp. 436, 437.

ping was given more sparingly. Indeed, when the negroes stood forth on the auction-block for inspection and for sale, every trace of the irons and the lash had been carefully removed from their bodies. From the auction-stand they were carried to the plantations, where, among negroes not much more civilized than themselves, they learned to speak a dialect that passed for English, and to perform the duties of a field-hand.

Under the kindest of masters the condition of the slaves was most pitiable. Those whose lot it was to give suck to the children, to fan the master, to wait at the table, to ride before the stick-back gig, or follow the cumbrous coach when the mistress went forth to ride, enjoyed, perhaps, the largest share of ease and comfort. Sometimes a negro of marked intelligence would be suffered to become a blacksmith or a mason, or be sent to a neighboring village to sweep chimneys or sell fruit; but the great body of slaves were still as barbarous as the blacks who ran wild on the Gambia or along the banks of the river Congo. They were still as ignorant, as superstitious, as devoted worshippers of stocks and stones, as their most remote ancestors. Spirits and ghosts, witches and devils, were to them as much realities as the men they spoke with or the wind they felt blow. The moon inspired them with peculiar awe; the darkness filled them with dread; nor would the boldest among them willingly go through a wood after sundown without a hare's foot in his hand. Of charms and evil eyes they lived in never-ending fear. Bright colors, gay clothes, glittering objects, were their delight. Of music and the dance they were passionately fond. With fragments of a sheep's rib, with a cow's jaw and a piece of iron, with an old kettle and a bit of wood, with a hollow gourd and a few horse-hairs, they would fabricate instruments of music and play the most plaintive airs.

Against the plottings of such men as these their masters defended themselves by brutal laws. Lashes were prescribed for every black who kept a dog, who owned a gun, who had a "periagua," who hired a horse, who went to a merrymaking, who attended a funeral, who rode along the highway, who bought, or sold, or traded without his owner's consent.* Slaves

---

* Virginia Laws, 1792, chap. 41, § 8. South Carolina Statutes at Large, vol I, p. 404, § 13. Georgia Laws, 1770, Act No. 204, § 12.

were forbidden to learn to write * or read writing, to give evidence against a white man,† to travel in bands of more than
seven unless a white man went with them,‡ or to quit the plantation without leave. Should they do so, the first freeman they
fell in with might give them twenty lashes on the bare back.#
If one returned a blow, it became lawful to kill him. ‖ For
wandering about at night or riding horses without permission,
the punishment was whipping, cropping, or branding on the
cheek.△ When his crime was murder or house-burning, the
justices might, if it seemed best, command his right hand to be
cut off, his head to be severed from the trunk, the body quartered, and the pieces hung up to public view. ◊ Next to murder, the worst offence a slave could commit was to run away.
Then the Legislature could outlaw him, and any free white that
met him might kill him at sight. ‡ To steal a negro was felony.
To take his life while punishing him was not. Indeed, if a
planter provided coarse food, coarse clothes, and a rude shelter
for his slaves; if he did not work them more than fifteen hours
out of twenty-four in summer, nor more than fourteen in winter, and gave them every Sabbath to themselves, he did quite as
much for their comfort as the law required he should. Before
the law a slave was a chattel; could be bought or sold, leased or
loaned, mortgaged, bequeathed by will, or seized by the sheriff
in satisfaction of a debt. Property he could neither hold nor
acquire. If the State gave him land for his services in the
war, the court bestowed it all upon the master. If he went

---

* Georgia Laws, 1770, Act No. 204, § 39. South Carolina Statutes at Large
vol. 7, p. 413, § 45.

† Maryland Laws, 1717, chap. 13, §§ 2 and 3. (1796) Cox v. Dove, 1 Martin
(N. Car.) Repts., 43. (1821) White v. Helmes, 1 M'Cord (S. Car.) Repts., 430.

‡ Georgia Laws, 1770, Act No. 204, § 38. South Carolina Statutes at Large,
vol. 7, p. 413, § 43.

South Carolina Statutes at Large, vol. 7, p. 398, § 3. Georgia Laws, 1770,
Act No. 204, § 38. See also § 5.

‖ South Carolina Statutes at Large, vol. 7, p. 399, § 5. Georgia Laws, 1770,
Act No. 204, § 5.

△ Maryland Laws, 1751, chap. 14, § 8. The letter R was branded on the
cheek. See also Laws 1754-'57-'62-'65-'73-'80-'87-'95-'98.

◊ Maryland Laws, 1729, chap. 4.

‡ Hayward's Manual, pp. 521, 522. In 1792 the outlawry of slaves was ex-
punged from the Virginia code.

forth and labored for a price, even with his owner's leave, the money was not his. Nothing could be left a slave by will. He could not call his life his own. To strike out his eye in the heat of passion, to cut out his tongue, to maim him, to cruelly scald him, or deprive him of a member or a limb, was, indeed, an offence. But the sole punishment was a fine of one hundred pounds currency. To kill him outright cost the owner but a little more. Within these limits it was lawful to load him with irons, to confine him for any length of time in a cell, and to beat him and whip him till the blood ran in streams from the wounds and he grew too weak to stand. Old advertisements are still extant in which runaway blacks are described by the scars left upon their bodies by the lash.* When such lashings were not prescribed by the court, they were commonly given under the eye of the overseer, or inflicted by the owner of the negro himself. In the great cities were often to be found men whose business it was to flog slaves. Such an one long lived in Charleston, and, when the beating was not done by contract, charged a shilling for each one whipped.†

While such scenes took place in the South, abolition began in the North. Of all the societies for promoting the abolition of slavery the world has seen, the oldest was that of Pennsylvania. Fourteen years after the founding of the colony the yearly meeting sent a minute to the Society of Friends.‡ Each member was advised not to buy any more negroes, and to be very heedful of the moral and religious training of those he had. But it was not till 1743 that the matter was seriously taken up. Then an annual query was started to find out how many members had really ceased to buy or bring in slaves. Many had done so. More had not. For fifteen years the Meeting waited patiently, and then began to punish all who disobeyed. Slave-buyers were forbidden to sit in the Meetings of Discipline, to take part in the Society's affairs, or to give one penny toward the relief of the destitute and the poor. When the war opened, every one owning a slave over lawful age was about to be cast out. Meanwhile, so many had

---

* North Carolina Gazette, November 7, 1795, and also January 2, 1796.

† Travels of Four Years, etc. John Davis, p. 90. Rochefoucauld. Travels, etc., vol. i, p. 565.   ‡ A protest against slavery was made at Germantown in 1688.

obeyed that, in 1775, there were, in the colony of Pennsylvania, thousands of freed negro slaves. But, to seize upon these, run them off and sell them again into slavery, soon became so common a crime that a few men of heart determined it should stop. A score of gentlemen, therefore, gathered, five days before the battle of Lexington, in the old Sun Tavern at Philadelphia. There they framed a constitution, and organized a body which they named "The Society for the Relief of Free Negroes unlawfully held in Bondage." Four meetings were held. Ere a fifth came, the war opened, and, during nine years, the society did nothing. At last, in 1784, the members once more assembled, and began a long career of activity and use. The cause of the negro for a time was popular. The Methodists took it up and bade every member of the society, where the law would permit, emancipate his slaves within a twelvemonth. Before a decade had gone by, abolition societies sprang up in Rhode Island, in Connecticut, in New Jersey, at New York, at Baltimore, in Virginia, at Washington, Pennsylvania, and even on Maryland's eastern shore. One State became free;* three others provided for a gradual abolition,† two more revised their emancipation statutes, ‡ and Congress passed the ordinance of 1787, which forbade slavery ever existing in the territory of the United States northwest of the river Ohio. In Massachusetts no act of abolition was ever passed. When the revolution ended it became the fashion to consider slavery as at an end, and, for the time and the manner of its extinction, to point to the State Constitution of 1780 and a phrase in the first article of the Declaration of Rights. "All men," says that instrument, "are born free and equal." This the courts afterwards declared meant abolition. The people chose to believe it, and the custom of buying and selling and owning slaves passed slowly away, like the custom of purchasing the time of redemptioners, or binding young lads to a trade.# The same year that the northwestern territory became free soil the Pennsylvania Society took a new name, sent a memorial to the Constitutional Convention on the subject of the

---

* New Hampshire.
† Pennsylvania, Rhode Island, Connecticut.   ‡ Virginia and Maryland.
# See Notes on the History of Slavery in Massachusetts. G. H. Moore.

slave-trade, begged the printers at Philadelphia not to adver-
tise the sale of negro slaves, and chose Benjamin Franklin its
president.   From it, too, came one of the memorials which, in
March, 1790, excited southern congressmen and led to the
first resolutions of the House of Representatives on slavery
and the slave-trade.   The wish of the society was defeated.
But, toward the close of 1791, the matter was once more urged
on the attention of the House.

The Federalist '90's

There were sharp differences between democrats and conservatives: between those who looked to Washington's Secretary of State, Thomas Jefferson, for leadership, and those who anticipated guidance from his Secretary of the Treasury, Alexander Hamilton. . . . Antagonisms were heightened by the spectacular rise of the uncompromising Jacobins, in Revolutionary France. . . . McMaster had many picturesque details to offer regarding the effect on American sympathizers by the French extremists, who used the guillotine with bloody effect. . . . American friends of the Jacobins called each other "Citess" (for the French *"Citoyenne"*) and "Citizen," and played seriously at being revolutionists. . . . They despised the British on double grounds: as their late foes and as enemies of the French. . . . This was the era of the Whisky Rebelsion in western Pennsylvania against taxation which seemed to the hot-heads unfair taxation without adequate representation. . . . Jay's Treaty with the British caused Republicans to assert that the Administration had sold out the American Revolution, and to encourage mobs to burn Washington in effigy. . . . It was the time of the frightful Yellow Fever, which put thousands in their graves, and caused the Federal Government, then housed in Philadelphia, to all but break up, as legislators fled the city to avoid the plague. . . . As England and France waged war, the United States struggled officially to remain neutral. . . . Words and phrases changed; a critic complained of people professing to be "bored," "infinitely hot," "making up their minds," "committing themselves," and pronouncing "virchue," "natchure," "fortchune," as well as (what did not survive) "quietchude," and "distchurbed." . . . Jefferson and Hamilton quarreled over the Government's right to and need for a national Bank. . . . The Patent Office modestly began a stream of operations which widened into a roaring flood of ingenious enterprises. . . . The cotton gin was invented, fatefully making slavery profitable. . . . Washington announced his retirement in 1796, and Democratic-Republicans and Federalists fought for the Presidency. . . . The candidate of one party, John Adams, received the first place; the candidate of the second party, Thomas Jefferson, gained the Vice-Presidency. . . . "Hail, Columbia" was first sung in 1798. . . . Bitter, libelous, irresponsible debate increased between the Government defenders and the out-of-power Jeffersonians, who accused the in-group of monarchical aspirations and a desire to return to the British Empire. . . . The Federalists sought to curb their rivals with the Alien and Sedition Laws and were fiercely denounced. . . . The Kentucky and Virginia Resolutions, sponsored by Jefferson and James Madison, even suggested that states were not constrained to obey laws they deemed unconstitutional. . . . Here was an argument which would return to trouble the country. . . . Vigorous Jeffersonian editors were actually jailed under the Sedition laws. . . . There were untidy land frauds in Georgia. . . . Revolutionary France had fallen into the hands of a Directory; the XYZ Affair—a corrupt French effort to exact tribute from America—brought on an unofficial war between the two countries. . . . Washington City was planned. . . . George Washington died. . . . In the Election of 1800, the Democratic-Republicans elected (such were possibilities at that time under the Constitution) *both* their party candidates to the office of President, Jefferson and Aaron Burr. . . . The defeated Federalists were thus able to decide in Congress which of their opponents they preferred! . . . Hamilton threw his power to Jefferson, earning the personal enmity of Burr who, four years after, would challenge him to a duel and shoot to kill. . . . The Great Revolution of 1800 (as Jeffersonians called the election) gave them both the Executive Office and Congress, and drove the resentful Federalists back to their New England stronghold. . . . They breathed states-rights and in some cases plotted secession from the Union. . . .

3

The Turn of the Century

THE charge of "pyrotechny" brought against the Federalists in 1801 was precisely such as they brought against the Republicans in 1797. The presidential election of 1796 was over, and the people, angry and excited, were restlessly awaiting the returns from distant States, when terrible fires broke out in quick succession at Savannah, at Baltimore, Philadelphia, and New York. That at Savannah occurred late in November, destroyed three hundred and fifty houses, and was generally believed to have been of accidental origin. But those elsewhere were held to be clearly the result of design.* The Jacobins, the Democrats, the shouters of Ça ira, the friends of the Sage of Monticello, had applied the torch. Unable to afflict the country with a French President, they were determined to afflict it with French liberty. Having commenced to burn cities, they would soon begin to murder citizens. Such was the penalty for refusing to lie down at the feet of the French Directory. If anybody ventured to attribute the fires to the severity of the winter, to sooty chimneys, and to the huge piles of wood that blazed and crackled on a thousand hearths, he was pronounced a Jacobin, and told that the weight of evidence was against him. One man at New York had found in his out-house coals of fire rolled in oiled rags.† Another had the bed on which his child slept set on fire. ‡ A third found his door badly scorched one morning.# An old lady had overheard an alarming conversation on the street. ‖ Two

---

* Gazette of the United States, December 23, 1796. Argus, December 15, 1796.
† Philadelphia Gazette, December 16, 1796.
‡ Ibid.   # Ibid.   ‖ Ibid.

young men were arrested going over the fields with combustibles and pick-locks hidden in their clothes.   Two more were caught setting fire to a house.*   The Common Council in alarm offered five hundred dollars for the detection of the incendiaries, and urged the citizens to meet and form companies to keep night-watch.†   The call was obeyed.   A great meeting was held at Rattoone's Tavern, and, when night came, every ward in the city was patrolled by armed bands. ‡   The watch was chiefly made up of young men, who, finding little to do, spent the nights in frolic and play.   They sang songs; they played tricks; they stopped and insulted wayfarers on the streets.#   When the watch of two neighboring wards met, a fracas was sure to ensue. ‖   The newspapers, meanwhile, were full of advice.   Citizens would do well to confine their servants.△   Those who had pumps in their yards should throw a little salt in them to prevent freezing during the cold nights. The watch ought to move the pump-handles a few times as they went past. ◊   The city charter was at fault.   The police regulations at fires were shockingly bad.   What business had strangers and women at such places?   Everybody knew that thieves took such occasions to plunder their fellow-citizens. Nothing could be easier, especially at night, than for women in long cloaks to conceal and carry off valuable articles from a burning house.   Let the citizens be enrolled, let them wear a badge at fires, and let neither women nor strangers come near. ‡

The law then required every householder to be a fireman. His name might not appear on the rolls of any of the fire companies, he might not help to drag through the streets the lumbering tank which served as a fire-engine, but he must at least have in his hall-pantry, or beneath the stairs, or hanging up behind his shop-door, four leathern buckets inscribed with his name, and a huge bag of canvas or of duck.   Then, if he were aroused at the dead of night by the cry of fire

---

* Argus, December 16, 1796.

† Ibid., December 17, 1796.   Philadelphia Gazette, December 16, 1796.

‡ Ibid., December 16, 1796.   Philadelphia Gazette, December 16, 1796.

Ibid., December 20, 1796.   ◊ Minerva, December 26, 1796.

‖ Minerva, December 22, 1796.   ‡ Ibid., December 12, 1796.

△ Argus, December 15, 1796.

and the clanging of every church-bell in the town, he seized
his buckets and his bag, and, while his wife put a lighted
candle in the window to illuminate the street, set off for the
fire.* The smoke or the flame was his guide, for the custom
of fixing the place of the fire by a number of strokes on a
bell had not yet come in. When at last he arrived at the
scene he found there no idle spectators. Each one was busy.
Some hurried into the building and filled their sacks with
such movable goods as came nearest to hand. Some joined
the line that stretched away to the water, and helped to pass
the full buckets to those who stood by the flames. Others
took posts in a second line, down which the empty pails were
hastened to the pump. The house would often be half consumed when the shouting made known that the engine had
come. It was merely a pump mounted over a tank. Into the
tank the water from the buckets was poured, and pumped
thence by the efforts of a dozen men. No such thing as a suc-
tion-hose was seen in Philadelphia till 1794. A year later
one was made which became the wonder of the city. The
length was one hundred and sixty feet. The material was
canvas, and, to guard against decay, was carefully steeped in
brine. The fire-buckets, it was now thought, should be larger,
and a motion to that effect was made in the Common Council.
But when it was known that the new buckets, if ordered, must
hold ten quarts, the people protested. Ten quarts would
weigh twenty pounds, and the bucket five pounds more. This
was too much, for, as everybody knew, the lines at a fire were
often made up of boys and lads not used to passing heavy
weights. Eight quarts was enough. Much could also be accomplished by cutting the city into fire wards and giving a different color to the buckets of each ward. They could then be
quickly sorted when the fire was put out.† At New London
five fire wardens took charge of the engines and all who aided
in putting out fires. To disobey a warden's order was to incur
a fine of one pound. If a good leathern bucket was not kept
hanging in some convenient place in the house, and shown to

---

* See an account of a fire in Boston. Travels in the United States of North
America. W. Priest, pp. 168, 171.
† American Daily Advertiser, January 17, 18, 1797.

the warden when he called, six shillings a month was exacted
as punishment.*   At New York, however, it was long before
the buckets gave way to the hose. There, if a householder were
old, or feeble, or rich, and not disposed to quit a warm bed to
carry his buckets to the fire, he was expected at least to send
them by his servant or his slave. When the flames had been
extinguished, the buckets were left in the street to be sought
out and brought home again by their owners. If the constables
performed this duty, the corporation exacted a six-shilling fine
for each pail. This was thought excessive, and caused much
murmuring and discontent. Some people undoubtedly, it was
said, were careless in looking for their buckets after a fire.
These could easily be made diligent by a small fine. A great
one was a strong temptation to the constables to hide away the
buckets to get the reward. Others again, having come down
the line empty, were tossed into the river so carelessly as to
fill and sink instantly. Innocent people were thus put to
needless expense. Let some one be appointed and paid to
fill the buckets properly. While so disagreeable a part was
voluntary, it was very hard to find a man to do it well. It
would be wise, also, to renew the old custom of inspecting
chimneys, stoves, and ash-houses.† They were fruitful sources
of fire.

That nothing should be left undone that could lessen the
chances of destruction by fire was most important. Few buildings and little property were at that time insured. The oldest
company in New York had existed but twelve years. Forty-
five years had not gone by since the first fire-insurance policy
in America began to run. Early in February, 1752, a notice
came out in the Pennsylvania Gazette inviting such prudent
citizens of Philadelphia as wished to insure their houses from
loss by fire, to meet at the Court-House. There, every seventh
day, subscriptions would be taken till the thirteenth of April.
Many came, and, on the April day named in the notice, chose
twelve directors and a treasurer. At the head of the poll stood
Benjamin Franklin. He has, therefore, often been supposed to
have founded the Philadelphia Contributorship for the Insurance of Houses from Loss by Fire. But the father of fire insur-

---

* Connecticut Gazette, November 26, 1795.   † Argus, December 14, 1796.

ance in the United States is, beyond a doubt, John Smith. The contributors took risks in Philadelphia, and in so much of the country as lay within ten miles of the town. The rate was twenty shillings on a hundred pounds. The policy was for seven years. The premium was in the nature of a loan. Every man who insured his dwelling or his shop left a few shillings with the treasurer, had his property surveyed, and, in a week's time, if all went well, deposited the premium. The contributors then nailed their "mark" to the front of his building. When the seven years were out the money was returned without interest, or the insurance renewed. It was announced, however, that the company would take no risks on houses surrounded by shade-trees. They interfered with the use of buckets, and the huge syringe which, at that time, every man carried to the fire with his pail. A rival, therefore, started up, took these dangerous risks, and assumed as the mark it fastened to patrons' houses the image of a green tree.*

The houses thus covered by insurance were, in general, of a comfortable but unpretentious sort. They were all alike, both without and within, and each had on the lower floor two connecting rooms. If the owner were a tradesman, the front room was his shop. If he were a lawyer, it was his office. If a doctor, it was there he saw his patients, compounded his prescriptions, and kept his drugs; for only the great practitioners then sent their patients to the apothecary. The rear room was for family use. There they met at meal-time, and in the evening there they sat and drank tea. Above stairs the front room extended across the whole house. People of fashion spoke of it as the tea-room or the drawing-room; but among those who affected no fashion it passed by the name of parlor. In it the tea-parties by invitation were held. On such occasion the hostess alone sat at the table. The guests were scattered about the room, and to them the servants brought tea and rusks and cake, and sometimes fruit and wine. When the gathering was less formal, when some friends or neighbors, as the custom was, had come in unbidden to tea, the little room behind the office or the shop was used. Then all sat about the long

---

* A Mutual Association Company for Assurance against Fire was started in Richmond in 1795. Richmond Chronicle, November 24, 1795.

table, and, tea over, listened to music and songs. Every man and woman who had even a fair voice was in turn called on to sing. The others, it was expected, could at least play. Among instruments the German flute was a favorite, and for women the four-stringed guitar; but not the violin. That was ungenteel, for Lord Chesterfield had pronounced it so. To the accompaniment of the guitar and flute the men sang hunting songs, and the women Scotch ballads and English airs. "Water parted from the Sea," "Fair Aurora, pray thee Stay," "In Infancy our Hopes and Fears," "Bess of Bedlam," and "Queen Mary's Lament," were favorites everywhere. There were those who heard with delight "Hark, away to the Downs" and "I Love them All."

There were others also who looked down on such innocent amusement with contempt. To their ears no music was pleasing which did not form part of some French opera, and was not to be heard at a concert in a tea-garden or a public hall. French manners had corrupted them. Since the fall of the Bastile, it was said complainingly, every Republican must dress like a Frenchman, and every Federalist like a subject of King George. If you happen to oppose the administration, you must go regularly to the shop of M. Sansculotte, before whose door is a flaring liberty-pole, painted tricolor and surmounted with a red cap of liberty, and have your hair cut *à la* Brutus; your pantaloons must fit tight to the leg and come down to your yellow top-boots, or, better yet, your shoes. If you persist in wearing breeches and silk stockings and square-toed boots, then are you an old fogy or a Federalist, which is the same thing, and must inscribe your brass buttons, "Long live the President."

The folly of the French dress was a source of never-ending amusement. Satire, raillery, invective, the lamentations of the weeping philosopher, and the exhortations of the preacher, were exhausted in vain. Dress became every season more and more hideous, more and more uncomfortable, more and more devoid of good sense and good taste. Use and beauty ceased to be combined. The pantaloons of a beau went up to his arm-pits; to get into them was a morning's work, and, when in, to sit down was impossible. His hat was too small to contain his handkerchief, and was not expected to stay on his head. His hair was brushed from the crown of his head toward his forehead, and looked, as a satirist of that day truly said, as if he had been fighting an old-fashioned hurricane backward. About his neck was a spotted linen neckerchief; the skirts of his green coat were cut away to a mathematical point behind; his favorite drink was brandy, and his favorite talk of the last French play. Then there was the "dapper beau," who carried a stick much too short to reach the ground, twisted his Brutus-cropped hair into curls, and, upon the very crown of his head, wore a hat of a snuff-box size. But the politest man on earth was the shopkeeping beau. He would jump over a counter four feet high to pick up a lady's handkerchief, made the hand-somest bows, said the best things, and could talk on any sub-ject, from the odor of a roll of pomatum to the vulgarity of not wearing wigs.

Even these absurdities were not enough, and, when 1800 began, fashion was more extravagant still. Then a beau was defined as anything put into a pair of pantaloons with a binding sewed round the top and called a vest. The skirts of the coat should be pared away to the width of a hat-band, and if he was doomed to pass his time in the house, he would require a heavy pair of round-toed jack-boots with a tassel before and behind. These provided, lift him, said the sat-irist, lift him by the cape of the coat, pull his hair over his face, lay a hat on his forehead, put spectacles on his nose, and on no account let his hands escape from the pockets of his pantaloons. Women were thought worse than the men. To determine the style of their dress, Fashion, De-cency, and Health, the statement was, ran a race. Decency lost her spirits, Health was bribed by a quack-doctor, so Fash-ion won.

Such must drink tea in the alcoves, the arbors, the shady walks of Gray's Garden.* They must visit Bush Hill, hear

---

* A traveller who visited the Garden in 1794 "ordered coffee, which I was informed they were here famous for serving in style. I took a memorandum of what was on the table; viz.: coffee, cheese, sweet cakes, hung beef, sugar, pickled salmon, butter, crackers, ham, cream, and bread." Travels in the United States, etc. Priest, p. 34.

the music, see the fireworks, and watch the huge figure walk about the grounds.* For them, too, were the Assembly and the play. The Assembly-Room was at Oeller's Tavern, and made one of the sights of the town. The length was sixty feet. The walls were papered in the French fashion, and adorned with Pantheon figures, festoons, pilasters, and groups of antique drawings. Across one end was a fine music-gallery. The rules of the Assembly were framed and hung upon the wall. The managers had entire control. Without their leave, no lady could quit her place in the dance, nor dance out of her set, nor could she complain if they placed strangers or brides at the head of the dance. The ladies were to rank in sets and draw for places as they entered the room. Those who led might call the dances alternately. When each set had danced a country dance, a cotillion might be had if eight ladies wished it. Gentlemen could not come into the room in boots, colored stockings, or undress.† At Hanover gentlemen were forbidden to enter the ball-room " without breeches," or to dance " without coats."

Equally fine in its decorations was the theatre. Travellers were divided in their opinion as to whether the finest house was at Charleston, ‡ or Boston, or Philadelphia. But it seems to have been at Philadelphia. Great sums had been laid out on the building. Gilders and painters, frescoers and carvers, had been brought from England to assist in the decoration, and, mindful of the opposition once made by the good people of the city, the managers put up

---

* A female figure which, after promenading the garden, " disappeared as by enchantment." Porcupine's Gazette, August 12, 1797.

† An Excursion to the United States of North America, etc. Henry Wansey, pp. 119, 120.

‡ The Charleston theatre is described in the General Advertiser, September 5, 1792. The stage was fifty-six feet long, the front circular, and provided with three rows of patent lamps. The galleries were built so that small parties could have a single box. Each box had a window and a Venetian blind. The three tiers of boxes were decorated with thirty-nine columns, and each column with a glass chandelier with five lights. The lower tier was " balustered "; the others panelled. The mouldings and projections were silvered. Three ventilators were in the ceiling. At a later date the public were informed that, " Agreeable to the regulation of the City Council, no people of color will be admitted to any part of the house." South Carolina State Gazette, November 19, 1795.

over the stage the words, "The Eagle suffers the little Birds to sing." * One who saw the place in 1794 declares that it reminded him of an English playhouse. The scenes, the plays, the names of the actors; the ladies, in small hats of checkered straw, or with hair in full dress or put up in the French way, or, if they chanced to be young, arranged in long ringlets that hung down their backs; the men, in round hats and silk-striped coats with high collars of English make, might well have produced that effect.† More than one of the players had often been seen by the crowds that frequented the Haymarket Theatre at London. No seats were reserved. No tickets were sold at the door. No programmes were distributed. No ushers were present. Gentlemen who left the theatre during the play, to drink flip at a neighboring tavern, were given printed checks as they passed out which, if they came back, would admit them. Out of this custom grew three evils. Some, not intending to return, gave away their checks to idle boys and disorderly persons, who thus gained admittance and annoyed the audience. Again, crowds of half-grown lads hung about the doors and, as every one came out, beset him with demands for a check. In this way the tickets passed into the hands of counterfeiters, and were sold for a shilling to persons of low character. All this, the proprietors declared, was ruinous to good morals, and, in a public appeal, begged their patrons not to give the checks to loungers. The curtain went up at an hour when the men of our time have scarcely returned to their homes. The entertainment was long and varied. Pieces now thought enough for one night's amusement were then commonly followed by farces and comedies, dances and tragedies, songs, pantomimes, and acrobatic feats. These were called interlocutory entertainments, and came in between the acts of the tragedy or before and just after the farce. Sometimes the jealousy of Othello would be relieved by the New Federal Bow-Wow, in which the singer would imitate in succession the surly dog, the knowing dog, the king dog, the sitting dog, the barking dog, till pit and gal-

---

* An Excursion to the United States of North America, etc. Henry Wansey, p. 114.

† Ibid., p. 113.

lery were convulsed with laughter.*   Again it would be a banjo
dance, or a hornpipe by some actress of note. If " Ça ira " were
sung, the Federalists would not be quiet till Yankee Doodle
was given, whereupon the gallery would join in the chorus.
On particular occasions the programme would be made to suit
the day. On the twenty-second of February, 1797, the Federal
Street Theatre at Boston made a great display of illuminations
and transparencies, covered the pit, and spread a fine supper
on a table which stretched from the boxes to the stage. The
Haymarket Theatre, not to be outdone, decorated its walls, had
an ode written for the occasion, and played the tragedy of
Bunker Hill.† A few months later, when, after many trials,
the famous ship Constitution left her ways, the evening performance at the Haymarket closed with " The Launch, or
Huzza for the Constitution," and a fine representation of the
ship. ‡ As much as three thousand dollars are known to have
been expended on the scenery of a single piece.# The income
of a single night reached sixteen hundred dollars. ‖

When the season was over in the cities, the players wandered over the country and performed in the large towns.
During the summer of 1796 part of the Old American Company stopped at Newport. But they were not to the liking of
the people. Few went to see them. They fell into debt, and
on the day of the last performance put up a cry for help.
Would the people of Newport take into their kind, generous,
and humane consideration the sufferings of the actors ? The
business during the whole summer had been poor. The
weekly outlay had not been met. No salaries had been paid
till the great nights when the Providence Company came
down. Would the town, therefore, please to honor and pat-
ronize their last play ? When the occasion came the Beaux
Stratagem, the Federal Bow-Wow, a comic opera called the
Poor Soldier, a hornpipe, slack-rope tumbling, and the pan-
tomime of the Death of Captain Cook, were all performed.^

---

* Massachusetts Mercury, November 3, 1797.

† Ibid., February 24, 1797.   ‡ Ibid., November 3, 1797.

Aurora, February 10, 1797.

‖ On another night the proceeds were $666.   Boston Gazette, June 25, 1796.

^ Newport Mercury, September 6, 1796.

The Providence Company that brought the great nights had long been playing a programme quite as varied. One night it was Road to Ruin, with the Grecian Fabulist, Bucks have at Ye All, and a musical piece, the Son-in-Law, thrown in.* On another evening the Midnight Hour, and Oscar and Malvina, a drama founded on Ossian's Tale, were played.† A third company, on its way to Philadelphia, informed the ladies and gentlemen of Hartford that it would play in the town for one night only. ‡ A fourth notified the people of East Hartford, East Windsor, and Glastonbury that it had come to Hartford, that it would play there, and had contracted with the ferryman to attend regularly at his dock when the play was done.#

These strolling players met at best with poor returns. The theatre was looked upon, and justly, as an institution of questionable morality. The playhouse was not then the quiet and well-ordered place it has since become. Both actors and audience took liberties that would now be thought intolerable. On one occasion, at Alexandria, whither a company always went in racing season, some of the players forgot their parts. They supplied the omissions with lines of their own composition, and even went so far as to recite ribald passages. Thereupon they were threatened with a pelting of oranges, eggs, and hard apples. ‖ At another time, at Richmond, the actors came upon the stage with books in their hands and read their parts. Some ventured to appear before the audience in a state of gross intoxication. Much of the illusion of the scenery, it was said, was yet further destroyed by the voice of the prompter, which could be heard in all parts of the house.△ From Charleston came complaints of the misbehavior of the young men. They would enter the theatre carrying what might well be called bludgeons, but what they had named tippies, would keep up an incessant rapping on the seats, and, when remonstrance was made, had been known to declare that a theatre,

---

* Providence Gazette, August 6, 1796.   † Ibid., September 10, 1796.
‡ Connecticut Courant, August 7, 1797.   # Ibid., August 14, 1797.
‖ Virginia Gazette and Alexandria Advertiser, August 5, 1790. For the manager's reply, see the Gazette of August 12, 1790.
△ Richmond and Manchester Advertiser, November 7, 1795.

like a tavern, was a place where a man, having paid the price
of admission, was free to do as he liked.* One evening a
fight took place in the gallery. The play was instantly
stopped, the offender seized, brought upon the stage, and exposed to public view. The performance then went smoothly on till a bottle was suddenly flung from the gallery to
the pit. This was too much. The men in the pit went up
into the gallery in a body, laid hold on the culprit, dragged
him on the stage, and demanded that a public apology should
be made. He refused, and was at once driven from the
house.†

In the theatres at the North it often happened that, the
moment a well-dressed man entered the pit, he at once became
a mark for the wit and insolence of the men in the gallery.
They would begin by calling on him to doff his hat in mark of
inferiority, for the custom of wearing hats in the theatre was
universal. If he obeyed, he was loudly hissed and troubled no
more. If he refused, abuse, oaths, and indecent remarks were
poured out upon him. He was spit at, pelted with pears, apples, sticks, stones, and empty bottles till he left the house.
As "the blades in the gallery" were poor marksmen, the
neighbors of the man aimed at were the chief sufferers. ‡ On
one occasion the orchestra was put to flight and some instruments broken. Then the manager came on the stage and
begged "the men in the gallery to be quiet; if they were
not, he should be compelled during all future performances
to keep the gallery shut."

Admittance to such performances was quite as costly then
as at present. The mass of the people, therefore, supported
amusements of a cheaper kind. Every year, as soon as the
post-roads were fit to be used, a score of showmen and acro-
bats, magicians, and natural philosophers, came up from the
South. They wandered from town to town, spent a few days
at the tavern, hired a room, charged a small sum for admission,

---

* Daily Evening Gazette and Charleston Tea-Table Companion, February 14,
1795.

† Ibid., February 14, 1795. On one of the handbills "The manager requests
that no gentleman will smoke in the boxes or pit." Columbian Herald or New
Daily Advertiser, May 3, 1796.

‡ General Advertiser, October 25, 1795.

and drew all the farmers for miles around. One had a lion,* another an ostrich,† another a cassowary, another a learned pig,‡ another a dwarf, another a buffalo,# another the first African elephant that ever was seen in the United States. The creature danced "Yankee Doodle," drew corks, ate, as the handbills set forth, ninety pounds of food and drank half a barrel of water each day. ‖ There were wax-figures and musical clocks, and " thunder-houses " ᐃ and automatons without number. ◊ Any man who could perform a striking experiment in physics, who knew enough of " catoptrics " to make a " penetrating spy-glass " or a " shade," who had acquired knowledge enough of electricity to build a "thunder-house" or construct an " electrical and perpetual lamp," ‡ was sure of a large and attentive audience. Parties of pleasure would be made up, and people go in scores to behold the wonders provided for their amusement by Seignior Falconi, or Seignior Cressini, or Seignior Jonalty. Gases were exploded by electricity; men were " electrified "; sea-fights were represented by "shades"; automatons were made to perform. Now the subject was the conflict of the Salamander and the Butterfly, which took place, it was boastfully said, in a pool of real fire ; ‡ now the figures were Citizen Sans Culotte and Mr. Aristocrat;‡ now they

---

* Impartial Herald (Newburyport), May 19, 1795.

† Virginia Argus, November 15, 1799. Aurora, November 10, 1795.

‡ Porcupine's Gazette, January 10, 1797.

Baltimore Daily Repository, February 7, 1793. City Gazette and Daily Advertiser (Charleston), January 7, 1797.

‖ Eastern Herald, May 2, 1796. Massachusetts Mercury, October 24, 1797.

ᐃ Columbian Mirror, April 30, 1795.

◊ At an exhibition at Lee's Coffee-House, at Hartford, the automatic figures were: A Butcher slaying an Ox; Beheading of John the Baptist; a Canary-Bird whistling Tunes; a Prussian Huzzar ; a Chimney-Sweep ; a Bullfinch and Canary-Bird "singing as natural as life." Connecticut Courant, August 7, 1797.

‡ Connecticut Gazette, November 5, 1795.

‡ A long description, with a wood-cut, appears in American Daily Advertiser, September 11, 1795.

‡ Citizen Sans Culotte and Mr. Aristocrat were two life-size figures, which, when wound up, turned somersaults, danced to music, saluted the company, and disappeared. Mr. Aristocrat could never be made to dance the Carmagnole, or to make any move when " Ça ira " was played. When the French excitement of 1794 was at its height, the figures were exhibited at Philadelphia in the rooms of Mr. Poor's Academy, a famous school for girls. The school was at 9 Cherry

were Mr. Aristocrat, Mr. Democrat, and Mrs. Moderate;
again they were Citizen Democrat, Mr. Aristocrat, and Miss
Modern, a young woman from Boston; now the French king
was guillotined in an automaton, to the delight of those that
came to the showman's room from nine in the morning until
nine at night.*   But the greatest automaton of all was the Indian Chief.   Till the chess-player appeared, his equal was not
seen.   Nor should the name of a Frenchman who diverted
the multitude be forgotten.   Did he live in our time he would
be known as an aëronaut.   But, in the language of his own
day, Blanchard was described as a man who experimented in
aërostatics.   When the balloon was still a new invention he

Alley, between Third and Fourth streets, "near the sign of the white lamb."
For some account of the figures, see American Daily Advertiser, March 10, 1794.

* The advertisement is worth citing in full as a specimen of its kind:

EXHIBITION

Of Figures in Composition at Full Length
(Corner of Second and Callowhill Streets),
—At the Sign of the Black Bear—

LATE King of France, together with his Queen, taking her last Farewell of him
in the Temple the day preceding his execution.   The whole is a striking likeness,
in full stature, and dressed as they were at the time.

The King is represented standing, his Queen on her knees by his right side,
overwhelmed with sorrow and ready to faint, the King looking tenderly at her.

Second is the Scaffold on which he was executed, whereon the King stands in
full view of the Guillotine; before him is a Priest on his knees with a Crucifix in
one hand and a Prayer-Book in the other; on the side of the Guillotine stands
the executioner prepared to do his duty.

When the first signal is given the Priest rises on his feet, the King lays himself on the block, where he is secured; the executioner then turns and prepares
to do his duty; and, when the second signal is given, the executioner drops the
knife and severs the head from the body in one second; the head falls in a bas-
ket, and the lips, which are first red, turn blue; the whole is performed to the life
by an invisible machine without any perceivable assistance.

Made by the First Italian Artist of the Name of

COLUMBA.

The workmanship has been admired by the most professed judges wherever it
has been seen.

*_** The proprietors humbly hope for the encouragement of the public, as
nothing shall be wanting on their part to render the exhibition *pleasing* and *satisfactory* to their patrons.

Price, 3s.   Children, half price.

To be seen from 9 o'clock in the morning until 9 at night.   Daily Advertiser,
November 21, 1794.

had gained fame as a daring voyager, had made many ascensions in France, had crossed the English Channel from Dover to Calais, had come to America in 1792, bringing with him a parachute, a balloon, four thousand two hundred pounds of vitriolic acid, and had informed the public that he would go up, God willing, from the prison-yard at Philadelphia on the ninth of January, 1793. Some doubts were expressed on the propriety of men and women of decent character attending at the prison; but they were speedily removed, and, when the time came, half the city was there. On that day no business was done, no trades were made, no shops were open, till the balloon was lost to sight. From sunrise till ten in the forenoon cannon were discharged incessantly. At nine the inflation be-began. The bag was of green taffeta; the "gaz" was that which is produced when vitriolic acid is mingled with iron chips. At ten Blanchard stepped into the car, received a paper from Washington, threw out the ballast, and was soon beyond reach of the shouts that came up from the multitude that covered the vacant lots and housetops of the city and stood upon the hills for miles around. Many galloped down the Point road in hope of overtaking him; but they soon came back, declaring that the balloon was out of sight. At seven in the evening he was once more in the city, paying his respects to the President. The experiment was pronounced a complete success. All manner of uses to which the balloon might be put were suggested, both in jest † and earnest. At Philadelphia money was raised to pay back the four hundred guineas the experiment had cost. ‡ From New York came a request that M. Blanchard would make a second ascent from the Battery Park.# He declined, made haste to put up a

---

* Independent Gazetteer, January 12, 1793.

    † "Grand Blanchard, lorsque tu voleras dans les airs,
        Va annoncer aux planettes de l'univers
        Que le François ont vaincu leurs ennemis intérieurs,
        Leur intrépidité a expulsé les extérieurs;
        Pénétre dans l'Olympe, et dis à tous les dieux,
        Que les François ont été les victorieux;
        Prie Mars que les armes de la France
        Ne laisse aux tirans aucune espérance."

‡ Independent Gazetteer, January 26, 1793.   # Ibid., March 2, 1793

huge rotunda in the rear of Governor Mifflin's house, and there for a time exhibited the balloon.* But trouble soon overwhelmed him. The boys stoned his balloon, and it collapsed.† Then he exhibited a parachute ‡ at Ricketts's Circus on Market street, and a carriage dragged by an automatic eagle at his rotunda on Chestnut street.# But the town gave him small support. He fell into debt, his property went to other hands, and for many years the country heard no more of parachutes and balloons.

In the museums was gathered material which did much for the education of the people. The Columbian was at Boston. A second was in an empty room in the garret of the State-House at Hartford. Another was in the City Hall at New York. The best was that of Mr. Peale, at Philadelphia. There were a mammoth's tooth from the Ohio, and a woman's shoe from Canton; nests of the kind used to make soup of, and a Chinese fan six feet long; bits of asbestos, belts of wampum, stuffed birds, and feathers from the Friendly Isles; scalps, tomahawks, and long lines of portraits of great men of the Revolutionary War. To visit the museum, to wander through the rooms, play upon the organ, examine the rude electrical machine, and have a profile drawn by the physiognotrace, were pleasures from which no stranger in the city ever abstained. There, too, was the circus where Mr. Ricketts delighted his audience with Gilpin's ride, or, mounted on the bare back of a galloping horse, danced a hornpipe, or went through the exercises of the manual of arms.

From sights such as these the countrymen went back to the enjoyment of the festivities of the rural towns. If they were so fortunate as to live to the westward of the city, the road commonly taken was the Lancaster pike. Running out from

* Independent Gazetteer, January 26, 1793.
† See his singular letter in American Daily Advertiser, May 29, 1793.
‡ Independent Gazetteer, June 8, 1793; also, The Courier, November 4, 1795.
# In the advertisement of this exhibition appears the request that "Gentlemen having dogs accustomed to the chase will please not bring them, as experience has shown they may be very dangerous to the Eagle." Ibid., August 24, 1793. Blanchard was the first of sensational advertisers. He carried on imaginary correspondences in the newspapers, made his private affairs public, and put a *fac simile* of his signature at the end of his letters that appeared in print,

Philadelphia to Lancaster, it was, by the testimony of all travellers, the finest piece of highway in the United States.* In
1792, when the desire to speculate was rife in the land, a number of gentlemen organized a company to build the road.
The charter was secured, the books were opened, and in ten
days two thousand two hundred and seventy-five subscribers
put down their names for stock. This was more than the
law allowed. The names were, therefore, placed in a lottery-
wheel, six hundred drawn in the most impartial manner, and,
with their subscriptions, the work was begun. But of road-
making the Americans of that day knew nothing. When the
land had been condemned, when the trees had been felled, and
the road-bed made ready, the largest stones and boulders that
could be found were dragged and rolled upon it. Earth and
gravel were then thrown on, and the work pronounced complete. But, when the heavy rains came, the errors of the road-
makers were plain to all. Great holes appeared on every side.
Huge stones protruded from the track, and, as the horses stum-
bled and floundered along it, numbers of them sank to their
knees between the boulders, and were drawn out with broken
legs. In this strait an Englishman, who had seen many a road
built on the Macadam plan, offered to undertake the work. The
company consented, and the road became the first turnpike in
the United States.

This fact alone was sufficient to awaken opposition and
alarm. That a company of private citizens should have authority to take land against the will of its owners; that they
should have a right to send a band of surveyors over the farms
of their neighbors to mark down a turnpike wherever seemed
most fit, through the barn-yards, or the wheat-fields, or the
orchards; and that, when it was built, they should forbid the
men whose land they had seized to drive so much as a lame
horse over the road till a toll had been paid, was, in the opinion of many, a most dangerous grant of power. The mal-

---

* "There is, at present" (1796), "but one turnpike-road on the continent,
which is between Lancaster and Philadelphia, a distance of sixty-six miles, and is
a masterpiece of its kind ; it is paved with stone the whole way, and overlaid with
gravel, so that it is never obstructed during the most severe season." Journal of
a Tour in Unsettled Parts of North America in 1796 and 1797. Francis Baily,
p. 107.

contents, therefore, held a meeting, one day in May, 1793, at the Prince of Wales Tavern. Some came to it because they felt aggrieved that the company had not bought strips of their lands, or given them work to do upon the road. Some had farms near Philadelphia. These feared that a good highway to Lancaster would enable farmers twenty miles away to compete with them in Market street on Wednesday and Saturday of each week. The chairman of the gathering was George Logan. The meeting passed a set of resolutions denouncing the Legislature for chartering the company. The chairman, with one to assist him, drew up an address to the people. Acts to incorporate a few men of wealth and give them power to violate property by digging canals and building turnpikes were, the resolutions declared, unjust and dangerous to the rights of the people. The justification of these unprecedented laws was, the address set forth, public good. This was pretence. The company had nothing of the kind in view. Sordid motives of private emolument were its only guide. The weakness of the legislators who suffered themselves to be misled by such tricks was pitiable. But the artifices of those who secured the passage of the laws were to be viewed with indignation and alarm. The Legislature was intrusted by the sovereign power, the people, with the duty of protecting them, their property, and their lives. Did the duty of protecting give the right to take away the property of one man and bestow it on another? The address closed with citations from Burlamaqui, from Blackstone, and the Laws of Edward III.

The next day a sharp reply was published. The movers of the enterprise, the answer said, well knew that Nature had placed great obstacles in their way. They expected the novelty of the work would create more. But they had never for a moment believed they would be opposed and hindered by the very men for whom they were doing so much. They had, indeed, seen Doctor Logan hurrying through the country, like a Bedlamite escaped from a cell, brawling in the taverns, vilifying congressmen, posting up handbills with the specious words Liberty, Property, and No Excise, and seeking, in a thousand ways, to stir up opposition to the laws of the land. In all this he had been acting as a private man. Now, however, he was transformed into the chairman of a meeting, and assisted by one Edward Heston. It was easy to see why Heston was present. He had long given the company a warm support, had sold it some of his land, and had served it as an overseer of the work at one dollar a day. But, finding he was about to be discharged, he had resigned, and was taking his revenge in opposition. That the Legislature had incorporated a few rich men was not true. No set of men in particular had been incorporated. The books of the company had been open to the public. Any one might have subscribed. Half the stock issued was, in fact, held by the farmers of Chester and Lancaster. As to the arguments from Blackstone, they were valueless. The Doctor had taken a sentence here and another there, and tacked them together. If he read Van Swieten in the same way, he would some day be prescribing fish-hooks, instead of rhubarb and calomel, for a child with worms. In one part of the New Testament were the words, " Judas went and hanged himself." In another, " Go thou and do likewise." Let the Doctor join these two sentences, and then follow the advice they contained.*

Despite the opposition, the road-building went on, and more than one man who came to the Prince of Wales Tavern in 1793 lived to see the Lancaster turnpike the pride of the whole State. To this day, in every town along the route, old men may be found who delight to recall the times when the pike was in its prime, when trade was brisk, when tavern-keepers grew rich, when the huge sheds were crowded with the finest of horses, and when thousands of Conestoga wagons went into Philadelphia each week creaking under the yield of the dairy and the produce of the famous Pennsylvania farms.

Nor was the reputation of the farms undeserved. Many of the settlers in the four counties through which the road ran were Germans, and wherever a German farmer lived there were industry, order, and thrift. The size of the barns, the height of the fences, the well-kept wheat-fields and orchards, marked off the domain of such a farmer from the lands of his shiftless Irish neighbors. His ancestor might, perhaps, have left a home in Alsace or Swabia, Saxony or the Palatinate, a well-

---

* American Daily Advertiser, May 25, 1793. For the replies of Logan and Heston, see the Advertiser of May 30, 1793.

to-do man. But he was sure, ere he reached Philadelphia, to be reduced to a state of beggary and want. Ship-captains and ship-owners, sailors and passengers, rifled his chests and robbed him of his money and his goods. Then, with no more worldly possessions than the clothes he had on his back, and the few coins and the copy of the Heidelberg Catechism, or Luther's Catechism, or Arndt's Wahres Christenthum, he had in his pockets, he was at liberty to earn the best living he could, save a few pounds, buy ten or twenty acres of forest-land, make a clearing, and begin to farm. The underbrush he grubbed. The trees he cut down, and, when he had burned them into convenient lengths, his neighbors came in to drink brannt-wein and help him log-roll. It was long before his house was anything better than a well-built cabin of logs. In it he lived in the simplest manner with the strictest economy. He came from a land where wood was dear. The huge open fireplace, the glory of a New England kitchen, seemed, therefore, to him to produce a shameful waste of fuel. His rooms were warmed and his food was cooked by the fire in a ten-plate iron stove which sent the smoke and gases up the flue of a solitary chimney that rose from the middle of the house.* His food was chiefly pork and rye, onions and sauerkraut, milk and cheese, turnips and Indian corn. Sometimes fresh meat was added. But no beeves nor sheep were slaughtered till every part of the carcass had been disposed of among the families on the neighboring farms.† With this exception, everything he ate grew upon his own land. Everything he wore was made under his own roof. The good wife and her daughters cultivated the garden-patch that lay near the house, trained the honeysuckles that shaded the door, spun the flax and woollen yarn, worked the loom, made the cheese and butter, and, when harvest came, toiled with the sickle in the field. If he had a servant on the farm, the man or woman was a redemptioner.

---

* Schoepf's Reise durch Pennsylvanien, 1783, p. 185.

† " I asked him where he purchased his meat. He says, 'When a farmer kills beef, mutton, or veal, he advertises his neighbors, who take what they choose, and he sells the remainder.'" New Travels in the United States of America. De Warville, p. 254.

In 1800 a redemptioner was always a person in the depths of poverty, who, for transportation to the United States, willingly became a slave. The time, the conditions, the recompense of the bondage, were fully expressed in the contract, and the contract placed on record.* Ship-captains and ship-agents would rarely accept a shorter term of service than three years. The redemptioners would rarely give more than eight; stipulated for meat, drink, lodging, and apparel, and the customary freedom suits when their time was out. One of their suits must be new, or ten pounds currency be given in its stead. Twenty pounds one-and-six was the price for which a redemptioner sold, whether man or woman, whether the time of service was long or short. Children brought eight to ten pounds, were to have at least one quarter at some day or night school, were to be taught to read and write, and, occasionally, some trade.† The whole relation of master to servant was prescribed by law. No redemptioner could be sold and sent out of Pennsylvania till he and two justices of the peace had given their consent. None could be assigned out of the county where service began till the servant and one justice approved. Should he labor faithfully and well for four years, he was, when his service ended, to receive from the master or the mistress two complete suits of clothes, a grubbing-hoe, a weeding-hoe, and a new axe. For each day he absented himself from labor without his master's leave, five days were to be added to his service-time. If he married without permission, he must serve

---

* The language of the contract was:

"This Indenture, made the .... day of ......, in the year of the Lord one thousand seven hundred and ...., between .... of the one part and .... of the other part, *witnesseth* that the said .... doth hereby covenant, promise, and grant to and with the said ...., executors, administrators, and assigns, from the day of the date hereof until the first and next arrival at ..... in America, and after, for, and during the term of .... years to serve in such service and employment as the said .... or .... assign, shall there employ ...., according to the customs of the country in the like kind. In consideration whereof the said .... doth hereby covenant and grant to and with said .... to pay for .... passage, and to find and allow .... meat, drink, apparel, and lodging, with other necessaries, during the said term, and at the end of the said term to pay unto .... the usual allowance, according to the customs of the country in kind. In witness whereof," etc.

† Registry of the Redemptioners, 1785–1817, in Pennsylvania Historical Society.

an additional year. If he ran away, any one who hid him or fed him or gave him keep for four-and-twenty hours, without sending word to a justice, was liable to a fine of twenty shillings for each day. To apprehend him was a meritorious act, and rewarded with ten shillings if he were ten miles from home, and twenty shillings if the distance were greater. To buy of him, to trade with him, to sell to him, unless the master first approved, was an offence in the eye of the law, and punishable by fine.

Save so far as these laws hindered, the ship-captains were free to do with their bondsmen what they pleased. They parted husband from wife; they separated children from parents; nay, one brute, when the yellow fever was devastating Philadelphia in 1793, shocked the people of Chester by sailing up the Delaware with a cargo of redemptioners, and seeking to sell them as nurses to the sick.

Among the Germans, as among farmers of all sorts, agriculture was believed to be much affected by the moon. Grain should not be sown, orchards should not be pruned, reaping should not begin, till the proper moon had reached its proper quarter and appearance. Whether it lay upon its back or stood upon its horn, whether it gave promise of drought or rain, were all matters of deep concern. When at last the crops had been gathered, the labor of transporting them began. Then the great wagons were brought from under the shed, and, while the men put on the load, the women made ready the provisions for the whole trip. The capacity of the vehicles was often four tons. Their covers of linen were high at each end and low in the middle. Their wheels were at times fifteen inches wide. The horses that tugged them through the mire of the country roads were of the far-famed Conestoga breed. These creatures were of English origin. Some emigrants who settled in Chester county brought a few horses with them. From the English in turn the Swiss Mennonites obtained that stock which, in the valley of the Pequea and along the banks of Conestoga Creek, they brought to a high state of perfection. The horse and the ox were the only draught animals in general use. The mule was almost unused. Twelve years had not passed since the first pair of jacks in

America landed at Portsmouth, in New Hampshire. The King of Spain had sent them to Washington, that mules might be bred at Mount Vernon.* In a few years the progeny of "Royal Gift" was scattered over the plantations of northern Virginia,† and regularly offered for sale on the race-course at Annapolis. ‡ Other jacks were afterward imported from Spain # by numbers of breeders, and finally great cargoes of mules. ‖ Yet the animals were little used north of the Virginia line.△ In every State the number of farmers who had ever in their lives beheld a mule was extremely small. Through the whole farming region of New England and New York ox-carts and ox-sleds were oftener met with than horses and wagons. There most of the vehicles went upon two wheels. Only in the large towns were chariotees and coachees, gigs, carriages, and stage-coaches to be seen.

The stage-coach was little better than a huge covered box mounted on springs. It had neither glass windows, nor door, nor steps, nor closed sides. The roof was upheld by eight posts which rose from the body of the vehicle, and the body was commonly breast-high. From the top were hung curtains of leather, to be drawn up when the day was fine, and let down and buttoned when rainy and cold. Within were four seats. Without was the baggage.◊ Fourteen pounds of luggage were allowed to be carried free by each passenger. But if his portmanteau or his brass-nail-studded hair trunk weighed

---

* See the letter of Washington to Count de Florida Blanca, December 15, 1795.

† Maryland Gazette, April 21, 1796.

‡ Ibid., September 19 and 26, 1793.

Ibid., November 5, 1795; also June 2, 1796.

‖ See an offer to deliver sixty or seventy in Boston ten days after contract. Independent Chronicle, June 13, 1796.

△ Notices of mules lost or for sale, or of jacks to cover, appear from time to time after 1795 in the newspapers in various parts of the country. Mules strayed. Connecticut Gazette, November 26, 1795. Notice of a "jack." Grafton, Minerva, and Haverhill Weekly Bud, May 26, 1796. For sale. Richmond Chronicle, October 27, 1795. To cover. North Carolina Gazette (Newbern), April 2, 1796.

◊ For some account of the stage-coach, see Journal of a Tour in the Unsettled Parts of North America. Francis Baily, pp. 107, 108. New Travels in the United States of America. Brissot de Warville, pp. 172–175. London edition, 1792. A fine picture of the "American Stage-wagon" is given in Weld's Travels. London edition, p. 15.

more, he paid for it at the same rate per mile as he paid for himself. Under no circumstances, however, could he be permitted to take with him on the journey more than one hundred and fifty pounds. When the baggage had all been weighed and strapped on the coach, when the horses had been attached and the way-bill made out, the eleven passengers were summoned, and, clambering to their seats through the front of the stage, sat down with their faces toward the driver's seat. On routes where no competition existed progress was slow, and the travellers were subjected to all manner of extortion and abuse. "Brutality, negligence, and filching," says one, "are as naturally expected by people accustomed to travelling in America as a mouth, a nose, and two eyes are looked for in a man's face." Another set out one day in March, 1796, to go from Frenchtown to New Castle, on the Delaware. Seventeen miles separated the two towns, a distance which, he declares, a good healthy man could have passed over in four hours and a half. The stage-coach took six. When it finally reached New Castle it was high noon, the tide was making, the wind was fair, and the boat for Philadelphia was ready at the wharf. Yet he was detained for an hour and a half, "that the innkeeper might scrub the passengers out of the price of a dinner." Dinner over, the boat set sail and ran up the river to within two miles of Gloucester Point. There, wind and tide failing, the vessel dropped anchor for the night. Some passengers, anxious to go on by land, were forced to pay half a dollar each to be rowed to the shore. At one in the morning the tide again turned. But the master was then drunk, and, when he could be made to understand what was said, the tide was again ebbing, and the boat aground.* Evening came before the craft reached Philadelphia. The passengers were forty-eight hours on board. Another came from New York by stage and by water. He was almost shipwrecked in the bay, lost some of his baggage at Amboy, was nearly left by the coach, and passed

---

* Says another: "After sailing down the Delaware about ten hours in the water-stage, our skipper ran us on a sand-bank. As there was no remedy but to wait patiently the flow of the tide, a party of us borrowed a boat and went a-shooting on the islands with which this part of the Delaware abounds." Travels in the United States of America, etc. Priest, p. 73.

twenty hours going sixteen miles on the Delaware. The captain was drunk. The boat three times collided with vessels coming up the river.* A gentleman set out in February to make the trip from Philadelphia to Baltimore. Just beyond Havre de Grace the axle broke. A cart was hired and the passengers driven to the next stage-inn. There a new coach was obtained, which, in the evening, overset in a wood. Toward daylight the whole party, in the midst of a shower of rain and snow, found shelter and breakfast at a miserable house three miles from Baltimore. But the host would not suffer one of them to dry his clothes by the kitchen stove. When an editor in the town was asked to publish an account of their trip he refused. The owners of the coach-line might, he said, hinder the circulation of his newspaper.† To add to the vexation of such delays "the Apostolic Assembly of the State of Delaware" had forbidden stage-coaches to cross their "hand's-breadth of territory" on the Sabbath. ‡ The worst bit of road in the country seems to have been between Elkton, in Maryland, and the Susquehanna Ferry. There the ruts were so deep that, as the wheels were about to enter one, the driver would call upon the passengers to lean out of the opposite side of the coach, to prevent the vehicle being overturned. "Now, gentlemen," he would say, "to the right." "Now, gentlemen, to the left." #

Yet another traveller had quitted Philadelphia for New York. All went smoothly till the coach drew near to the town of Brunswick. There one of a rival line was overtaken, and a

---

* The History of the United States for 1796, pp. 274, 275.

† American Annual Register, pp. 34, 35. "The complaint is not confined to a single journey, and much less to a single passenger. Many coaches were last season overturned. Many passengers were bruised." Baily, p. 36. "Waited at Baltimore near a week before I could proceed on my journey, the roads being rendered impassable." Journal of a Tour in Unsettled Parts of North America in 1796 and 1797. F. Baily, p. 107. For accident near Havre de Grace, see p. 108. For one near Newport, in Delaware, see pp. 109, 110.

‡ American Annual Register, or Historical Memoirs of the United States for the Year 1796, pp. 36, 37. The punishment was £50 fine and six months imprisonment.

Travels through the State of North America and the Provinces of Upper and Lower Canada during the Years 1795, 1796, and 1797. By Isaac Weld, Jr. London edition, p. 22.

race begun.   At Elizabethtown a young woman, well mounted, rode up behind the coach and attempted to pass.   In an instant half the men on the stage began to revile her most shamefully, raised a great shout, frightened her horse, and all but unseated her.   One, indeed, ventured to expostulate.   But he was quickly silenced by the question, "What! suffer anybody to take the road of us?"*   At New York three of the passengers found lodgings in a single room at an inn.   The custom was a general one, and of all customs was the most offensive to foreigners.†   No such thing, it was said, was ever seen in the British Isles.   There every decent person not only had a bed, but even a room to himself, and, if he were so minded, might lock his door.‡   In America, however, the traveller sat down at the table of his landlord, slept in the first bed he found empty, or, if all were taken, lay down on one beside its occupant without so much as asking leave, or caring who the sleeper might be.#   If he demanded clean sheets, he was looked upon as an aristocrat, and charged well for the trouble he gave; for the bedclothes were changed at stated times, and not to suit the whims of travellers.

---

* The History of the United States for 1796, p. 274.

† "Four beds in a room crowded pretty close together; these beds laid on a kind of frame without any curtains, and the room itself, without any ornament save the bare white walls, indicated, without any other assurance, my removal into a strange country." The inn alluded to was the Eagle Tavern at Norfolk. Baily's Journal of a Tour in Unsettled Parts of North America in 1796 and 1797, p. 100. "What can be the reason for that vulgar, hoggish custom, common in America, of squeezing three, six, or eight beds into one room?" Letter from a gentleman in Philadelphia to his friend in Baltimore, dated April 25, 1796. The History of the United States for 1796, p. 276.

‡ The History of the United States for 1796, p. 276.

"An American sits down at the table of his landlord, and lies down in the bed which he finds empty, or occupied by but one person, without in the least inquiring, in the latter of these cases, who that person may be." Travels through the United States of North America. Duc de la Rochefoucauld-Liancourt, vol. i, p. 68. "There [a Nashville tavern] we met with good fare, but very poor accommodations for lodgings; three or four beds of the roughest construction in one room, which was open at all hours of the night for the reception of any rude rabble that had a mind to put up at the house; and if the other beds happen to be occupied, you might be surprised when you awoke in the morning to find a *bedfellow* by your side whom you had never seen before, and perhaps might never see again. All complaint is unnecessary, for you are immediately silenced by that **all**-powerful argument, *the custom of the country.* . . ." Journal of a Tour,

It was not against every tavern, however, that this reproach could be brought. Many a New England village inn could, in the opinion of the most fastidious of Frenchmen, well bear comparison with the best to be found in France. The neatness of the rooms, the goodness of the beds, the cleanliness of the sheets, the smallness of the reckoning, filled him with amazement.* Nothing like them were to be met with in France. There the wayfarer who stopped at an ordinary over night slept on a bug-infested bed, covered himself with ill-washed sheets, drank adulterated wine, and to the annoyance of greedy servants was added the fear of being robbed.† But in New England he might with perfect safety pass night after night at an inn whose windows were destitute of shutters, and whose doors had neither locks nor keys. Save the post-office, it was the most frequented house in the town. The great room, with its low ceiling and neatly sanded floor, its bright pewter dishes and stout-backed, slat-bottomed chairs ranged along the walls, its long table, its huge fireplace, with the benches on either side, where the dogs slept at night, and where the guests sat, when the dipped candles were lighted, to drink mull and flip, possessed some attraction for every one. The place was at once the town-hall and the assembly-room, the court-house and the show-tent, the tavern and the exchange. There the selectmen met. There the judges sometimes held court. On its door were fastened the list of names drawn for the jury, notices of vendues, offers of rewards for stray cattle, the names of tavern-haunters, and advertisements of the farmers who had the best seed-potatoes and the best seed-corn for sale. It was at the " General Greene," or the " United States Arms," or the " Bull's Head," that wandering showmen exhibited their automatons and musical clocks, that dancing-masters gave their lessons, that singing-school was held, that the caucus met, that the colonel stopped

Baily, p. 414. Weld complains of being crammed into rooms where there was scarcely sufficient space to pass between the beds. Travels through the States of North America during the Years 1795, 1796, 1797. Isaac Weld, Jr., pp. 35, 84.

* New Travels in the United States of America. Brissot de Warville, pp. 123, 124. London edition, 1792. The tavern to which he particularly alludes was at Spencer.   † Ibid., p. 124.

during general training. Thither came the farmers from the back country, bringing their food in boxes and their horses' feed in bags, to save paying the landlord more than lodging rates. Thither, many a clear night in winter, came sleigh-loads of young men and women to dance and romp, and, when nine o'clock struck, go home by the light of the moon. Thither, too, on Saturdays, came half the male population of the village. They wrangled over politics, made bets, played tricks, and fell into disputes which were sure to lead to jumping-matches, or wrestling-matches, or trials of strength on the village green. As the shadows lengthened, the loungers dispersed, the tavern was closed, and quiet settled upon the town. At sundown the Sabbath began. Then the great Bible was taken from its shelf and devotion opened with Scripture-reading, with psalms, and a long season of self-examination and prayer. By eight o'clock every farmer's household was asleep. On the morrow no meals were cooked. No labor but the most necessary was done. Not the most innocent pleasures were allowed. To gather flowers in the fields, to stroll through the woods, to sit on the river-bank, was sinful. The whole family went in a body to meeting. When the distance was as great as four miles, the farmer would mount his horse and take his wife on the pillion behind. When he drove the two-wheeled cart, his wife enjoyed the comforts of a chair.* The boys walked barefoot. The girls bore their shoes and stockings in their hands, and, as they neared the meeting-house, stepped into the bushes to draw them on.† The horse-block where the pillion-riders got down was sometimes in the training-field, and sometimes hard by the steps that led to the meeting-house door. ‡ The sides of the building were unpainted, the roof was shingled, and often destitute of steeple or bell. The main door opened on a broad aisle that led to the high pulpit, with its green cushions and funnel-shaped sounding-board that hung, like an extinguisher, from the roof. A narrow aisle crossed the broad one midway and joined the doors on either side. Close to the

* Lewis and Newhall. History of Lynn, p. 348.
† Kingman. History of Bridgewater, pp. 373, 374.
‡ Reminiscences of a Nonagenarian, pp. 15, 16. History of Old Braintree and Quincy, p. 327.

four walls was a row of pews, separated by a continuous aisle from the body of the church. Beneath the pulpit sat the deacons, and just before them were the deaf-seats and benches for the old and feeble who owned no pews. In the front gallery sat the singers. The young women filled the wall-pews of the right-hand gallery. The little girls had benches. Spinsters and elderly women of the flock were given the first row of seats. In the left-hand gallery were the young men and boys.* There, too, was the tithing-man.

This great functionary was still chosen in the old way, and still attempted to carry out the duties ordered by law. Once each year the freemen of the township met, and elected persons of good substance and of sober life to be tithing-men. To them the community looked for a strict enforcement of the Sunday laws. They were to see to it that the taverns were shut, that the village was quiet, that none behaved with levity, that no artificer nor laborer did a stroke of work, and were to ask of all who travelled on the Sabbath their names, their purposes, and whither they were bound. But the day when men would answer such questions was gone. The tithing-man who, in 1800, rushed from the meeting-house to stop the driver of a coach or a four-wheeled carriage or a sleigh, and bid him give his name, was likely to get a surly answer, and be left standing in the road while the transgressor drove rapidly away. Pious men complained that the war had been a great demoralizer. Instead of awakening the community to a lively sense of the goodness of God, the license of war made men weary of religious restraint. The treaty of peace had not been signed, the enemy were still in the land, when delegates to the General Court of Massachusetts boldly said the Sabbath was too long. Country members demanded a Sabbath of thirty-six hours; town members would give but eighteen, and had their way. The effect was soon apparent. Levity, profaneness, idle amusements, and Sabbath-breaking increased in the towns with fearful rapidity. What, the sober-minded cried out, is to become of this nation? Before the war nobody swore, nobody

---

* Reminiscences of a Nonagenarian, pp. 15, 16. History of Old Braintree and Quincy, p. 234. History of Pittsfield, pp. 157, 158. The Town of Roxbury, pp. 285, 286. History of Spencer, p. 89.

used cards. Now every lad is proficient in swearing, and knows much of cards. Then apprentices and young folks kept the Sabbath, and, till after sundown, never left their homes but to go to meeting. Now they go out more on the Sabbath than on any other day in the week. Now the barber-shops are open, and men of fashion must needs be shaved on the Lord's day. They ride on horseback; they take their pleasure in chaises and hacks. How much better, they say, is this than sitting for two hours in a church hearing about hell? Who would not rather ride with a fine young woman in a hack than hear about the devil from Adam's fall?

Against this impiety, the impiety of the nineteenth century, the tithing-man continued fighting stoutly to the last. He was the rear guard of New England Puritanism, covering it as it slowly retreated into the past.

When the deacons had taken their seats, when the congregation had all come in, a sudden rush into the men's gallery served to announce that the minister was near. As he walked gravely down the broad aisle, whispering would cease, and, in the midst of profound silence, the sexton would hasten to his seat on the pulpit-steps. Then the minister would rise and read two lines of a psalm, a deacon would repeat them, the precentor with a pitch-pipe would set the key, and the congregation and the choir join in the song. The singing would now be thought abominable. The congregation that could drone ten tunes was an exception. York and Windsor, Martyrs, Hackney and St. Mary's, commonly made up the list. The days of " deaconing," it is true, were soon to end. The Bay Psalm-Book had already given place to Watts's Hymns. Singing-schools had become general. Choirs had been introduced, and with them had come a longing for the music of the organ and the bass-violin.

The hymn sung, a prayer followed; then a sermon, and after the sermon the benediction and a long pause. The reverend man would then quit the pulpit, take his wife on his arm, and, followed by his children, go bowing and smiling out. The congregation were then at liberty to leave. Some, who came from afar, would be carried off to partake of a cold lunch at a friend's, and there wait for the service of the afternoon. Others would eat their luncheon in the pews. Such waiting in summer was thought little of. But in winter not the sturdiest among them could call it pleasant. Not a meeting-house was warmed. Not a chimney, not a fireplace, not a stove was to be seen. Stories have come down to us of a minister who, in the depth of winter, preached in great-coat and mittens, and complained that his voice was drowned by persons stamping and knocking their feet to keep warm.* Yet nothing was done to improve this. In Connecticut a few obtained " winter privileges " and stayed away. Others were suffered to put up " Sabbath-day houses," or " noon-houses," † hard by the meeting-house on the road. They were rude structures, sixteen feet square, with a door on one side and a window on another. To them, when morning service was ended, the people would flee to eat and warm themselves by an open fire that almost took up one side of the house. Indulgences of this kind were not approved of in Massachusetts. There even old and feeble women were forced to be contented with tin foot-stoves and a few hot coals. The expenses of maintaining the meeting-house were great enough without the addition of fires and stoves. The chief outlay was the settlement of the minister and his pay. The settlement was a sum of money bestowed when he assumed charge of the church. Rarely did it exceed two hundred pounds currency, and was payable, in four annual instalments, in boards and shingles, corn or produce, or whatsoever the congregation saw fit. His salary might be any amount from seventy-five to one hundred and forty pounds, Massachusetts currency. ‡ Translated into the language of the Federal coinage, seventy-five pounds would have been expressed by two hundred and fifty dollars. This translation, however, seldom

---

* Davis. History of Wallingford, pp. 414, 415.

† History of Warwick, p. 99. History of Waterbury, p. 228.

‡ For the salary of New England ministers, see History of Belfast. $300. Williamson, pp. 232, 233. G. A. and H. W. Wheeler, History of Brunswick, Topham and Harpswell, p. 409, £85. History of Norwich, p. 471, £135. Emerson's History of Douglas, p. 97, £132. Fox, History of Township of Dunstable, p. 167, £53 6s. 6d. ($180). Windsor, History of Duxbury, p. 207, £80. Taylor, History of Great Barrington, p. 323, £200. Felt, History of Ipswich, Essex, and Hamilton, p. 278, $367. Clark, History of Norton, p. 174, £80. Blake, History of Warwick, pp. 82, 83, £70 in silver. In New England, $3.33 made a pound currency.

took place. A few great towns, a few importers and merchants, a few men of enterprise and push, made use of the
Federal terms. But the people still adhered to the ancient
way, and bought, sold, and kept their accounts in pounds, shillings, and pence.* Travellers from abroad were amazed at
this, and smiled to see a tradesman, who wished to pay three
shillings four and a half pence to his customer, put down on
the counter a quarter, an eighth, and a sixteenth of a Spanish
milled dollar, two half-pence of George II and one of George
III. † Six dimes would, in New England, have served as well.
Dimes, however, were scarce. Numbers of men had never seen
one. Their circulation was confined to the seaports and the
Eastern towns. Not one was to be met with in the cabins of
the far West.

What was then known as the far West was Kentucky,
Ohio, and central New York. Into it the emigrants came
streaming along either of two routes. Men from New England took the most northern and went out by Albany and
Troy to the great wilderness which lay along the Mohawk
and the lakes. They came by tens of thousands from farms
and villages, and represented every trade, every occupation,
every walk in life, save one : none were seafarers. No whaler
left his vessel ; no seaman deserted his mess ; no fisherman
of Marblehead or Gloucester exchanged the dangers of a life
on the ocean for the privations of a life in the West. Their
fathers and their uncles had been fishermen before them, and
their sons were to follow in their steps. Long before a lad
could nib a quill, or make a pot-hook, or read half the pre-
cepts his primer contained, he knew the name of every brace
and stay, every sail and part of a Grand Banker and a Che-
bacco, all the nautical terms, what line and hook should be
used for catching halibut, and what for mackerel and cod. If
he ever learned to write, he did so at " writing-school," which,
like singing-school, was held at night, and to which he came,
bringing his own dipped-candle, his own paper, and his own

* Travels in the United States of America, commencing in the Year 1793 and
ending in 1797. W. Priest, p. 65.

† Ibid, p. 66. Owing to the great number of counterfeits in circulation, the
half-pence of George III passed at 360 to the dollar. Ibid., p. 66.

pen. The candlestick was a scooped-out turnip, or a piece of board with a nail driven through it. His paper he ruled with a piece of lead, to save the cost of a graphite lead-pencil. All he knew of theology, and much of his knowledge of reading and spelling, was gained with the help of the New England Primer. There is not, and there never was, a text-book so richly deserving a history as the Primer. The earliest mention of it in print, now known, is to be found in an almanac for the year 1691. The public are there informed that a second impression is " in press, and will suddenly be extant," and will contain, among much else that is new, the verses " John Rogers the Martyr," made and left as a legacy to his children. When the second impression became extant, a rude cut of Rogers lashed to the stake, and, while the flames burned fiercely, discoursing to his wife and nine small children, embellished the verses, as it has done in every one of the innumerable editions since struck off. The tone of the Primer is deeply religious. Two thirds of the four-and-twenty pictures placed before the couplets and triplets in rhyme, from

> " In Adam's fall
> We sinned all,"

to

> " Zaccheus, he
> Did climb a tree
> Our Lord to see,"

represent biblical incidents. Twelve words of " six syllables " are given in the spelling-lesson. Five of them are abomination, edification, humiliation, mortification, purification. More than half the book is made up of the Lord's Prayer and the Creed, some of Watts's hymns, and the whole of that great Catechism which one hundred and twenty divines spent five years in preparing. There, too, are Mr. Rogers's verses, and John Cotton's " Spiritual Milk for American Babes "; exhortations not to cheat at play, not to lie, not to use ill words, not to call ill names, not to be a dunce, and to love school. The Primer ends with the famous dialogue between Christ, Youth, and the Devil.

Moved by pity and a wish to make smooth the rough path to learning, some kind soul prepared " A Lottery-Book for

Children." The only difficulty in teaching children to read was, he thought, the difficulty of keeping their minds from roaming, and to " prevent this precipitancy" was the object of the Lottery-Book. On one side of each leaf was a letter of the alphabet; on the other two pictures. As soon, he explained, as the child could speak, it should thrust a pin through the leaf from the side whereon the pictures were at the letter on the other, and should continue to do this till at last the letter was pierced. Turning the leaf after each trial, the mind of the child would be fixed so often and so long on the letter that it would ever after be remembered.

The illustrations in the book are beneath those of a patent-medicine almanac, but are quite as good as any that can be found in children's books of that day. No child had then ever seen such specimens of the wood-engraver's and the printer's and the binder's arts as now, at the approach of every Christmas, issue from hundreds of presses. The covers of such chap-books were bits of wood, and the backs coarse leather. On the covers was sometimes a common blue paper, and sometimes a hideous wall-paper, adorned with horses and dogs, roosters and eagles, standing in marvellous attitudes on gilt or copper scrolls. The letter-press of none was specially illustrated, but the same cut was used again and again to express the most opposite ideas. A woman with a dog holding her train is now Vanity, and now Miss Allworthy going abroad to buy books for her brother and sister. A huge vessel with three masts is now a yacht, and now the ship in which Robinson Crusoe sailed from Hull. The virtuous woman that is a crown to her husband and naughty Miss Kitty Bland are one and the same. Master Friendly listening to the minister at church now heads a catechism, and now figures as Tommy Careless in the " Adventures of a Week." A man and woman feeding beggars become, in time, transformed into a servant introducing two misers to his mistress. But no creature played so many parts as a bird which, after being named an eagle, a cuckoo, and a kite, is called, finally, Noah's dove.*

Mean and cheap as such chap-books were, the pedler who

---

* For the privilege of examining a fine collection of such books, I am indebted to the American Antiquarian Society, and to Mr. N. Paine, of Worcester, Mass.

hawked them sold not one to the good wives of a fishing village. The women had not the money to buy with; the boys had not the disposition to read. Till he was nine a lad did little more than watch the men pitch pennies in the road, listen to sea stories, and hurry at the cry of "Rock him," "Squael him," to help his playmates pelt with stones some unoffending boy from a neighboring village. By the time he had seen his tenth birthday he was old enough not to be sea-sick, not to cry during a storm at sea, and to be of some use about a ship, and went on his first trip to the Banks. The skipper and the crew called him "cut-tail," for he received no money save for the fish he caught, and each one he caught was marked by snipping a piece from the tail. After an apprenticeship of three or four years the "cut-tail" became a "header," stood upon the same footing as the "sharesmen," and learned all the duties which a "splitter" and a "salter" must perform. A crew numbered eight; four were "sharesmen" and four were apprentices; went twice a year to the Banks, and stayed each time from three to five months.

Men who had passed through such a training were under no temptation to travel westward. They took no interest; they bore no part in the great exodus. They still continued to make their trips and bring home their "fares," while hosts of New Englanders poured into New York, opening the valleys, founding cities, and turning struggling hamlets into villages of no mean kind. Catskill, in 1792, numbered ten dwellings and owned one vessel of sixty tons. In 1800 there were in the place one hundred and fifty-six houses, two ships, a schooner, and eight sloops of one hundred tons each, all owned there, and employed in carrying produce to New York. Six hundred and twenty-four bushels of wheat were brought to the Catskill market in 1792. Forty-six thousand one hundred and sixty-four bushels came in 1800. On a single day in 1801 the merchants bought four thousand one hundred and eight bushels of wheat, and the same day eight hundred loaded sleighs came into the village by the western road.* In 1790 a fringe of clearings ran along the western shore of Lake Champlain to the northern border, and pushed out through the

* Hampshire Gazette, April 1, 1801.

broad valley between the Adirondacks and the Catskills to Seneca and Cayuga Lakes. In 1800 the Adirondack region was wholly surrounded. The emigrants had passed Oneida Lake, had passed Oswego, and, skirting the shores of Ontario and the banks of the St. Lawrence, had joined with those on Lake Champlain. Some had gone down the valleys of the Delaware and Susquehanna to the southern border of the State. The front of emigration was far beyond Elmira and Bath. Just before it went the speculators, the land-jobbers, the men afflicted with what in derision was called "terraphobia." * They formed companies and bought millions of acres. They went singly and purchased whole townships as fast as the surveyors could locate, buying on trust and selling for wheat, for lumber, for whatever the land could yield or the settler give. Nor was the pioneer less infatuated. An irresistible longing drove him westward, and still westward, till some Indian scalped him, or till hunger, want, bad food, and exposure broke him down, and the dreaded Genesee fever swept him away. The moment such a man had built a log-cabin, cleared an acre, girdled the trees, and sowed a handful of grain, he was impatient to be once more moving. He had no peace till his little farm was sold and he had plunged into the forest, to seek a new and temporary home. The purchaser in time would make a few improvements, clear a few more acres, plant a little more grain, and then in turn sell and hurry westward. After him came the founders of villages and towns, who, when the cabins

---

* Such a speculator is described in the Wilkesbarre Gazette, October, 1796. ". . . He has been to Bath, the celebrated Bath, and has returned both a speculator and a gentleman, having spent his money, swapped away my horse, caught the fever and ague, and, what is infinitely worse, that horrid disorder which some call the terraphobia.

"We hear nothing from the poor creature now (in his ravings) but of the captain and Billy, of ranges, of townships, numbers, thousands, hundreds, acres, Bath, fairs, races, heats, bets, purses, silk stockings, fortunes, fevers, agues, etc., etc. My son has part of a township for sale, and it is diverting enough to hear him narrate its pedigree, qualities, and situation. In fine, it lies near Bath, and the captain himself once owned, and for a long time reserved, part of it. It cost my son but five dollars per acre; he was offered six in half a minute after his purchase; but he is positively determined to have eight, besides some precious reserves. One thing is very much in my boy's favor—he has six years' credit. Another thing is still more so—he is not worth a sou, and never will be, at this rate. . . ." A Farmer.

about them numbered ten, felt crowded and likewise moved away.   Travellers through the Genesee valley tell us they could find no man who had not in this way changed his abode at least six times.   The hardship which these people endured is beyond description.   Their poverty was extreme.   Nothing was so scarce as food; many a wayfarer was turned from their doors with the solemn assurance that they had not enough for themselves.   The only window in many a cabin was a hole in the roof for the smoke to pass through.   In the winter the snow beat through the chinks and sifted under the door, till it was heaped up about the sleepers on the floor before the fire.

Just behind the pioneers came the more thrifty settlers, a class long since historical and now almost extinct.   During eighty years the emigrant train, so often portrayed both by painters and by travellers, has been gradually disappearing beyond the Alleghanies, beyond the Mississippi, beyond the Missouri, beyond the Rocky Mountains into the region of the extreme Northwest.   To-day it can seldom be seen out of Washington and Oregon, and has reached the shores of Puget Sound. In 1800 the high-peaked wagons with their white canvas covers, the little herd, the company of sturdy men and women, were to be seen travelling westward on all the highways from New England to Albany, and from Albany toward the lakes.   They were the true settlers, cleared the forests, bridged the streams, built up towns, cultivated the land, and sent back to Albany and Troy the yield of their farms.   With them the merchants of the East kept up a close connection, exchanging rum and molasses, hoes, axes, iron pots, clothing, everything of which they stood in want, and receiving lumber, wheat, pot and pearl ashes in return.   Favored by this great trade, Troy grew and prospered at an astonishing rate.   The place may be said to have begun its existence in 1786, when a few men of push induced the owners of the Van Der Heyden farms to sell them some plots, and on these put up a few houses, and named the village Vanderheyden.   From the very start it began to thrive.   In 1791 it was made the county-seat; yet, even then, it was so small that the inhabitants were every Sunday summoned to church in the store by blasts upon a conch-shell.   Two years later Troy had a court-house and a jail, a church, the only paper-mill north of the Highlands, and in 1797 a weekly newspaper. The next year the Northern Budget was drawn away from Lansingburg and became a Troy weekly paper. In his appeal to the citizens the editor declares that, with the utmost economy, the expenses of his office are thirty dollars a week, and they sustained him. In 1799 the taxable property was over eight hundred and fifty thousand dollars. Grain and lumber was the source of this wealth. No sleigh that came into Troy with boards or logs, no wagon that rolled up to a granary with bags of grain, was suffered to go away loaded. Along the river-bank were great storehouses filled with bins. On the land-side was the lifting-tackle, by which the sacks of corn or wheat were raised to the loft and placed in the pan of the clumsy scales. The counter-weights were stones, and to weigh with them was a problem in arithmetic. On the water-side projected long spouts, through which the grain was poured into the sloops and schooners beneath. In the great flour-mills of Pennsylvania, grain elevators, with buckets not larger than a common teacup, were in use.

The second pathway over which thousands of emigrants rushed westward lay through the valley of the Ohio. As early as 1794 the trade between Pittsburg and Cincinnati had become so paying that a line of packet-boats began to ply between the two towns. They made the trip once a month, were bullet-proof, and, for defence against the Indians, carried six cannon throwing a pound-ball each, and were plentifully supplied with muskets and ammunition.

When Wayne quieted the Indians, the stream of emigration turned northward, and the territory northwest of the river filled rapidly. At the time the first census was taken there could not be found from the Ohio to the Lakes, from Pennsylvania to the Mississippi, but four thousand two hundred and eighty human beings. The second census gave to Ohio Territory alone a population of forty-five thousand three hundred and sixty-five. The numbers in Kentucky in the same period had swollen from seventy-three thousand six hundred to two hundred and twenty thousand nine hundred and fifty. This was nine thousand greater than in the State of New Jersey. The figures of the census are expressive of the enormous exodus from New England.* The total increase of population in the five States of that section, including Maine, was two hundred and twenty-nine thousand. In the five Southern States the gain was four hundred and sixteen thousand. Of the New England States, four lost and one retained rank. Of the five Southern States, two lost rank, two gained rank, and Virginia remained first. Such was the emigration to New York that it rose from the fifth to the third State in the Union. North Carolina fell from the third in 1790 to the fourth in 1800. Thousands of her people had gone over the mountains to settle along the Cumberland, the Holston, and the Kentucky border, there to live a life of poverty, sacrifice, and independence. The centre of population had moved westward forty-one miles.†

---

* A comparison of the census of 1790 with that of 1800 will show the enormous increase of population in the West most clearly. The slow rate of increase of the New England States as compared with the Carolinas and Georgia, Virginia and Pennsylvania, is a good indication of the great emigration from New England.

	1790.		1800.	
United States........................		3,929,214		5,308,483
Connecticut.........................	8	237,946	8	251,002
Delaware............................	16	59,096	17	64,273
District of Columbia................	..	....	19	14,093
Georgia.............................	13	82,548	12	162,686
Indiana (Territory).................	..	....	21	5,641
Kentucky............................	14	73,677	9	220,955
Maine (District of; belonged to Massachusetts)........................	11	96,540	14	151,719
Maryland............................	6	319,728	7	341,548
Massachusetts.......................	4	378,787	5	422,845
Mississippi (Territory).............	..	....	20	8,850
New Hampshire.......................	10	141,885	11	183,858
New Jersey..........................	9	184,139	10	211,149
New York............................	5	340,120	3	589,051
North Carolina......................	3	393,751	4	478,103
Ohio (Territory)....................	..	....	18	45,365
Pennsylvania........................	2	434,373	2	602,365
Rhode Island........................	15	68,825	16	69,122
South Carolina......................	7	249,073	6	345,591
Tennessee...........................	17	35,691	15	105,602
Vermont.............................	12	85,425	13	154,465
Virginia............................	1	747,610	1	880,200

† The centre of population is the centre of gravity of the population of the country, or "the point at which equilibrium would be reached were the country

Beyond the Blue Ridge everything was most primitive. Half the roads were "traces," and blazed. More than half the houses, even in the settlements, were log-cabins. When a stranger came to such a place to stay, the men built him a cabin, and made the building an occasion for sport. The trees felled, four corner men were elected to notch the logs, and while they were busy the others ran races, wrestled, played leap-frog, kicked the hat, fought, gouged, gambled, drank, did everything then considered an amusement. After the notching was finished the raising took but a few hours. Many a time the cabin was built, roofed, the door and window cut out, and the owner moved in before sundown. The chinks were stopped with chips and smeared with mud. The chimney was of logs, coated with mud six inches thick. The table and the benches, the bedstead and the door, were such as could be made with an axe, an auger, and a saw. A rest for the rifle and some pegs for clothes completed the fittings.

The clothing of a man was, in summer, a wool hat, a blue linsey hunting-shirt with a cape, a belt with a gayly-colored fringe, deer-skin or linsey pantaloons, and moccasons and shoe-packs of tanned leather. Fur hats were not common. A boot was rarely to be seen. In winter a striped linsey vest and a white blanket coat were added. If the coat had buttons, and it seldom had, they were made by covering slices of a cork with bits of blanket. Food which he did not obtain by his rifle and his traps he purchased by barter. Corn was the staple, and, no mills being near, it was pounded between two stones or rubbed on a grater. Pork cost him twelve cents a pound, and salt four. Dry fish was a luxury, and brought twenty cents a pound. Sugar was often as high as forty. When he went to a settlement he spent his time at the billiard-table, or in the "keg grocery" playing Loo or "Finger in Danger," to determine who should pay for the whiskey consumed. Pious men were terrified at the drunkenness, the vice,

---

taken as a plane surface, itself without weight, but capable of sustaining weight, and loaded with its inhabitants, in number and position as they are found at the period under consideration; each individual being assumed to be of the same gravity as every other, and, consequently, to exert pressure on the pivotal point directly proportional to his distance therefrom." For the manner of finding the centre of population, see the Population volume of the Tenth Census.

the gambling, the brutal fights, the gouging, the needless duels they beheld on every hand. Already the Kentucky boatmen had become more dreaded than the Indians. "A Kentuc" in 1800 had much the same meaning that "a cowboy" has now. He was the most reckless, fearless, law-despising of men. A common description of him was half horse, half alligator, tipped with snapping-turtle.

On a sudden this community, which the preachers had often called Satan's stronghold, underwent a moral awakening such as this world had never beheld.

Two young men began the great work in the summer of 1799. They were brothers, preachers, and on their way across the pine barrens to Ohio, but turned aside to be present at a sacramental solemnity on Red river. The people were accustomed to gather at such times on a Friday, and, by praying, singing, and hearing sermons, prepare themselves for the reception of the sacrament on Sunday. At the Red river meeting the brothers were asked to preach, and one did so with astonishing fervor. As he spoke, the people were deeply moved, tears ran streaming down their faces, and one, a woman far in the rear of the house, broke through order and began to shout. For two hours after the regular preachers had gone the crowd lingered, and were loath to depart. While they tarried, one of the brothers was irresistibly impelled to speak. He rose and told them that he felt called to preach; that he could not be silent. The words which then fell from his lips roused the people before him " to a pungent sense of sin." Again and again the woman shouted, and would not be silent. He started to go to her. The crowd begged him to turn back. Something within him urged him on, and he went through the house shouting and exhorting and praising God. In a moment the floor, to use his own words, "was covered with the slain." Their cries for mercy were terrible to hear. Some found forgiveness, but many went away "spiritually wounded" and suffering unutterable agony of soul. Nothing could allay the excitement. Every settlement along the Green river and the Cumberland was full of religious fervor. Men fitted their wagons with beds and provisions, and travelled fifty miles to camp upon the ground and hear him preach.

The idea was new; hundreds adopted it, and camp-meetings began. There was now no longer any excuse to stay away from preaching. Neither distance, nor lack of houses, nor scarcity of food, nor daily occupations prevailed. Led by curiosity, by excitement, by religious zeal, families of every Protestant denomination—Baptists, Methodists, Presbyterians, Episcopalians—hurried to the camp-ground. Crops were left half gathered; every kind of work was left undone; cabins were deserted; in large settlements there did not remain one soul. The first regular general camp-meeting was held at the Gasper River Church, in July, 1800; but the rage spread, and a dozen encampments followed in quick succession. Camp-meeting was always in the forest near some little church, which served as the preachers' lodge. At one end of a clearing was a rude stage, and before it the stumps and trunks of hewn trees, on which the listeners sat. About the clearing were the tents and wagons ranged in rows like streets. The praying, the preaching, the exhorting would sometimes last for seven days, and be prolonged every day until darkness had begun to give way to light. Nor were the ministers the only exhorters. Men and women, nay, even children, took part. At Cane Ridge a little girl of seven sat upon the shoulder of a man and preached to the multitude till she sank exhausted on her bearer's head. At Indian Creek a lad of twelve mounted a stump and exhorted till he grew weak, whereupon two men upheld him, and he continued till speech was impossible. A score of sinners fell prostrate before him.

At no time was the "falling exercise" so prevalent as at night. Nothing was then wanting that could strike terror into minds weak, timid, and harassed. The red glare of the camp-fires reflected from hundreds of tents and wagons; the dense blackness of the flickering shadows, the darkness of the surrounding forest, made still more terrible by the groans and screams of the "spiritually wounded," who had fled to it for comfort; the entreaty of the preachers; the sobs and shrieks of the downcast still walking through the dark valley of the Shadow of Death; the shouts and songs of praise from the happy ones who had crossed the Delectable Mountains, had gone on through the fogs of the Enchanted Ground and entered the land of Beulah, were too much for those over whose minds and bodies lively imaginations held full sway. The heart swelled, the nerves gave way, the hands and feet grew cold and, motionless and speechless, they fell headlong to the ground. In a moment crowds gathered about them to pray and shout. Some lay still as death. Some passed through frightful twitchings of face and limb. At Cabin Creek so many fell that, lest the multitude should tread on them, they were carried to the meeting-house and laid in rows on the floor. At Cane Ridge the number was three thousand.

The recollection of that famous meeting is still preserved in Kentucky, where, not many years since, old men could be found whose mothers had carried them to the camp-ground as infants and had left them at the roots of trees and behind logs while the preaching and exhorting continued. Cane Ridge meeting-house stood on a well-shaded, well-watered spot, seven miles from the town of Paris. There a great space had been cleared, a preachers' stand put up, and a huge tent stretched to shelter the crowd from the sun and rain. But it did not cover the twentieth part of the people who came. Every road that led to the ground is described to have presented for several days an almost unbroken line of wagons, horses, and men. One who saw the meeting when it had just begun wrote home to Philadelphia that wagons covered an area as large as that between Market street and Chestnut, Second and Third. Another, who counted them, declared they numbered eleven hundred and forty-five. Seven hundred and fifty lead tokens, stamped with the letters A or B, were given by the Baptists to communicants; and there were still upward of four hundred who received none. Old soldiers who were present, and claimed to know something of the art of estimating the numbers of great masses of men, put down those encamped at the Cane Ridge meeting as twenty thousand souls. The excitement surpassed anything that had been known. Men who came to scoff remained to preach. All day and all night the crowd swarmed to and fro from preacher to preacher, singing, shouting, laughing, now rushing off to listen to some new exhorter who had climbed upon a stump, now gathering around some unfortunate who, in their peculiar language, was "spiritually slain." Soon men and women fell in such numbers that it became impossible for the multitude to move about without trampling them, and they were hurried to the meeting-house. At no time was the floor less than half covered. Some lay quiet, unable to move or speak. Some talked, but could not move. Some beat the floor with their heels. Some, shrieking in agony, bounded about, it is said, like a live fish out of water. Many lay down and rolled over and over for hours at a time. Others rushed wildly over the stumps and benches, and then plunged, shouting Lost! Lost! into the forest.

As the meetings grew more and more frequent, this nervous excitement assumed new and more terrible forms. One was known as jerking; another, as the barking exercise; a third, as the Holy Laugh. "The jerks" began in the head and spread rapidly to the feet. The head would be thrown from side to side so swiftly that the features would be blotted out and the hair made to snap. When the body was affected, the sufferer was hurled over hindrances that came in his way, and finally dashed on the ground to bounce about like a ball. At camp-meetings in the far South, saplings were cut off breast-high and left "for the people to jerk by." One who visited such a camp-ground declares that about the roots of from fifty to one hundred saplings the earth was kicked up "as by a horse stamping flies." There only the lukewarm, the lazy, the half-hearted, the indolent professor were afflicted. Pious men, and scoffing physicians who sought to get the jerks that they might speculate upon them, were not touched. But the scoffer did not always escape. Not a professor of religion within the region of the great revival but had heard or could tell of some great conversion by special act of God. One disbeliever, it was reported, while cursing and swearing, had been crushed by a tree falling on him at the Cane Ridge meeting. Another was said to have mounted his horse to ride away, when the jerks seized him, pulled his feet from the stirrups, and flung him on the ground, whence he rose a Christian man. A lad who feigned sickness, kept from church and lay abed, was dragged out and dashed against the wall till he betook himself to prayer. When peace was restored to him, he passed out into his father's tanyard to unhair a hide. Instantly the knife left his hand, and he was drawn over logs and hurled against trees and fences till he began to pray in serious earnest. A foolish woman who went to see the jerks was herself soon rolling in the mud. Scores of such stories passed from mouth to mouth, and may now be read in the lives and narratives of the preachers. The community seemed demented. From the nerves and muscles the disorder passed to the mind. Men dreamed dreams and saw visions, nay, fancied themselves dogs, went down on all fours, and barked till they grew hoarse. It was no uncommon sight to behold numbers of them gathered about a tree, barking, yelping, "treeing the devil." Two years later, when much of the excitement of the great revival had gone down, falling and jerking gave way to hysterics. During the most earnest preaching and exhorting, even sincere professors of religion would, on a sudden, burst into loud laughter; others, unable to resist, would follow, and soon the assembled multitude would join in. This was the "Holy Laugh," and became, after 1803, a recognized part of wor·ship.*

---

* Fragmentary accounts of the Great Revival in Kentucky will be found in Surprising Accounts of the Revival of Religion in the United States of America, in Different Parts of the World, and Among Different Denominations of Christians, with a Number of Interesting Occurrences of Divine Providence, 1802. Gospel News, or A Brief Account of the Revival of Religion in Kentucky and several other Parts of the United States, 1802. History of Cosmopolite, or the Four Volumes of Lorenzo's Journal concentrated in One, 1816. Smith, History of the Cumberland Presbyterians. History of Methodism in the Western States. Davidson. History of the Presbyterian Church in Kentucky. Lyle's Diary.

American Loyalties
and Disloyalties

Jefferson delivered one of the greatest of all Inaugural Addresses, appealing for unity and denouncing "entangling alliances." . . . It is a curiosity of our history that this phrase should be associated with Washington's Farewell Address—though it does not appear anywhere in that paper. . . . The battle over the purchase of Louisiana—an empire, not a state—took detailed pages of McMaster's prose. . . . Incredible though it may seem, the acquisition of this vast territory, extending to the Rocky Mountains, was bitterly resisted by opponents of the Jeffersonian Administration. . . . They complained that we did not need the land. . . . that there was no Constitutional justification for the Purchase (Jefferson himself guiltily agreed). . . . that the nation was being saddled with intolerable debt. . . . that it would drain the manpower from the east. . . . among other arguments. . . . In 1803, Merriwether Lewis and William Clark (so often, sadly, confused with his brother George Rogers Clarke) made their immortal exploration of the new American possessions. . . . Zebulon Pike made his stirring march to the Peak which memorializes him. . . . McMaster wrote with gusto of western settlement into Ohio. . . . Kentucky. . . . Michigan. . . . Alabama. . . . and beyond. . . . Meanwhile, the suffrage expanded. . . . Jefferson made attacks on the Supreme Court, a Federalist haven, even more serious than those attempted by Franklin D. Roosevelt a hundred and thirty years later. . . . An associate justice of the Supreme Court, Samuel Chase, was actually impeached, but the Administration leaders failed to convict him. . . . "Judge-breaking" took place in various parts of the nation. . . . Jefferson was re-elected in 1804, but headed a split party of states-rights partisans and of nationalists. . . . It was indicative of the utter defeat of the Federalists on the national scene that they could not take advantage of a state of affairs in which the Virginian, John Randolph, a leading Republican, denounced President Jefferson for having departed from Jeffersonian principles. . . . Aaron Burr became involved in dubious schemes in the west and principal in a great treason trial presided over by Chief Justice John Marshall. . . . The former Vice-President and political leader was freed, but his career was over. . . . It was a distraught time during which the President of the United States refused to honor a summons from the Chief Justice, and in which an associate of Burr, General James Wilkinson, commander of American forces in the west, was shown to be receiving a pension from the Spanish Crown. . . . War between England and Napoleon raised questions of Freedom of the Seas, created problems Woodrow Wilson would have to face more than a century later. . . . British and French warships waylaid American vessels and boarded them. . . . British impressment of American seamen into His Majesty's Fleet roused patriotic indignation, rendered somewhat ironic by the fact that seamen were the lowest of the low, without status or honor at sea or ashore. . . . Jefferson made his grand effort to stay neutral by proclaiming an Embargo. . . . Ships at home could not involve us in incidents. . . . Unfortunately, this policy hurt New Englanders's commerce; "Dambargo," they called it. . . . and all but made it a point of honor to defy it. . . . William Cullen Bryant, aged twelve and a son of Federalists, wrote a furious satire on the Embargo which his proud parents published. . . . Our brilliant young War Hawks, including Henry Clay of Kentucky, and John C. Calhoun, then an unreserved nationalist and expansionist from South Carolina, pressed Jefferson's successor, James Madison, to declare war on Great Britain. . . .

4

The People Move West: Roads and Canals, 1812

AFTER nine-and-twenty years of peace the people of the United States were thus a second time at war with Great Britain. Before attempting to narrate the events of that singular struggle it will not be amiss to describe the marvellous prosperity which, in spite of French decrees and British orders, in spite of embargoes, in spite of acts of non-intercourse and acts of non-importation, of confiscations, of burnings, of plunderings, of the unwise conduct of congresses, presidents, and legislatures, had during these nine-and-twenty years been built up by the thrift, the energy, the self-reliance of the people.

Between the day when our fathers celebrated, with bonfires and with bell-ringing, the return of peace, and the day when, discordant and disunited, they read the proclamation renewing war, the area of our country had expanded from eight hundred thousand square miles to over two millions; the people had increased from three millions and a quarter to seven millions and a quarter; the number of States, from thirteen to eighteen; and five Territories—political divisions unknown in 1783—had been established. Forty-nine treaties and conventions had been made with the Indians, their title to occupancy extinguished, and vast stretches of country, once their hunting-grounds, had been thrown open to settlement, and were being rapidly covered with villages and with farms. Had a line been drawn around the frontier in 1790, it would, judging from the best evidence now attainable, have been thirty-two hundred miles in length, and would have enclosed a settled area of two hundred and forty thousand square miles.

Had a similar line been drawn in 1812, it would have been but twenty-nine hundred miles long, yet it would have enclosed a settled area of four hundred thousand square miles. The frontier line now ran due west through southern Maine from Eastport to the head-waters of the Connecticut river, across New Hampshire and Vermont, around the Adirondacks on the north to the St. Lawrence, down the St. Lawrence and the southern shores of Lakes Ontario and Erie to the Cuyahoga river, where Cleveland stood and the Indian boundary-line began. Beyond this no white man could go for purposes of settlement. The frontier therefore followed the Indian boundary across central Ohio and eastern Indiana to the mouth of the Kentucky, went down the valley of the Ohio to the Mississippi, up that river to the Missouri and back to the Tennessee, which it followed to its source in the mountains, crossed the mountains to their eastern slopes, and, heading the waters of the Santee and the Savannah, skirted the Altamaha to the sea. Separated from the frontier by great tracts of wilderness were the outlying settlements at Detroit, at Michilimackinac, at Green Bay, at the mouth of the Arkansas river, in the Territory of Mississippi, and in the new State of Louisiana. Roughly speaking, four fifths of the whole area of the United States had not a white settler upon it.

The region whence the Western settlers came was, of course, the Atlantic seaboard, for the foreigners who each year landed on our shore were still very few in number. Yet it must not be supposed that the movement of people from the Atlantic States had been uniform or steady. The returns of the third census show that from Rhode Island, from New Jersey, from Delaware, and Maryland, migration had almost ceased, and that in them the percentage of the increase of population for the census period ending in 1810 was very much greater than for that ending in 1800. From Massachusetts and Connecticut the movement had been steady, and no material change is noticeable in their percentages at the two periods. Elsewhere the migration had been heavy, and had gone chiefly into the States of New York, Ohio, Kentucky, and Tennessee.

In entering these States the emigrants had, as before, marched forward in three great streams. The northern, made up largely of people from New England, Pennsylvania, and Maryland, had pushed out into western New York, and had dotted the whole region from Utica to Buffalo with towns and villages. In 1790 New York, from a meridian * through Seneca Lake westward to the Canadian boundary, was one huge county.† Before 1812 that same region had been cut into seven. In 1790 there were in the entire State but sixteen counties. In 1812 there were forty-five counties, four hundred and fifty-two towns, and more than three hundred villages of at least thirty families each. Buffalo now existed, and Lewiston and Batavia, and Maysville at the head of Chautauqua Lake. The town of Erie had been founded in Pennsylvania, and Cleveland in Ohio.

The second stream during the last ten years had poured down the Ohio valley, had peopled all southern Ohio, had raised Indiana to a Territory of the second grade, had overrun Kentucky and Tennessee to the Indian boundary, and, reaching the banks of Tennessee river, had begun to push southward into what is now Alabama. The third stream had gone as far as the Altamaha river, where the Indian country stopped it.

From this rush of people into the new country came economic consequences of a most serious nature. The rapidity of the movement and the vastness of the area covered made it impossible for the States to do many of the things they ought to have done for the welfare of their new citizens. The heaviest taxes that could have been laid would not have sufficed to cut out half the roads, or build half the bridges, or clear half the streams necessary for easy communication between the new villages and for successful prosecution of trade and commerce.

In the well-populated parts of the country along the seaboard the people seemed disposed to remedy the evil themselves, and for some years after the close of the Revolution numbers of lotteries were started to build bridges and improve roads. This was noticeably the case immediately after the adoption of the Constitution. The funding of the Federal

---

* Beginning at the eighty-second mile-stone on the Pennsylvania line.
† Ontario.

debt, the assumption of the State debts, the restoration of public credit, called out from their hiding places hundreds of thousands of dollars nobody supposed existed. Investments were sought in every direction. Banks were opened, canal companies were started, turnpike companies were chartered, and their stock subscribed for in a few hours. It seemed for a time that internal improvements were to be the economic feature of the last years of the century; but suddenly the European war began. France opened her West Indies. A splendid carrying trade sprang up. Money was instantly diverted to ships and commerce, and many a plan for internal improvement languished and was abandoned. But the movement of the people westward not only went on, but went on with increasing rapidity. The high price of wheat, of corn, of flour, due to the demand for exportation, sent thousands into the Genesee country and the borders of Lake Champlain to farm, and from them came back the cry for better means of transportation. The people of the shipping towns were quite as eager to get the produce as the farmers were to send it, and with the opening of the century the old rage for road-making, river improvements, and canals revived. The States were still utterly unable to meet the demand, and one by one were forced to follow the policy begun by Pennsylvania in 1791 and spend their money on roads and oridges in the sparsely settled counties, and, by liberal charters and grants of tolls, encourage the people of the populous counties to make such improvements for themselves. The wisdom of this policy was apparent. The success of the Lancaster Pike encouraged it, and, before the first decade of the nineteenth century closed, most of the landed and well-settled States were voting money, setting apart the proceeds of land sales, or establishing lotteries to open roads on the frontiers, while their citizens were forming stock companies to do the same thing between the old towns and the seaboard. The prospect of increasing the value of the back lands by establishing good roads, the hope of great dividends to be derived from the tolls, the fascination of speculating in stock, induced scores of communities to risk their capital in turnpike ventures. Once aroused, the rage for turnpiking spread rapidly over the whole country. In a few years a sum almost equal to the domestic debt at the close of the Revolution was voluntarily invested by the people in the stock of turnpike corporations. By 1810, twenty-six had been chartered in Vermont and more than twenty in New Hampshire, while in all New England the number was upward of one hundred and eighty. New York by 1811 had chartered one hundred and thirty-seven. Their combined capital was over seven millions and a half of dollars. Their total length was four thousand five hundred miles, of which fully one third was constructed. Albany resembled a great hub from which eight pikes went out north, east, south, and west. Five more joined the villages of Newburg, Kingston, and Catskill on the Hudson with points on the Delaware and the Susquehanna, and cut off some of the trade which would otherwise have gone to Baltimore and Philadelphia. New Jersey had chartered thirty roads. Pennsylvania had given letters-patent to thirty-three. Maryland, in the hope of turning aside to Baltimore some of the rich trade which came down from the Genesee country and passed through Carlisle to Philadelphia, had chartered three roads to extend from Baltimore to points on the Mason and Dixon line, and many more to points on the Potomac.

Yet even this did little to remedy the evil. The cost of transportation was enormous. To move a barrel of flour down the Susquehanna from the Genesee country to Columbia cost twenty-five cents. To send it thence by land to Philadelphia, a distance of seventy-four miles, cost one dollar. To float it down the Susquehanna from Columbia to Frenchtown, at the head of the Elk, then haul it over the peninsula to the Delaware, and so to Philadelphia, cost seventy-five cents more. Shippers of merchandise from the Chesapeake to Philadelphia paid for transportation across the peninsula from Frenchtown to Newcastle rates that now seem extortionate. That for wheat was six cents per bushel; that for flour was twenty-five cents per barrel; for tobacco, two dollars a hogshead; that for freight in general, two dollars a ton. What little freight went from New York to Lewiston, almost entirely a water route, paid forty dollars a ton, with tolls extra. To haul a ton from Philadelphia to Pittsburg, an all-land route, cost one hundred and twenty-five dollars. Had flour been sent over this route at the same rate per mile that was paid in carrying it from Columbia, the charges on each barrel would have been five dollars. To move a bushel of salt three hundred miles over any road cost two dollars and a half. For wagoning one hundred-weight of sugar three hundred miles the tariff was five dollars. Taking the country through, it may be said that to transport goods, wares, or merchandise cost ten dollars per ton per hundred miles. Articles which could not stand these rates were shut from market, and among these were grain and flour, which could not bear transportation more than one hundred and fifty miles. The causes of these rates were the terrible state of the roads and the high rate of tolls. Four horses at least were necessary to drag a wagon loaded with two tons any distance. For such a wagon the toll in New England was, on the average, twelve and a half cents for each two miles. In New Jersey one cent per mile for each horse was exacted. In Pennsylvania the rate of toll depended on the width of the tire of the wheels and the number of the horses, and varied from one sixteenth of a dollar to two cents per horse for each ten miles. Maryland used the same rates. On the Manchester turnpike in Virginia the rate for a loaded wagon was twenty-five cents for twelve miles.

Long carriage at such tariffs, so far as many products were concerned, was simply prohibitory. Flour, grain, corn, produce in general, was therefore forced to find a market somewhere within a radius of one hundred and fifty miles. The consequence was that as the States bordering on Canada became populated they turned to Quebec and Montreal for a market, and hundreds of thousands of dollars' worth of lumber, grain, flour, and potash were every year shipped down the St. Lawrence instead of down the Hudson or the Susquehanna. The channels of trade opened by the smugglers in the embargo days had never been closed. They had indeed been most carefully improved, and by 1812 the trade of northern New Hampshire, Vermont, and New York was in the hands of England. One half of the fur trade of the Northwest, all the produce of Vermont as far south as Middlebury, and of every county of northern New York from Essex and Clinton on Lake Champlain to Niagara on the Niagara River, was gathered at Montreal. The gazettes of Albany contained many advertisements of the rates of transportation. A barrel of flour could be carried from Ogdensburg to Montreal for eighty-eight cents, from Salina one dollar, from Cayuga a dollar and a half, and the same from Buffalo. As English goods came into Canada duty free, the cheapness with which they could be obtained formed another incentive to continue this trade, and the two sections of New York, no longer connected commercially, seemed in a fair way to be some day disconnected politically.

What was true of New York was doubly and trebly true of the whole country. The time had come when the great geographical sections of this country must be united, if they were to be united at all, by something stronger than the Constitution. No one who studies the history of those interesting times can fail to be struck with the utter want of anything approaching to a national feeling. Slowly but surely the sections were developing local interest and drawing farther and farther apart. The economic question of the hour was plainly how to counteract this tendency by a system of interstate commerce which should unite them with a firm bond of self-interest. That Congress had power to regulate commerce between the States was not disputed; but how far it could go in regulating the highways of commerce was yet to be settled.

Since the beginning of government under the Constitution, demands for internal improvements at public expense had often been made on Congress There had been calls for more piers in the Delaware below Philadelphia; for piers in the Merrimac at Newburyport; for piers in Barnstable Bay; for the removal of sand-bars at the mouth of Christiana Creek; for the removal of shoals in Nantucket Harbor; for a bridge across the Potomac; for a canal in the city of Washington; for a canal around the falls of the Ohio; for a survey of the rivers of Louisiana; for help to finish the Alleghany Turnpike, the Highland Turnpike, the Chesapeake and Delaware Canal; and to publish a map of the coast of Georgia.

The petitioners in the matter of the survey of the Georgia coast were three men named Parker, Hopkins, and Meers. They had, so the memorial informed the House, made a careful survey of the coast and inland navigation of Georgia and

South Carolina. The cost had been greater than they could bear. Their funds were gone, and, lest the work should be lost, they asked for money to engrave a map. The committee having the memorial in charge at first reported in favor of a loan of money. But this was so seriously opposed that the report was disagreed to and a new one submitted. The whole coast, the committee now said, from Florida to Chesapeake Bay, had never been surveyed with the degree of accuracy its importance to commerce and navigation demanded. Georgia in particular was almost unknown. Her harbors were numer· ous. Great quantities of lumber, ship-timber, indigo, rice, cotton, and tobacco went out from her ports each year. Yet her inland navigation had never been explored, nor the shift· ing of her bars and channels observed with accuracy. North Carolina and South Carolina were perhaps better known to our own sailors; but they, too, had never been carefully mapped, and, as many a shipwreck proved, were dangerous and terrible to strangers. That accurate charts, with the soundings, the appearance of the land, the entrance to the harbors, the channels of inland navigation, all carefully marked on them, would be of great public utility was not to be disputed. That the preparation of them ought to be encouraged was certain; for how could the public wealth be better used than in promoting undertakings which tended to increase the sources whence that wealth flowed? The committee felt justified, therefore, in urging that the President should be authorized to secure from individuals complete and well-made charts of the coast from St. Mary's river to Chesapeake Bay; that the revenue cutters, when practicable, should be employed in making such surveys as could not be purchased from individuals, and that, when the survey of the coast of each State was finished, the charts should be published.*

All admitted that the plan was commendable; yet so little interest was taken that the business was not again considered till the next session, when two reports were made.† During

---

* Annals of Congress, 1794–'95.   House of Representatives, February 27, 1795.

† Annals of Congress, 1795–'96.   House of Representatives, December 29, 1795, and May 14, 1796.

the interval the plan had greatly developed. Parker, Hopkins, and Meers had begun by asking for three thousand dollars
to engrave maps of the Georgia coast from St. Mary's river
to Savannah. The Committee on Commerce and Manufactures now recommended that every bay, sound, harbor, and
inlet of the whole Atlantic coast should be surveyed and
mapped. If well-made charts of any part of the coast could
be had from individuals, the President was to buy them. If
not obtainable, the President was to employ surveyors to make
them, and use the revenue cutters where necessary. The end
of the session was so near when this report was read that consideration was put off till, as it was supposed, Congress should
meet again. But Congress met and adjourned many times,
and six years slipped by before the House once more took
action on a coast survey. An act was then passed providing
for the erection of a number of light-houses. Some of them
were to be on Long Island Sound, and, that the sites for
them might be the better determined, the Secretary of the
Treasury was bidden to employ fit persons to survey the
Sound.[*] The result was a fine chart, which ought to have
encouraged Congress to go on with the work so well begun.
This, indeed, it seems to have done ; for, almost precisely four
years later, the Secretary was instructed by two other acts to
have careful surveys made of the shores of Orleans Territory
from the mouth of the Mississippi to Vermilion Bay,[†] and of
the coast of North Carolina from Cape Fear to Cape Hat-
teras.[‡] In presenting the bill for the Carolina survey the
committee expressed an earnest hope that Congress would not
let the next session pass without ordering a complete survey
of the coast from the St. Croix to the Mississippi, and along
the Gulf to the westernmost confines of Louisiana.[#] The wish
was fully realized. The next session did not close without just
such a law as the committee wanted, and on February tenth,
1807, Jefferson signed the bill which founded the coast survey.
Fifty thousand dollars were set apart for surveys and charts
on which, the law especially provided, should be put down not

---

[*] Act of April 6, 1802.   [†] Act of April 20, 1806.   [‡] Act of April 10, 1806.
[#] Report of the Committee on Commerce and Manufactures, February 27,
1806.

merely the shore line, but all the islands, shoals, roads, places of anchorage within twenty leagues of our coast, together with the courses and distances between the chief capes and head-lands.

The time chosen for beginning this noble work was most opportune, for there was then in the presidential chair a man who truly appreciated the importance of the undertaking, and at the head of the Treasury department a man whose powers of organization and administration were not second to those of Hamilton. Acting together, these two men drew up a plan for the survey, and sent it for criticism to seven men whose opinions were worth considering. One was Robert Patterson, director of the Mint. Another was Andrew Ellicott, who, after serving on many surveys of great importance, then filled the post of Secretary of the Land Office of Pennsylvania. Ferdi-nand Rudolph Hassler, a mathematician of note, was the third. John Garnett, Isaac Briggs, Rev. James Madison, president of William and Mary College, and Joshua Moore, of the Treasury Department, made up the seven. As submitted to these men, the plan consisted of three parts: A number of headlands, of capes, of prominent light-houses, of remarkable features along the coast, and the entrance to the chief harbors were to be se-lected and their latitudes and longitudes determined astronomi-cally. There was to be a trigonometrical survey to connect these points, and a hydrographical survey to determine the channels, bars, shoals, and depth of water off the coast and in the bays, sounds, and harbors. If this plan seemed practical, the men consulted were asked to name persons fitted to carry out the work.* The answers were so satisfactory that, by the fall of 1807, Patterson, Hassler, and Briggs were at work se-lecting the instruments to be used, and making ready the de-tails of the survey. Instruments of the kind and degree of accuracy needed could not then be had in the United States. Hassler was therefore ordered to proceed to England and super-intend their manufacture in London. But before he could start the embargo was laid, the restrictive system followed, and August, 1811, came ere he set sail. The war opened soon

---

* Albert Gallatin to Robert Patterson and others, March 25, 1807.

after, so that it was not till November, 1815, that he reached
the United States and delivered a great collection of mathematical books and mathematical instruments to the director
of the Mint at Philadelphia.

While thus assisting commerce by sea, Congress was not
unmindful of the needs of commerce by land. To such a
course, indeed, it was pledged by the solemn compact made
with Ohio. When that State was about to enter the Union,
her people agreed that public lands sold within her borders
should not be taxed for five years after the day of sale. In
return for this, Congress agreed to spend five per cent of
the net proceeds of such sales in road-making. Some of
the roads were to be in the State, others were to join the
Ohio river with navigable waters emptying into the Atlantic. As three per cent. was speedily appropriated for road-
making within the State,* but two per cent. was left to be
expended on highways without. Yet, small as the percentage
was, it had, by December, 1805, produced twelve thousand six
hundred dollars.† A Senate committee was then appointed
to consider the best manner of using it, and reported in favor
of a road from Cumberland, on the Maryland side of the
Potomac, to a point near Wheeling, on the Virginia side of
the Ohio. This route, the committee were careful to state,
was chosen from among several because it seemed best suited
to the present needs of the people of Ohio, and because, starting at Cumberland, on the eastern slopes of the mountains, it
would not interfere with systems of internal improvements
then being carried on by Pennsylvania and Maryland.‡ No
fault was to be found with the location of the road, and, as
the money was lying idle in the Treasury, a bill to regulate
the laying out and making of a road from Cumberland to the
State of Ohio readily passed both Houses and became law.#
Thirty thousand dollars were appropriated for beginning the

---

* Act of March 3, 1803.

† The fund began to accumulate on July 1, 1803. Between that date and
September 30, 1805, inclusive, the net proceeds of land sales in Ohio was $632,-
604.27, two per cent. of which was $12,652.

‡ Report of the committee communicated to the Senate, December 19, 1805.

March 29, 1806.

work. Three commissioners were appointed to select the route. Applications were at once made to the States of Maryland, Virginia, and Pennsylvania, for leave to build the road, and the summer and autumn of 1806 was spent by the commissioners in travelling over ground to determine the alignment. Starting at Cumberland just where Wills Creek joins the north branch of the Potomac, the commissioners decided that the route should be over Wills Mountain at Sandy Gap, and along the line, but rarely on the bed, of Braddock's old road to the Big Crossing of the Youghiogheny, over Laurel Hill, across the Great Meadows, past the site of Fort Necessity, and on to the Monongahela at Red-Stone-old-Fort, or, as it had long since been called, Brownsville, and thence, by as direct a course as the country would permit, to the Ohio, near Wheeling. It now became the duty of the President to approve or disapprove the work of the commissioners, but Jefferson would not act till the three States had consented that he should have a free choice of routes. Pennsylvania did not consent till the early spring of 1807. Summer came, therefore, before the commissioners were again in the field. Their instructions were to change the alignment, bring the road through Unionville, and cut it out, for half its width, from Cumberland to Brownsville. More money was appropriated in 1810, and still more in 1811. Nevertheless, the work dragged on so slowly that the first contracts for actually building the road-bed were not signed till May, 1811. Four men then contracted for ten miles, beginning at Cumberland, and bound themselves to have their work completed by August first, 1812.

Thus, when the war for commercial independence opened, Congress had yielded to the demands of the East and of the West, and had begun to make internal improvements at Government expense. Hassler at London seeking books and instruments with which to found the Coast Survey, the workmen in Maryland ploughing and grading, pounding and rolling the National Pike, excited no comment whatever. It is quite likely that not one third of the people of the United States were aware of what was going on. Yet the political, the economic consequences of the era of internal improve-

ments thus opened have outlasted every result of the war in
which the people were about to engage.

What Congress was willing to do was, however, but a trifling part of what it was asked to do. Many of the applications
were easily disposed of. An adverse report, a postponement
till another session, was enough to end such demands as that for
the improvement of the harbor of Nantucket or for a pier in
Barnstable Bay. But occasionally an appeal for aid came in
which could not be disposed of by the report of a committee
or the vote of one House. Such was the memorial of the
president and directors of the Chesapeake and Delaware Canal.

This was a company chartered by the States of Maryland,
Delaware, and Pennsylvania to dig a canal across the neck of
the peninsula which parts the waters of Delaware and Chesapeake Bays. The scheme seemed so likely to be profitable
that no difficulty was found in getting subscribers, and four
hundred thousand of the five hundred and twenty thousand
dollars of capital stock were quickly taken. Engineers were
then employed, the alignment determined, and work begun
on a large feeder, when the stockholders took alarm. One
hundred thousand dollars had been spent in buying water
rights, making surveys, and digging a feeder, yet not a clod
had been turned along the line of the main canal. Seeing one
quarter of their subscriptions gone with nothing, in their
opinion, to show for it, the stockholders refused to pay their
assessments. Suits followed, and in December, 1805, the
directors, in distress, appealed to Congress for help. In their
memorial they excused the call on the ground that the work
was of general, not merely local importance. It was the
beginning of a great system of inland navigation binding
together eleven States. One glance at the map was enough to
show that if the Chesapeake and Delaware Canal was dug,
another much-talked-of canal, the Delaware and Raritan, would
surely be cut across New Jersey. A continuous inland water-
way would then be opened from Hampton Roads to Narra-
gansett Bay and the head-waters of the Hudson and the Mohawk. Nay, more. The Dismal Swamp Canal, then building,
would extend the line to Albemarle Sound and the bays and
inlets of South Carolina. Another canal from Buzzard's Bay

to Massachusetts Bay would open the route to Boston, while a few years would suffice to see the Hudson joined with Lake Champlain, and the Mohawk with Lake Ontario. The economic value of such a work was set forth by statistics. Each State, it was said, produced something which the others wanted. Coal abounded on the navigable waters of the James, and was wanted in every maritime city on the coast and in every inland city where mills and factories existed. Flour and wheat, corn and meal, were products of the Middle States, and were wanted southward and eastward. Tobacco grew in a few States and was consumed in all. The fish, the oils, the lumber produced in the East, were much in demand in the South. But the enormous cost of land transportation and the immense distance by water had seriously hindered this interchange. From the head of Chesapeake Bay to Philadelphia by sea was a journey of five hundred miles, and could not be performed under a week or ten days. The consequence was that coal from Liverpool sold for less at Philadelphia than coal from Richmond. A ton of merchandise was frequently brought from Europe for forty shillings sterling, or about nine dollars. But the same sum of money would not move the same ton thirty miles on land. Let the canals be opened and this hindrance would be removed. Twenty-one miles of Chesapeake and Delaware Canal would save five hundred miles around the peninsula. Twenty-seven miles of canal between Trenton and New Brunswick would save three hundred miles of sea travel to New York. Dangers of the sea and dangers of the road would not exist. Insurance rates would fall, freight rates would be reduced, and a flourishing interstate commerce arise.

In the Senate the memorial found many friends and was warmly supported. They could not, however, venture to give money. The Treasury was, indeed, full to overflowing. But the House was bent, not on spending, but on distributing the surplus, and had already appointed a committee to report upon a plan. There were, moreover, many who doubted the constitutionality of voting money to dig canals. But that any one should object to give away land for such a use did not seem likely. Great blocks of it had often been given for church purposes, for schools; to the refugees from Canada;

to the French at Gallipolis; to the Marquis Lafayette; to Lewis and Clarke; to the Revolutionary soldiers; nay, to Ebenezer and Isaac Zane for building a road in Ohio. Why not, then, for building a canal in Delaware? But the committee having the memorial in charge did not propose to give land. They proposed to buy the shares of the company which had not been taken at two hundred dollars each and pay for them in land. A bill for this purpose was brought in,* but went over till February, 1807, when consideration was again put off till the next session.†

While the bill was still under debate John Quincy Adams moved ‡ that the Secretary of the Treasury be directed to report a plan for a general system of internal improvements. He was to consider the opening of roads, the removal of obstructions from rivers, and the building of canals. He was to make a statement of the number and character of works of public utility then existing in the country, and was to name such as, in his opinion, were worthy of Government aid. The motion did not pass. Nevertheless, within ten days a senator from Ohio secured the passage of a resolution precisely similar in character.#

With these instructions from the Senate before him, Gallatin set to work. A series of questions regarding the number, length, route, cost per mile of canals and roads, rate of toll, gross receipts, and substance of their charters, was drawn up and sent to the collectors of the ports, with orders to secure full answers. From the information thus obtained, Gallatin prepared that famous report on Roads, Canals, Harbors, and Rivers which is still ranked among the best of his official papers. By those who have never read that report, or, having read it, know nothing of the history of the times in which it was made, the work of the Secretary has been greatly overestimated. There was little in it that was new. A map, he said, would show that the United States possessed—were it not for four interrupting necks of land—a tide-water inland naviga-

---

* Journal of the United States Senate, January 28, March 21, April 12, 1806.

† Journal of the Senate, January 13, 15, February 5, 10, 24, 1807.

‡ Journal of the Senate, February 23, 1807.

March 2, 1807.

tion secure from the violence of storms and the attacks of
enemies, and stretching from Boston to the southern confines
of Georgia. These necks were the isthmus of Barnstable,
New Jersey from the Raritan to the Delaware, the peninsula
between the Delaware and the Chesapeake Bays, and the low
marshy tract which separated Chesapeake Bay from Albemarle
Sound. Were they all cut through by canals, the combined
length of the four water-ways would not be one hundred
miles, nor the cost much over three millions of dollars. The
plan was old. The directors of the Chesapeake and Delaware
had urged it on Congress in their memorial in 1805, Bayard
had explained it in his speech in 1806, and canal companies
had been chartered to carry it out.*

The second suggestion of the Secretary was that of a
great turnpike along the Atlantic coast from Maine to Georgia.
This, too, was old, and had but a year before been presented
to the Senate in a resolution. Having thus disposed of the
subject of communication north and south, Gallatin took up
that of communication east and west and southwest. Four
great rivers flowing into the Atlantic should, he thought, be
improved to the head of possible navigation and then joined
by four great roads over the mountains with four other rivers
of the Mississippi valley. The rivers selected were the
Juniata and the Alleghany, the Potomac and the Monongahela,
the James and Kanawha, and the Santee or Savannah and the
Tennessee. There should also be a canal around the falls of
the Ohio, and good roads from Pittsburg to Detroit, to St.
Louis, and New Orleans. Northward and northwestward the
Hudson should be joined with Lake Champlain, and the Mohawk with Lake Ontario. A canal should be dug around
Niagara that sloops might pass from Ontario to Lake Michigan. The cost of this splendid system of inland water-ways
would be twenty millions of dollars. The sum was indeed a
vast one; yet the United States could well afford to spend it.
Her Treasury was full. Her surplus was yearly five millions

---

* Dismal Swamp Canal, 1787 and 1790. Chesapeake and Delaware Canal,
1797, 1801, 1802. Delaware and Raritan Canal, 1796. The route from Boston
Harbor to Long Island Sound was surveyed by order of the General Court of
Massachusetts, March, 1806.

of dollars. She might therefore, without embarrassment, draw two millions a year for ten years from the public Treasury; or, better still, set apart the proceeds of the sales of public lands.

The report was read on the sixth of April, 1808. A time less propitious could not have been chosen. The embargo had been on three months. The first and second supplementary acts had been passed. Trade and commerce were at an end; the whole frontier was in commotion; Jefferson was on the point of declaring the people of the region around Champlain to be in a state of insurrection; while the surplus of which the Secretary spoke was fast melting away. Under these circumstances the Senate did no more than order that twelve hundred copies of the report should be printed, and that six should be given to each member of Congress.

From the information thus spread broadcast during the summer, a plentiful harvest of petitions was gathered in the autumn. Every corporation which, under the plan of Gallatin, seemed even remotely entitled to aid, now made ready to seek it. The Carondelet Canal, the Chesapeake and Delaware Canal, the Ohio Canal, the Susquehanna Bridge Company, the Susquehanna and Tioga Turnpike Company, the Philadelphia, Brandywine and New London Turnpike Company, sent in memorials. Toward them all the Senate was well disposed. But a different disposition ruled the House, and there not one of the Senate bills was passed.

Such action did not discourage petitions, and with the opening of the eleventh Congress a new crop came to the tables of the Vice-President and the Speaker. And now the House began to give signs of yielding. Among the men who at that session took seats for the first time in Congress was Peter Buell Porter. He was a native of New England and a graduate of Yale. He had studied law in Connecticut, had caught the rage for Western emigration, and was then engaged in the business of transportation on the Niagara frontier. He represented the western district of New York, was perfectly familiar with the peculiar needs of the people, and had studied their political and economic condition as only a man of education could. The friends to internal improvements in the Senate consulted him freely, and it is not unlikely persuaded him to become the champion of the movement in the House. However this may be, he undertook the task, and a bill for the internal improvement of the country by-roads and canals, a bill in the making of which he had a hand, having come down from the Senate, he seized the opportunity and presented the whole subject in a fine speech. The people of the United States, he began by saying, were parted by a geographical line into two great and distinct sections : the people who dwelt on the Atlantic slope of the Alleghanies and were made up of merchants, manufacturers, and agriculturists, and the people who dwelt on the western slopes and were exclusively farmers. It was the fashion to assert that this mountain barrier, this diversity of occupation, and the differences of character to which they gave rise, would lead to a separation of the States at no very distant day. In his humble opinion, this very diversity, if used skilfully, would become the means of producing a closer and more intimate union of the States than ever. At that very moment the people of the West were suffering, and suffering badly, for the want of a market. There was no vent for their surplus produce at home. All were farmers and produced the same articles with the same ease. Now, this want of a market had already done harm not only to the industry, but also to the morals of the people. Such was the fertility of their farms that half their time spent in labor was sufficient to produce enough to satisfy their wants. To produce more there was no incentive, for they knew not what to do with it. The other half of their time was therefore spent in idleness and dissipation. No question, surely, of greater importance could possibly come before the House than the question : How can this evil be removed ? How can a market, and an incentive to labor, be provided for the people of the West ? His answer was, by a canal from the Mohawk to Lake Ontario ; a canal around the falls of Niagara ; a canal from the Cuyahoga to the Muskingum ; and another past the falls of the Ohio at Louisville.

The first result of such a system of inland navigation would be a fall in the cost of transportation. This would enable farmers to send to market grain and flour now shut out by the expense of land-carriage. Wheat was one of the staples of the lake country, and was grown there with greater certainty and in greater perfection than in any other part of the United States. Yet wheat was selling on the lakes for fifty cents per bushel. This depression was due solely to the fact that it cost one dollar a bushel to send it to New York. Let a canal be cut from Lake Ontario to the Mohawk, and the cost of moving would fall to twenty-five cents a bushel, while the price on the lakes would rise to one dollar. But it cost the farmer from thirty to forty cents to grow a bushel of wheat. When he sold it for fifty cents his profit was, therefore, but ten cents. When he sold it for a dollar, his profit would be sixty cents, an increase of six hundred per cent.

Then would the farmer be able to pay for his land. The people who had settled on the public domain were indebted to the Government to the amount of several millions of dollars. Without a market they could never free themselves from debt. Without internal improvements they could never reach a market, and without the help of Congress there could never be internal improvements. Neglect this opportunity to secure the affections of the Western people, refuse to extend to them the benefits their situation so strongly demanded, and they would, some day, accost the Government in language higher than the Constitution. Let them see millions expended for the encouragement of commerce, while constitutional doubts were expressed concerning the right to expend one cent for the advancement of agriculture; let them see banks established for the accommodation of the merchant, but no canals dug for the accommodation of the farmer, and they would very soon take possession of their country and with physical force defy all the tax-gatherers that could be sent against them. If they were to be attached to the Union they must be attached through their interests. If the Government shunned all communication with them save that which sprung from the relation of debtor and creditor, let no man doubt that this relationship would very speedily be ended. When Porter had finished his speech he moved for a committee to consider the fitness of appropriating land, or the proceeds thereof, to building roads and canals of national importance. The House, without a division, agreed, and appointed a committee of twenty.* From them came a bill essentially the same as one which, not many weeks before, had been reported in the Senate. In substance, this bill provided that the Government should take one half of the capital stock of any corporation which had been, or which might be, chartered to dig any of the canals or build any of the roads suggested by Gallatin. Having done this much, Congress would do no more, and the session passed without action. Nor was the following session more fruitful of results. The Senate made a land grant to the Chesapeake and Delaware Canal, refused a grant to the Havre de Grace bridge, and ordered a subscription to the stock of the Ohio Canal. But again the House would do nothing, and the eleventh Congress was in turn beset with petitions, old and new.

Twenty years before, in the early days of the rage for canals, Pennsylvania had chartered two companies. One was to join the waters of the Schuylkill and Delaware. The other was to construct a canal from the Schuylkill to the Susquehanna. Each had raised money; each had made surveys; each had bought land, dug some miles of trench, become embarrassed, and fallen into decay. From this condition the directors and stockowners were suddenly roused by the report of Gallatin in 1807.† Regarding this report as a pledge of Federal aid,‡ the Legislature of Pennsylvania united the two companies in one, called the new corporation the Union Canal Company of Pennsylvania, and gave it power to extend its route from the Susquehanna to Lake Erie. As soon as the new charter was secured, the affairs of the old companies were put in order, and Congress asked to help on the enterprise. But, of all beggars, the sturdiest, the most unblushing was the State of New York. There, too, after years of effort on the part of individuals, the State was roused to activity by the report of Gallatin. Encouraged by the near prospect of Federal aid, the Legislature instructed a commission to explore a route for

---

* Annals of Congress, 1809-'10, February 9, 1810, p. 1401.

† Memorial of the President and Managers of the Union Canal Company. Annals of Congress, 1811, 1812, pp. 2159-2161.

‡ Ibid.

inland navigation from the Hudson to Lakes Erie and Ontario.*
The commission reported † and the Legislature promptly
passed an act to provide for the improvement of the internal
navigation of the State. ‡ In it nine well-known men were
named canal commissioners.# Among the many duties assigned them was that of applying to Congress and the Legislatures of the neighboring States for aid and co-operation in
the undertaking. The answers were not encouraging. Tennessee instructed her senators and requested her representatives to vote for congressional aid. New Jersey was deeply
interested in the canal, but could not help it herself, and saw
no reason for asking the Federal Government to do so. Connecticut thought it inexpedient to act on the request. Vermont put off consideration. Massachusetts and Ohio followed
the example of Tennessee. The acting Governor and the
judges of Michigan Territory did not approve of the route.
The special committee sent to Washington to lay the application before Congress reported failure. Madison they found
troubled with constitutional scruples. Gallatin thought land
might be given, but not money. Some congressmen thought
the scheme too vast; some were jealous of New York; some
were eager for a constitutional amendment giving Congress
power to charter banks and build canals without consulting
the States. In the end New York received nothing. The
Senate did not act. The House, taking up the memorials of
the Chesapeake and Delaware Canal, of the Union Canal, of
the commissioners from New York, declared that the state
of the country was not such as to justify grants of land or
gifts of money for the purpose of building canals. Though
incensed by the refusal of land, the commissioners were not
disheartened, and recommended the Legislature to borrow
money abroad and begin the work without delay. ‖

---

* Appointed by joint resolutions, March 13–15, 1810.

† Report of the Commissioners, etc., Albany, 1811.

‡ Act of April 8, 1811.

Gouverneur Morris, Stephen Van Rensselaer, De Witt Clinton, Simeon De
Witt, William North, Thomas Eddy, Peter B. Porter, Robert R. Livingston, Robert Fulton.

‖ Report of the commissioners appointed by an act of the Legislature of the
State of New York, etc., passed April 8, 1811, etc. Albany, 1812.

A Dubious War, a Doubtful "Era of Good Feelings"

McMaster absorbed himself in his usual style in war-time peccadilloes and campaigns. . . . Smuggling on the frontier. . . . The derivation of "Uncle Sam." . . . Opposition to the war. . . . Riots in Baltimore against Federalist critics of the Administration. . . . Federalists bitterly remembered the hue and cry which had been raised against them by Republicans for their enforcement of the Sedition Laws. . . . The shameful loss of Detroit to the British was recounted, as well as the more satisfying Battle of Lake Erie, with its unforgettable message dashed off by Oliver Hazard Perry to General William Henry Harrison. . . . "Dear General. We have met the enemy, and they are ours. Two ships, two brig, one schooner, and one sloop. Yours with very great esteem." . . . Other actions on land or sea heartened or dismayed Americans. . . . Especially distressing was the burning of the nation's capital, Washington, the fleeing of the President and his entourage before the British. . . . Less well-known is the burning of the capital of Upper Canada at York, by American soldiers, to be sure acting without orders. . . . The Battle of New Orleans was a consolation prize, though it took place *after* the signing of the treaty of peace, at Ghent, and did not affect its deliberations. . . . Its main accomplishment was to start General Andrew Jackson on his road to the White House. . . . The Hartford Convention, product of New England's hatred of "Jemmy Madison's War," with its hints of secession, further hurt Federalist prestige. . . . Americans emerged from the war politically exhausted. . . . North and South, Jeffersonians and even Federalists momentarily took solace from having a new President, James Monroe, who harked back to some of the traditions of the Revolutionary War. . . . But there were currency and tariff questions to disturb sectional feelings. . . . Troubles with Algerian pirates, who exacted tribute from the American Government, until put down by American forces in sharp and decisive actions. . . . Quarrels over banking regulations, and relations between state banks and the Federal government. . . . There was now a Second Bank of the United States. . . . Quarrels over fisheries with the English in the northeast, and over furs in the northwest. . . . There was an unhappy war with the Seminole Indians of Florida; it kept General Jackson in the public eye, and involved a transgression of Spanish sovereignty. . . . Most near to American feelings were the hard times which attended the economic crash of 1817. . . .

5

The Darker Side of Life

THE serious consequences which the hard times I have attempted to describe produced in the seaboard States were displayed in a most interesting manner by the census of 1820. Indeed, no counting of the people which, up to that time, had been made in this country is so well deserving of careful examination, for in it are the results of a migration westward the like of which was not seen again for many years. The entire population now numbered more than nine and a half millions. One million and six hundred thousand of these lived in New England, two millions and seven hundred thousand in the Middle States, two millions and nine hundred thousand in the Southern States, while more than two millions and a quarter dwelt beyond the Alleghany Mountains. In every one of the Atlantic States from Maine to Georgia the ratio of the increase of population had fallen save in Connecticut and South Carolina, and even in them the increase was but a fraction of one per cent. In Delaware the census takers could find but seventy-five more people in 1820 than were in the State in 1810. Virginia was no longer first in rank. New York was now the most populous State in the Union, and had added four hundred and thirteen thousand human beings to her inhabitants. No other State had approached this. Ohio came next in increase with an addition of three hundred and fifty-one thousand, which raised her from thirteenth to fifth place. Massachusetts, which ten years before was fifth, had become seventh. Kentucky was sixth with one hundred and fifty-eight thousand more people than in 1810. Tennessee had one hundred and sixty-one thousand more; but both these States had contributed largely to swell the population in Indiana, Illinois, and Missouri.

In passing westward the people followed the three great highways of emigration as heretofore. The northern stream has now traversed all Ohio, has joined Cleveland with Detroit, and has populated the entire southern shore of Lake Erie. The middle stream, pushing down the valley of the Ohio, has peopled all the southern half of Ohio, and much of the southern part of Indiana and Illinois has crossed the Mississippi and moved up the Missouri almost to the western boundary of the United States. The third stream—which, unable to cross the country of the Creeks and Cherokees in Georgia, had for thirty years past been moving down the Cumberland and the Tennessee, and had just reached northern Mississippi in 1810—has gone down the Mobile river and its branches, leaving a wide strip of populated country across Alabama from its northern border to the Gulf and has entered southern Mississippi. Indiana, Illinois, Alabama, Mississippi, and Missouri have become States in the Union, and raised the number to twenty-four.*

East of the mountains three States † had each over a million of people, and, taken together, had almost as many inhabitants as thirty years before were to be found in the whole United States. Not a little of this increase in the case of New York was due to migration from other States and from abroad. The Erie Canal, now half-way toward completion, was visibly attracting settlers to the interior of the State. Within ten years, and despite the war, three hundred and fifteen new towns and one hundred and sixty-one new villages had sprung up, and eight new counties had been established. The city of New York had become the favorite spot for landing emigrants from England and Ireland, and, as most of those who came went no farther, the growth of the city since the war had been portentous. During the first half of the decade, when her trade and commerce were gone, her bay.

---

* Indiana was admitted December 11, 1816; Mississippi on December 10, 1817; Illinois on December 3, 1818; Alabama on December 14, 1819; Missouri on August 10, 1821.

† New York, 1,372,111; Pennsylvania, 1,047,507; Virginia, 1,065,117.

blockaded and the business of her merchants ruined, she had almost stopped growing. A census taken for municipal purposes in 1816 returned but forty-two hundred more people than were reported by the census of 1810. But with the return of peace strangers came streaming in from every quarter and added twenty-three thousand * to her population in four years. In no other great city in the Union did the increase approach these figures. Some added far less to the number of their inhabitants from 1810 to 1820 than they did from 1800 to 1810. In Boston the increase was eight thousand during the one decade and eleven thousand in the other.† In Albany the gain fell from four thousand in the first to three thousand in the second decade,‡ and in Baltimore from twenty thousand to seventeen thousand.# Philadelphia, which in 1810 had a population about equal to that of New York gained but twelve thousand between that time and 1820. But most remarkable of all was the depopulation of Charleston, where there were but eighty more inhabitants in 1820 than there were in 1810.‖ War and the hard times had checked the growth of the great seaboard cities. During no other census period has the population of the cities failed to increase at a much more rapid rate than the population of the rural districts; but between 1810 and 1820 the ratio of increase was precisely that of the period preceding, which was four and nine tenths per cent.

Although the population of the seaboard had grown but slowly, the pauper, dependent, and petty criminal classes had multiplied with what seemed alarming rapidity. Some declared that the war, and above all the general idleness which followed the war, had demoralized the lower classes. All admitted that crime, profaneness, desecration of the Sabbath, intemperance and pauperism, prevailed everywhere to an ex-

---

* In 1810 the population was 96,372; in 1816 it was 100,619; and in 1820 it was 123,700.

† Boston in 1800 had 24,000; in 1810, 32,000; and in 1820, 43,000.

‡ Albany had 5,000 in 1800, 9,356 in 1810, and 12,360 in 1820.

Baltimore had 26,000 in 1800; 46,000 in 1810; 63,000 in 1820.

‖ The Federal census gave a population of 24,700 in 1810; a local census in 1817 gave 23,950; and the Federal census of 1820 returned 24,780.

tent which called loudly for public interference. As early as 1813 a Society for the Suppression of Intemperance had been formed in Massachusetts, each member of which pledged himself to discountenance the use of liquor at entertainments, funerals, and auction sales, and on no account to furnish laborers with grog during haying time, as was then the custom. So too the Presbytery of Cayuga, in New York, in 1813 urged the formation in the different counties of moral societies for the enforcement of the laws against Sabbath-breaking, swearing, and tippling. But it was not till the distress produced by the hard times of 1816 caused such general misery among the idle and dependent classes that the people went earnestly to work to seek for the causes of pauperism. As might have been expected, they found them in intemperance and in ill-regulated and ill-advised charity, and at once began an attack on each. In the great cities, where the suffering was most keen, the citizens had been called on to come to the aid of such charitable organizations as existed, and in response had contributed winter after winter in the case of New York and Philadelphia as much as ten thousand dollars for the relief of the destitute. That such calls might be prevented in the future, the committees intrusted with the use of the money were asked to investigate the condition of the poor, find out, if possible, the causes conducive of pauperism, and report a remedy. At Philadelphia the Committee of Superintendence addressed the ward and district committees and asked them to ascertain what kind of persons were most improvident; what they alleged to be the cause of their poverty; how much liquor, pawnbrokers, and soup societies contributed to it; if the poor could be induced to deposit their surplus earnings in savings-banks; how many children industrious parents could support; how many were willing to go into the interior of the State in search of work, if assisted; and how many indigent parents were willing to bind their children to tradesmen or send them out to service in families,* and with the information so gathered made a most interesting

---

* Circular of the Committee of Superintendence, Philadelphia, February 21, 1817.

report. They found that a radical change in the mode of administering charitable relief was most imperative. The number and variety of benevolent associations which Philadelphia supported were so great that, when joined to the provision made by law for the care of the poor, they made the city a veritable "emporium of beggars." Not only was a dependent pauper class created thereby at home, but a temptation was actually offered to every idle vagabond in the neighboring counties of the State to come in and live on the city. Nothing could stop this but a better system of granting relief; the judicious care of orphans from their infancy; the education of indigent children at county expense; the discouragement of the use of liquor, and a rigid execution of the law against dram-shops and tippling houses. That such desirable results might be secured it was necessary to keep public attention ever on them, and to do this it was suggested that a society be formed for the sole purpose of improving "the condition of the poor, and removing or preventing the causes that produce mendicity." Before the meeting which listened to this report and suggestion adjourned, a committee was chosen to propose by-laws and a constitution,* and so founded the Pennsylvania Society for the Promotion of Public Economy.† Among its many committees was one to suggest such methods of effecting savings in the diet, fuel, and clothing of the poor as should lessen consumption and tend to avert the evils of poverty; another was to report on the suppression of tippling houses and the promotion of sobriety and industry; a third was to examine the poor laws; a fourth was to concern itself with the management of prisons; while a fifth was to ascertain if the laws establishing public schools were properly administered, and if not, report such improvements in the mode of educating the poor as might seem worthy of public indorsement. The Constitution of Pennsylvania enjoined it on the Legislature to see to it that, "as soon as conveniently may be," schools should be "established throughout the State in such a manner that the poor may be taught

---

* American Daily Advertiser, May 10, 1817.
† Ibid., May 22, 1817.

gratis." But although the Constitution had been law for more than twenty-six years, the Legislature had never obeyed the injunction. Large sums had indeed been voted to endow " seminaries of learning," and in 1809 it was made lawful for parents who could not pay for the education of their children to send them to the most convenient school, and have them taught at the cost of the county.* Three years' experience under the law proved so burdensome to the tax payers of Philadelphia that in 1812 the city and county were exempted from its working, and the select and common council given authority to establish public schools.† But the war opened and nothing had been done when, in 1817, the Society for the Promotion of Public Economy appointed its committee on public schools. A plan, based on the system of Lancaster, was quickly prepared by the committee; an appeal was made to the Legislature ‡ by the society, and the law secured which made the city and county of Philadelphia the first school district of Pennsylvania, and established in it public schools.#

The action of the people at New York was almost identical with that at Philadelphia. Hard times had produced destitution and want far beyond the means of the benevolent societies to relieve. A public meeting was therefore called, money raised, soup-houses opened, and a committee appointed to examine into the causes of the increase of pauperism. The cause was not far to seek, and the committee soon came to the old conclusion that nothing was so fruitful a source of poverty as rum. A careful examination of the reports on the condition of the poor for ten years past revealed the alarming fact that paupers were increasing more rapidly than population. Fifteen thousand, or one seventh of the population of the city, were actually living on charity. About one sixteenth of them were worthy persons reduced to poverty by the depressed state of commerce. Another sixteenth were paupers from a variety of causes. But seven eighths were people reduced to abject poverty by the inordinate use of liquor. As far back as 1809

---

* Act of April 4, 1809.
† Act of March 31, 1812.
‡ Journal of the Pennsylvania House of Representatives, 1817–'18, p. 69.
# Act of March 3, 1818.

the Humane Society found eighteen hundred licensed dram-shops scattered over the city retailing liquor in small quantity, and offering every inducement to the poor to drink. Suppos-ing the number of such tippling houses had not decreased and that each sold two dollars and a half worth of rum every day, the enormous sum of one million six hundred thousand dol-lars * would, in the course of a year, be paid down by the la-boring classes for drinks. If laid out in flour at ten dollars a barrel this would buy one hundred and sixty thousand barrels, or more than enough to supply the entire population of the city with bread for a year. Should the receipts of the dram shops average three and a half dollars a day, the money expended in these annually would buy not only all the bread, but all the fuel consumed in New York city in a twelvemonth. Facts such as these were sufficient, the committee thought, to convince anybody that eighteen hundred dram-shops scattered over a city of a hundred thousand people, and drawing from the poor-est and most dependent classes several millions of dollars a year, was an evil so portentous as to require instant and serious at-tention. To go on year after year contributing food, clothes, money, was idle. It increased pauperism, which could only be lessened by reforming the method of dispensing charity, by stamping out grog-shops and corner groceries, and by educat-ing the children of shiftless and worthless parents in houses of industry. All this required public support, persistent effort, a careful study of the existing conditions of the poor, and money, and was very properly the work, not of a committee, but of a society which, it was earnestly recommended, should be formed at once. Such a body, known as The Society for the Prevention of Pauperism in the City of New York, was accordingly formed early in 1817 with a large number of well-known citizens for managers.

As soon as the managers were appointed they organized, and chose nine standing committees to report on idleness and sources of employment, on intemperance, on lotteries, on houses of ill fame, on pawnbrokers, on charitable institutions, on gam-bling, and on ignorance. But when the committees had gath-

---

* $1,642,500.

ered all the information they could and the managers had digested it in a report, the causes especially conducive of pauperism were declared to be drink, lotteries, pawnbrokers, and the many charitable institutions of the city. Drunkenness was singled out and described as the cause of causes. More than sixteen hundred licensed groceries then existed in the city, in any one of which any human being of any age could buy liquor in small quantities. If each one of these sixteen hundred dealers sold two hundred and fifty cents' worth each day, the amount of money so wasted in a year would be nearly one million five hundred thousand dollars,* a sum large enough to build fifty churches worth twenty thousand dollars apiece, and still leave enough to erect school-houses and pay for the education of every child in the city.

The lotteries were almost as bad as the dram-shops and tippling houses. The time spent in making inquiries regarding them and in attending at the lottery offices, the feverish anxiety that seized on the adventurer from the day he bought his ticket, the depression and disappointment that so invariably followed the drawing, diverted the laborer from his work, weakened his moral tone, consumed his earnings, and soon brought him to pauperism. But worse than the authorized lottery were the self-created lottery insurances, where young and old were enticed to spend little pittances under the delusive expectation of a gain, the chance of which was as low as it was possible to conceive.

To place the many noble charitable institutions with which the city abounded in the same category with lotteries, dramshops, and pawnbrokers, was most unfortunate. They had been founded by the purest motives of true philanthropy, and had unquestionably relieved thousands of human beings from pinching want, cold, hunger, and even untimely death. But was it not true that all of this good was offset by the evils that flowed from the expectations they aroused, by the relaxation of industry their display of benevolence produced, and by encouraging a reliance on charitable aid in evil days which ruined, in the minds of the laboring classes, that wholesome

---

* $1,460,000.

anxiety to provide for the future which alone can save them from a state of absolute dependence on the community?

As a means of checking these evils, the managers suggested that street begging be stopped, that the petty dram-shops be closed, that houses of industry be established, that more churches be built and more Sunday-schools opened in the outer wards of the city, and that the poor be encouraged to invest their money in savings-banks, benefit societies, and life insurances.*

The public, as was to have been expected, turned a deaf ear to the report. But the managers persevered, and in the course of another year founded a Saving Fuel Fund Society, and a savings-bank—the first in New York and the third in the United States—secured new regulations from the city regarding pawnbrokers and lottery offices, and aroused the Common Council to call on the Mayor for information on the subject of grog-shops and tippling houses. His report showed that there were then in the city nineteen hundred licensed grog-shops, and at least six hundred where rum was sold without a license. Each of these twenty-five hundred was frequented by the poorest and most vicious classes, and, what was worse, by the very men and women who as street beggars and out-door poor were themselves dependent on public charity for support. That such a condition of affairs existed in a country so vast in extent, so easily cultivated, with a population so thinly spread, where taxes were so light, where rank was unknown, where industry was so richly rewarded, and where all were eligible to the highest offices in the Government—must be due, the managers believed, to a radical defect in the laws and institutions. Year after year, therefore, they continued to call for the stoppage of street begging by the refusal of the public to yield to applications for relief, for the arrest of beggars and for their removal to houses of industry.

While the two societies were hard at work at Philadelphia and New York, a general movement in behalf of temperance and better morals swept over the Atlantic States. At last the

* First Annual Report of the Managers of the Society for the Prevention of Pauperism in the City of New York, February 4, 1818.

people seemed to be aware that of the hundreds of wretches who filled the poorhouses and workhouses or were supported by taxation as "out-door poor," the larger part were habitual drunkards. The newspapers began to print long communications on the cost of intemperance, on the vast sums spent each year for liquor, and on the good the thirty-three millions of dollars so wasted annually would do in founding churches and libraries, schools, seminaries, and starting in life young men of correct habits. The Portland Society Auxiliary to the Massachusetts Society for Suppressing Intemperance reported that out of eighty-five persons in the workhouse, seventy-one became paupers through drink. In another town forty-nine out of fifty-one tenants of the workhouse were habitual drunkards. The people of Waldoboro, Maine, in town meeting assembled, gave it as the sense of the town that drunkenness prevailed to an extent which was ruinous to morals and destructive to health ; that a speedy check must be put to it, and instructed the select-men to enforce the laws against taverners. A grand jury at Albany drew a picture of their city quite as dismal, and presented the immense number of dram-shops and corner groceries where liquor was retailed by the cent's worth as an evil and a nuisance to society. Members of the jury could recall a time when not a dram-shop or corner grocery existed ; but so common had they become since the war that they were fast destroying good morals and religion, and reducing a large class of the community to beggary and dependence on public support.* The farmers of upper Providence township in Pennsylvania met in the school-house just before harvest time and agreed not to give liquor to their field hands, nor to use it in the hay-field or during the harvest, nor to allow any one in their employ to use it.† When the local elections took place in Philadelphia an earnest call was made on the voters to attend the elections of constables, as they were the men whose duty it was to suppress unlicensed dram-shops and tippling houses.‡ In Baltimore a citizen petitioned the Legislature

---

* Albany Gazette, June 13, 1817.   Presentment made June 11.

† American Daily Advertiser, June 20, 1817.

‡ Ibid., March 21, 1817.

for relief. Within the bounds of Baltimore there were, he
said, some five hundred tippling houses, each holding out
every sort of allurement to the laborer to spend his earnings
for rum. To them went not only laborers, both black and
white, but servants of both sexes, and even apprentices.* The
Legislature gave his petition no attention, but public sentiment was aroused and the Mayor in a message to councils
urged them to establish a house of industry as a remedy for
pauperism and vice.† The Moral Society in the Pendleton
district of South Carolina insisted that the justices of the peace
should execute the laws providing for the punishment of cursing, swearing, and Sabbath-breaking.

Had the times improved, public interest in the reformation
of morals would undoubtedly have subsided. But the times
grew worse, and with each succeeding winter the people in the
cities were required over and over again to make contributions for the relief of the destitute. These repeated drains
upon their pockets kept them ever mindful of the suffering of
their less fortunate fellow-men, and did not a little to convert
what might have been a temporary effort on the part of a few
kind-hearted gentlemen into an important part of a great
humanitarian movement. The five years which followed the
war were most favorable to such a movement. Never in the
history of our country had the sufferings of the dependent
and unfortunate classes been so forcibly and persistently
brought to the attention of the public, for never before had so
many worthy citizens been reduced to want. Under such circumstances it is not surprising that one of the first manifestations of a kindlier spirit was lessening the severity of the laws
for the imprisonment of debtors. No class of the community
deserved consideration more. For years past they had been
treated with a cruelty and barbarity disgraceful to the humanity of our ancestors. For the smallest debt possible to
contract, though it were but a cent in value, the body of the
debtor, whether man or woman, would be seized by the credit-
or and cast into jail. By an old law, which went back to the
days when Pennsylvania was a colony, magistrates were allowed

* New England Palladium, January 31, 1817.   † Federal Gazette.

cognizance, without appeal, of debts under forty shillings or five dollars and thirty-three cents in amount. When the indebtedness exceeded that paltry sum the debtor was entitled by law to a stay of execution. But no such happiness awaited the poor wretches who owed a sixpence or a shilling, and who each year were dragged to prison by thousands on what were truly called "spite actions." Once behind the prison walls they were consigned to a fate harder than that which awaited the worst criminal. Murderers and thieves, forgers and counterfeiters, were fed, clothed, and cared for at the expense of the State; but for the unhappy man whose sole offence was his inability to pay a trifling debt of a few cents no such provision was made. The food he ate, the shreds that covered him, the medicine he took—nay, the very rags he wrapped about his sores *—were provided, if provided at all, by his friends, by the public, or by some Humane Society, or Society for alleviating the Miseries of Public Prisons. The room in which he was confined with scores of other offenders was utterly without furniture of any sort. In it were neither beds, nor cots, nor tables, nor chairs, nor so much as a bench or stool. He sat on the floor, ate off the floor, and at night lay down to sleep on it like a dog, without mattress, blanket, or covering; and this misery he endured till he died, or his debt was paid, or his creditor released him. Against this at length humanity revolted, and in 1792 a change for the better was ordered.† "Whereas," says the law then enacted, "many persons confined for debt in the prison called the debtors' apartment, in the city of Philadelphia, are so poor as to be unable to procure food for their sustenance, or fuel, or covering in the winter season, and it is inconsistent with humanity to suffer them to want the common necessaries of life," the State must come to their relief. It was then ordered that the inspector should provide fuel and blankets for such debtors as, by reason of their dire poverty, could not get them; and should make an allowance of seven cents a day for food, and charge this

---

* See, for instance, the appeals in Baltimore Federal Gazette, February 25, 1804, and November 9, 1804.

† Act of April 4, 1792.

against the creditors. If any creditor refused to pay after ten days' notice, his debtor was to be discharged. For twenty-two years the community seem to have thought that this mild concession was all that humanity required, for no further change was made till 1814.* Then was passed the "Bread Act," under which each prisoner whose debts did not exceed fifteen dollars was entitled to a discharge after an imprisonment of thirty days. Such as were destitute were to have a daily food allowance of twenty cents, payable every Monday morning by the creditors. On failure to pay it for a space of three days, the debtor could apply to the judge of the Court of Common Pleas for his release. All this seemed fair enough. But the duty of carrying the petition was assigned to no one in particular, and as a fee of one dollar and a half was exacted for fulfilment of the process, many a prisoner was detained long after his spiteful creditor had ceased to feed him. From documents presented to the Senate of New York in 1817, it appears that the keeper of the debtors' jail in New York city certified that during 1816 nineteen hundred and eighty-four debtors were confined, and that upward of six hundred were always in the prison or on its limits. The sheriff of the county certified that eleven hundred and twenty-nine were imprisoned for debts under fifty dollars; that of these, seven hundred and twenty-nine owed less than twenty-five dollars each, and that every one of them would have starved to death but for the kindness of the Humane Society. Indeed, he had more than once been forced to buy fuel out of his own pocket to keep them from freezing. One man who had been confined for a debt of fifty dollars remained in the jail three years before death ended his misery, and during this entire time was fed by the Humane Society. Another had been imprisoned six years and supported by charity.

In the face of such evidence the Legislature relented, and in 1817 forbade the imprisonment of debtors for sums less than twenty-five dollars. This led the way, and State after State followed. In 1818 New Hampshire exempted her inhabitants from arrest for debts under thirteen dollars and

---

* Act of March 26, 1814.

thirty-three cents.   A year later Vermont abolished imprisonment for debts under fifteen dollars.   Pennsylvania and Kentucky were not ready to go so far; yet each amended her
laws and exempted women.*   When the new States in the
West framed their constitutions prior to admission into the
Union, each one of them made it part of the fundamental law
of the State that no citizen should be imprisoned for debt
unless he refused to give up his estate.†   The relief afforded,
the misery averted, by this humane legislation cannot now be
truly appreciated.   Nothing done by the States since they
provided for the gradual or complete abolition of slavery did
so much to alleviate human suffering, unjustly and often
maliciously inflicted, as the abolition of imprisonment for
petty debts.

But nothing which philanthropy had been able to devise
had tended in the least to suppress pauperism or diminish its
great cause—intemperance.   Statistics of the cities, and indeed
of the populous counties, revealed a condition of affairs which
was getting worse instead of better.   Year by year the inmates
of workhouses and almshouses increased at a far more rapid
rate than the inhabitants of the cities.   Winter after winter
the same demands were made on the public for contributions
to keep the destitute from starvation.   In the cities the children of the pauper and dependent classes had now become so
numerous as to seriously threaten the peace of the community.
Bands and gangs of young boys and lads roamed the streets,
stealing, destroying, and insulting passers-by.   At last, in Philadelphia, matters were brought to a climax by the hard winter
of 1820–'21.   The distress exceeded anything ever before
experienced.   The Northern Soup Society; the Southern
Soup Society; the Western Charitable Association; the Indigent Widows' and Single Woman's Society—all the innumerable charitable societies were taxed to their utmost.   Yet the
number of paupers seemed greater than ever, and brought out
the usual earnest appeals to the humane for help.   Farmers

---

* Laws of Pennsylvania, Chap. XXXII, February 8, 1819. Laws of Kentucky,
Chap. DCXXXIX, February 14, 1820.

† See the Constitutions of Indiana, 1816; Mississippi, 1817; Illinois, 1818;
Alabama, 1819.

who came to the city with food for market were urged to give flour, meat, and vegetables. Citizens of New Jersey and Delaware were asked to remember how much they had benefited by the trade of Philadelphia, and contribute liberally to her distressed poor. But the destitution was too great for such slow means of relief, and once more a general call went forth for a meeting of citizens at the City Hall to take steps for the relief of the suffering poor. In some of the wards such meetings had already been held, and committees had been appointed to receive and solicit donations of food, wood, and clothing. But at the public meeting committees for each of the fourteen wards and the adjoining districts and townships were chosen, and a general system of collection begun.*

As the work of relief went on it was found that no charges which the committees had to meet were heavier than those for fuel. More than twenty-five hundred dollars was expended for wood alone.† As not a little of the destitution arose from improvidence, it occurred to those concerned in affording relief that this item of expense could be greatly reduced by the formation of a Fuel-saving Society. Its purpose was to furnish the poor in winter with wood bought with funds provided by themselves. Every workingman and woman was to be encouraged to deposit a small sum each week with the society, and receive in winter as much fuel as the money so deposited would buy at the low rates for which the society as a wholesale purchaser could sell it.‡ The public gave the scheme a hearty approval, and the society went promptly to work.

But the criminals and habitual paupers were yet to be cared for. The question of pauperism seemed so hard to deal with that the Legislature was appealed to, and a law secured which bade the Governor appoint a committee of nine to investigate the causes of pauperism in Philadelphia, and report to the next Legislature. While these gentlemen were at work another series of public meetings was called to devise a plan for improving the morals of a certain class of the youth of the city.#

* American Daily Advertiser, January 31, 1821.
† Ibid., June 13, 1821.
‡ Ibid., May 15, 1821.
# American Daily Advertiser, June 18, 25, 27, 1821.

It was not a little surprising, the call said, that no association had been formed to save young children from falling into vicious ways. The great number of idle boys who frequented the wharves on Sunday playing pitch and toss and other games destructive of morals, and who during the week spent their time in pilfering goods landed on the wharves from the ships, was an evil as serious as any which had received public attention. It ought to be stopped, and as a few citizens were determined to make the attempt to do so, all who were like minded were asked to meet them at the Mayor's office on a certain day in June.* So few attended that it was thought best to renew the call, and at the same time to state the evils complained of, which were breaches of the Sabbath, and the means by which they were effected. The first thing we hear, it was said, on the Sabbath morning is the ringing of bells on the steamboats on the Delaware river, to invite our youth to go to Camden, where they may engage in every sort of mischief and dissipation. Gardens and places of public resort are kept open, and oyster cellars and dram-shops, which are so many receptacles for the worthless and profligate of all descriptions.†

At the adjourned meeting it was resolved to urge the people in the wards and districts to take up the matter, investigate it, and send delegates to a general meeting where some plan for curing the evil might be considered and digested. Never, it was said, had the increase of vice and immorality been so alarming. Not one person in a hundred is aware of the frightful extent of juvenile crime among us. The number of children whose constant occupation is theft is enough to make one shudder. There is very good reason to believe that many of the fires which afflict our city so often are kindled by these youthful villains. The Mayor has done wisely to call on the people to investigate this subject for themselves, and the people will do wisely to follow the advice of the Mayor. That the citizens should act in a body was impossible. The promoters of the investigation, therefore, made a formal call for ward meetings to elect delegates to a general convention,‡ to which the

---

* American Daily Advertiser, June 5, 1821.
† Ibid., June 12, 1821.
‡ Held July 9, 1821.

Mayor addressed a most interesting letter. He called attention
to the great number of children and apprentices thrown out of
work by the hard times, who roamed the streets and wharves,
picking up and carrying away every article their strength and
adroitness enabled them to secure, and stated that he alone in
the course of three months had sent twenty boys of from ten
to eighteen to prison for larceny. He complained of the
second-hand shops and pawnbrokers where stolen goods were
sold for a tenth of their value. He pointed out the dangers
of the tippling houses and corner groceries, where liquor was
sold by the cent's worth to children of five years old, and paid
for often with stolen goods, and asked for a serious consideration of the flagrant breaches of the Sabbath.

This letter the meeting referred to a committee which reported a month later.*

The authors of the report earnestly advised that the community, in place of being content with the punishment of
crime when committed, should go further and seek to destroy
the sources of crime, which were six in number. At the very
head and front stood the tippling houses. With an audacity
that was simply unparalleled they fixed themselves in the
places of greatest resort, and in open violation of the law conducted their unlicensed business. They preyed not only on
the laboring class, whose savings were needed for the support
of families, but on servants, on young men, and even on children. They encouraged idleness, fraud, and vice; tempted
men to waste their earnings, reduced families to beggary, and
inflamed those passions which led straight to crime.

Almost as dangerous were the oyster cellars. As a city
institution they had but lately come in. Early in the century
the lover of oysters was forced to get a supply on the oyster
boats at the wharves, or seek the oyster man, who drove his
wagon up one street and down another, and, provided with
crackers, salt, and pepper, fed his customers at the street corners with oysters opened at the cart's tail. As population increased and the city spread, this primitive method was too
slow. The cartman was unable to supply the demand and

* August 6, 1821.

gave place to a host of wheelbarrow-men, who occupied the
street corners in the busy hours of the day and tempted every
passer-by. But to this method, in turn, there were objections,
for the streets were often hot and dusty and the business entirely interrupted in times of severe cold and rain. These considerations finally induced one of the oyster men to take up his
quarters in a cellar, and, finding that he succeeded, the whole
fraternity followed. Once there, the business quickly underwent a change, and the oyster cellar became the club-house, the
tavern, the exchange of apprentices, serving men, and idlers.
Liquor was sold without license, and acts were done which for
very shame would not have been allowed in a tippling house or
a tavern. Under the pretence of a fondness for oysters, young
men—from the school-boy to the clerk in the counting-house
—resorted to these places and learned to drink, to smoke, to
swear, and to gratify their sensual passions.

Next were the shops for the purchase and sale of second-
hand articles. In them everything from a brush, broom, or an
old bottle to a jewel of the first water were bought at a great
undervaluation and without asking a question. They became
in consequence the receptacles of that unlawful business which
the pawnbrokers could not transact. They were open markets
for the sale of stolen articles and a great incentive to pilfering
and petty thefts.

But of all the sources of youthful crime none was so prolific
as the neglect of education. Crowds of idle and disorderly
boys infested the streets, wharves, vacant lots, and ponds, where
they engaged in games, sports, and mischief to the ruin of
their morals and the annoyance of the community. They swore
and drank, resorted to oyster cellars, formed parties for the
redress of each other's wrongs, and stole in open day.

The best remedy for these evils was, the committee thought,
a stricter enforcement of the laws and the establishment of an
asylum where the mechanical arts should be taught to boys.
The advice was heartily approved by the meeting, and a committee appointed to draft a law and submit it to the next
Legislature.

However effective this remedy might be in the future, it
could do nothing for the suppression of the evils of the present,

which were fast becoming unbearable. House-breaking, till-robbing, assaults on peaceable citizens were of almost daily and nightly occurrence. With the opening of the new year, there-fore, the young men had a public meeting and chose seven of their number for each city ward and assigned to them the duty of rousing the people to take vigorous "measures to suppress the alarming nightly depredations on the persons and property of our citizens." * As the men engaged in these depredations were believed to be usually negroes, the African Methodist Church called a meeting of colored people, who pledged them-selves to aid the Mayor in his efforts " to detect and suppress the villanies and vice carried on in this city." †

The time had come, it was evident, for a reform in the gov-ernment of large cities. Philadelphia was attempting to con-trol a population of a hundred thousand by the same primitive methods which had been in use when she did not contain twenty thousand. She had grown to be a city without ceasing to be a village, and what was true of her was true of her neighbors. At New York the Society for the Prevention of Pauperism found thirteen thousand paupers in the city main-tained by public charity. Prostitution was so rife that the women formed a society and opened a home for girls, between five and ten years of age, whose parents were drunkards, taught them to read, write, and sew, and, when old enough, sent them to service with respectable families, or bound them to a trades-man. At Providence, where the cost of the poor was twenty thousand dollars a year, a town meeting ordered a committee to devise a plan for providing paupers with work and not with free livings. New Hampshire required the select-men of each town to post the names of tipplers in every tavern and fined anybody ten dollars who sold them liquor.

From such earnest efforts to prevent pauperism and crime there sprang most naturally a discussion and revision of the means then employed to reform criminals and lessen the rep-etition of crime; in short, of the criminal codes and peniten-tiary systems in use in the States. Imperfect as they were,

* American Daily Advertiser, February 18, 1822.
† Ibid., February 16, 1822.

our ancestors might well have been proud of them, for barbarous as they now seem there was then no other country on the face of the earth where they were so mild, so rational, and so wisely suited to their ends. The earliest attempt at a reform in penal jurisprudence in America was made by William Penn, a name that ought never to be mentioned without a grateful recognition of his many noble efforts to lessen the burdens and promote the happiness and comfort of mankind. The charter which was given him by Charles distinctly required that the penal laws of Pennsylvania should be like those of England; but, with a courage that did him honor, Penn put the injunction at defiance; abolished forfeitures in cases of suicide; abolished the deodands that followed murder; abolished capital punishment for robbery and burglary, arson and rape; forgery and levying war upon the Governor; substituted imprisonment with hard labor, and sent to England a code so humane that Queen Anne and her council promptly vetoed it. A feeble and unavailing struggle followed, and down to the opening of the Revolution sixteen species of crimes were punishable with death in Pennsylvania. But with independence a better era began, and in 1786 and again in 1790 and 1794 Pennsylvania reformed her code, swept away every trace of English cruelty, made treason and murder alone punishable with death, built the State Prison at Philadelphia, and with it began the penitentiary system of the United States. New York was next to feel the humane spirit of the new era. There, too, for any one of sixteen crimes men and women might be put to death. But in 1796 * her Legislature abolished capital punishment in fourteen cases and ordered State prisons to be erected at Albany and New York.† Thenceforth no period of four years elapsed but some State followed these happy examples, ‡ and in doing so they imitated not only all that was good, but all that was bad in the system of Pennsylvania. The prisons were usually huge buildings cut up into cells of two sizes. Those for the use of convicts doomed to solitary confinement were eleven by eight feet, were heated

---

* Law of March 26, 1796.   † That at Albany was not built.

† Virginia in 1800; Massachusetts in 1804; Vermont in 1808; Maryland in 1811; New Hampshire in 1812; Ohio in 1816.

by stoves placed without the grated doors, were lighted by little windows, and provided with necessaries, for no prisoner once within his cell ever crossed its threshold till he was pardoned or had served out his term. Those for the use of convicts whose sentence did not require solitary confinement were often twenty by eighteen feet in area, and into them were crowded every night boys and men without discrimination. The sexes were indeed kept apart. But with this all attempt at classification ended, and murderers awaiting sentence, thieves and highwaymen, swindlers and poor debtors, boys convicted of petty larceny, men held as witnesses—were all herded together in one common crowd. These little rooms had originally been designed to accommodate six or eight prisoners. But so crowded had the jails become that as many as thirty and even forty were to be found in each of them. The New York prison, which was intended to hold three hundred, had seven hundred, and the Governor was actually forced to pardon old convicts in order to make room for the new.* During 1818 two hundred and eighty were turned out in order that three hundred might be admitted.†

Evidence of the dreadful condition into which the prisons all over the country had long been sinking is abundant. As far back as 1809 the Humane Society of New York sent a committee to visit the Bridewell, or City Prison, and report what they saw. The picture which they drew is indeed a horrid one; but it is well to present it as evidence of what then went on in half the jails and penitentiaries of the country. In a room used as the women's apartment seventy-two prisoners guilty of twenty different crimes—vagrants and prostitutes, thieves and drunkards, offenders sentenced for sixty days, paupers who had misbehaved at the almshouse, women committed on suspicion or held as witnesses, black and white, old and young—were indiscriminately mingled together. Some, destitute of garments of every kind, went about with nothing but a dirty blanket wrapped around them. All were very ragged, all were very dirty, and, having no beds, were forced to

---

* Report of a committee to the New York Senate, March 7, 1817.

† Report of the Committee on Criminal Law and the Employment of Criminals on the Canals, to the New York Senate, 1822.

sleep on the floor.   Their food consisted on three days in the
week of meat and potatoes, and at other times of mush and
molasses.   The mush was brought in a great tub around which
the prisoners gathered and fed themselves, some with spoons,
some with tin cups, some with their hands, while one of the
number, armed with a whip, was appointed by the keeper to
maintain order.

The men's apartment was worse, for the inmates were as
foul and destitute as the women and far more brutal.   In one
of the rooms, where blacks and whites were confined, the captain—the man chosen by the jailer to keep order—was a negro,
who told the committee that he was often forced to strip and
beat his companions into obedience.   As he spoke he pointed
to a corner where lay a prisoner heavily chained by his orders.
But the worst case of all was that of a wretch who for more
than ten years had been confined in the dungeons on the
ground floor ; yet neither keeper nor turnkeys could tell for
what offence.   He was blind and insane, and so ragged that
the committee remarked on it, and were assured that as often
as a shirt was given him it was eaten by the rats.*

Aroused by this report, some unknown citizen visited the
debtors' jail and drew of that a picture almost as dreadful.
The building consisted of four stories and a cellar cut off from
each other by strong doors.   Underground in the cellar were
the damp, unwholesome dungeons, unventilated and unlighted,
save by little openings high up in the wall near the ceiling.
Into these were thrust such wretches as were condemned to
solitary confinement, and, from time to time, such unhappy
women as could not find lodgings in the women's apartments.
The ground, or first floor, was occupied by the families of the
jailer and the turnkeys, and by the bar, where liquor was sold
to the prisoners at a high price.   The second or middle floor
was given up to well-to-do debtors who could contribute to a
stock purse for cleaning, lighting, and whitewashing the hall,

---

* Report of a Committee of the Humane Society appointed to inquire into
the Number of Tavern Licenses ; the Manner of granting them ; their Effect upon
the Community ; and other Sources of Vice and Misery in this City ; and to visit
the Bridewell.   Prefaced with an Address to the Citizens of New York.   December 27, 1809.

and by so doing made themselves members of the "Middle Hall Society." On the third floor was the great mass of debtors, most of whom were supported by the Humane Society, for neither State nor city made any provision for giving them so much as a crust of bread. Their hall was without light at night, and often without fire in winter. Yet in it, during 1809, were confined eleven hundred and fifty-two persons, not one of whom owed twenty-five dollars.* During 1808, the Embargo year, when trade and commerce were much depressed, upward of thirteen hundred debtors had been imprisoned, and were fed and clothed by the Humane Society.†

The prisons and the discipline in force in them had not kept pace with the growth of population and the spirit of the times. The history of the New York penitentiary so well illustrates this fact, and is so closely resembled by that of every similar institution then in the land, that it is well worth while to follow it. From the reports made by those in charge it appears that down to 1803 the ends for which it was established were accomplished. But in that year the report contained the ominous words, "There will soon be a want of room." This was the first sign of coming trouble, and thenceforth for eighteen years the record is one of growing failure. In 1804 it fell into debt, and the cost of keeping the prisoners was eleven thousand dollars more than the product of their labor. In 1805 the debt increased, and overcrowding of the convicts began. A year later the effects of overcrowding is noticed; complaint is made that "lessons of vice are inculcated"; that no reform is seen; and the suggestion is offered that no offenders be sent to the prison whose term of confinement is under five years. During 1807 and 1808 the vices of the system were yet more fully developed. The cells are packed; the hospital is crowded with sick; numbers of convicts are in for second offences; and twenty thousand dollars are wanted to make up the deficit in expenses. Alarmed at this

---

* 591 for debts under $10.00.
 235 " " between $10.00 and $15.00.
 326 " " " 15.00 " 25.00.

 1,152

† Theophilanthropist, No. 3, March, 1810.

steadily growing debt, the visiting judges and the Governor begin the vicious practice of making the number of discharges equal to the number of commitments, and in 1810 one hundred and thirty are pardoned in order to make room for one hundred and seventy-one admitted. But even this afforded no relief. The deficit and the number of convicts went on increasing, and in 1814 it was found that old offenders who had been pardoned were in again for second and even third offences. Then was it that the Legislature, for the first time in many years, gave serious attention to the state of the prison, ordered a new one to be built at Auburn, and in 1816 appointed three men to investigate and suggest reforms. They told the Legislature that want of room and the consequent necessity of pardon was the greatest evil of the system; they described the prisoners as corrupting and being corrupted by each other; asserted that men left the prison more confirmed in their vicious propensities than when they entered it; and admitted that the penitentiary had failed to accomplish the great object for which it had been created. Between 1810 and 1815 seven hundred and forty had been released by pardon, and only seventy-seven by the expiration of their sentences. Of all who, in that period, had been incarcerated for a second or third offence, more than two thirds were men who had been pardoned.

The experience of New York was not extreme. Wherever the penitentiary system was in use the same complaints were heard. Whoever was in any way concerned in prison discipline—judges, grand juries, governors, lawyers, secretaries of state, societies for the suppression of crime, committees of investigation—all agreed that the penitentiary was a failure. Indiscriminate herding had defeated reform, and turned what ought to be an institution for the betterment of morals into a seminary of every vice. Culprits came out more depraved and desperate than when they went in. The young were advanced in the path of guilt; the old were hardened in their baseness; morals were destroyed; conscience was blunted, and the ranks of the criminal classes steadily recruited.* It was

* Report of the Committee on the Penitentiary System to the Pennsylvania Senate, 1821. Report on the Penitentiary System in the United States, prepared

from such associates and in such surroundings that the young learned to commit the fearful crime of sodomy; to make molds for counterfeiting small coin; to pick locks and construct skeleton keys; to alter banknotes, and become skilful in the art of picking pockets.

Great results had been expected from the penitentiary system. Failure to realize them was therefore followed by astonishment, by disappointment, and by a complete revulsion of public feeling. A belief now prevailed that the kindhearted and benevolent gentlemen who had persuaded the community to mitigate the severity of the penal code had been led astray by their benevolence; that the system was wholly wrong; that nothing but evil had come of it; and that it could not be too soon abolished. Some in their disappointment cried out for a return to the barbarous practices of twenty years before, and declared that they longed for the day when malefactors would again be pelted in the stocks and flogged at the whipping post, and when the number of criminals would be lessened, not by reformation but by hanging. Others were for the transportation of criminals—for a Botany Bay—and when asked where it should be, invariably answered, At the mouth of the Columbia river in Oregon. But wiser counsels prevailed. State legislatures, prison discipline societies, societies for the suppression of vice, well-known philanthropists, took up the matter, and, guided by their reports and pamphlets, public opinion gradually settled to the belief that reformation of a criminal was not impossible, that a return to capital punishment was a step backward, and that solitary confinement, by day and by night, of men whose sentences were not for life was an expedient worth trying.

It was at this time that the tread-mill, a device borrowed from England, was introduced into the prisons. A hot controversy was waged by the physicians over the question of its effect on the physical organization of man; but it held its

under a resolution of the Society for the Prevention of Pauperism in the City of New York, 1822. I have borrowed largely from this. On the Prisons of Philadelphia, by a European, 1796. Statistical View of the Operation of the Penal Code of Pennsylvania, to which is added a view of the present state of the Penitentiary and Prison in the city of Philadelphia, 1817.

place for many years. Societies for the reformation of juvenile delinquents; prison-discipline societies; houses of refuge; public schools; new prisons, constructed in accordance with humane ideas—appeared in many States, and the first quarter of the nineteenth century closed with a serious effort for the prevention of crime and the education and reformation of criminals.

Again the cry for the abolition of imprisonment for debt arose in the Eastern States, and a flood of literature setting forth the cruelty and barbarity of the system was poured forth on the community. The cause now found friends even in Congress, where, session after session, efforts were made to secure the abolition of imprisonment for debt by process from a United States court. The speech made by R. M. Johnson, on one occasion when the subject was under debate in the Senate, was considered so fine an effort that the Society for the Relief of the Distressed in Boston published it with an appendix full of information concerning the sufferings of debtors. From this statement it appears that between the first day of January, 1820, and the first day of April, 1822, three thousand four hundred and ninety-two persons were imprisoned for debt in Boston; that two thousand of them were deprived of liberty for sums less than twenty dollars; that four hundred and thirty were women; and that the suffering and distress occasioned to the families of the persons imprisoned involved more than ten thousand human beings. One brute had a woman, who owed him twelve dollars, dragged to jail with an infant at her breast. There she and her child remained in a crowded room for twenty days, by which time the infant had become insane and was carried away by a stranger to breathe its last, while the miserable mother remained in confinement. Nothing short of the payment of the debt would induce the creditor to release her. Yet another creditor imprisoned a woman for a debt of three dollars and sixty cents, and forced her to leave two children under two years of age behind her in what had once been her home. An instance, the Society declared, was known to them of a man who was lodged one bitter winter night in the Cambridge Jail, where he froze to death before morning;* and another of a debtor imprisoned for thirty years. When his case was brought to light his friends had utterly forgotten him; but they came nobly to his relief, and raised the three thousand dollars necessary to pay the jail fees which had accumulated during the long period of confinement.

The one region of our country which showed no signs of moral awakening was the District of Columbia. In it when the quarter century closed were the most barbarous criminal code and the foulest prison in the United States. On the Virginia side of the District thirty crimes were punishable with death, and on the Maryland side fourteen. A white man who broke into a storehouse, warehouse, or tobacco house, and stole to the value of five shillings, or escaped from jail when confined under charge of felony, could, under the law, be put to death. But a slave who maliciously burned a house, though it were a privy, not only could but must be hung, and when dead have his head cut off, his body quartered, and the fragments displayed in the most public places in the District.

The jail was as bad as the code. Through the middle of it, from end to end, ran a broad passage with eight cells on a side. Under each cell was an arched sewer. With this sewer the cell was connected by a hole which was cut through the brick floor and served as a privy. In these sixteen rooms, not one of which was over eight feet square, the marshal of the district was often forced to confine seventy and even eighty persons; the innocent with the guilty; the old with the young— nay, not infrequently the witness with the criminal against whom he was to testify. A member of Congress who visited the prison declared, in his place in the House, that in one cell there were seven persons—three women and four children; that they were almost naked; that they had neither bed nor chair, nor stool, nor any other of the common necessaries of life, and were compelled to sleep on the damp brick floor without any other covering than a few dirty blankets.

Nothing, perhaps, illustrates the neglected state of the prisons so fully as the fact that no effort worthy of mention had

* Appendix by the Society for the Relief of the Distressed to a pamphlet edition of the speech of R. M. Johnson, on a proposition to abolish imprisonment for debt, delivered in the Senate, January 14, 1823.

been made toward giving their inmates moral and religious instruction.   In New Jersey, in Pennsylvania, in Maryland, and Virginia no chaplain was provided by the State, and not a cent was expended for religious services even on Sunday.   Now and then some society, or some individual, shocked at this state of affairs, would see to it that the Bible was read a few times and a few sermons preached.   But periods of three and five months would pass without a service.   New Hampshire, whose penitentiary was a source of revenue, and often paid from one to five thousand dollars a year into her treasury, spent twenty-five dollars annually for religious instruction.   Massachusetts appropriated two hundred dollars.   Vermont set apart one hundred dollars, and made a weavers' shop of the prison chapel.

Such indifference is the more remarkable because at that very time great religious activity was displayed in every part of the country.   The missionary societies were flourishing and busy.   Bible societies were being formed in towns and cities ; a National Bible Society was in existence, and money was being freely given to send Bibles and teachers into the West, where there was far less need of them than in the prisons of the East.

Increasing Growth,
Hardening Dissension

Evangelical societies arose, dedicated to bringing Christianity to the frontier. . . . The sects competed for followers: Methodists, Baptists, Congregationalists, Presbyterians, among many others. . . . The American Bible Society pressed its own particular crusade of distributing copies of Holy Writ to those bereft of it. . . . The American Colonization Society began its remarkable effort in 1816 to start a stream of Negroes returning to Africa to begin its conversion to Protestant Churches. . . . It was generally imagined that this movement would herald the deterioration of the slavery system, and it attracted philanthropic talents and the patronage of the United States government. . . . The settlement and growth of Liberia were expected to measure the success of colonization. . . . Only later did it dawn upon anti-slavery elements that colonizers seemed more intent on sending already free Negroes to Africa, than putting pressure on slaveholders to emancipate their slaves. . . . Expansionism and slavery suddenly, in 1820, confronted the country with another sectional crisis: Ought Missouri, first Territory applying for admission as a State outside the Old Northwest, enter the Unon with slavery? . . . The passion of the Congressional debate, as maintained by excited northerners and southerners, alarmed patriots. . . . Personalities, rather than parties, dominated the era, and continued to suggest a fragmented nation. . . . A third term for Monroe seemed an alternative to chaos to some of his admirers, those especially who were impressed by his famous Doctrine against further European colonization of the Americas. . . .

Volume Five of McMaster's *History* is particularly rich for his purposes since (despite slavery as an American institution) democracy was expanding rapidly in all fields: socially, economically, politically. . . . A number of major candidates presented themselves for the Presidency in 1824:

> John Quincy Adams,
> Who can write,
> And Andrew Jackson,
> Who can fight.

—as well as William H. Crawford of Georgia—who would almost certainly have been elected, had he not been stricken during the campaign—and Henry Clay, among others. . . . None gained an electoral majority, and the election was once more, as in 1800, thrown into the House of Representatives for decision. . . . There, Henry Clay became President-maker, and he chose Adams. . . .

6

The Spirit of Progress and Reform

FIFTY years had now gone by since the farmers of Massachusetts made the first appeal to arms in the struggle for independence, and forty-nine since the thirteen colonies threw off allegiance to Great Britain and founded the Republic of the United States. Our country when independence was obtained was a very little one. It nowhere touched the Gulf of Mexico. It just touched the Mississippi. Its population numbered scarcely three million and a half of souls, and nowhere within its bounds was a city of forty thousand people. Since that time its domain had been extended across the continent; the waves of the Pacific now beat upon its western confines; the waters of the gulf now washed the shores of three great States and one Territory; while on the soil of the Republic dwelt six million of the happiest people on earth. The States had multiplied from thirteen to four-and-twenty. Four * cities boasted of more than forty thousand inhabitants each, and two † of more than one hundred thousand. Fourteen had each more than ten thousand, while scores of towns which in 1825 contained a thousand and more population did not exist in 1776.

Quite as marvellous was the social betterment. No man, whatever his station in life, whatever his business, trade, or occupation, was without its influence. Life along the seaboard was getting easier. Much of the old hardship of earlier times was gone. Increase in population and in wealth, joined with improved means of communication, had greatly expanded

---

* New York, Philadelphia, Boston, and Baltimore.
† New York (1820), 123,706.   Philadelphia (1820), 112,772.

business opportunities. New industries, new trades, new occupations had arisen, and now afforded ways of gaining a livelihood unknown in the time of Washington. Manufactures had grown up since 1807, and had dotted the Eastern and Middle States with a thousand mills and factories. Steamboats were now on lake and river. Canals now joined great waterways, while a network of turnpikes spread out in every direction from the chief cities. These civilizers had so abridged distance that in 1825 the frontier and the seaboard almost touched. Boston was but two days from New York, New York but eleven hours from Philadelphia, and Philadelphia but five days from Pittsburg and fifteen hours from Washington. Freight could now be moved from New York to Buffalo through the Erie Canal for four cents a ton per mile, tolls included. These rates revolutionized business. The field a merchant or a manufacturer could cover by his enterprise seemed boundless. The whole West, as well as the East, became his market, and transportation companies for the handling of freight had been established in order to enable him to reach that market. Banks were multiplying. Insurance companies, steamboat, turnpike, and canal companies, mills, and factories were springing up on every hand. Simple as these things seem, they changed the whole course of life.

Tens of thousands of men who under the old conditions would have been doomed to eke out a scanty livelihood by farming, or by cobbling, or by toiling in the crowded ranks of unskilled labor, now found new occupations opening before them. They became mill hands and operatives; they turned machinists and mechanics; they served as engineers and firemen on the steamboats, as clerks and book-keepers in banks and insurance companies; they handled freight, tended the gates on the turnpikes or the bridges on the canals; drove the horses that dragged the canal boats, or found employment in some of the older industries which, such as tailoring and printing, shoemaking, stage-driving, hatmaking, and carpentry, had been greatly expanded since the war.

The rise of new industries and the development of old caused an immense increase in the number of working-men and working-women. The growth of this class brought up questions of reform, and with 1825 the labor movement began. Less hours of labor, higher wages, better treatment, payment in honest money and not in depreciated bank paper, became the demands of the time. Some of these were as old as the Republic. Journeymen shoemakers, journeyman tailors and carpenters over and over again had struck, or "turned out," during the past forty years. Now the grievance was the employment of non-union men; now it was low wages; again, it was giving out work to women. Twice the purpose of the strike was to secure a shorter working-day. The first of these movements occurred in 1791, when the members of the Union Society of Carpenters at Philadelphia ordered a turnout. They complained that in summer they were forced to toil from sunrise to sunset for five shillings a day, and in winter were put on piecework, and demanded that the year through a working-day should be from six in the morning to six at night, with an hour for breakfast and another for dinner; or, what was the same thing, ten hours of labor. Nothing came of the movement, they were forced to yield, and in all likelihood not one of them ever lived to see the time when the working-man did not labor thirteen hours out of the twenty-four. During the summer, when the sun rose early, every cobbler, every carpenter, mason, stone-cutter, every laboring man, was hard at work at four o'clock in the morning. At ten an hour was taken for lunch, and at three another for dinner, after which work went on till, according to the almanac, the sun had set.

The second protest against so long a working-day was made in 1822 by the journeymen millwrights and machine workers of Philadelphia. They met at a tavern, and passed resolutions that ten hours of labor were enough for one day, and that work ought to begin at 6 A. M. and end at 6 P. M., with an hour for breakfast and one for dinner. Their action went no further, and led to no immediate result. But the fact that the men who formed the meeting were machinists was one of many signs of the expansion of labor. Yet another was afforded in 1824 in New York city. A tariff bill was then before Congress, and the people all over the seaboard States were supporting or opposing it in memorials and petitions. New York, as a great commercial city, was full of anti-tariff men, and by them a meeting was called and held in the City Hall. But a band of weavers from Paterson, from Westchester, and from the mills in the city marched to the Hall, took possession, interrupted the proceedings with cries of " No British goods! " " Tariff, tariff! " " American manufactures ! " " Protection to domestic industries ! " smashed some chairs, tore up some benches, broke lamps and windows, and went away. The rioters, it was said in explanation, were aliens, weavers imported from Great Britain, men who had not been long enough in the United States to acquire citizenship. The statement was true, and, trifling as was the affair, it showed that the time had come when the ranks of labor were being recruited abroad; that the importation of foreign operatives had begun; and that a new element was introduced to still more complicate the industrial questions pressing for settlement.

The condition of the working-man stood in need of betterment. In the general advance made by society in fifty years he had shared but little. Many old grievances no longer troubled him, but new ones, more numerous and galling than the old, were pressing him sorely. Wages had risen within ten years, but not in proportion to the increase in the cost of living. In some States he was no longer liable to imprisonment for debt, unless the amount was larger than fifteen dollars, and in others than twenty-five. If he was so fortunate as to save a few cents out of the pittance he earned, and lived in either of the four great cities, there were savings banks in which he might with reasonable safety deposit the fruits of his economy and receive interest thereon. These were decided gains. Nevertheless, his lot was hard. The hours of labor were still from sunrise to sunset. Wages were not always paid weekly or monthly, but often at long and irregular intervals, and frequently in bad money. His ignorance of finance and of the tricks of business men made him the recipient of counterfeit notes and bills of broken banks, or of institutions of such doubtful soundness that the paper he was forced to receive at its face value would not pass with the butcher or the baker save at a heavy discount. When his employer failed, no lien law gave him a claim on the product of his labor. In many States he was still disfranchised. In all, he was liable under the common law of England to be punished for conspiracy if by strikes, by lockouts, or by combination with others he sought to better his condition or raise his pay. One thing he did not lack—he now had friends ready and willing to help on his cause.

The pleas they put forth in his behalf dwell at great length on the awful misery of drunkenness; declare that the poverty of the working-classes is the real cause of intemperance; call for legislation to " prevent the rich from swallowing up the inheritance of the poor "; hold up as a warning the " injurious consequences to the community of individuals amassing large landed property "; point out the dangers to which factory operatives are daily and hourly exposed; and ask for cleaner shops and healthier mills and lodgings.

Such pleas had small effect on the public, but much on the working-man and woman, who, after 1825, began to organize in earnest. Social unions of various crafts were formed in all the seaboard cities and manufacturing centres north of Baltimore. In New England the women weavers and cotton operatives led the way. In New York city the ship carpenters and calkers, following the example of the machinists of Philadelphia, in their turn began to agitate for a ten-hour day. So energetic was the labor movement that in 1828 an attempt was made in the New York Legislature to secure a mechanics' lien law, and a report strongly favoring such a measure of relief was presented. In Philadelphia the workingmen, breaking old ties, entered politics on their own behalf and formed a labor party. At a public meeting in August it was formally resolved to urge the working-men to support no candidate for a seat in the Legislature or in the city councils who would not pledge himself to further the interests and demands of " the working-classes," and a call was issued for organization.* The city and county were marked off into four districts, from each of which delegates were sent to a general

* United States Gazette, August 14, 1828.

convention which nominated assemblymen, common council-men, and auditor.*

The tickets were defeated; but the organization continued, and ere another year went by made two demands for reform—one that the managers of the House of Refuge, who had just introduced mechanical occupations into their institution, should see to it that the mechanics and working-men of Philadelphia suffered no injury; and another that the State of Pennsylvania should establish a system of free republican schools, open to the children of the rich and of the poor without distinction.

Judged by the standard of public instruction as now maintained in Pennsylvania, the demand of the working-men was reasonable and just. The constitution of the commonwealth, framed a generation before, required that the children of the poor should be educated at the public cost. The injunction was mandatory; the meaning was plain. Yet no steps were taken to carry it out till 1809, when a law was enacted requiring the assessors of taxes to make a census of the children whose parents were too poor to educate them, send the boys and girls to the nearest school, and assess the cost on the tax-payers. Even this wise provision was neglected. Some districts had no schools of any kind; in others the funds were embezzled, misapplied, perverted, or the law but partly executed, for the people refused to accept the benefit conferred lest their children should be looked on and treated as paupers. Meanwhile the cities increased in population, and the number of children growing up in absolute ignorance became so large that in 1818 a second step forward was taken, and the city and county of Philadelphia, the city and borough of Lancaster, and the city of Pittsburg were formed into three districts, with free schools in which children whose parents were too poor to educate them were taught reading, writing, arithmetic, and geography. No child whose parents could pay his schooling was admitted, and this in the eyes of the working-men was an offensive class distinction. It separated the children of the rich from those of the poor, and said to the latter, " You

* United States Gazette, August 21 and October 1, 1828.

are paupers." That some men should be rich and others poor was inevitable, but to build up class hatred was not necessary, and no surer way of preventing it could be devised than a system of equal republican education, with free schools open to the children of all citizens alike.

The efforts which working-men were thus making to secure great social reforms, and especially their demands for free public schools, now warmly enlisted in their cause another body of reformers, known as the Free Enquirers, who were regarded at that day by conservative people with the same horror and detestation that anarchists and socialists are regarded in ours. The origin of this movement for free inquiry goes back to a little community of men and women who gathered in 1825 at New Harmony, near the Wabash river, in Indiana. The founder of the community, Robert Owen, was a native of Wales, where he was born in 1771. Forced to earn his living while still a lad, he became a clerk in a draper shop near London at ten, went to Manchester at fourteen, was made manager of a cotton mill at eighteen, and at twenty-seven bought the mills at New Lanark, in Scotland, from David Dale, whose daughter he married.

From the day when as a mere lad he entered the Manchester mills his mind seems to have been full of schemes for the social betterment of the laboring classes, held down by ignorance, by squalid poverty, and by lack of character. Once in control at New Lanark, Owen put his plans in operation, and after long opposition built and opened what he called an Institution for the Formation of Character, but what was, in fact, a great school for the instruction of children from the time they were infants till they were boys and girls of twelve. He shortened the hours of daily labor in the mills, introduced rules to enforce morality and promote cleanliness and good habits; he added to the comfort and happiness of all, and little by little established co-operation on the community system of living. The fame and the success of the New Lanark experiment spread far and wide. Co-operation, "unrestrained co-operation on the part of all the members for every purpose of social life," became the reform hobby of the hour, and Owen the great teacher of a new economy. Co-operative economical societies sprang up all over England and Scotland, and attracted the attention of men in the New World.

Among those whose attention was so attracted was an agent for the sale of a village built in the far West by one of the many religious communities which then flourished in the United States. The founder of this sect was George Rapp, the son of a small farmer and vine-dresser of Würtemberg, in Germany, where he was born in 1757. He was a man far more inclined to read and think than to plough and reap, and having no books save the Bible, he read it constantly, with the result so common in the case of bright men with little education. He began to see new meanings and to catch new ideas. Religious doubts tormented him; then firm convictions took their place, and a sense of duty arose which drove him to make known the new truths he had discerned for the good of mankind. He was moved to preach first in his own house, and then in public. But when he began to preach the clergy began to persecute, and as persecution continued, his followers increased in number and in earnestness. At last, wearied with the perpetual struggle for the rights of conscience, Rapp turned to the one land where men were free to worship as they pleased, and prepared to lead his followers to the United States of America. In 1804, with his son and a few friends, Rapp came to Baltimore, travelled over Maryland, Pennsylvania, and Ohio, and finally chose a tract of land in the valley of the Conoquenessing, twenty-five miles northwest of Pittsburg, in Pennsylvania, and on it in 1805 seven hundred Rappites built the village of Harmony. Hitherto they had formed a religious body. Now they became a community, put all property into a common fund, adopted a simple style of dress, plain houses and plain living, and agreed that each should labor for the good of all.

As time passed the site of Harmony proved to be ill-chosen, for the soil and climate were unsuited for vine-growing, the only industry in which the people were skilful, and the town had no water communication with the outside world. A new home was therefore sought in the far West, and found in the valley of the Wabash, whither, in 1815, the society migrated and built a second Harmony. Once more the site proved far from satisfactory. The wild rush of population westward brought them neighbors of a most unpleasant sort; malaria, or " the shakes," was worse than the neighbors, and so disheartened the people that in 1824 an Englishman named Richard Flower was offered five thousand dollars to find a purchaser for the land and houses. Flower went straight to Great Britain, sought out Owen, and sold him the town of Harmony, with all its mills, houses, factories, and thirty thousand acres of land, for one hundred and fifty thousand dollars. Three thousand acres were under cultivation, eighteen were covered by full-bearing vines and flourishing orchards, while the village itself was well built and well laid out, with broad streets and a public square, around which were brick buildings used by the Rappites for schools, churches, and community purposes.

The purchase concluded, Owen, in December, 1824, came over to the United States, and, while the Rappites were on their way to a new home, which they built in Beaver County, Pennsylvania, and named Economy, he began preparations for the founding of the first Owenite community in our country. That his scheme and his views might be as widely known as possible, he went to Washington, secured the use of the Hall of Representatives, and in it, on two evenings,* delivered long addresses to most distinguished audiences. In making such appeals, it was his custom to begin by attempting to show that the construction of modern society was all wrong; that the prevalence of error, prejudice, vice, and crime was due to the practice of bringing up the young in a system of society which he called the individual, or selfish; and that there were two sets of circumstances which entirely regulated the formation of a man's character. The one was his religious belief, and the other was his education. Every child was possessed of a body and a mind over which he had no control; whether that mind was moulded for good or for ill depended on the circumstances with which the parents sur-

* Two Discourses on a System of Society as delivered in the Hall of Representatives of the United States on the 25th of February and the 7th of March, 1825, etc. By Robert Owen, of New Lanark. The plan for a community is given on pages 42–52.

rounded the child.* " Had you," he would say, " on my right
hand been brought up under the influence of such circumstances as are to be found at the foot of the Rocky Mountains,
you would all have been Indians, save as to the color of your
skins. Had you on my left hand been exposed from infancy
to the circumstances which prevail in China, you would all
have been Chinese, except in form and figure." Any social
system, then, which ignored the power of circumstances was
wrong. That system which was based on " the science of circumstances " was right. As to religion, it should be a rational
one, founded on matter of fact and the evidences of the senses
—in short, the revealed word of God. Any events recorded
in books professing to be of divine origin which were in opposition to this principle were false. The Scriptures were not
divine nor written by men under divine influence, nor did
they more than any other writings contain the revealed word
or will of God. All religions, the Christian included, were
founded in error, and, so far from being fitted to promote
happiness and virtue among mankind, they had the opposite
tendency. If the human race, then, was to be made virtuous
and happy, the old system must be done away with, for its
institutions and its prejudices could not exist together with
the principles of the new.†

It was for this reason, therefore, that he urged the formation of communities in which should be associated persons
in sympathy with his views. The number in any community
should never be less than five hundred nor more than two
thousand, and they should begin by purchasing a tract of
twenty thousand acres of good land. In the centre should
be four buildings, each a thousand feet long, so placed as to
form the four sides of a hollow square. From the middle of
each side a building should project into the square, and in it
should be the dining-hall, the kitchen, the laundry, the store-
rooms—in short, all the domestic appliances needed for the
comfort and convenience of those living in the dormitory to
which it was attached. The school-rooms, lecture-rooms, lab-

* National Advocate (N. Y. C.), November, 1825. American Daily Advertiser, November 22, 1825.
† American Daily Advertiser, November 30, 1825.

oratories, the chapels, concert-halls, and ball-rooms should be in the centres and corners of the buildings. On the first and second stories should be dormitories, and on the third floor the quarters of unmarried persons and children over two years of age, for at that time of life they were to be taken from their parents, lest they should acquire the foolish ideas and habits of the old society.* Around the village thus arranged should lie the farms. Every member should have equal rights and privileges according to age, and be fully supplied with the comforts and necessaries of life. Nobody should own any land, or houses, or cattle, for all property was to be held in common. There should be no churches, no sects or creeds, no religious worship, but moral lectures, and such a system of public education as would foster in the young a love of justice, morality, and truth. For the very young there should be dancing, singing, and military drill. For those older in years, such studies as music and history, drawing and astronomy, geography, botany, and agriculture. The school-room should be not a barn, but a picture gallery and a museum. Learning should cease to be a task and become a source of wonder and delight.

From Washington, Owen went on to New Harmony, to which he had invited " the industrious and well-disposed of all nations " to come, and in April, 1825, met a motley gathering of men and women in New Harmony Hall, as he called the old Rappite Church. To these he unfolded his plan for the regeneration of society through co-operation. He told them that it was idle to expect that men trained as they had been should be able to pass at one bound from an irrational to a rational system of society. A half-way house, a period of probation, was necessary to fit them for the practice of co-operation; that he had determined, therefore, to form them into the Preliminary Society of New Harmony, give them a constitution which should continue for three years, and leave the management of affairs in the hands of a preliminary committee. To all this the people gladly agreed, for they were really the guests

---

* A drawing of such a village was published in London in 1826 under the title, " A Bird's-eye View of one of the New Communities at Harmony, in the State of Indiana, North America."

of Owen.* The land they tilled, the seed they planted, the houses in which they lived, the medicines they consumed, the goods they obtained at the store, all belonged to Owen. At his expense one hundred and thirty children were boarded, clothed, and taught, and a band maintained in order that the people might dance every Tuesday and listen to a concert every Friday evening.

After starting the New Harmony Preliminary Society on its way, Owen went back to New Lanark, and left the people to their own devices. In November of 1825 he returned, and, after lecturing in New York and Philadelphia, and gathering in each a small band of recruits, he started westward. Ice detained the party for a month on the Ohio, but in January, 1826, it reached New Harmony in safety.

A traveller who saw the village at this time describes it as a scene of idleness and revelry. There were, he declares, a thousand persons of every age, sex, and condition gathered in the town, with no visible means of support save the generosity of the visionary Mr. Owen. In the school, which was held in the old brick church of the Rappites, were three hundred and thirty children, who were under no control whatever, for the plan of education was that of Pestalozzi, in which the sole punishment for bad behavior was a short confinement. The teachers, he was amazed to find, had thrown aside the Christian faith, and taught doctrines not unlike those held by the German Illuminati at the opening of the French Revolution. In and about the village no man seemed to be busy. The houses were falling into a state of dilapidation, the gardens were full of weeds, the fences were down, and the curious labyrinth constructed by Rapp had been destroyed by cattle. †

The picture, it is true, may have been overdrawn, yet reorganization was necessary, and the Preliminary Society was promptly abolished. Another society was then formed and called the New Harmony Community of Equality, and a

* General Rules and Regulations proposed by Mr. Owen for the Independent Community, subject to such alterations as circumstances may require. Ohio Monitor, May 7, 1825.

† Missouri Republican, American Daily Advertiser, December 1, 1825.

new constitution was made. The principles now laid down for the guidance of the Community of Equality were, for those days, socialistic in the extreme. There was to be the utmost freedom of speech, absolute equality of rights and equality of duties, common ownership of property, co-operation to the fullest extent, and a rigid practice of economy. That these ends might be secured, the pursuits of daily life were classified, and six departments created and named—agriculture, manufacture, and mechanics; literature, science, and education; domestic economy; general economy; commerce.*

Under the watchful eye and fostering care of Owen the community now for the first time showed signs of prosperity. Idleness and waste gave place to industry and thrift such as had not been seen since the Rappites left New Harmony. Every man, every woman was busy in some chosen occupation. The streets were no longer full of groups of idle talkers. The meetings at Harmony Hall were held for business, and not for the vain display of oratory. To the community, moreover, had come men of marked ability. There were now gathered Charles Alexander Le Seur, a naturalist of note, an authority on turtles and fishes, and one of the company on the Péron during her voyage around the world; George Francis Vigo, the painter; Gerard Troost, the Dutch geologist; Thomas Say, the conchologist, who had been with Long across the plains; Robert Dale Owen; and William Maclure, of Philadelphia, a man of means, a geologist of distinction, and a firm believer in co-operation and the Pestalozzian system of education. He was often heard to assert that the community system must prevail; that the cities of the East had seen their best days; that houses and lots in them would no longer rise in value; that they would soon be literally deserted; and that, as he expressed it, men then living would see the day when foxes would stare from the windows of the crumbling buildings of Philadelphia. His mission was to conduct a school of industry in which " the arts that conquer the forces of Nature " should be taught.

The new constitution and the establishment of the six

---

* United States Gazette, March 21, 1826.

departments had been cheerfully accepted by the people. But the next reforms to be introduced bred trouble. First came a decree prescribing uniformity of dress. For men, the outer garments were to be a collarless jacket, drawn on over the head, pantaloons buttoned to the jacket, and a belt around the waist. The women were to wear pantalets, and a sleeveless frock that came down to the knees. Against this many of them openly rebelled, refused to wear the costume, and would have nothing to do with those who did. Still, the great projector did not lose heart. Such things were but the fruit of the irrational system in which the human race had been trained since the first man set foot on earth. They were painful and hard to endure, yet they must be borne with the patience of a reformer.

As such Owen took up his burden, and on the fourth of July, 1826, went one step further, and made a Declaration of Mental Independence which shocked and horrified far more people than it ever converted. Man, he said, up to that hour, all the world over, had been a slave to a trinity of the most monstrous evils that could possibly be combined to inflict mental and physical evils on the whole race. One was private or individual ownership of property; another was absurd and irrational systems of religion; the third was the marriage tie, which, he declared, ought to be made without any ceremony and terminated at the pleasure of those concerned. This was too much. His theories about property and co-operation, the arrangements of buildings, and the education of children were matters of opinion. In a land of toleration he might hold any religious belief or none. But the moment he touched the marriage rite he touched public morality, and his views were denounced from one end of the country to the other. Newspaper after newspaper attacked him. People whose friends, sisters, daughters had gone to New Harmony were shocked and alarmed. One anxious mother, whose three daughters were members of the Community, wrote to Maclure in great stress of mind to know what this declaration meant. He assured her that he had been six months in New Harmony, yet had seen no immorality, no vice; that he knew of no place where the married were so faithful and the young so chaste, " and for the best of reasons, for the bribe to abuse is taken away by all the cares, anxieties, and troubles of matrimony and a family of children being entirely removed by the Community educating, supporting, and providing for them." *

Hitherto the Community had been singularly prosperous. Emigrants had come in so fast that to provide them with lodgings had been found impossible, and those contemplating settlement had been warned to wait.† But now all was changed. Discord took the place of harmony, and in a little while three communities—New Harmony, Macluria, and Feiba Peven, a name which was gibberish for the latitude and longitude of New Harmony—existed on the land Owen bought from Rapp. Before another six months elapsed Owen was selling property to individuals, sign-boards were appearing, shops were opening, fences were going up, and New Harmony was taking on all the characteristics of a village of the unregenerated sort. Before a year had passed, Owen, discouraged by the wreck he saw about him, bade his followers farewell, and left them to their fate.‡ Many remained and formed little communities on lands held on long leases. Some were driven off as worthless. Numbers went home, or settled at Nevillsville, in Ohio. To-day the traveller who visits New Harmony can find no trace and scarce a reminiscence of the days of the Owenite Community of Equality.#

While these things were happening at New Harmony, other communities of a like kind were springing up on the frontier. ‖ Some enthusiasts at Cincinnati, carried away by the eloquence of Owen, bought land and founded the Yellow Springs Community in Ohio.ᴬ Others were started at Blue Springs, Indiana; at Forestville, Indiana; at Kendal, near Canton, Ohio; at Pittsburg; at Coxsackie, New York; at Haverstraw, New York; at Valley Forge,◊ Pennsylvania; and at

---

* Maclure's letter is printed in the United States Gazette, September 27, 1826.

† New Harmony Gazette, May 17, 1826. United States Gazette, June 9, 1826.

‡ American Daily Advertiser, May 31, June 6, July 3, 1827.

For satires on the Owenite movement, see Paulding's Three Wise Men of Gotham, and a dramatic piece, The New Lights of Harmony.

‖ Brief accounts of most of these are given in Noyes's American Socialism.

ᴬ This community disbanded within a year. New England Palladium, January 10, 1826.

◊ Preamble and constitution of the Friendly Association of Mutual Interests.

Nashoba, in Tennessee, which in many respects exceeded them all in interest. The foundress was Frances Wright, one of the early advocates in our country of what would now be called woman's rights. She was born at Dundee, in Scotland, but at the age of nineteen, animated by a strong desire to see the great Republic, she came to the United States and passed two years in New England. From girlhood she had been a devoted admirer of republics and the rights of man, an admiration which her life in New England intensified, and which she fully expressed on her return to England, in 1820, by publishing her views of society and manners in America. From England she went to France, and spent three years in the family of Lafayette. There, if possible, her partiality for our country was yet more increased, and in 1824 she returned to the United States, landed at a southern port, and, if her biographer may be trusted, became aware for the first time that slavery existed in the Republic she had fondly believed was founded on the rights of man. Horrified at the discovery, she set herself the task of finding some way of showing the people of the South that it was not impossible to gradually abolish slavery. She had been assured on every hand that the negro was incapable of education, that he would never work unless forced to, and that the whites would never be safe in the midst of a population of free Africans. To dispel this delusion, Miss Wright bethought herself of applying to the slave the same system of social education that Owen had applied to the laboring classes in Scotland. With this end in view, she visited the Rappites, made a study of the system of the Shakers, was present at New Harmony when the Rappites left and the Owenites began to arrive, and in the course of 1825 framed a plan of action. She proposed that sections of the public domain, or Congress land, as it was called, should be purchased in the cotton States; that colonies of one or two hundred slaves should be settled on each; that a system of co-operative labor on the community plan should be introduced, and the negroes and their children educated and made fit for freedom. The labor performed by each slave was to be rated at its full market value; the cost of food and clothes was to be deducted and the surplus set aside as a fund for the purchase of his freedom and that of his children, who mean-time were to be trained in a " school of industry." *

That an example of such a community might be set, Miss Wright, in the autumn of 1825, purchased a tract of twenty-four hundred acres on the Wolf river, thirteen miles from Memphis, and there planted a town which she called Nashoba. Her purpose was threefold: She wished to found a community in which the negro slave should be educated, trained, and made fit for freedom; she wished to emancipate him when educated, and so set an example which, if followed, would in the end abolish slavery in the South; and she wished to bring together in one village men and women of all nationalities who were eager to devote their lives to the search for truth and rational happiness. Money was freely given, and the experiment was tried. But Nashoba shared the fate of New Harmony, and in 1829 Miss Wright took her negroes off to Hayti, whither another abolitionist, Benjamin Lundy, was entreating his countrymen to send their manumitted slaves.

After the failure at Nashoba, Miss Wright went to New Harmony, and with Robert Dale Owen edited the Nashoba and New Harmony Gazette. But in the autumn of 1828 she entered the lecture field and made a tour of the chief cities, delivered courses of free lectures on education, manners, morals, and religion, and shocked her auditors by the boldness of her projects and the immorality of her teachings. Some were horrified at the appearance of a woman on the lecture platform; some thought her opinions on free education and the wisdom of co-operation little better than the vagaries of a lively imagination; but when she urged the abolition of the marriage rite, told her audiences that incompatibility of temper was good ground for divorce, and that no distinction ought to be made between legitimate and natural children, the cry for her suppression grew so fierce that it soon became almost impossible to secure a lecture hall, a church, a court-house, or a school in which to deliver her lectures. Yet she

* Genius of Universal Emancipation. United States Gazette, December 16, 28, 1825.

was not without followers. "Fanny Wright Societies" were formed in many towns and cities, the reforms she advocated were seriously undertaken, and New York city made the centre of the new movement. There an old wooden church was purchased, and, under the name of Hall of Science, it became the headquarters of the sect. To it in 1829 the New Harmony Gazette was removed and issued as the Free Enquirer. It claimed to be a weekly newspaper under the influence of no religious sect, controlled by no political party, and muzzled by no fear of lack of patronage. It was to be free to inquire into every social abuse; free to express any opinion it pleased on any subject social, moral, religious, or political; and was to be the friend of the working-man in his efforts to secure his rights.

Scarcely was the Free Enquirer established when the campaign opened and the working-men were summoned to meet and organize for defence of their rights. Hundreds responded, and before adjournment a committee of fifty was appointed to prepare a plan of organization and an address. At another meeting a month later an Assembly ticket was put in the field, and resolutions, which did duty as the platform of the Working-man's party, were adopted.* On this occasion Robert Dale Owen was present, acted as secretary, and was accused later with having had much to do with drafting the platform. This he denied, but the anti-religious, the communistic, the agrarian doctrines it contained leave no doubt that the Free Enquirers were in control, and had used the name of the working-man to make popular a social system which concerned him but little.

In the opinion of the reformers, the first appropriation of the soil of New York to private possession was "barbarously unjust." It was feudal in character, for those who were given enormous grants were in reality lords, and those who received little or nothing were no better than vassals. The hereditary transmission of wealth on the one hand, and of poverty on the other, thus provided for, had brought down to the generation then living all the ills of feudalism, and these were the

---

* The meeting was held October 19, 1829.

causes of present calamities. Banks and bankers were next denounced. A hundred broken banks, a thousand kinds of counterfeit notes, an army of bankers, " the greatest knaves, impostors, and paupers of the age," who had promised to redeem thirty-five million of papers with four million of specie, admonished the people to destroy banks altogether. A third form of privilege which ought to be destroyed was the exemption from taxation of churches, church property, and the property of priests under fifteen hundred dollars, for it was nothing short of a direct and positive robbery of the people. Auctions ought also to be regulated. As then conducted, they were a source of immense and unjust revenue to the auctioneers, who, without any return to the public beyond a small tax, divided two and even three millions of dollars among them each year. When the resolutions were adopted, an " Association for the Protection of Industry and for the Promotion of National Education " was formed, and every member pledged to support no man at the polls who would not support the cause of the people in the Legislature.

The seriousness of this movement, and the eagerness with which laborers, mechanics, clerks, men who belonged to every class of the great body of toilers, hastened to give it encouragement and support now brought into existence a new journal, and in October, 1829, the first number of The Workingman's Advocate made its appearance. The editors were two young mechanics who had caught the spirit of the age and were eager for the reform of society. "We think," said they in the prospectus of the Advocate, " we see in the existing state of society around us something radically wrong. We see one portion living in luxury and idleness. We see another engaged in employments which are useless or worse than useless. We see a third part—and it is the most numerous—groaning under the oppressions and miseries inflicted on it by the other two, and we see all suffering from the effects of vice produced by luxury and indolence, and of ignorance caused by poverty. We are therefore opposed to monopolies, exemptions, exclusive privileges. We consider it an exclusive privilege for one part of the community to have the means of education in college while another is restricted to the common schools, or forced by dire poverty to have no education at all. We are therefore in favor of a system of education equally open to all men." On the same principle the Advocate was opposed to banks in general, and to the Bank of the United States in particular, was against imprisonment for debt, against the ownership of land in large quantities by private individuals, and in favor of a lien law.

Shocking as these demands seemed to the clergy, the men of property, and the conservative part of the community, they were regarded as mild by a half-crazy Quaker named Russell Comstock, who now came forward as the agitator of reforms still more sweeping and radical. As described by himself in his handbills and advertisements, he was a " Ciderist," a steady friend to the downtrodden and oppressed, the enemy of monopolists, and a firm believer in equal rights for men and women. No man, he thought, was fit to be an assemblyman or a State senator who did not believe in the establishment of national schools, where children should be taught trades and morality, but not religion; who was not willing to see the wife put on a par with her husband; who did not advocate a lien law for working-men, the abolition of imprisonment for debt, a bankrupt law for the benefit of honest debtors, and the gradual abolition of all laws for the collection of debts. These were the principles of what he called " pure republicanism"; and that they might be tested he issued a call for a public meeting one day in October, and asked that all who came should be prepared to pledge themselves to give his pure republicanism a hearty support.

On the appointed day and hour quite a crowd gathered about the City Hall, from the steps of which Comstock made a long speech in explanation of his views. His hearers were so delighted that they nominated him for President, for State senator, for member of the Assembly, and would probably have gone on down the list of officers had not the constable arrested Comstock for disturbing the peace and carried him before a magistrate.* But he was not to be suppressed, and up to the day of election scattered handbills broadcast over the city.

---

* New York American, November 6, 1829.

Though his efforts did him little good—he received but one hundred and thirty-seven votes for member of the Assembly—they went far to arouse the working-men to support the ticket the committee of fifty had placed in the field. It was then the custom in New York to open the polls on three consecutive days. At the close of the first day it seemed so likely that the Working-men's Ticket would triumph that the journals which upheld the Republican cause called loudly on the friends of good order to rally. The general impression prevails, said one newspaper, that the ticket for Assembly got up by the disciples of Fanny Wright, and wrongfully called the Mechanics' Ticket, has received a large proportion of the votes given yesterday. Some have declared that it is far ahead of every other. Be this as it may, it becomes the friends of good order in this community, of whatever party, to go to the polls and by their votes prevent so shameful a result. Shameful it would be if even a moderate support were given to tickets prepared by persons who scoff at morality and demand a system of public robbery.* " We understand," said another, " with astonishment and alarm that the ' Infidel Ticket,' miscalled ' the Working-men's Ticket,' is far ahead of every other Assembly ticket in the city. What a state of things have we reached! A ticket got up openly and avowedly in opposition to all banks, in opposition to social order, in opposition to the rights of property, running ahead of every other! Is not this sufficient to startle men who have regard for the fundamental laws of society?" † On the second and third days the friends of religion and order thus appealed to did rally, and but one candidate on the Mechanics' Ticket, Ebenezer Ford, was elected.‡

The great vote cast for Ford—6,166—alarmed the community. All the horrors of anarchy seemed at hand. The " Fanny Wright Ticket," the " Infidel Ticket," was denounced, and the Legislature called on to unseat Mr. Ford. The leaders of this miscalled Mechanics' party, the people

---

* New York American, November 6, 1829; New York Evening Post, November 3, 1829.

† Courier and Enquirer, November 3, 1829.

‡ New York Evening Post, November 9, 1829.

were told, held that everything was wrong in the present state
of society, and that the whole system must be changed.
Their object was represented to be to turn the State into an
Owenite Community, confiscate all land and hold it for the
general use of the people, strike down religion, and abolish
marriage.

So horrid a picture of socialism disturbed the mechanics,
who now made haste to publicly disavow all connection with
Owen, with Fanny Wright and the Free Enquirers, and at a
ward meeting passed resolutions denying all sympathy with
the " Infidel Party "; repelling with scorn the charge that
they were hostile to the civil, moral, and religious institutions
of the country; and declaring agrarian laws to be debasing,
wicked, and dishonest. The New York Typographical Society
went further yet. Some time before the election the newly
formed Association for the Protection of Industry and the
Promotion of National Education sent to every organized
trade in the city a copy of the plan of the association, a pamphlet on National Education, by Robert Dale Owen, and a
request that the society would join in the effort to secure the
needed reforms. It was high time, the accompanying letter
said, that the friends of equal rights made a firm stand against
the unrepublican influences of the day. Labor was not only
unprotected, but was oppressed, despised, and stripped of its
just reward. There was no system of education affording
instruction to the children of the rich and poor alike; none
free from clerical and sectarian influences and class distinc-
tions; none suited to induce in the rising generation habits
of industry, plant principles of morality, or awaken feelings
of brotherly love. Yet it was possible to obtain a better system
of education and proper protection to industry if those most
concerned would bestir themselves. Let tracts be written
and scattered among the working-classes; let associations be
formed all over the land, and a regular correspondence carried
on between them; let the clergy be watched, and the needed
legislation would soon be obtained.

The Typographical Society, in common with the other
trade associations, having received these documents, proceeded
to consider them, and noticing that the pamphlet was written

by Owen, and the letter signed by Owen as secretary of the association, supposed he was also the author of the plan, and appointed a committee to report as to who he was and in what his scheme consisted. The committee assured the typesetters that Robert Dale Owen was a Scotchman, that he probably had never been naturalized, and that he had been assisted in his labors "by one Fanny Wright, also an exotic of some notoriety."

It does seem unaccountably strange, said the report, that a native of that part of the world where thousands are every day groaning under oppression should leave these unfortunates, come over to the New World, and in the midst of a people enjoying the fullest liberty proclaim himself the apostle of equal rights and tender them the hand of friendship against their oppressors. Such insolence might well be treated with contempt were it not for the fact that a band of choice spirits of foreign origin have united and, taking advantage of our mild laws, are sowing the seeds of discontent and rebellion. It is true that there is some distress among laboring people. It is true that labor is not as well paid as in times past; that a man working with his hands is now unable to earn as much as he once could. But in our country, at least, the distress is caused not by anything Owen would reform, but by the introduction of labor-saving machinery during the last thirty years. Has Owen any remedy to propose? Far from it. He calls on the working-men to associate for defence of their rights when no rights are endangered. The report ended with a repudiation of his plan and a denial of all sympathy with his purposes.* The Painters' Society, on the other hand, took a different view, admitted that much Mr. Owen said was true, and was disposed to favor his plan for free education. At Philadelphia, where the working-men supported a ticket at the October election for city and county officers, they too denied the charge of sympathy with Miss Wright as warmly as their fellow-laborers in New York. "We view," so ran a resolution adopted at a public meeting after the election, "the re-

---

* New York Evening Post, December 8, 1829. Free Enquirer, December 19 1829.

port charging us with being disciples of Miss Wright, and connecting religious points with our contention, as a base fabrication propagated by our enemies; we disclaim all adherence to Miss Wright's principles, and hold them foreign to our views, and appeal to the fact of the existence of the Working-men's party on the principles it now professes for nearly a year before she appeared among us."

But it mattered little whether the working-men avowed or disavowed sympathy with the Free Enquirers. The fact remained that a serious reform movement was well under way, and was spreading and gaining in importance daily. All over the country journals were appearing to advocate it, and societies were forming to labor in its behalf. In New York city the Telescope was busy exposing the designs of the clergy, and holding up to public view the dangers of ecclesiastical encroachment. At Rochester the Spirit of the Age was denouncing imprisonment for debt and capital punishment, and calling loudly for a mechanics' lien law. At Canton, in Ohio, the Farmers' and Mechanics' Society of Stark County had been founded to spread the new doctrines and agitate for co-operation and reform. At St. Louis there was a Society of Free Enquirers. In Alabama "The Ladies Bill," to give women the right to hold after marriage property which belonged to them before, was warmly debated in the Legislature, and in Tuscaloosa another Spirit of the Age upheld the cause of the people as vigorously as its Rochester contemporary. The Southern Free Press, of Charleston, South Carolina, announced its principles to be "No sect, no creed, open to all," and declared that it would collect such information as was useful to mechanics and working-men, and would look to them for support. "Our great object," said the editor in his prospectus, "will be to urge you to break down the barrier which separates your children from those of lordly aristocrats by the establishment of national schools." At New Castle, in Delaware, an Association of Working People was formed with a membership open to any person twenty-one years of age who was engaged in any branch of productive labor. How is it, said the preamble to their constitution, that all classes save the laboring are heard in the Legislature? The commercial, the agricultural, the manufacturing ask for protection, and it is granted. But what is accorded the working-man? Nothing. Yet who needs protection more? The price of labor is hourly going down because of the numbers thrown out of employment by labor-saving machinery. The cost of every article of consumption meantime is increased by taxation. " Does not the present system under such circumstances tend to increase the poverty of the poor and add to the riches of the rich? " Let us then be represented in the Legislature. Let us unite at the polls and give our votes to no candidate who is not pledged to support a rational system of education to be paid for out of the public funds, and to further a rightful protection of the laborer. At Wilmington, Delaware, was another Free Press likewise pledged " to be open to all for the free, chaste, and temperate discussion of subjects connected with the welfare of the human family." Its mission was " to arouse the attention of working-men to the importance of co-operation in order to attain the rank and station in society to which they are justly entitled by virtue of industry, but from which they are excluded by want of a system of equal republican education." In New York city two new journals of a strongly agrarian sort began their career early in 1830. The one, The Friend of Equal Rights, demanded the equal division of property among the adults of a family at the age of maturity. The other, the Daily Sentinel, was devoted " to the interests of mechanics and other working-men," and at once became a political power. Indeed, it was started for the sole purpose of becoming such a power.

The late election in the city made it clear that the working-men had, in the language of our time, bolted their party, had supported a ticket which was not put forward by any political faction, and had done so because they were discontented, and because they did not believe that their grievances would ever be removed by the men then in power. Six thousand votes cast solidly for or against any of the three parties then struggling for control in the city and State was too serious a matter to be treated lightly, and each of the three began to strive eagerly for the support of the working-man.

These three parties were the friends of Adams and Clay,

who called themselves the Administration party; the friends of Jackson and Van Buren, who were known as the regular Republicans, and the Antimasons. The Republicans, with a show of public virtue to which they could lay small claim, sought to destroy the union of Working-men and Free Enquirers, and, in the hope of doing so, raised the cry of Infidel party, and called on the priests and ministers of every sect to stop the new movement. They expressed horror at the communistic and agrarian doctrine of the so-called Mechanics' party and its organ, the Daily Sentinel, and summoned manufacturers, business men, land-owners, farmers, " bank gentlemen," and friends of law and order to rally to the support of popular government; they held ward meetings and county conventions, and under the name of mechanics and working-men protested against the doctrines of Frances Wright and Robert Dale Owen. But all in vain.

From the city the movement spread to the State, where it was taken up by the leaders of every one of the innumerable knots of anti-regency, anti-Van Buren, Antimasonic and Clay Republicans. At the charter election in Albany, in the spring of 1830, the working-men united on a ticket and carried four wards out of five. In Troy the same course was pursued, and " not one regency man," it was boastfully said, was elected. For this they were ridiculed by the Republican or Jackson press as " workies," and were held up as Federalists, as " the old enemy in a new disguise," as men bent on the destruction of society. When the autumn came and the time approached for the election of State officials, a convention was called to meet at Salina and name working-men's candidates for Governor and Lieutenant-Governor. Seventy delegates from thirteen counties responded, and put Erastus Root and Nathaniel Pitcher in the field, but neither would accept. To this convention New York city sent two delegations, one of which was rejected; whereupon it met and nominated a rival working-men's ticket, on which were the names Smith and Hertlett. Neither of these men were serious candidates. The strength and the weakness of the party was in New York city, where, in September, a meeting was held in the North American Hotel. All who were in favor of a republican system of education; all who approved of the abolition of imprisonment for debt; who believed in protection to American industries; who were against the auction system; against monopolies, regency dictation, and Tammany management; all who were ready to resist encroachments on the rights of the people, were bidden to come and frame a ticket for Congress and the Assembly. This was a serious movement, and to the ticket then and there made was given the name North American Clay Working-men's Ticket. The platform declared it to be the duty of the Government to extend the means of education as widely as the population; complained of the militia system as an unnecessary and useless oppression of the laboring man; described imprisonment for debt as a relic of barbarism, and called for its abolition; demanded the protection of American industry; * and indorsed Francis Granger, the Antimasonic candidate for Governor. In return for this the Antimasons a little later formally approved the municipal part of the North American Clay Working-men's Ticket, and the union between the two factions, denounced by the Jackson newspapers as the Paul Cliffords and Jonathan Wildes of politics and morality, was complete.

From this union of petty opposition, malcontents, and aspiring politicians—a union of what in derision was called Clayism, antimasonry, and Workeyism—two classes of would-be workmen were carefully excluded: those who followed Fanny Wright and those who followed a leader named Skidmore, editor of the Daily Sentinel. The Fanny Wright party —the Infidel party, as they were called by their opponents; the Liberal Working-men's party, as they named themselves— held a convention at Syracuse and nominated Ezekiel Williams for Governor. The Skidmore or Agrarian Working-men, or, as they wished to be known, the Poor Man's party, chose James Burt, a farmer, and Jonas Humbert, a baker, as candidates for Governor and Lieutenant-Governor, and at the November election gave them one hundred and fifteen votes. Williams received two thousand. The Working-men and Antimasons polled nearly eight thousand votes.

* New York American, November 2, 1830.

Of all the political parties that have ever attained importance in our country, the most remarkable was the Antimasonic. The events which brought it into existence, the rapidity with which it rose to power, the limitation of its power to the New England belt of emigration, its sudden decline, and the traces of its existence left on our political institutions, all combine to make its history of no common interest.

Some time in the spring of 1826 rumors were current in western New York that William Morgan, a stone-mason of Batavia, had written a book revealing the secrets of freemasonry, and that David C. Miller, a printer in that village, was putting the work to press. Morgan was a native of Culpeper County, Virginia, where he was born in 1776. By trade he was a stone-mason and bricklayer, and, having by industry and frugality saved a little money, he began business as a small shopkeeper at Richmond. Wearying of this, he moved to York, in Upper Canada, where, in 1821, he became a brewer, and was fast acquiring a competence when fire consumed his brewery, reduced him to poverty, and led him to remove first to Rochester and then to Batavia. There he once more became a bricklayer, was made a member of the lodge of Royal Arch Masons at Le Roy in 1825, and in 1826 signed a petition praying for the establishment of a chapter at Batavia. Before the petition was presented some objection was made to his signature, because if a charter were granted he would in consequence become a member of the new lodge, where his presence would be most undesirable. A second petition was therefore written and presented without the signature of Morgan, who, when the charter arrived and the chapter was organized, was deeply mortified to find that he was not a member. Then it is probable he determined to be avenged not only on his fellow-townsmen who had excluded him from their lodge, but on the whole masonic fraternity, and formed the plan of writing a book revealing the secrets of masonry. However this may be, it is certain that in March, 1826, a contract was made with David C. Miller, editor of the Republican Advocate, a weekly newspaper published at Batavia, binding Morgan to write a book which Miller was pledged to print and publish.

As reports of the intended publication passed from mouth to mouth the respectable part of the community gave them no heed, or regarded the forthcoming book as a catchpenny for hawkers and pedlers. But there were among the Masons a few hot-heads, who took alarm, and, having made up their minds that the book should never appear, went on to carry out their decision, and began with intimidation. Many patrons of Miller's newspaper suddenly withdrew their subscriptions; suits were commenced against him to enforce the payment of small debts; and threats were made which led him to believe that an attack on his office was meditated. Even Morgan did not escape, and one day in August an abusive " notice and caution " was published in a Canandaigua newspaper called the Ontario Messenger, and was reprinted in the Batavia Spirit of the Times and the People's Press.

The publicity thus given to the matter now attracted the attention of a man of some means, who believed that, rightly managed, the book would prove to be a source of great profit. He came to Batavia accordingly, took lodgings at the tavern, represented himself as a Canadian, gave his name as Daniel Johns, and soon offered to join Miller in the publication of Morgan's book. The offer was gladly accepted. Johns was admitted to the partnership, advanced forty dollars, and obtained possession of some of the manuscript. The little he saw was enough to convince him that the book would never succeed, and a demand was at once made on Miller for a return of the money. Failing in this, Johns sued out a warrant before a magistrate of Le Roy. On the night of that same day some fifty men, under the lead of a resident of Canandaigua, met at a tavern in Stafford and marched thence to Batavia for the purpose of breaking into the printing office and destroying the manuscript and printed sheets of the book; but something deterred them, and no attack was made till the night of Sunday, September tenth, when the two buildings used by Miller as printing offices were discovered to be on fire. The flames were extinguished, and on examination it was found that an incendiary had been at work. The sides of the buildings were smeared with turpentine. A brush used for the purpose was picked up near by, and balls of cotton and whisps of straw soaked with turpentine were found under the stairways. Meantime early in the morning of this same Sunday Nicholas G. Chesebro, of Canandaigua, a hatter by trade, and one of the coroners of Ontario County, obtained from Jeffrey Chipman, justice of the peace, a warrant for the arrest of Morgan on a charge of stealing a shirt and cravat from an innkeeper named Kingsley. Armed with this, and attended by the constable and a small posse, Chesebro repaired to Batavia, and on Monday, September eleventh, Morgan was apprehended. The prisoner had been arrested for debt in July, was at that time on the limits of the jail, and could not lawfully be taken without them. But it mattered not, and in utter defiance of law he was carried to Canandaigua, and there discharged by the justice when it was proved that the shirt and cravat were borrowed and not stolen. The next minute he was rearrested for an old debt of two dollars and sixty-five cents due an innkeeper, confessed judgment, and, stripping off his coat, asked the constable to levy on it. The request was refused, and Morgan was sent to the common jail. There he remained till about nine o'clock on the night of September twelfth, when a man named Loton Lawson appeared at the jail, paid the debt, persuaded the jailer's wife, who was in charge in her husband's absence, to liberate the prisoner, and came out of the jail with Morgan on his arm. When a few yards from the door, Morgan was seized by a number of men, and, despite his struggles and cries of murder, was hurried into a carriage. Many persons living near heard his cries, and one man, hurrying from his house to ascertain the cause, met Edward Sawyer and Nicholas G. Chesebro, who were standing by quiet spectators of the scene, and asked what was the matter. Chesebro answered, "Nothing, only a man has been let out of jail and has been taken on a warrant and is going to be tried." Thus assured, he did not interfere, and the carriage was driven to Rochester. Just beyond the town a change of carriage, horses, and driver was made, after which Morgan was taken westward along the ridge road toward Lewiston. As the journey proceeded the utmost secrecy is said to have been observed. Public houses were avoided as much as possible, the blinds of the carriage

were always pulled down, and horses furnished by Masons
living along the road were exchanged in secluded places.
When Niagara County was reached, Eli Bruce, the high
sheriff, took the party in charge, and went with the carriage
to Lewiston.   There, in the dead of night, Morgan was put
into another carriage, which was driven by way of Youngstown
to Fort Niagara, about a mile beyond the town.   The fort had
been unoccupied since the troops left it in May, 1826, but was
in charge of a keeper.   Save this man and his wife and a Mr.
Giddins, who kept the ferry and lived directly on the bank
of the river, no human beings dwelt near the fort, into the
stone magazine of which Morgan is said to have been hurried
near dawn on the morning of September fourteenth.   At this
place all trace of him disappears, and what then became of him
has never been revealed to this day.

When Morgan was arrested at Batavia, and in defiance
of law was taken to Canandaigua, one of the witnesses to the
proceedings was David C. Miller, who protested vigorously
against the outrage.   For this and for his connection with
Morgan and the book, it was now determined to quiet Miller.
On Tuesday, September twelfth, accordingly, about noon a
band of some sixty men, armed with cudgels, appeared in
Batavia and put up at one of the taverns, while Jesse French,
a constable, went off armed with the process sworn out by
Daniel Johns four days before, arrested Miller at the printing
office, and brought him to the house where the mob was gathered.   After some delay, he was placed in a wagon guarded
by armed men and taken to Le Roy, where, about nine at
night, he succeeded in forcing his captors to bring him before
the justice who issued the warrant.   But as neither constable,
warrant, nor plaintiff appeared, he was discharged, and made
his way back to Batavia.

Burning with indignation, Miller now published a long
account of his treatment by the Masons and of the abduction
and probable murder of Morgan, and appealed to the public
to vindicate the majesty of the law.   His friends quickly responded, an investigation was begun, and an agent * sent to

---

* Miller's account taken from his newspaper of September 18, 1826, is reprinted in the second edition of Illustrations of Masonry.

Canandaigua, where sworn statements were secured from the wife of the jailer, from a prisoner, from some people who resided near the jail, and finally from Mrs. Morgan. The publicity given to this testimony was followed by great excitement and by a series of public meetings, at one of which a committee was chosen to gather information. By its authority a short statement of the facts was written and published, with the request that every newspaper editor would give the notice a few insertions, and that anybody having information regarding Morgan's fate or present whereabouts would send it to the committee. The Governor was next appealed to, and went through the idle form of issuing a proclamation calling on the civil authorities to spare no pains to arrest the offenders and to prevent such outrages in future.

As time passed and the mystery remained as impenetrable as ever, the excitement spread to other counties, and committees of investigation were soon at work in Livingston, Ontario, Monroe, and Niagara. By these the Governor was again appealed to, and late in October he offered a reward of three hundred dollars for the discovery of the offenders and one hundred dollars for the discovery of each and every one of them, and two hundred dollars for authentic information of the place where Morgan had been conveyed. Still the mystery was not solved, and when the November session of the Court of General Sessions was held at Canandaigua the grand jury could do nothing more than find two indictments against Chesebro, Lawson, Sawyer, and John Sheldon. The trial began on the first of January, 1827, in the Court of Oyer and Terminer, before Judge Throop, and aroused intense interest in all the western counties of the State. For days before the court met the taverns at Canandaigua and the nearby towns were crowded to excess by counsel, witnesses, and those drawn thither by curiosity. Seventy applicants for lodgings were turned away from one tavern during one day.

The charges against the defendants were two in number—conspiracy to seize Morgan, and conspiracy to carry him to foreign parts and there secrete and confine him. Chesebro, Sawyer, and Lawson plead guilty, and were sentenced, Lawson to two years, Chesebro to one year, and Sawyer to one month imprisonment in the common jail of Ontario County. Sheldon stood trial, was found guilty, and was confined in the jail for three months. Had the men been acquitted, the disgust and indignation of that part of the community which owed no allegiance to masonry could not have been greater. In its opinion the whole masonic fraternity was now in league to shield the murderers of Morgan. The sentence of the court was described as an insult to an enlightened people; the newspapers were accused of suppressing facts, of holding back information, and of taking no notice of any public proceeding concerning Morgan. At Seneca the people, in mass meeting assembled, resolved that all secret societies were dangerous to freedom; that masonry was especially so, as Masons had now shown themselves ready to murder their fellow-men in the interests of their order; that no Mason should be supported for any public office; and that every newspaper which did not publish full accounts of Morgan meetings must be proscribed. The committees appointed by the towns, convinced that the trial had been a farce, that the pleas of guilty were to stop investigation, and that the affidavits of Chesebro, Sawyer, and Lawson did not begin to disclose all they knew, called for a convention at Lewiston for the purpose of determining what steps should be taken to restore Morgan to his country, his freedom, and his family; to discover and punish those who had by violence and fraud deprived him of his liberty and perhaps of his life; to disclose the extent of the conspiracy; and to make known to the public the motives which prompted the conspirators to acts ruinous to our free institutions.

While the Lewiston committee was gathering information, all manner of guesses as to the fate of Morgan were made. One newspaper asserted that he was kept at Fort Niagara a few days and then put to death. Another maintained that three men took him into Canada; that Captain Brant, a son of the Mohawk chief whose name is forever joined with the massacres in Wyoming and Cherry Valley, was asked to send him to the northwest coast; that when Brant refused, some British officers were urged to take him down the St. Lawrence, and that when they declined Morgan was killed and his body flung into the river. Yet another version represents him as led, bound and blindfolded, to Newark, Upper Canada, only to be brought back to the fort and executed.

So firm was the belief that Morgan had at one time at least been taken over the border, that the Lieutenant Governor of Upper Canada offered a reward of fifty pounds for information as to his whereabouts,* and Brant publicly denied that he had ever been asked to dispose of Morgan.† At the request of the Lewiston committee, Governor Clinton now issued a third proclamation, offering one thousand dollars for the discovery of Morgan if alive, and, if dead, two thousand dollars for the discovery of the murderers.‡

When the spring local elections came on, the excitement against the Masons took on a political form. It was now not uncommon to find five, six, even seven columns of a newspaper filled with accounts of Morgan meetings, and the assertions and counter-assertions of private citizens. The people of one town resolved not to support a Mason for any office, State, county, or town; those of a second declared that they deemed " Freemasons unfit for any office of confidence "; those of a third dismissed their minister because he belonged to the fraternity; the resolution adopted at Poultney reads: " We will not hear any person preach unless the said preacher should refuse to meet with any lodge of Freemasons, and openly declare that masonry is bad "; at Middlebury a town meeting was warned " for the purpose of taking into consideration the late masonic outrages and to make nominations to fill the different offices in this town."

To such a height had the popular feeling been raised that the county committees, finding that sometimes, as in the case of Niagara County, the grand juries were packed and would not indict, and at others, as in Monroe County, the grand juries could secure no direct testimony, though much circumstantial evidence, and so failed to return a bill, appealed by petitions to the Legislature. These early in March were laid before the Assembly, and sent to the Committee on Courts of Justice. But finding that a majority of the members were

---

* American Daily Advertiser, February 19, 1827.
† York Observer, February 26, 1827.   ‡ March 19, 1827.

Masons, it asked to be discharged, and the papers went to another. The report when made closed with a statement that, having failed to devise a tribunal for the investigation of the outrage, a tribunal with jurisdiction over the whole extent of country covered by the conspiracy, with power to enforce the attendance of witnesses, with right to imprison such as refused to obey, and with authority to arrest and hold for trial, yet not infringe the chartered privileges of the humblest citizen, nothing was left but to recommend a joint committee of investigation and a reward of five thousand dollars for the discovery of Morgan if living, and a like sum for the apprehension of his murderers if he were dead. Resolutions embodying these suggestions were, however, voted down by a great majority of nearly three to one.*

The refusal of the Legislature to act, the continued failure of grand juries to indict, the silence of the masonic newspapers, or, what was worse, the imperfect reports of Morgan meetings, and even positive assertions that Morgan was not dead, served but to increase the excitement. The whole population of Ontario, Monroe, Livingston, Genesee, Erie, Niagara, and Orleans Counties seemed arrayed as Masons and Antimasons. In Genesee, where the feeling was especially strong, a great meeting of citizens of the county was held at Batavia, and every voter pledged to support none but Antimasons. Three thousand people, men and women, were estimated to have been present. This was followed by a call from the " Morgan Committee " for a convention at Warsaw to nominate a candidate for the State Senate.

Without the limits of New York, Antimasonry excited little or no interest. In many places it was regarded as a shrewd electioneering movement. At others it was believed that the commotion had been stirred up in order to sell a new edition of an old book, and that Morgan had been abducted by his friends.

To disprove these rumors and, if possible, confirm the belief that he had been murdered, the Lewiston committee

---

* Albany Argus, April 12, 1827. The report of the committee is in Niles's Register, April 14, 1827, vol. xxxii, pp. 120, 121.

kept boats and vessels busy for months dredging the Niagara river and the shore of Lake Ontario. But no body was found till one day in October, when a hunting party discovered a corpse stranded on the lake shore some forty miles from Fort Niagara. A coroner was at once sent for, an inquest was held, and, as the body was in such an advanced stage of decomposition as not to be recognizable, a verdict of drowning was rendered and the remains buried on the beach. In ordinary times an event so common would have passed unnoticed. But these were no ordinary times, and the report of the coroner was no sooner published than the Lewiston committee began to suspect that the dead man had been Morgan. Hurrying to the spot, the grave was opened, and what seemed a strong resemblance to Morgan was recognized. The coroner thereupon assembled a new jury, examined Mrs. Morgan and a host of men who knew her husband, and, influenced by the testimony so collected, a verdict was rendered by the jury that the body was that of Morgan. The corpse was then removed with great ceremony to Batavia, where it was interred in the presence of an immense crowd.

The account of these proceedings soon reached Canada and came before the eyes of the friends of a man named Timothy Monro, who in September was drowned by the upsetting of his boat in the Niagara river. The description of the body, and especially of the clothing and the bundle of tracts in the pockets, convinced them that the corpse found on the beach was not that of Morgan, but of Monro. So sure were they that they came to Batavia, persuaded the coroner to hold a third inquest, and presented evidence so overwhelming that a third verdict was obtained, and the unknown dead declared to have been Timothy Monro. The fate of Morgan then remained as impenetrable a mystery as before.

By this time Miller had published the now famous " Illustrations of Masonry by One of the Fraternity who has devoted Thirty Years to the Subject "; the Lewiston committee had given to the world a long " Narrative of the Facts and Circumstances relating to the Kidnapping and Presumed Murder of William Morgan," and in the local elections some seventeen thousand votes had been cast for Antimasons. To secede from the fraternity and make a public declaration of the fact became the most popular act an aspiring politician, a doctor with small practice, or a tradesman with little business could perform. So great was the defection that in February, 1828, a convention of seceding Masons was held at Le Roy. Morgan's " Illustrations of Masonry " was there declared to be a fair and full exposition of the first three degrees; a committee was appointed to prepare and publish all degrees above that of master; a memorial was ordered to be sent to Congress complaining of the use of Fort Niagara for the imprisonment of Morgan, and a second convention called to meet July fourth. Shortly after the delegates had gone home yet another body, representing the Antimasons of the twelve western counties of New York, assembled in the same town. The address which it issued to the people of the State set forth that the existence in such a country as ours of any society whose purpose, principles, and measures are secret is hostile to the spirit and dangerous to the existence of free institutions; that masonry was such a society, and had showed itself ready to subvert law and defy justice in furthering its own ends; that the entire subjection all over the Union of the press to masonry was an evil which called for correction; that it was necessary for the people to establish free presses with editors ready and willing to uphold the rights of citizens and the laws of the land; and that a convention of Antimasons ought to meet at Utica and take measures to destroy masonry as an institution, to establish free presses, assert the supremacy of the law, and protect the rights of citizens against the vindictive persecutions of masonic bodies.*

This was a serious movement. A presidential election was at hand; congressmen, a Governor, a State Legislature were to be chosen, and the political results of the convention were quickly apparent. When the memorial from Le Roy reached Congress, no committee wanted to receive it, and a good excuse was found for sending the paper to the President.

When Pitcher, who by the death of De Witt Clinton in

---

* Proceedings of a Convention of Delegates opposed to Freemasonry, which met at Le Roy, Genesee County, N. Y., March 6, 1828.

February had become Governor of New York, heard of the proceedings at Le Roy, he lost no time in urging the Legislature to act, and easily obtained authority to appoint a special commissioner to investigate the Morgan affair. When the memorial from the convention was laid before the Legislature, it was found to contain a request that, as the masonic oaths were profane and impious, no oaths should be allowed unless administered by a public officer. This was not granted, though an act to do so was passed by the Assembly.

Much stress was now laid on the character of the masonic oaths, and no pains were spared to excite the animosity of the churches and array them against masonry. Its oaths were depicted as shockingly unchristian, its ceremonies as sacrilegious, and the whole institution as antireligious in that it profaned Holy Scripture by using it for unholy purposes, made religion a performance of outward duties, confounded knight-errantry with Christianity, and was regarded by its members as a saving institution.*

To the American proud of his country and her free institutions, to the firm believer in democracy, the appeal was made from the standpoint of politics. He was assured by men who had once been Masons that the very design and purpose of freemasonry were hostile to the principles of our Government and the welfare of society. He was told that it exercised an absolute jurisdiction over the lives and persons of its members, and, with the recollection of the Morgan case in mind, he believed the statement. He was assured that it arrogated to itself the right to administer oaths and to punish for offences unknown to the law; that it hid crime and protected the guilty; assumed titles and dignities not compatible with republican institutions; and created an aristocracy odious in the sight of a free people. †

---

* Two oaths were cited as especially offensive: "Furthermore do I promise and swear that I will aid and assist a companion royal arch Mason wherever I shall see him engaged in any difficulty, so far as to extricate him from the same, whether he be right or wrong." "I swear to advance my brother's best interests by always supporting his military fame and political preferment in opposition to another."

† Proceedings of the Convention of Seceding Masons, held at Le Roy, July 4, 1828.

The effect of such charges was lasting. Gradually a firm conviction took possession of the public mind that masonry was all it was said to be; that it did exercise a too powerful influence on the press; that it did control the acts of tribunals of justice in civil as well as in criminal cases; and that judges, juries, justices of the peace, and even referees had been forced to do its will.

In this state of the public mind the antimasonic convention assembled at Utica in August to take measures, so the call said, to destroy masonry as an institution, and, fully satisfied that no help would be given by either the friends of Adams or of Jackson for such a purpose, it disregarded both parties, nominated candidates of its own for Governor and Lieutenant-Governor of New York, and appointed a general committee to call future conventions if necessary. The candidates selected were Francis Granger and John Crary. Granger, who had already been nominated for Lieutenant-Governor by the Adams party, declined, and at a second convention of Antimasons at Le Roy, Solomon Southwick was chosen in his stead, and polled more than thirty thousand votes.

Meanwhile the excitement had spread to Vermont, where, in the congressional election of 1829, seven thousand votes were cast by the Antimasons. The whole New England belt from Boston to Buffalo fairly teemed with antimasonic newspapers.* A new political party had arisen to complicate still more the political situation in New York, and, indeed, in all the States from New England to Ohio.

---

* There were thirty-two in New York State.

7

Flush Times

THE social and economic conditions of the working people in the cities—conditions out of which the early labor movements grew—did indeed call loudly for reform. Ten years of rapid industrial development had brought into prominence problems of urban life and municipal government familiar enough to us, but new and quite beyond solution in 1825. The influx of paupers to partake of the benefits of the many charitable societies; the overcrowded labor market; the steadily increasing number of unemployed; the housing of the poor; the rise of the tenement house; the congestion of population in limited areas, with all its attendant vice and crime; and the destitution produced by low wages and lack of constant employment, had already become matters for serious consideration. An unskilled laborer, a hod-carrier, a wood-sawyer, a wood-piler in a city was fortunate if he received seventy-five cents for twelve hours of work and found employment for three hundred days in a year. Hundreds were glad to work for thirty-seven and even twenty-five cents a day in winter who in spring and summer could earn sixty-two and a half or perhaps eighty-seven and a half cents by toiling fourteen hours. On the canals and turnpikes fifteen dollars a month and found in summer and one third that sum in winter were considered good pay. In truth, it was not uncommon during the winter for men to work for their board. Nothing but perfect health, steady work, sobriety, the strictest economy, and the help of his wife could enable a married man to live on such wages. But the earnings of women were lower yet. Many trades and occupations now open to them either had no existence or were then confined to men. They might bind shoes, sew rags, fold and stitch books, become spoolers, or make coarse shirts and duck pantaloons at eight or ten cents a piece. Shirt-making was eagerly sought after, because the garments could be made in the lodgings of the seamstress, who was commonly the mother of a little family, and often a widow. Yet the most expert could not finish more than nine shirts a week, for which she would receive seventy-two or ninety cents. Fifty cents seems to have been the average.

To the desperate poverty produced by such wages many evils were attributed. Intemperance was encouraged, children were sent into the streets to beg and pilfer, and young girls were driven to lives of shame to an extent which but for the report of the Magdalene Society in New York and the action of the people * elsewhere would be incredible. The cities, in short, were growing with great rapidity, and were exhibiting every phase of life.

At New York, now the metropolis of the country, the growth of the city was astonishing to its own citizens. The population numbered one hundred and sixty-two thousand, an increase of forty thousand in five years. To keep pace with such an inpouring of strangers was hardly possible. More than three thousand buildings were under way in 1825; † yet such was the press that not an unoccupied dwelling house existed in the entire city, and it was quite common to see families living in houses with unfinished floors, with windows destitute of sashes, and in which the carpenters had not hung a single door. Nor was this an accident. Year after year the same thing occurred, and on one first of May—the great " moving day "—three hundred homeless people gathered in the park with their household goods and were lodged in the jail till the houses they had rented were finished and made habitable.

* At Portland the people on three occasions gathered and pulled down houses of ill fame. Portland Argus, November 11 and 14, 1825. A similar riot occurred in Boston. New York Evening Post, August 1, 1825.

† Most of these houses were built by speculators, and were erected so cheaply and hastily that several fell down while in course of construction; others were torn down by order of the authorities.

In the upper wards entire blocks of fine brick buildings had arisen on sites which in 1820 were covered with marshes or occupied with straggling frame huts of little value. In the neighborhood of Canal Street a new city stood on what a few years before was the shore of a stagnant pool. In Greenwich new streets had been opened, and all along the Bowery new houses had been put up. Never in the history of the city had its commerce been greater. Ten million dollars had been collected in duties in one year, a sum larger by eighty thousand than in the same time had been gathered at the custom-houses of Boston, Philadelphia, Baltimore, Norfolk, and Savannah combined. Sixteen packets plied regularly between the city and Liverpool. Four more were engaged in trade with Havre. Seven were in the Savannah line, ten in the Charleston line, and four in the New Orleans, while innumerable brigs, sloops, schooners, and steamboats made stated trips to every seaport of importance on the coast. The city, it was said boastfully, was visited by merchants of every clime and from every part of the United States, so that New York might truly be called the mart of nations. Nor was this an idle boast. Five hundred new mercantile houses were said to have been established in the city in the early months of 1825, a statement well borne out by the crowded condition of the mercantile newspapers. The Gazette in seven days contained 1,115 new advertisements,* and in one issue, a week later, printed 213, and stated that 23 others were left out for want of space.†

There were now twelve banks in the city, with an aggregate capital of thirteen millions of dollars, paying dividends of from five to eight per cent., and ten marine insurance companies with a capital of ten million dollars. Yet even these were not enough to transact the volume of business, and when the Legislature met applications were made for charters for twenty-seven more banks with a combined capital of twenty-two and a half millions, and for thirty-one corporations of all sorts with a total capital of fifteen millions.

Thirteen hundred sailing vessels entered the port yearly.

---

* New York Gazette, April 14 to 21, 1825.
† New York Gazette, April 26, 1825.

Such as came from Great Britain were always crowded with emigrants, of whom more than five thousand arrived annually. Since 1819 some thirty-four thousand aliens had been landed in the city. Seven eighths of these were artisans, laborers, and skilled workmen, and, while some found homes in the West or went off to other cities or to inland towns, a large proportion remained and constituted an element hard to govern, for the machinery of government was of the rudest kind. Despite its growing wealth and commercial importance, New York was in many respects but a town. Population had poured into it with such rapidity that it had become large in area before it had ceased to be small in customs, usages, and the administration of affairs. Over it presided a mayor, a recorder, the aldermen, and a few officials in charge of what have since become departments of city government, some of which now expend more money each year than in 1825 was used in governing the entire State. The mayor was elected by the aldermen, who, one from each ward, were elected by the people, and were required two at a time to serve as judges in the Court of General Sessions for the city and county. The few departments in existence were of a humble kind, and were aided in the discharge of the duties assigned them by the citizens. There was a superintendent of streets, but he had little to do with cleaning them. Every occupant of a dwelling house or other building, every owner of a vacant lot on any paved street, must twice a week, from April to December, scrape and sweep the pavement before his premises as far as the middle of the roadway, must gather the dirt in a heap, and on it must place the ashes and rubbish brought out from his house or cellar. The city was responsible for nothing but the removal of the rubbish and the sweeping of paved streets before unoccupied houses at the cost of the owner. Between December and April no street-cleaning was attempted, and the sole scavengers became the hogs, who were suffered to range at large provided they had rings in their noses.

There was a rude sort of fire department, consisting of the chief engineer and his assistants, of the firewardens, and the firemen, hosemen, hook-and-ladder men, whose duty it was to drag the engines to the burning building and attach the hose. Each firewarden was assigned to a particular engine, was responsible for the supply of water, and formed the citizens in two lines stretching from his engine to the nearest pump or well. Up one line went the full buckets; down the other came the empty ones. These buckets belonged to the citizens. Each occupant of a house was still required to have in his front hall the old-fashioned leather bucket marked with his initials, the number of his house, and the name of his street. If his house had three or less fireplaces, he must keep one bucket; three to six fireplaces, two buckets; six to nine fireplaces, four buckets; which on the alarm of fire he must put out on the sidewalk to be carried off by the first passer-by. After the fire had been extinguished the owner must seek his property at the City Hall. At night the watch cried the name of the street in which the burning building was, and every occupant of a house put a lighted candle in his window.

The peace of the city was kept in the day by the constables, and in the night by the watch. The city was marked out into four districts, over each of which presided two " captains of the night watch." One served every other night, had command of as many watchmen as the Common Council saw fit to give him, assigned the men to their " rounds," and saw that they kept sober and were diligent.

The high constable, the constables, and the marshals enforced the ordinances, some of which are curious enough to be mentioned. In the crowded part of the city—that south of Grand Street on the east side and Vestry Street on the west —no horse attached to a carriage, gig, chaise, or coach could be driven faster than " slow trot," and must turn every corner walking. No drayman or cartman could sit on his wagon unless by reason of old age a special dispensation was given him by the aldermen. He must walk beside his horse. No team driven tandem could go faster than a walk. On Sunday drivers of vehicles and horsemen must walk very slowly past churches and places of worship during divine service. If a congregation pleased, chains could be hung across the street before the place of worship during service, and all passing of horses and carriages stopped. Nobody could fish on the Lord's Day; nor drive nor wade a horse into the waters of either river; nor deliver milk between nine in the morning and five in the afternoon; nor buy nor sell; nor bring anything into nor take anything out of the city.

Restrictions of this sort were by no means peculiar. Indeed, there was little in the city government of New York that could not be paralleled in that of Philadelphia. There, too, were a mayor, a recorder, fifteen aldermen, and select and common council. The people elected councils. But the Governor of Pennsylvania appointed the recorder and the aldermen to hold office during good behavior, and the councils each year elected one of the aldermen to serve as mayor. Even in the selection of so important an officer as the constable the people had little to say. Annually the voters of each ward were required to elect two persons fit to be constables, and one of them must be appointed to the office by the mayor.

In Philadelphia, as in New York, occupants of houses must have the pavement before their premises swept to the middle of the street every Friday or pay a fine of five shillings. These sweepings the city would remove; but ashes, mud, shavings, or refuse not arising "from common housekeeping" must be removed at the cost of the housekeeper. There, too, each tenant must have fire buckets and a canvas bag hanging in his hall, and must lend a hand in the extinguishment of fires. There, too, on Sundays the streets were chained in the neighborhood of churches and houses of public worship. There, too, the constables preserved the peace during the day and the superintendent of the night watch and his men guarded the city by night.

To the watch belonged the care of the oil, wicks, lamps, and utensils used in illuminating the streets, and the duty of lighting the lamps each night at sundown and keeping them burning till dawn.

As far back as 1816 an effort was made to introduce gas, and the manufacture of what was called carbonated hydrogen was begun by a Dr. Kugler. Peale promptly put the apparatus in his museum, and informed the public that on certain nights the hall would be illuminated with "gas-lights which will burn without wick or oil." The managers of the new theatre next introduced it into their building as an attraction. Finally, a citizen put one of Kugler's gas machines in his dwelling house, and invited councils to come and see the new light. A committee was accordingly sent, and, after visiting Peale's Museum, the theatre, and Mr. Henry's residence, recommended that a standing committee on gas-light should be appointed to watch the progress of the new invention and report from time to time.

The public having satisfied its curiosity, the new light shared the fate of the velocipede just then exhibited in the museum, and was forgotten. In 1820, however, attention was again drawn to gas by the Masons, who, when they built their new hall, lighted it with Kugler's carbonated hydrogen. The whole neighborhood complained of the stench, and voted the Lodge Gas Works a nuisance. But the experiment proved so successful that in 1822 the Masons applied to councils for leave to lay pipes in the streets and furnish gas to such as were willing to burn it. The petition was rejected. Councils had no desire to encourage an innovation so dangerous, so offensive, and one likely to injure the business of candle makers and oil-dealers.

In other cities the friends of the new light fared better. Gas as a means of street lighting was adopted by Boston in 1822, and by New York in 1823, when the New York Gas-Light Company was incorporated. The work of actual introduction was slow, for there was not a foundry in the country where long iron pipes were cast, and every foot of the street main was brought from England.

An exhibition of Kugler's gas at Peale's Museum in Baltimore in 1816 led to the formation of a gas-light company in that city in 1817. There also the process of pipe-laying was slow, so that 1820 came before the company began business with three customers.

Now that Philadelphia had fallen behind her sister cities in enterprise, another attempt was made to introduce gas, and in 1825 a bill to incorporate the Philadelphia Gas-Light Company and give it power to lay pipes in the streets and furnish gas was reported in the Legislature. But again public prejudice defeated the scheme. Gas was denounced as an unsafe, unsure means of illumination; its manufacture was described as a nuisance, and its use cited as one of the follies of the age. Common lamps were good enough.* Two years later, when the matter was once more before the public, the struggle waxed hotter. Some one said that if gas was used to light the streets crime would be lessened. This was scoffed at, and the public was reminded that a burglar with a spade could in a few minutes destroy a gas main and leave whole squares in darkness. A burglar, it was answered, can blow out the lamps and leave whole squares in darkness. The night watch, was the reply, can relight a lamp, but not a gas-jet when the main is cut. When gas, said another, was tested in 1820, and the Masons built works in the rear of their hall, the stench tainted provisions and sickened whole families, and drove people from Peale's Museum. Peale denied the statement, and asserted that when his museum was illuminated with gas the cost was least, the attendance greatest, and his income doubled.† The application was rejected by councils, and Philadelphia was without gas till 1837.

Much the same difficulty attended the introduction of a new fuel destined in time to increase the comforts of life, facilitate the use of steam, and revolutionize manufactures. That anthracite coal abounded in Pennsylvania had been known for more than thirty years, and as early as 1792 a tract of land was purchased in Lehigh County at a place where the coal cropped out and could be quarried at the surface, and the Lehigh Coal Mine Company was formed, and the vein opened. Like scores of other enterprises called into existence by the revival of confidence and the good times that followed the establishment of Government under the Constitution, the Lehigh company was far in advance of the ideas of the people and the conditions of the day. There was no market, and no way to get to market had one existed. The company, however, built a road from its mine to a landing on the river nine miles away, and when the water was high enough sent its first shipment to Philadelphia. But to a people who had wood in

---

* United States Gazette, February, 1825.
† American Daily Advertiser, February 2, 13, 14, 15, etc., 1827.

plenty, and whose stoves and fireplaces were suited to its use, the new fuel seemed unnecessary, and the experiment failed completely. At last, in 1798, a navigation company was organized to clear the Lehigh of obstructions, and, as one hindrance was about to be removed, interest in the mine revived, and the Lehigh company leased its property to several men, who in their turn gave up the enterprise as hopeless till the war with Great Britain and the blockade of the coast made Virginia coal scarce, and turned the attention of a wire-making firm at the Falls of the Schuylkill to the possibility of using the stone coal of Pennsylvania. Then for the third time the attempt was made, and five ark loads were started from Mauch Chunk. Three were wrecked on the way; two reached the city in safety, and were sold at twenty-one dollars a ton to the wire-makers, who then had before them the task of discovering how the coal should be ignited. Failure attended every effort till, at the close of a whole night spent in the attempt to light a fire in the furnace, the workmen shut the door and started for home in disgust. One of them, however, left his coat, and on returning a little later to get it was astonished to find the coal burning brightly and the furnace red hot. The problem of the draught was solved, and the way opened for the development of the coal and iron industries of Pennsylvania. Thenceforth anthracite was brought down in wagons, and in 1819 was advertised for sale in Philadelphia at eight dollars and forty cents a long ton. Meantime the Lehigh Navigation Company was chartered, a new coal company was organized, and in 1820 three hundred and sixty-five tons of anthracite reached Philadelphia. Two new industries—grate-making and grate-setting—now sprang up, and so increased the use of the new fuel that by 1825 demands were made that householders must be forbidden to throw their coal ashes into streets to be blown into the eyes and mouths of pedestrians by every passing gust.

In New York the prospect of a great consumption of coal seemed so good that the New York Schuylkill Company was formed, and a small quantity offered at eight dollars and a half a ton. At first it went off slowly, as householders were loath to undergo the expense of replacing andirons with grates. The company thereupon gave grates to such consumers as were willing to be beholden to it, and then, the economy of coal having been proved, the sale was rapid, and the demand so great that at one time four thousand tons were stored in the city, and made, it was boastfully said, the largest coal heap in the United States.

To New Yorkers the new fuel was most welcome, for the price of wood was rising because of the quantity consumed by the steamboats. Thirteen that plied on the Hudson burned sixteen hundred cords a week. The ferry-boats used fourteen hundred more, making a total of three thousand cords per week, or one hundred thousand for the eight months the river was open. Each steamer on the Sound consumed sixty cords a trip, and, though all the immense quantity required for the purposes of transportation on river, bay, and Sound was not furnished by New York city, so much came from it that fuel had grown to be a heavy item in household expenses.

Now that the Supreme Court had destroyed the monopoly so long held by the Fulton-Livingston Company, and had opened the waters around New York to all vessels moved by steam no matter to whom they belonged, a sharp competition had resulted, and a fuel more economical than wood was needed by the steamboat companies. Already the effect of competition was visible. The fare to Providence had fallen to three dollars, and to Albany to a dollar, and on one line to seventy-five cents, provided no meals were furnished. The old Fulton Company met this by placing on their route a "safety barge," which was hailed as one of the remarkable improvements of the day. The Lady Clinton, as the barge was named, was a vessel of two hundred tons, with neither sails nor steam nor any means of propulsion, and was used exclusively for the transportation of passengers. Within was a spacious dining room ninety feet long, a deck cabin for ladies, state-rooms, a reading-room, and over all a promenade deck one hundred feet long shaded by an awning and provided with comfortable settees. As the barge had no means of locomotion, it was towed by the Commerce, one of the regular steamers of the line, and made the trip to Albany twice a week in sixteen hours. Passengers, said the advertisement, on the safety barge will not be exposed in the least to any accident which may happen by reason of fire or steam on board the steamboat. The noise of the machinery, the trembling of the vessel, the heat from the boilers, the furnace, and the kitchen—in short, everything which may be considered unpleasant or dangerous on a steamboat are wholly wanting on the barge.* Success attended the venture from the start, and as quickly as possible a companion, the Lady Van Rensselaer, was put on the route.

A journey northward by daylight on such a vessel was indeed a pleasure, for along no other river in all the land could be found scenery so magnificent and places of such historic interest. These—as the Commerce, pouring forth great clouds of smoke and cinders from its tall stack, crept northward at a speed which would now be thought insufferably slow, with the Lady Clinton tugging at the long hawser in the stern— some self-appointed cicerone was sure to point out to the traveller. Now it was the spot on the west bank, where Hamilton fell in the ever-memorable duel with Burr; now Harlem Heights; now Fort Lee, on the summit of the Palisades, or Fort Washington, on the east bank, places famous as the scenes of gallant fights in the war for independence; now the beauty of the Palisades, rising hundreds of feet above the river and stretching away northward for twenty miles a solid wall of rock to Tappan Bay, where near the little village of Tappan had once been the grave of Major André. As the boats sped on across Tappan Bay and Haverstraw Bay to Stony Point and West Point, the story of Arnold and André and the great conspiracy was retold in all its detail. At Catskill village a landing was always made for the accommodation in summer of passengers bound for Pine Orchard, a " resort of fashion " on the mountain side, where the Catskill Mountain Association had built a fine hotel overlooking the valley of the Hudson for sixty miles around. Long before Catskill village was reached night had come on, and the first streaks of dawn were visible when the Lady Clinton made fast to the dock at Albany, where the travellers scattered, and took passage on

---

* Albany Argus, August 9, 1825.

some of the thirteen stage lines which ran out of the city in as many directions.

Albany was now a city of sixteen thousand inhabitants, and in commercial and industrial importance was second to no other in the State save New York. Her streets were crowded with emigrants gathered from every part of the East and bound for the growing towns of the West. Now that the Erie Canal was open and in use, the canal boats, steamboats, sloops, and schooners that clustered around her wharves made an array of water craft which in number and tonnage could not be equalled by any seaport in the Union. No event in the history of the State surpassed in lasting importance the completion of the canal. After eight years of persistent labor, " the big ditch," so constantly the subject of ridicule, was finished, and in June the gates at Black Rock were opened and the waters of Lake Erie for the first time were admitted into the western division. Later in the month the capstone of that splendid chain of locks at Lockport was laid with masonic ceremonies, but it was not till October that the canal from end to end was thrown open to the public.

The celebration of the opening began at Buffalo, where, on the twenty-sixth of the month, a procession of citizens and militia escorted the orator and the invited guests to a gayly decorated fleet lying in wait on the canal. On the Seneca Chief, which headed the line, were two painted kegs full of water from Lake Erie. Behind it were the Superior, the Commodore Perry, the Buffalo, and the Lion of the West, a veritable Noah's ark, containing a bear, two eagles, two fawns, two Indian boys, birds, and fish—all typical of the products of the West before the advent of the white man. When the address had been made the signal was given, and the Seneca Chief, drawn by four gray horses, started eastward on a most memorable journey. As the fleet moved slowly along the canal, saluted by music, musketry, and the cheers of the crowd on the bank, the news was carried to the metropolis by the reports of a continuous line of cannon placed along the canal to Albany and down the Hudson to New York. When the last gun was fired at the Battery, the forts in the harbor returned the salute, and the news that New York had heard the tidings was sent back to Buffalo by a second cannonade. The progress of the little fleet was one continuous ovation, as town after town along the route vied with each other in manifestations of delight.   From Albany an escort of gayly dressed steamboats accompanied the fleet down the river to New York, where the entire population, increased by thirty thousand strangers, turned out to receive it, and whence thousands, boarding every kind of craft, went down the bay to Sandy Hook.   There Governor Clinton, lifting the kegs from the deck of the Seneca Chief, poured their contents into the sea, saying as he did so: " This solemnity at this place, on the first arrival of vessels from Lake Erie, is intended to indicate and commemorate the navigable communication which has been accomplished between our Mediterranean Seas and the Atlantic Ocean, in about eight years, to the extent of more than four hundred and twenty-five miles by the public spirit and energy of the people of the State of New York, and may the God of the heavens and the earth smile propitiously on this work and render it subservient to the best interests of the human race."

This ceremony over and a grand salute fired, the boats returned to the city, where a fine industrial parade, to which each trade society furnished a float with artisans at work, closed the day.   At night there were balls, parties, dinners, and illuminations.

The canal thus opened to the world, which was, in truth, little more than a large ditch, for it was but four feet deep and forty feet wide, was connected with the Hudson by a basin made by inclosing a part of the river between the shore and a pier forty-three hundred feet long.   From this basin the canal passes along the west bank of the Hudson nearly to the mouth of the Mohawk, which it follows to Schenectady.   This part was used solely by freight boats.   No canal packet, as the passenger boats were termed, ever came east of Schenectady, because of the many locks between it and the Hudson.   Travellers bound west by water were carried by stage from Albany to Givens's Hotel, which stood a few rods from the canal in Schenectady.   Shortly before eight in the morning and seven in the evening two blasts on a horn would give notice that the Buffalo packet was about to start, whereupon the west-bound

travellers would hurry from the hotel and board a vessel not
unlike a Noah's ark. The hull was eighty feet long by eleven
feet wide, and carried on its deck a long, low house with a flat
roof and sloping sides, which were pierced by a continuous row
of windows provided with green blinds and red curtains. At
the forward end was a room six feet long containing four
berths, and called the " Ladies' Dressing Room." Behind it
was a room thirty-six feet long, which was used as a cabin
and dining-room by day and a bedroom by night. Precisely
at nine o'clock the steward and his helpers would appear
loaded down with adjustable berths, sheets, pillows, mattresses,
curtains, and in a little time the cabin would resemble the
interior of a modern sleeping car. Each berth was a narrow
wooden frame with a strip of canvas nailed over it, and was
held in place by two iron rods which projected from one side
and fitted into two holes in the wall of the cabin, and by two
ropes attached to the other side of the frame and made fast
to rings in the ceiling. In this manner the berths were suspended in tiers of three, one over the other, along the two
walls of the cabin, making thirty-six in all, with curtains hung
before them. If more than four women were on board, and
there usually were, one or two tiers in front of the " Ladies'
Dressing Room " were cut off for their use by an opaque
curtain. When the passengers outnumbered the berths, the
men slept on the dining table or the floor.

Behind the cabin was the bar, and in the rear of this was
the kitchen, always presided over by a negro cook.

When the weather was fine, the travellers gathered on the
roof, reading, sewing, talking, and playing cards, till the
helmsman would shout, " Bridge! bridge! " when the assembled company would rush headlong down the steps and into
the cabin, to come forth once more when the bridge had been
passed. To walk on the roof, if the packet was crowded, was
not possible. It was the custom, therefore, to jump ashore as
the boat rubbed along the bank, and walk on the towpath till
a bridge was reached, and then jump on board as the boat
glided from beneath.

Three horses, walking one before the other, dragged the
boat four miles an hour, and by dint of relays every eight

miles Utica was reached in just twenty-four hours. According to the inscription on the china plates of the packet boats, Utica, the site of which thirty years before was a wilderness, was then " inferior to none in the western section of the State in population, wealth, commercial enterprise, active industry, and civil improvements." At this thriving town other packets were taken to Lockport, whence passengers bound for Niagara went by stage to the Falls. At the end of the fourth day from Schenectady the jaded traveller reached Buffalo, three hundred and sixty-three miles by canal from Albany. The debt entailed on the State by this noble work, and by another joining Lake Champlain and the Hudson, was a trifle under eight millions of dollars, carrying an annual interest of four hundred and twenty-eight thousand, to meet which the State had pledged a duty on salt and sales at auction.* But, to the astonishment of the most eager advocates of inland navigation, before the canal was finished the tolls began to exceed the interest charges. In 1825 five hundred thousand, and in 1826 seven hundred and sixty-five thousand dollars, were paid in tolls. Fifty boats starting westward from Albany day after day was no uncommon sight. During 1826 nineteen thousand boats and rafts passed West Troy on the Erie and Champlain Canals. The new business created by this immense movement of freight cannot be estimated. Before the Champlain Canal was opened there were but twenty vessels on the lake. In 1826 there were two hundred and eighteen bringing timber, staves, shingles, boards, potashes, and giving employment to thousands of men in navigation, shipbuilding, and lumbering. Rochester became a flour-milling centre, and turned out one hundred and fifty thousand barrels a year. Even Ohio felt the impetus, and boats loaded with pig-iron

---

* Governor Clinton, in his message in 1826, stated that the debt created by the Erie and Champlain Canals was $7,944,770.90, on which the interest was $427,673.55, and that the fund available for the extinguishment of the debt was:

Tolls	$771,780 10
Auction duties	200,737 31
Salt duties	77,405 83
Other sources	7,635 19
Total	$1,057,558 43

from Madison County were seen in the basin at Albany. Orders for cherry boards and dressed lumber were received at Buffalo from Hartford and from dealers in Rhode Island. The warehouses along the canal bank at Buffalo were filled with the products of the East and the West; with wheat, grain, lumber, posts and rails, whiskey, fur and peltry bound for the markets of the Atlantic, and with salt, furniture, and merchandise bound for the West.

To the people of the West the opening of the canal was productive of vast benefit.   Said a Columbus newspaper: " It takes thirty days and costs five dollars a hundred pounds to transport goods from Philadelphia to this city; but the same articles may be brought in twenty days from New York by the Hudson and the canal at a cost of two dollars and a half a hundred.   Supposing our merchants to import on an average five tons twice a year; this means a saving to each of five hundred and sixty dollars."   It meant, indeed, far more: it meant lower prices, more buyers, a wider-spread market, increased comfort for the settlers in the new States, and, what was of equal importance, an impetus to internal improvements which should open up regions into which even the frontiersman would not go.

As section after section of the Erie Canal was finished and opened to travel, and the day of its completion came nearer and nearer, a mania for internal improvements swept over the commercial States, and one by one many of the long-discussed projects began to take shape.   On July fourth ground was broken in Ohio for a canal to join Lake Erie and the Ohio river.   A fortnight later a goodly company from the counties of Ulster, Sullivan, and Orange in New York assembled at the summit level of the Delaware and Hudson Canal, and with music, prayers, and speeches beheld the beginning of that great work.*   The Delaware and Chesapeake was well under way; the Chesapeake and Ohio was about to be commenced; while plans were on foot for canals to join New Haven and Northampton, Providence and Worcester, Boston with the Connecticut river, and Long Island Sound with Montreal by way of the

---

* Albany Argus, July 26, 1825.

valley of the Connecticut river, Vermont, and Lake Mem-
phremagog. Indeed, early in 1826 a convention of delegates
from the towns of New Hampshire and Vermont met at Concord to consider the expediency of such an enterprise.* Massachusetts, alarmed at the prospect of a diversion of her trade to
New York, had already appointed a commission to examine
into the possibility of cutting a canal from Boston harbor to the
Hudson, that she might tap the great western trade on its way
down to New York.† In a message on the subject, the Governor told the General Court that trade was passing from
Boston. The cheapness of transportation from Albany to New
York, and the abundant and variously supplied market at the
basin of the Erie Canal, had drawn west, he said, the produce
of the green hills of Berkshire and the rich valley of the
Housatonic. If the navigation of the Connecticut were improved as proposed, the produce of that valley would go to
enrich a seaport of Connecticut, while the Blackstone Canal,
joining Worcester and Providence, would open a new way
from the interior of Massachusetts to the coast of Rhode
Island, and all the trade of western and central Massachusetts
would be taken from Boston. Land transportation from Boston to Worcester or Providence then cost ten dollars a ton;
but by the canal a ton of freight could be hauled from Worcester to Providence for three dollars and thirty-three cents.

Philadelphia was in much the same condition as Boston.
Her western trade was seriously threatened. The day seemed
at hand when articles of her own manufacture would be sent
by sloop to Albany and by canal to the West, when she would
be outstripped by cities on the shore of Lake Erie, and would
find herself surpassed in trade and manufactures by Pittsburg.
If the great western carrying trade—an industry to which the
interior of the State owed no small part of its prosperity—was
not to be taken away by New York, a short and cheap route
to the Ohio river must be opened, and opened quickly.

Thus impelled by necessity, the community went seriously to work on the problem before it, and was soon engaged

---

* New England Palladium, January 13, 1826.
† Ibid., January 3, 1826.

in discussing the relative merits of railroads and canals. As
far back as 1811, John Stevens, of Hoboken, a man who richly
deserves to be called the father of the American railroad, applied to the Legislature of New Jersey for a railroad charter.
None was granted, and the following year he turned to New
York, where the Erie Canal Commissioners had just been appointed, and by means of a memoir, with plans and estimates,
endeavored to persuade the commission to build a railroad
and not a canal across the State to Buffalo.* Again he failed,
but the events of the next few years greatly changed public
opinion.   War with Great Britain destroyed the coastwise
commerce, and developed an enormous inland-carrying trade.
The sight of thousands of wagons hurrying across New Jersey with military stores and ammunition; the sight of great
fleets of " the ox-marine " † scudding along between New
York and Trenton; the report that two million dollars had
been paid during the war for the cartage of goods, wares, and
produce between the Hudson and the Delaware, convinced
Jerseymen that a highway of transportation was really needed
across their State.   When, therefore, Stevens again applied to
the Legislature, he met with no difficulty in securing, in 1815,
the first railroad charter ever granted in the New World.‡
His road was to join the Delaware and Raritan rivers, and
serve to connect the steamboat lines from Philadelphia to Bordentown with those from New Brunswick to New York. But
the project was far ahead of the times; the money wherewith
to build it could not be secured, and Stevens was again doomed
to disappointment.   Nevertheless, the idea of moving vehicles
by steam on a railway was taking root, and in 1819 another
projector yet more advanced applied to Congress for aid with
which to test the utility of his invention.*   He had, he said,
devised in theory a way of moving wheeled carriages by steam

---

* Documents Tending to Prove the Superior Advantages of Railway and Steam
Carriages over Canal Navigation.   New York, 1812.

† History of the People of the United States, vol. iv, pp. 220–221.

‡ Laws of New Jersey, Thirty-ninth Session, Second Sitting, Statute 68, 1815.

This man was Benjamin Dearborn, of Boston.   His memorial was presented
to the House of Representatives February 12, 1819.   Journal of the House of
Representatives, Fifteenth Congress, Second Session, p. 258.

on level railroads at the rate of a mile in three minutes, and of using vehicles so large that passengers might walk in them without stooping, and be furnished with accommodations for taking their meals and their rest during the passage, as in packets.* The boldness of his aims marked him out as a dreamer on whom practical congressmen were not disposed to waste either time and money, and, with the reference of the memorial to the proper committee, Dearborn and his railway were forgotten.

Stevens meanwhile had not lost heart. After failing in New York and New Jersey, he turned to Pennsylvania, and addressed a letter † on railroads to the Mayor of Philadelphia, who sent it to Councils, a body which manifested not the slightest interest in the matter. With business men, however, he fared better. To them the situation was serious. The New York canal was well under way. The appearance of the steamboat on the Mississippi put it within the power of the West to ignore the East, and trade directly with the world through New Orleans. If western trade was to be held against such competition, some cheap means of transportation to Pittsburg must be opened, and this the railroad seemed likely to furnish. It was not so costly as a turnpike; it would not freeze in winter, as did the water in the canals. Some men of means and prominence were persuaded to give the enterprise a trial, and in December, 1822, Stevens and his friends applied to the Legislature for a charter. To have attempted to build a railroad across the State of Pennsylvania from the Delaware to the Ohio would have been rash in the extreme. Half the distance was all they thought of covering, and, as there were good pikes from Philadelphia to Harrisburg and a canal almost completed from the Schuylkill to the Susquehanna, the proposed railroad was to begin at Harrisburg and end at Pittsburg. The House of Representatives, however, would not hear of this.

---

* "For obtaining these results, he relies on carriages propelled by steam, on level railroads, and contemplates that they be furnished with accommodation for passengers to take their meals and their rest during the passage, as in packets; that they be sufficiently high for persons to walk in without stooping, and so capacious as to accommodate twenty, thirty, or more passengers, with their baggage."   † January 5, 1821.

The valuable trade of the Susquehanna valley, despite turn-pikes and canals, was flowing steadily to Baltimore, and, in hope of diverting it to Philadelphia, the House insisted that the railroad should extend from Philadelphia to Columbia, a town on the Susquehanna, twenty-seven miles south of Harris-burg, and carried their point.*

The preamble of the act of incorporation sets forth that John Stevens had memorialized the Legislature for authority to build a railroad; that he had made many discoveries and improvements in the manner of building such highways; and that it was because of such improvements that the privileges asked for were granted. Some of these privileges now seem curious enough. The charter was to be in force for ten years; the rails were to cross all pikes and roads on causeways; and the company might charge seven cents a ton per mile on freight moving westward and half that sum on freight bound east.

With the granting of the charter the enterprise came to a standstill. The community seemed to be ignorant of what was meant by a railroad. Indeed, when a correspondent of one of the newspapers asked, " What is a railroad?" the editor answered, " Perhaps some other correspondent can tell." No-body did tell,† and the public remained unenlightened till the Pennsylvania Society for the Promotion of Internal Improve-ment within the Commonwealth published such information as it could gather concerning railroads in Great Britain. A committee of the society took the pains to explain that it had purchased treatises and essays on the subject, and had con-sulted well-informed individuals, only to find that, while many valuable facts were obtained, no connected view could be given. The society, therefore, had determined to send an agent to Europe to inspect and report on the railroads then in use, with a view to enabling the public to understand one of the most valuable internal improvements of the day, and in the meantime to call attention to the best description that

---

* Journal of the Senate, 1822–'23.   Journal of the House of Representatives, 1822–'23.   Laws of Pennsylvania, Chapter CXLVIII, 1823.

† In the United States Gazette for April 30, 1823, is a long article indorsing the proposed railroad, but no description.

had come to hand.* Accompanying the text were cuts showing plans and cross sections of the rails and road-bed.

The information thus given to the public was immediately
increased. Some one in Baltimore wrote two papers on the
construction of railroads, and the manner of drawing wagons
along them by steam locomotives,† and deposited a model of
a track with locomotive and cars in the Exchange Reading
Rooms. Somebody in Philadelphia published a series of essays
on Railways, Roads, and Canals.‡ The Society for the Promotion of Internal Improvements printed the report of its
agent, strongly indorsing railroads #—a report which the
friends of canals made haste to attack and refute, only to be
in turn answered. In the midst of the discussion one public
meeting was held at Philadelphia to consider the expediency
of building a railway from the Schuylkill to the Delaware,
and another to discuss the project of joining the two rivers
near the city by a canal. Each approved its own scheme, and
each instructed a committee to prepare plans and estimates
of cost.

Such part of the community as took any interest in the
commercial and industrial welfare of the State was thus rent
into two opposing factions—the friends and advocates of
canals and the friends and advocates of railroads. For the
time being the victory was with the friends of canals. Forced
on by public feeling, the Legislature of Pennsylvania, in 1824,
empowered the Governor to appoint three commissioners to
explore a route from Philadelphia to the Ohio. The result of
the exploration was a recommendation that the Alleghany
and the Conemaugh rivers on the west side of the mountains,
and the Susquehanna and the Juniata on the east side, should

---

* Abstract of a review of the plans submitted to the Highland Society, Edinburgh, for the premium or award of a piece of plate, valued at fifty guineas, for
the best essay, model, or drawing which might tend to the advancement of the
railway system.

† These papers may be found in the Baltimore American for March, 1825.
That describing the use of steam and giving a cut of the locomotive and train was
reprinted in the United States Gazette, March 9, 1825.

‡ United States Gazette, March 24, 28, 30, 1825.

United States Gazette, August 12, and September 5, 16, 1825. Lycoming
Gazette, August 24, 1825.

be opened to the foot of the mountains by canal and slack-water navigation, and that they should be joined by a canal passing through a tunnel four miles long under the Alleghanies. Lest the Legislature might not know what a tunnel was, the commissioners described it as " a passage like a well dug horizontally through a hill or mountain."

The utmost interest in the work of the commissioners was manifested all over the State. In January, 1824, a public meeting at Philadelphia * called for canals from the Susquehanna to Lake Erie and to the Ohio, and petitioned the Legislature not to delay the work.† In May another meeting issued a call for a Canal Convention to be held at Harrisburg in August. Fifty-six counties sent delegates, who declared that canals were needed; that the money appropriated for them would not be an expenditure, but an investment; that all local objects leading to a diffusive and unconnected use of public funds ought to give way for the present; and that public opinion would fully sustain the Legislature in all its efforts in behalf of internal improvements.‡ The Legislature had already established a regular board of canal commissioners,# and a year later ordered them to proceed at once to build " The Pennsylvania Canal " at State expense, and made a first appropriation of money. On July fourth, 1826, ground was broken at Harrisburg, and Pennsylvania, after a long struggle, began the construction of her highway to the West.

Now that the State was seriously at work, the old idea of the railroad revived, and in 1826 the charter granted to Stevens was repealed, and the Columbia, Lancaster, and Philadelphia Railroad was incorporated, only to share the fate of its predecessor. Then the State, convinced that private enterprise was not equal to the task of railroad-building on a great scale, took the work into her own hands, bade the canal commissioners make surveys for such a road || and build ᐃ it from Philadelphia through Lancaster to Columbia, and, if possible, finish the work in two years. By the same act they were instructed to examine a route for a railroad over the Alleghany

* American Daily Advertiser, January 28, 1825.   † Ibid., February 10, 1825.
‡ Ibid., August 9, 1825.   # April 11, 1825.
| 1827.   ᐃ 1828.

Mountains from Huntingdon on the east to Johnstown on the west side—a route which in time became celebrated as the Portage Railroad, and was long one of the engineering wonders of America.

Two years had wrought a marvellous change in the place which railroads held in public estimation. The scheme which in 1823 and 1826 seemed too visionary to be seriously thought of, and which failed because nobody was rash enough to advance the needed money, was high in favor in 1828 all over the seaboard States. New York had chartered the Mohawk and Hudson to join Albany and Schenectady, and had given the company authority to use " the power and force of steam, of animals, or of any mechanical or other power." * Massachusetts had incorporated the Granite Railway Company,† whose track was to extend from Quincy to tide-water,‡ had appointed a Board of Commissioners of Internal Improvements to survey one route for a railway from Boston to the boundary line of Rhode Island # and another from the same city to the boundary line of New York near Albany,‖ and had listened to reports urging that each road when built should be operated by horse power.△ In New York city a railway up the Hudson was seriously meditated. The objectors protested that it would never pay; but the projectors declared that success was certain, because rails could be used in winter when ice made transportation by water impossible. At Hoboken John Stevens built a circular railway, and demonstrated be-

---

* Laws of New York, Chapter CCLIII, 1826.

† Laws of Massachusetts, Chapter CLXXXIII, 1826.

‡ In many treatises on the history of railways, the Quincy road is called the first railway in America. This is a mistake. As early as 1809 Thomas Leiper built a railway from his quarry to the Delaware, and used it for eighteen years. History of the People of the United States, vol. iii, pp. 494, 495. Later still, but before 1823, Conroe, of Philadelphia, had another from his ice-house to the Delaware. Railways had long been used on the bridges of Pennsylvania to reduce the jar of rolling loads, while many of the fire companies in Philadelphia had tracks across the sidewalks in front of their houses.

Resolves of the General Court of Massachusetts, Chapter LXXXVI, March 2, 1827.

‖ Ibid., Chapter VII, June 14, 1827.

△ Ibid., Chapters XLVI and XLVIII.

yond dispute that a locomotive could drag a train round a
curve.*   Pennsylvania chartered five railroads.†   The business men of Baltimore, fully aware that the activity of Pennsylvania threatened their western connections, called a public
meeting,‡ at which it was resolved to form a company and
seek a charter for a railway to the West.   The charter was
obtained,# and on the fourth of July, 1828, the corner-stone
of what is now the Baltimore and Ohio Railroad was laid with
imposing ceremonies at Baltimore.‖

Meanwhile the merchants of Charleston, South Carolina, became enthusiastic, called a public meeting, and sent
a memorial to the Legislature praying for State aid and a
charter.   The State was asked to bear the cost of the survey
of a route from Charleston to Hamburg—a town on the
Savannah river, opposite Augusta—grant an act of incorporation, and exempt the property of the company from taxation.
After a brief contest the act was passed.^   Almost at the same
time the old idea of a railroad from Camden to some point
on the rivers emptying into New York Bay was revived in
earnest in New Jersey.   There, too, a public meeting was
held, at Mount Holly, and a memorial adopted.   Situated as
the State was, between two great centres of trade and commerce, and blessed with resources of her own waiting to be
developed, it was a reproach to the enterprise of her citizens,
the resolutions declared, that no line of interstate communication had been extended across her territory.   Such a link in
the chain of internal intercourse along the Atlantic coast was
of the utmost importance to New Jersey.   Therefore the
meeting earnestly recommended the Legislature to grant a
charter, and a liberal one, to a company for the construction
of a railway from Camden to Amboy.◊   Like meetings were

---

* A model of the locomotive, together with the original tubular boiler and a
drawing of the circular track, are in the National Museum at Washington.   The
date was 1826.

† Laws of Pennsylvania.

‡ February 12 and 19, 1827.

Laws of Maryland, Chapter CXXIII, February 28, 1827.

‖ Niles's Weekly Register, July 12, 1828, vol. xxxiv, pp. 316–328.

^ Laws of South Carolina.   ◊ New Jersey Mirror, January 16, 1828.

now held at Burlington, Bordentown, Princeton, Trenton, and similar memorials sent up to the Legislature in behalf of four proposed railroads,* none of which were chartered. Virginia had already surveyed a route for a railroad from the coal pits of Chesterfield County to the banks of the James river opposite Richmond,† and had incorporated the Chesterfield Railroad Company.‡ In Delaware, the people of Wilmington and vicinity met and discussed the expediency of a railroad from Elkton to Wilmington.#

Though many were planned, the work of construction went slowly on. The period 1825 to 1830 was one of preparation, and closed with but thirty-six miles of railroad in the country. The mechanical difficulties were great. The supply of engineers, of instrument-makers, of iron, was out of all proportion to the demand. When the Pennsylvania commissioners began work the president of the board reported that he had " made most diligent search and anxious inquiry after an engineer," and had not succeeded. When the Baltimore and Ohio Railroad Company was about to begin the building of its road-bed, Congress was asked to grant it permission to import the strap iron for its rails free of duty, because the quantity wanted — some fifteen thousand tons — could not be had in the United States. The statement was flatly denied by the friends of American manufactures. Nevertheless, the Senate passed a bill remitting the duties.‖

The only roads on which the work of track-laying went steadily forward were the Hudson and Mohawk, the Philadelphia and Columbia, the Baltimore and Ohio, and the South Carolina, and about as much was built in a year as can now be laid with ease in one day. Everything was experimental. The best form of road-bed, the strongest and

---

* Camden to Amboy, Bordentown to South Amboy, Trenton to New Brunswick, Elizabethtown Point to Easton.

† Resolutions passed at a General Assembly of the Commonwealth of Virginia. Resolution No. 4, December 10, 1827.

‡ Laws of Virginia, Chapter XCIII, February 27, 1828.

January, 1828.

‖ Journal of the Senate, p. 328.

most durable kind of rail, the most economical sort of motive power, were problems yet to be solved. According to
the ideas then prevalent, there must be no steep grades, as
few curves as possible, and these of the sharpest and worst
sort. At first the rails were long wooden stringers, protected
on the upper surface from the wear of the wheels by strap
iron nailed on.* Then they were great blocks of granite,
resting on granite ties,† and plated on the upper inner surface
with strap iron bolted or riveted on; and, finally, " edge rails "
of rolled iron on stone blocks and stone sills, or edge rails on
stone blocks and wooden sills.‡ Even when the rails were
laid what was the best kind of motive power had not been
determined. The astonishing success of Stephenson's locomotives on the Stockton and Darlington Railroad in England, and the signal triumph of his Rocket over all other
competitors in the Liverpool and Manchester contest, convinced many that steam was the proper agent to use. But
every experiment with a locomotive ended in failure. The
Stourbridge Lion was imported from England and tried on the
rails of the Delaware and Hudson Canal and Railroad Com-

---

* When the road had been graded, a series of trenches two feet long, two feet
deep, and twenty inches wide was dug on either side of the road and filled with
broken stone rammed down. These were joined in pairs by other trenches cut
across the road-bed and also filled with broken stone, on which cross-ties were laid
with the utmost care and accuracy. On top of the ties, and four feet apart, were
the wooden rails, six inches square and from twelve to twenty feet long, plated on
their upper surfaces with strap iron two and a half inches by five eighths of an
inch by fifteen feet.

† A committee of the New York Legislature thus describes the Baltimore and
Ohio track : " A line of road is first graded, free from short curves, as nearly
level as possible. A small trench is formed for each track, and filled with rubble
on which are laid granite blocks one foot square and as long as possible. The
upper end and inner surface of each track are dressed smooth, as well as the ends
of the blocks where they join. Bars or plates of wrought iron, half an inch thick,
are laid on the granite blocks or rails in a line with the inner surface, and fastened
with iron bolts or rivets entering four inches into the blocks, and eighteen inches
apart."

‡ The " edge rails " were usually fifteen feet long, three and a half inches high,
and weighed about forty-one pounds to the yard. The chairs into which the
rail fitted weighed about fifteen pounds each, and rested either on stone blocks
(12″ × 12″ × 20″), on stone stringers, twenty inches deep, or were made fast to
wooden cross-ties or longitudinal sleepers.

pany, only to be thrown aside.* The Tom Thumb was built by Peter Cooper, and run on the Baltimore and Ohio Railroad to prove that a locomotive could pass around a sharp curve,† and was soon forgotten. A locomotive built by Stephenson was exhibited in New York city, but never drew a car. The early railroad managers were quite content to use the horse.

While the people on the seaboard were thus promoting communication between the States by every means in their power by public meetings, by conventions, by subscriptions to the stock of railroads and canals, and by appeals to their Legislatures to undertake at public expense internal improvements too costly to be carried on by private enterprise, the Federal Government was besought year after year to do its share toward opening cheap communication with the remote parts of the far West.

The veto of the Bonus Bill by Madison in the last hours of his administration checked but did not cool the ardor of the friends of internal improvement. A more liberal spirit, a less strict construction of the Constitution was hoped for from his successor—a hope somewhat deferred by a passage in the first annual message of Monroe.‡ Putting aside early impressions, I have given the subject, said he, all the deliberation required by its importance and a just sense of my duty; I am convinced that Congress does not possess the right, and suggest, therefore, that the States be asked to adopt such an amendment to the Constitution as will give Congress the right in question.

The response of the House to this suggestion was prompt. Before a week had elapsed the proposed amendment was moved,# and before a fortnight ended a long re-

---

* August 8, 1829. See History of the First Locomotives in America. W. H. Brown. Pp. 83, 87.

† The experiment is fully described in Brown's History of the First Locomotives in America, pp. 108–122.

‡ Messages and Papers of the Presidents. Richardson. Vol. ii, p. 18. See also History of the People of the United States, vol. iv, p. 423.

" Congress shall have power to pass laws appropriating money for constructing roads and canals and improving the navigation of watercourses. *Provided, however,* that no road or canal shall be constructed in any State, nor the navigation of its waters improved, without the consent of such State. *And provided, also,*

port was made in which the objections of Monroe were answered.*

Thus was the issue as to the constitutional power clearly drawn between the House and the President. It now remained to be determined whether or not the House would go further and make an appropriation, a step which it showed a readiness to take by adopting two resolutions calling for information. One asked the Secretary of War for a plan for the application " of such means as are within the power of Congress " for the construction of roads and canals that would be of use for military purposes in time of war. The other called on the Secretary of the Treasury for a similar report on roads and canals not especially designed for military purposes, and for a list of such public works then building or contemplated as might be deserving of congressional aid.

Calhoun responded with a long report,† which the House laid on the table, and two years passed before anything more was heard of a national system of internal improvements.‡ By that time the progress made in digging the Erie Canal, and the persistent demands of State after State for aid in the construction of some road or canal or the improvement of some watercourse or harbor,* once more forced the subject on the attention of the House, and a committee made bold to present a bill. Taking up the reports of Gallatin in 1808, and of Calhoun in 1819, it recommended a line of canals from Boston to Savannah; a great highway from Washington to New Orleans; a canal around the falls of the Ohio at Louisville, another from Lake Erie to the Ohio, and a third from

---

that whenever Congress shall appropriate money to these objects the amount thereof shall be distributed among the several States in the ratio of representation which each State shall have in the most numerous branch of the National Legislature."

* Report in part of the Committee of the House of Representatives of the United States on so much of the President's Message as relates to roads, canals, and seminaries of learning. House Documents, No. 11, Fifteenth Congress, First Session, vol. ii. See also History of the People of the United States, vol. iv, pp. 423–426.

† Report on Roads and Canals, January 7, 1819.

‡ January 10, 1821, a Committee of the House reported a bill.

May 4, 1822.

the Potomac at Washington to the Potomac at Cumberland; and good means of communication of some sort between the Susquehanna and the rivers Seneca and Genesee; between the Tennessee and the Savannah, and the Tombigbee and Alabama. That so grand a system might be undertaken intelligibly, the bill provided for the appropriation of a sum of money " to procure the necessary surveys, plans, and estimates." To have passed it would have been idle, for ere the session closed Monroe sent back a bill far less radical in character with his veto.

The national road from Cumberland in Maryland to Wheeling on the bank of the Ohio in Virginia was fast going into decay for want of regular superintendence and repairs. The Postmaster-General, who rode over it from end to end, declared that in some places the bed was cut through by wheels; that in others it was covered with earth and rocks that had fallen down from the sides of the cuttings; and that here and there the embankment along deep fillings had so washed away that two wagons could not pass each other. A bill was therefore sent to the President providing for the establishment of toll-gates at regular intervals along the road for the collection of tolls, and setting apart the money so gathered as a fund with which to meet the cost of repairs. But, in the opinion of Monroe, a power to establish turnpikes with gates and tolls, and to enforce the collection of tolls, implied a power to adopt and execute a general system of internal improvement, and this he did not consider Congress possessed. That his views might not be misunderstood, the veto was followed by a long message reviewing the history and explaining the meaning of the Constitution.*

All hope of a national system of internal improvements during the rest of Monroe's term was now ended. Maryland, indeed, attempted to revive the project, and bade her senators and representative introduce a constitutional amendment,† pledge her to a hearty support of internal improvements,‡

---

* Views of the President of the United States on the Subject of Internal Improvements. Richardson. Messages and Papers of the Presidents, vol. ii, pp. 144–183. † Resolution of January 11, 1823.

‡ Resolution communicated January 3, 1823.

and urge an appropriation to repair the Cumberland Road.* But all to no purpose. The utmost that could be obtained was an act appropriating money for surveys, plans, and estimates for such canals and roads as the President might deem of national importance from a commercial or military point of view or necessary for the transmission of the public mails,† and in the last hours of his administration another extending the Cumberland Road from Canton to Zanesville, and providing for a survey for a further extension to the capital of Missouri.‡

The completion of the National Pike was, in its day and time, a matter of much importance. It began at Cumberland, on the banks of the Potomac, passed through Hagerstown in Maryland, and Uniontown, Brownsville, and Washington in Pennsylvania, and across Virginia to Wheeling on the Ohio. With the pike from Baltimore to Cumberland, it made a great through line of communication between the East and the West, and was already the favorite highway with travellers bound for the Ohio Valley.

Such a journey was usually begun by taking boat at Philadelphia, going down the Delaware to New Castle, crossing by stage to Frenchtown on the Elk river, a tributary of Chesapeake Bay, and then boarding another steamboat for Baltimore. Twenty years had seen a marvellous betterment in the means and speed and cost of travel. Steamboats, turnpike, ferryboats, bridges, and, above all, competition, had accomplished wonders on the routes between the great seaboard cities. But no corresponding improvement had taken place in the comforts and conveniences of the inns and taverns at which the traveller was forced to stop. We lodged, said one traveller, at the City Hotel, which is the principal inn at New York. The house is immense, and was full of company; but what a wretched place! The floors were without carpets, the beds without curtains. There was neither glass, nor mug, nor cup, and a miserable little rag was dignified with the name of towel. At another inn the same traveller was shown to a

---

* Resolution of December 18, 1822.   † Approved April 30, 1824.
‡ March 3, 1825.

room with nine other men. " I secured a bed to myself," said
he, " the narrow dimensions of which precluded the possibility of participation, and plunged into it with all possible
haste, as there was not a moment to be lost." His companions " occupied by triplets the three other beds which the
room contained." * When you alight at a country tavern,
says another, it is ten to one that you stand holding your
horse, bawling for the hostler, while the landlord looks on.
Once inside the tavern, every man, woman, and child plies
you with questions. To get a dinner is the work of hours. At
night you are put with a dozen others into the same room,
and sleep two or three in a bed between sheets which have
covered twenty wayfarers since they last saw the tub. In
the morning you go out-of-doors to wash your face, and then
repair to the bar-room to behold your countenance in the only
looking-glass the tavern contains.† Much allowance must indeed be made for the tales of travellers. Yet the combined
testimony of them all is that a night in a wayside inn was
something to be dreaded, and to this the western highways
afforded no exception. Saving the inns and such discomfort
as came from rising at three o'clock in the morning and sitting for sixteen hours in a crowded coach, still made on the
pattern of twenty years before, a ride from Baltimore to
Wheeling was most enjoyable. The road-bed was hard, the
horses were fine, and the scenery as the road crossed the mountains was magnificent.

Beyond the mountains every year wrought wonderful
changes. In the river towns and on the farms bordering the
Ohio and its tributaries life had become much easier. The
steamboats supplied the large settlements already claiming to
be cities, while smaller craft carried goods, wares, and merchandise to every farmhouse and cluster of cabins. The Ohio was
now dotted with floating shops. At the sound of a horn the
inhabitants of the village or the settler and his family would
come to the river to find a dry-goods boat fitted with counters,
seats, and shelves piled with finery of every sort making fast

---

* Personal Narrative of Frederick Fitzgerald De Roos, 1826, pp. 5, 85, 86.
† Miner's Journal, November 28, 1825.

to the bank. Now it would be a floating lottery office, where tickets were sold for cotton or produce; now a tinner's establishment, within which tinware articles of every description were made, sold, and mended; now a smithy, where horses and oxen were shod and wagons repaired; now a factory for the manufacture and sale of axes, scythes, and edge tools.

The great river was more than ever the highway of travel. The huge barge of an earlier day, almost as large as a sea-going schooner, with its arched and outlandish-looking deck and its crew of five-and-twenty men, had fallen into disuse. But the keel-boat, still the favorite for waters too shallow for steamboats, and the broad-horn were more numerous than ever. Some of the " broads," called family boats, were twenty-five by one hundred feet, had pens for cattle, and neat cabins and rooms for the " movers " fitted with tables and chairs, beds, and a stove, and were constantly to be seen floating down the river in an almost endless procession with old and young, cattle, horses, swine, and fowls all in the same bottom.

When such an emigrant reached the town nearest his destination he would sell his broad and buy some sort of a conveyance, cover it with canvas or linen smeared on the inside with tar to make it water tight, go to the United States Land Office, enter his quarter or half-quarter section, and then set off for his farm. As he went slowly along, driving his cattle before him, he would come night after night to inns especially designed to meet the needs of men such as he. At each would be a room with an earthen floor and a huge fireplace, but no furniture, no conveniences of any sort, and in this his wife would cook the evening meal and the family would sleep.

When at last, after all manner of adventures, both serious and amusing, the site of the future home was reached, the settler would cut down a few saplings, build a " half-face camp," and begin his clearing. The " half-face camp " was a shed whose three sides were of logs laid one on another horizontally, whose roof was of saplings covered with branches or bark, and whose fourth side, in front of which was the fire hole, was open save in wet weather, when it was closed by hanging up deerskin curtains. In this camp the newcomer and his family would live while he grubbed up the bushes and cut down trees enough to make a log cabin. If he were a thrifty, painstaking man, he would smooth each log on four sides with his axe, and notch it half through at each end so that when they were placed one on the other the faces would nearly touch. Saplings would make the rafters, and on them would be fastened plank laid clapboard fashion, or possibly split shingles.

An opening, of course, was left for a door, although many a cabin was built without a window, and when the door was shut received no light save that which came down the chimney, which was always on the outside of the house. To form it, an opening eight feet long and six feet high was left at one end, and around this a sort of bay window was built of logs and lined with stones on the inside. Above the top of the opening the chimney contracted and was made of branches smeared both inside and out with clay. Generally the chimney went to the peak of the roof; but it was by no means unusual for it to stop about halfway up the end of the cabin.

If the settler was too poor to buy glass, or if glass could not be had, the window frame was covered with greased paper, which let in the light, but could not be seen through. The door was of plank with leather hinges, or with iron hinges made from an old wagon tire by the nearest blacksmith or by the settler himself. There was no knob, no lock, no bolt; but instead a wooden latch on the inside, which could be lifted by a person on the outside by a leather strip which came through a hole in the door and hung down. When this latch string was out, anybody could pull it, lift the latch, and come in. When it was drawn inside, nobody could enter without knocking. The floor was made of " puncheons," or planks split and hewn with an axe from the trunk of a tree, and laid with the round side down. The furniture was such as the settler brought with him or made on the spot.

The household utensils were of the simplest kind. Brooms and brushes were of corn husks. Corn was shelled by hand or by rubbing the ear on the rough side of a piece of tin punched full of holes, and called a " gritter," which was then used to grate the kernels into meal. More commonly the corn was carried in a bag slung over the back of a horse to a mill maybe fifteen miles away, or was pounded in a wooden hominy mortar with a wooden pestle, or ground in a hand mill made by placing one flat stone on a tree stump and hanging another over it in such wise that the upper stone could be rubbed around and around on the lower. Few implements were of more importance to the frontiersman than a sharp axe; but to sharpen it he used a grindstone consisting of a thick wooden disk into the circumference of which when green he had driven particles of fine gravel and sand.

Cooking stoves were unknown. Game was roasted by hanging it with a leather string before an open fire. All baking was done in a " Dutch oven," on the hearth, or in an " out oven," built, as its name implies, out of doors. The Dutch oven was a huge iron pot with an iron lid turned up at the rims. When in use it was buried in ashes, and hot coals were piled on the lid. To build an " out oven," chips and little sticks were heaped up near the house in an oblong mound some three feet long, two feet wide by the same in height, and covered over with a thick layer of clay, which, by setting fire to the wood, was burned hard as a brick. The oven was then ready for use. When about to be used, it was first made very hot by filling it with chips and allowing them to burn to ashes. The ashes were then swept out, the bread or the pies to be baked were put in, and something placed over the door and smoke hole to keep the oven from cooling too quickly.*

---

* "I know of no scene in civilized life," says a Kentucky pioneer, "more primitive than such a cabin hearth as that of my mother. In the morning, a buckeye back-log, a hickory fore-stick, resting on stones and irons, with a johnny-cake on a clean ash board, set before the fire to bake; a frying-pan, with its long handle resting on a split-bottom turner's chair, sending out its peculiar music, and the tea-kettle swung from a wooden lug-pole, with myself setting the table, or turning the meat, or watching the johnny-cake, while she sat nursing the baby in the corner, telling the little ones to hold still and let their sister Lizzie dress them. Then came the blowing of the conch-shell for father in the field, the howling of old Lion, the gathering around the table, the blessing, the dull clatter of pewter spoons in pewter basins, the talk about the crops and stock, the inquiry whether Dan'l could be spared from the house, and the general arrangements for the day. Breakfast over, my function was to provide the sauce for dinner; in winter, to

The land about the cabin was cleared by grubbing the
bushes and chopping down trees under a foot in diameter and
burning them. Big trees were " deadened," or killed, by cutting a " girdle " around them two or three feet above the
ground, deep enough to destroy the sap vessels and so prevent
the growth of leaves. When the settler was a shiftless fellow,
he would make no attempt to clear away the dead trunks, but
would suffer them to stand till, in the course of years, they
became so rotten that one by one they fell to pieces or were
destroyed by the wind and storms.*

In the ground thus laid open to the sun were planted corn,
potatoes, or wheat, which, when harvested, was threshed with
a flail and fanned and cleaned with a sheet. At first the corn
and wheat raised would be scarcely sufficient for home use.
But as time passed there would be some to spare, and this
would be wagoned to the nearest river town and sold or exchanged for " store goods." Many an early settler made the
shoes his family wore from leather of his own tanning, clothed
himself and children in jeans of his own manufacture, and in
linen every fibre of which had been grown on his own land,
and had been pulled, rotted, broken, hackled, spun, and
bleached by the members of his household.

If the site selected by the emigrant were a good one, others
would soon settle themselves near by, and when a cluster of
cabins had been formed some enterprising speculator would
appear, take up a quarter section, cut it into town lots, and
call the place after himself, as Piketown, or Leesburg, or
Wilson's Grove. A storekeeper with a case or two of goods
would next arrive, then a tavern would be built, and possibly
a blacksmith shop, a saw-mill, and a grist-mill, and Piketown
or Wilson's Grove would be established. Many such ventures
failed; but others succeeded, and are to-day prosperous villages.

It was in such far-away settlements that frontier life ap-

open the potato or turnip hole, and wash what I took out; in spring, to go into
the field and collect the greens; in summer and fall, to explore the truck patch, or
our little garden." Drake. Pioneer Life in Kentucky.

* For a delightful account of life in the West read Recollections of Life in
Ohio by William C. Howells.

peared in its least attractive form. Common hardships, common poverty, common ignorance, and the utter inability to get anything more out of life than coarse food, coarse clothes, and a rude shelter, reduced all to a level of absolute equality which existed nowhere else. The well-to-do and the destitute, the idle and the industrious, the judge and the criminal, the preacher, the circuit-rider, and the drunkard were all members of one common family. If any man rose to importance among his fellows, he did so because he possessed those physical and moral qualities which command respect alike in an Indian tribe, in a negro village in the heart of Africa, and in communities of civilized men.

The autobiographies, the reminiscences, the recollections of the early settlers abound in stories and anecdotes which exhibit, far better than any description could, the free-and-easy manners bred of this equality. The story is told of a member of the Territorial Legislature who up to the time of his election had always worn leather; but, thinking his buckskin clothes unbecoming a law-maker, he, with the help of his sons, gathered hazel-nuts, bartered them at the cross-road store for a few yards of blue strouding, and called on the women of the settlement to make him a coat and pantaloons. The material was just enough for a very short coat and a long pair of leggings, and in this garb he attended the session.[*]

When John Reynolds went down to hold his first Court in Washington County he found himself among old friends and companions in arms, who treated him accordingly, and when he was seated and the Court about to be opened, the sheriff, who was astride of a bench, cried out, "Boys, the Court is now open; John is on the bench."[†] "I knew a judge," says another, "who when asked for instructions would rub his head with his hands and say to the lawyers, ' Why, gentlemen, the jury understand the case; they need no instruction. No doubt they will do justice between the parties.' "[‡] "Judge," said the foreman of a jury that failed to agree, "this is the difficulty: The jury want to know whether what you told us

---

[*] Nicolay and Hay.   Abraham Lincoln, vol. i, p. 65.

[†] Reynolds.   My Own Time, p. 138.

[‡] History of Illinois.   Ford,   P. 83.

when we first went out really was the law, or whether it was only just your notion." " Mr. Green," said a judge to the prisoner, " the jury in their verdict say you are guilty of murder, and the law says you are to be hung. Now, I want you and all your friends down in Indian Creek to know that it is not I who condemns you, but the jury and the law. Mr. Green, the law allows you time for preparation, and the Court wants to know what time you would like to be hung." After the date had been fixed to the satisfaction of the two at that day four weeks, and the judge had been satisfied that four weeks from that day was not Sunday, the prosecuting attorney asked the Court to pronounce a formal sentence and exhort the prisoner to repentance. To this the judge answered: " Oh, Mr. Turrney, Mr. Green understands the matter as well as if I had preached to him for a month. He knows that he has got to be hung this day four weeks.—You understand it in that way, Mr. Green, don't you?" " Yes," said the prisoner, and so ended the discussion. A jury finding it could not agree on a verdict because one of the twelve was the confederate of a gang of horse thieves it was trying, brought him to reason by making serious preparations to hang him.

Trials in those days were held in somebody's log cabin or in the bar-room of a tavern, and when the jury retired to deliberate it was to the shade of some near-by tree or to a log especially prepared for them. Judge and bar rode the circuit together, and a lawyer was fortunate if at the end of his ride his daily earnings amounted to what would now be the wages of an unskilled laborer. An attorney of that day assures us that on his first circuit he was paid five dollars in one county for prosecuting criminals; that on his way to the next county he was almost drowned in crossing a river, but found some compensation in being retained in another trial which yielded him five dollars more; that in the third county there were no cases before the Court; that he then rode sixty miles over the unbroken prairie to Quincy, where he made another five dollars; and that, passing on to Pike County, he there found nothing to do, and was glad to be the guest of the hospitable sheriff.*

---

* Life of Lincoln. Nicholay and Hay, vol. i, pp. 61–62.

Yet his lot was the common lot of lawyers, not a few
of whom had attained to some distinction in the older States
long before they moved to Illinois. To such men the chance
of political preferment was the great attraction. In a frontier community, where no industries had been established,
where neither trade nor commerce consumed the thoughts
and energies of the ambitious and aspiring, where newspapers were scarce and books were little known, politics was
almost a daily vocation. Wherever a body of men were
gathered together, at the log tavern, at the cross-roads, at
the store in the settlement, at the horse-races, or at a " raising," measures and candidates were the all-absorbing theme
of never-ending discussion. No party organization, no caucus, no machine existed, and in the absence of such appliances the personal element counted for much, and the successful politician was he who knew the people face to face,
and who won their votes because his character compelled
esteem. If he wished to be a governor or a judge, a member
of the Legislature, a sheriff, or a senator, he said so plainly,
published an address, made a personal canvass from house to
house, asked for the votes he needed, and argued the matter
with the refractory. He was the candidate of no party. He
was the nominee of no convention, and looked on every vote
cast against him as a personal affront. On one occasion the
State treasurer, after a protracted struggle in the Legislature,
failed of re-election. But the vote had scarcely been counted
when he entered the chamber, took off his coat, and soundly
thrashed, one by one, four men who voted against him. Both
friends and opponents considered this as no more than the
occasion required, and he was promptly made clerk of the
Circuit Court.*

Violence of this sort was of too common occurrence to
excite even comment. " Men," said a pioneer, speaking of the
good old times, " would fight for the love of it, and then shake
hands and be friends." There is no reason to doubt the statement, for almost everything which passed as pleasure and
amusement was rude and boisterous, and often bordered on

---

* History of Illinois. Ford, p. 81.

the brutal. Whatever brought men together—a raising, a husking, a log-rolling, a horse-race, a wolf hunt, or a wedding—was sure to be the occasion of rough games and practical jokes. One who was himself a frontiersman, and who knew his class well, assures us that " these men could shave a horse's tail, paint, disfigure, and offer it for sale to the owner. They could hoop up in a hogshead a drunken man, they themselves being drunk, put in and nail fast the head, and roll the man down hill a hundred feet or more. They could run down a lean and hungry wild pig, catch it, heat a ten-plate stove furnace hot, and, putting in the pig, could cook it, they dancing the while a merry jig." * It would be a great mistake to suppose that the community which tolerated such misdeeds and the men who took part in them were depraved and vicious. Nowhere else was the standard of morality higher or more fully attained. Nowhere else did religion have a firmer hold. Churches, indeed, were few, but the circuit-rider was everywhere.

His vocation was rarely a matter of accident or choice. He had been called to it by the voice of the Lord God of Israel. Judged by his own estimate of himself, he was a brand snatched from the burning. He had committed no particular sin; he had broken no commandment; yet he had in his own eyes begun life a sinner, and had long refused to listen to the voice of the Lord pleading with him. But at last he had come to his senses, and after a spiritual experience as terrible as that of Bunyan, had passed safely through the Dark Valley and had reached the House Beautiful. Thenceforth he regarded himself as an instrument of God for saving the souls of men, and went to his work sustained by a faith that never wavered and animated by a zeal that never flagged.

For the work which lay before him he needed little other equipment. There were, he readily admitted, many paths to grace; but the safest and the surest was that pointed out by John Wesley, to whom he looked up as the greatest teacher the world had seen since the advent of Christ. For educa-

* Life of Lincoln. Nicholay and Hay, vol. i, pp. 53, 54.

tion, for book-learning he had no inclination. He knew the Bible as he knew his own name, accepted the good book with childlike credulity, and expounded its teachings with the utmost literalness in the plainest words and with an intensity of manner that carried conviction and aroused repentance in the rudest frontiersman. This, with a good constitution, a horse, and a pair of saddle-bags, was equipment enough. What he should eat or wherewith he should be clothed concerned him not. "The Lord will provide" was his comfortable belief, and experience justified his faith. His circuit was of such extent that he was constantly on the route; but it mattered not. Devoted to his calling, he rode his circuit in spite of every obstacle man or Nature could put in the way. No settlement was so remote, no rain was so drenching, no river so swollen, no cold so bitter, as to deter him in his work, or to prevent him from keeping an engagement to preach to a handful of frontiersmen. Over such men his influence was boundless. We read in the accounts of camp-meetings of great crowds of the plainest and roughest of men held spellbound by his rude oratory, or thrown prostrate with an excitement which did not by any means pass away with the occasion. It is not too much to say that the religious life of the middle West to-day bears distinct traces of the efforts of the Methodist itinerants in the early years of the century.

In common with their fellow-citizens in other Western States, the people of Illinois in 1824 were passing through a period of hard times, the inevitable consequence of cheap money, overspeculation, and debt. Twelve years before, while Illinois was still a Territory, money was rarely to be seen. Beaver, deer, and raccoon skins did duty as a circulating medium. But when the great emigration of 1816 swept over the Territory, the Legislature, following the custom of the day, chartered two banks of issue, and forced its notes on the people by enacting that if a creditor would not take them the collection of the debt was stayed. Notes of the banks of Ohio, Kentucky, Tennessee, and Missouri received the same consideration, and money at once became cheap, plentiful, and worthless.

Times grew flush, credit could be had to an unlimited

extent for the asking, and, as emigrants came thronging in, land and property of every sort rose rapidly in value. A spirit of wild and reckless speculation seized on the people. Towns without number were laid out on paper, lots were purchased on credit, houses were built on promises, and Government lands were entered in enormous quantities under the credit system then in force. The merchant, confident that the stream of emigrants would never stop, bought vast quantities of goods on time, and sold them on trust to the people, who felt sure of gathering great profits from the settlers yet to come. Everybody was extravagant, hopeful, and in debt. But the day of reckoning came sooner than was expected. By 1819 paper, having driven out specie, began to depreciate, the banks began to waver, credit disappeared, and the Legislature was called on for help. The usual replevin laws and stay laws were used, and a monster Bank of Illinois, with two millions of capital, was chartered. All was in vain. Not a dollar of its stock was ever taken, and when, in 1820, the banks of the neighboring States went down in bankruptcy, those of Illinois at once suspended, and the visions of prosperity vanished. The emigrants who came, driven West by hard times in the East, were as penniless as the old pioneers; the paper towns were never settled; trade languished; real estate was utterly unsalable, while the contracts made in a time of hopeful enthusiasm began to mature. Embarrassed on every hand, the people again appealed to the Legislature, and in 1820 the Illinois State Bank, with a capital of half a million dollars, based on the credit of the State, was chartered. It was preeminently a people's bank, for the act expressly provided that its bills should be loaned to the people in sums of one hundred dollars on personal security, and over one hundred and up to one thousand on real estate; that they should be receivable for taxes, costs, and fees; and that unless a creditor would write on his execution the words " Bills of the State Bank of Illinois or either of its branches will be received in discharge of this execution," the debtor was entitled to three years' stay by replevy. The State was laid off into four districts, with a branch of the bank in each, and three hundred thousand dollars were distributed on the basis of population.

Every man who could get security made haste to borrow his hundred, and every man with real estate mortgaged it for a thousand. Coin now disappeared, and dollar bills torn into pieces were used for small change. Depreciation began at once, and went on till the paper of the bank was not worth twenty-five cents on a dollar.

Across the Ohio in Kentucky the financial situation was worse. In truth, politically, financially, and industrially, that State was the most distressed member of the Union. Her State bank paper would rarely pass at fifty cents on the dollar; her people were bankrupt, her relief system was a failure, and, in a desperate effort to sustain it, the Legislature had used methods and gone lengths revolutionary and anarchical in the extreme.

Storm Center: Jacksonians
and State Politics

McMaster traced aggressive tendencies North and South. . . .
In Georgia, official attacks developed against the presence and
land-tenure of the Cherokee Indians. . . . Abolitionists emerged in
the North defining moral issues in the slavery system. . . . Northern
states agreed on the undesirability of slavery within their borders,
but as clearly agreed on the need to maintain firm discrimination
against Negroes. . . . The sensitivity of southerners to their slave
property rights caused new laws to erupt south of Mason-Dixon.
. . . South Carolina seized free Negroes from on board ships entering her ports, and imprisoned or sold them. . . . It removed Negroes
from British vessels, in defiance of international treaties. . . . There
was nothing the Federal Government could do. . . . Anti-slavery
leaders became more distinct in their protests. . . . but slave coffles
passed by the Capitol of the United States unmolested. . . . The
tariff became a major issue, South Carolinians holding, with other
southerners, that only free trade could give them independence of
northern manufacturers. . . . Henry Clay's "American System"
promised to parcel out favors to all sections, protecting American
manufacturers, and also satisfying southerners in various ways. . . .
The System also promised ultimately to make Clay President. . . .
The Jacksonians in Congress reduced the Adams Administration
to impotence. . . . They insisted that the will of the people had been
flouted by Congress's choice of Adams: the result of a "corrupt
bargain" with Clay, who became his Secretary of State. . . . Skillful
Jackson managers stymied Adams's plans for internal improvements

of roads and canals. . . . They withheld money from Clay for delegates to a Pan-American Congress. . . . Southern Jacksonians were
especially unwilling to tolerate recognition of nations which would
send to it delegates of mixed or Negro blood. . . . They sought to
concoct a tariff program which would win Jackson votes. . . . The
1828 tariff—"The Tariff of Abominations"—was the result of a
complicated campaign which, as the witticism had it, had no industrial purpose except "the manufacture of a President." . . . The
South, studying defiance, denounced the Tariff as unconstitutional;
Calhoun formulated his doctrine of Nullification. . . . In effect, a
state could refuse to recognize a Federal law which transgressed its
sovereignty. . . . Democratic politics continued intensively to create
issues and crises, though in a framework which extended from
Europe to Oregon, and beyond. . . . Thus, American resentment of
English patronage was deep. . . . McMaster dealt at length with
its unmitigated contempt for American ideals and performance.
. . . Our slavery system made a mockery of our alleged freedoms,
the English thought; and as for our culture, McMaster helped to
make even more famous than it was the extraordinary diatribe of
the English wit, Sydney Smith, which asked, in part: "Where are
their Foxes, their Burkes, their Sheridans, their Windhams, their
Horners, their Wilberforces? where their Arkwrights, their Watts,
their Davys? . . . their Scotts, Campbells, Byrons, Moores, or
Crabbes? Their Siddonses, Kembles, Keans, or O'Neils? . . . In the
four quarters of the globe, who reads an American book? or goes
to an American play? or looks at an American picture or statue?
. . . What have they done in the mathematics? who drinks out of
American glasses? . . . or sleeps in American blankets? . . ." Mc-
Master (and American cultural leaders) had answers, but, in
McMaster's case, for full effectiveness, they had to be abstracted
from the total research he so lavishly laid before his readers. . . .
Many of his subsequent chapters dealt indirectly with aspects of
these charges. . . . McMaster depicted the rise of the common
school. . . . He offered the details of the ever-increasing suffrage:
the debates, the partisans, the political duels by which the suffrage
came. . . . The ever-increasing westward movement, despite strong
and eloquent dissent. . . . With relish, he abstracted from the
Register of Debates in Congress the speeches of men who believed

that the west ought to be left alone, or left to others. . . . A member of Congress from Tennessee summed up much skeptical opinion:

> When we contemplate the vast extent of the fertile territory which spreads to the east and south of the Rocky Mountains, we may well be led to wonder what can lead any adventurer to seek the inhospitable regions of Oregon, unless, indeed, he wishes to be a savage. At what period do gentlemen suppose the population of this happy republic will have filled up the fair and fertile territory within our present limits? At what distant day will the pursuits of agriculture and the train of the mechanic arts have taken full possession of this immense region? . . . But it is said that if we do not take possession some other power will. Well, suppose they do; what will we lose? It is a territory we ought not to inhabit, and one I hope we never shall inhabit. Why? Because it is situated at such an immeasurable distance from the seat of Government that there never will, there never can be, any intervening links to unite it with the rest of the country. . . . It seems to me the decree of Nature herself that the Rocky Mountains shall be the western boundary of this Republic. . . .
>
> But suppose it possible to settle such a country. The next step will be to organize it into a Territory, and then you will be called on to turn this Territory into a State. And what then? It can be but a few years before such a State must of its own weight fall off from this Confederacy. You have no practical means to connect such a State with the rest of the Republic. No delegate or representative can come thence to this House and return within a twelvemonth. Let his journey average twenty-five miles a day, and it will take him three hundred and sixty-eight days to come here and go back. His mileage will amount to nearly four thousand dollars, and be paid him for no other service than travelling. No, sir, let those restless spirits who cannot be content to cultivate their native soil, let such beings go to Oregon, but let them go at their own risk.

Twenty years later, McMaster noted, a delegate from the Territory of Oregon was sitting in the House of Representatives. . . .

McMaster plunged into the turbulent era of Jacksonian politics. . . . the belligerent President's Inauguration, and his inauguration of the Spoils System. . . . The monumental irrelevancy of Peggy Eaton. . . . The controversy over Texas: "Texas should be bought"; Texas should not be bought." . . . The great Hayne-Webster debates, the deep impression made on the country by Web-

ster's unmatchable appeal for the preservation of the Union. . . .
Its effect on Jackson, whose own challenge to Calhoun—"Our
Federal Union. *It must be preserved"*—marked his supreme moment. . . . Exciting developments, from railroad building to the
innovations of the Mormon Church. . . . Jackson put down Nullification in South Carolina. . . . or threatened to. . . . He attacked
the Second National Bank of the United States, possibly to some
effect, in any event riding as stormy an issue as domestic politics
had heretofore offered. . . . The momentous abolitionist movement
went underway: a wave of reform totally different from, and opposed to that which Jackson had to offer. . . . Wild speculation in
western lands was suddenly halted by Jackson's Specie Circular,
forcing investors to pay their Government debts in gold or silver.
. . . Jackson, in 1837, left the White House to his heir, Martin
Van Buren, with a heritage of the Panic of that year: the worst
economic crash in American history to that time. . . . State politics
brought out troops in Pennsylvania. . . . The attempt, in upper
New York State, to preserve the Dutch patroonships, a feudal system of land grants held in perpetuity, required militia to attempt
to maintain outmoded and resisted law. . . . The Whigs studied
demagogy, in order to challenge the Democrats at the polls. . . .

8

The Election of 1840:
Log Cabin and Hard Cider

THE most remarkable and exciting campaign our countrymen had yet witnessed was by this time drawing to a close.
The difficulty which troubled the Whigs at the outset was
that of uniting the many factions, old and new, which divided
their ranks and those of the Democrats.   There were anti-
renters, anti-slaverymen, and Abolitionists; there were the
friends of Harrison, the friends of Webster, the friends of
Clay; there were the Conservatives in New York bitterly
opposed to Van Buren; the men in Maine who denounced the
Government for its failure to settle the boundary question,
and voters everywhere who attributed the hard times to the
refusal of the Government to come to their aid.   All along
the border from Vermont to Michigan were thousands of
voters who looked on Van Buren as a British tool because
he had suffered the burning of the *Caroline* to pass un-
avenged, and had sent troops to prevent the patriot invasion
of Canada.   Could all these factions be united under one
chief a Whig victory was certain.   But how could they be
united, and under what chief?

As early as July of 1837 the Ohio State Convention of
Whigs suggested that delegates from all the States should
meet at Pittsburg on the second Monday in June, 1838, and
select candidates to be supported for the presidency and
vice-presidency in 1840.   The delegates from each State
were to be equal in number to its Senators, and Representatives, were to be chosen in such manner as the people saw
fit, and no nomination was to be made unless by a majority
of all the States represented by at least one delegate.   Ohio

Whigs preferred Harrison, but would support the choice of the Convention.*

No attention was paid to this call, and nothing more was heard of a national Whig Convention till March of 1838, when the friends of Harrison in Pennsylvania met and appointed a central committee to further his interests. But the State Convention at Harrisburg which nominated Harrison in December, 1835, had also appointed a central committee. These two bodies now united, formed the Democratic Republican Central Committee of Pennsylvania, and in April called for a national convention to meet at Pittsburg on July fourth, not to nominate Harrison, for the committee considered him as already nominated, but to aid his election.†

Great opposition at once appeared in Ohio. " This movement," said one Whig journal, " is premature, shortsighted, and suicidal. To express approbation of Harrison, to use all means to secure his nomination by a national convention was fair; but let there be no partial convention to effect an organization of the friends of any one man. Let one and all, Harrison-Whigs, Clay-Whigs, Webster-Whigs, cling to a national convention as the sheet anchor of Whig hopes and follow the banner there raised. In the present state of affairs for any portion of the Whig party to nail its banner to the mast of one man and declare its determination to vote for him, is to say it loves men better than principles."

Aroused by this show of Harrison sentiment, the friends of Clay in Philadelphia met, declared their preference for him and urged the Whig members of Congress to call a national convention and fix the time and place.‡ Thus prompted they did so, and suggested Harrisburg as the place, and the first Wednesday in December, 1839, as the day, for the meeting of the convention, and that each delegation be equal to the representation of its State in both houses of Congress. Efforts were thenceforth made in all parts of the

---

* Niles's Register, July 27, 1837, Vol. LII, p. 329.
† National Intelligencer, April 20, 1838.
‡ National Intelligencer, May 10, 1838.

country to prevent expression of preferences for any man and so unite those who for any reason hated the administration. A Boston journal insisted that the question of choosing a candidate should be left with the convention. Young men assembled at Utica declared that the time had not come when it was proper for a public assemblage to express any preference for a candidate for the office of Chief Magistrate. The people were calmly and deliberately discussing that question.* A Richmond journal urged Whigs to attend to the coming Congressional elections and leave other issues alone.† A Kentucky journal insisted that no man, no State, should say there was but one man on whom the great Whig party could be brought to unite. He who was unwilling to give a Whig vote unless for a particular person was no Whig, but a man-worshiper. Let the assembled patriotism of the country in 1839 settle the question of Van Buren's successor. When the Philadelphia Whigs met to rejoice over the Whig victory and the election of Seward in New York, they approved of the national convention and appealed to Whig brothers everywhere to leave the choice of a candidate to the delegates.‡

In November, the Democratic Anti-Masonic national convention met in Philadelphia and, on motion of Thaddeus Stevens, unanimously nominated Harrison and Webster.# The body was in no sense national and was attended by few delegates from States other than Pennsylvania. Harrison, nevertheless, accepted the nomination, and in his letter laid down what he considered true Whig principles.‖ The President, he believed, should have but one term, and no control over the treasury, should exert no influence on elections, should suffer no Federal officeholder to take part in elections, should never use his high office for purely partisan purposes, should always give reasons for removals from office, and should limit the veto to such bills as were unconstitutional, or infringed the rights of the States, or, when

---

* National Intelligencer, July 20, 1838.   † Ibid., July 13, 1838.
‡ National Intelligencer, December 3, 1838.
# Public Ledger, November 15, 1838.
‖ National Intelligencer, February 14, 1839.

great interests were involved, required more deliberation or a reference to the people.

As the winter drew to a close Whigs in many of the State legislatures felt called on to express their preferences, and thenceforth little heed was paid to the plea for uninstructed delegates. A convention of Whig members of the Massachusetts legislature and delegates from towns having no Whig representatives in the General Court named Webster as its choice, but pledged the Whigs to abide by the decision of the national convention.* Members of both branches of the legislature of Louisiana declared for Clay, but, having appointed delegates to the national convention, bade them unite in support of any other man who received the votes of a majority of the convention.† In Connecticut, before the legislature ended its session, the Whig members named Clay as their first choice; but, as principles were more than man, and country more than party, they would cheerfully support the candidate of the party.‡ The Whig State convention of Pennsylvania having adopted a resolution declaring Clay the preferred candidate, an attempt was made to strike out his name and insert that of Harrison, and when it failed the Harrison men presented a written protest and left the hall.# The friends of Harrison in the State legislature thereupon called for a State convention of the anti-Van Buren party to be held at Harrisburg in September. New Jersey Whigs were for "principles, not men," and made no recommendation. Neither did the conventions in Vermont, New Hampshire, or Rhode Island. Convinced that he did not have the smallest chance of a nomination by the party, Webster, who had gone abroad, now addressed a letter to the people of Massachusetts ‖ and withdrew his name, to the great delight of the followers of Harrison and Clay.

The anti-Van Buren union and harmony convention, as it was commonly called, when it met at Harrisburg in Sep-

---

* National Intelligencer, March 4, 1839.
† National Intelligencer, March 30, 1839.   ‡ Ibid., June 14, 1839.
# Held June 14, 1839, National Intelligencer, June 22, 1839.
‖ National Intelligencer, July 6, 1839.

tember, chose delegates to the national convention, adopted
resolutions, bade a committee write an address, and declared
that no one save Harrison could unite the anti-Van Buren
party and rescue the country from misrule.   The reasons for
this statement were fully given in the address.   " There are
in the party of opposition," it was said, " many branches:
Abolitionists, anti-Masons, Democrats, Whigs, and men who,
prompted by gratitude for arduous military services, supported Andrew Jackson.   Can Mr. Clay unite these?   He
cannot.   The position taken by him in a recent speech in the
Senate must of necessity drive from him all Abolitionists.
A like difficulty existed with the anti-Masons.   Not only
have they persistently refused to support Mr. Clay, but they
have gone so far in opposition as to nominate General Harrison.   Could the Jackson men attached to the Whig party
forget the bitter opposition of Mr. Clay to their hero?

" To General Harrison no such objections exist.   Look at
the election returns for evidence of the popular estimate of
Mr. Clay and General Harrison.   In 1832 Mr. Clay was
beaten in Ohio, in New Jersey; in Indiana and in Maryland
had a majority of but ninety-two, and in Delaware of but
one hundred and sixty-six.   In 1836 General Harrison carried each of these States by handsome majorities, and cut
down the Democratic majority in Pennsylvania from twenty-
four thousand to forty-three hundred.   Van Buren, to be
sure, was elected in 1836.   Then he had the halo of Jackson's popularity.   But how is it now?   Has a bankrupt treasury, a wretched currency, profligate use of public money,
insolent meddling of Government officers with elections, the
many evils of his administration added to his popularity? "

In New York the outlook for Clay was far from good.
Early in February an old friend informed him that the great
body of the New York Whigs preferred him before all
others, and that the Whig Legislature stood ready to openly
declare him its choice, but were restrained by a class of politicians who thought it unwise to make a public declaration
at that time.   Chief among such Whigs were Seward and
Thurlow Weed, then the most important political leaders in
the State.   Disturbed by this warning Clay decided to do

what he had the year before declined to do, and accepted an invitation to visit New York. The time chosen happened to be that selected by Van Buren for a like political tour. Each party sought to surpass the other in enthusiasm for its chief, and the journey of each leader resembled a political progress. All went well with Clay till Saratoga was reached. There he met Weed who told him, as politely as possible, that he could not carry New York, and that for the good of the party he should withdraw in favor of a candidate on whom all the opponents of the administration could unite. That Weed was correct in his estimate need not be doubted; for neither anti-Masons, Abolitionists, nor Conservatives were likely to cast one vote for Clay. But he was willing to take his chances, and the two men parted; Clay fully determined to remain a candidate, and Weed as fully determined to defeat him.

The animosity which the Conservatives felt for Van Buren was expressed in an address by their State convention. The President was charged with responsibility for the panic of 1837 and all the ills it brought, because he had refused to recall the specie circular; with a cruel neglect of the paternal and protecting duties of government by refusing to assemble Congress till the Government was bankrupt, and, after bringing insolvency on the land, with adding to the manifold evils by recommending the sub-treasury, and withholding the fourth instalment of the surplus. He was a political apostate; he had forgotten his promise to follow in the footsteps of his illustrious predecessor, and was no longer worthy to be called a Democratic Republican. He was the enemy of credit, the enemy of banks, the uncompromising advocate of metallic currency. He proposed to put the public revenue in the hands of the Executive, through agents appointed by him and removable at his will, unite the purse and sword, increase his means of corruption, and by uniting in his person the command of the army and navy, and the keeping and the spending of the public money, gather to himself every attribute which defines a monarch and creates a tyrant. "Suppose we had a metallic currency," it was said, "would our condition be improved? There is in this country about

sixty millions of specie. Our circulation, even in these times
of distress, is not less than five hundred millions. How much
more freely then will we breath when the President has
brought us down to sixty millions? The man who now gets
a dollar a day will then get a shilling, and think himself fortunate to get that. The man who has ample means will
be reduced to insolvency, and the man who owns a farm and
owes for one-eighth of it will lose his estate and be brought
to want. Shall the People or the Executive control public
measures? Shall we have a Government by the people or
by officeholders? Shall we have prosperity or ruin and
misery? These are the questions you must answer."

The Whig convention in Virginia declared for Clay and
Tallmadge,* as did that of North Carolina.† Those of
Michigan, of Tipton County, Tennessee, and of New York
City preferred Clay, but would support the choice of the
convention.‡ That Clay was the party favorite was by this
time quite clear; but it was equally clear that he was not
the available candidate and that if the many factions opposed to the administration were to be united under the
Whig banner, it would have to be carried by another chief.
A rumor, current in August, set forth that Seward, Weed,
and the New York Whigs would abandon Clay and take up
Winfield Scott.# But it came from a Locofoco journal, was
denounced as a foolish attempt to divide and conquer the
Whigs, and was soon forgotten. Yet it was true, and when
the great Whig convention met in December, General Scott
was given the votes of New York, New Jersey, and Vermont.

The first day of the Harrisburg convention was taken up
with matters of organization. On the second the work of
selecting a candidate began. The Massachusetts delegation
presented an order of business which proposed that the delegates from each State should assemble, appoint each a committee, and then ballot for President and Vice-President;

* Niles's Register, October 19, 1839, p. 127.
† National Intelligencer, November 18, 1839.
‡ Ibid., November 23, 1839.
# The New Era. National Intelligencer, August 3, 1839.

that the result should then be made known to the committee, which should announce it to a general meeting of the
committees from all the States; that in this way the State
delegations should continue to ballot until a majority of the
States should have voted in favor of some one particular candidate whose name should then be laid before the convention
for further action.   No little opposition was made to this
plan; but it was adopted, with an amendment that the vote
of the majority of each delegation should be reported as the
vote of the State, which should be its full electoral vote.

On the third day, in order that the balloting might go
on, adjournments were taken again and again till near midnight, when the chairman of the committee of three from
each State reported that two hundred and fifty-four votes
had been cast; that one hundred and twenty-eight were necessary to a choice; that Winfield Scott had received sixteen,
Henry Clay ninety, and William Henry Harrison one hundred and forty-eight.*

The committee was then given leave to sit again and
ballot for a Vice-President.   When the convention assembled
on the morning of the fourth day member after member rose
to eulogize Clay.   " The first choice of my constituents,"
said one, " was Henry Clay; and my constituents are uncompromising; but it is in their hostility to Martin Van Buren.
They left me uninstructed who to vote for save on the first
ballot, and now I stand on the broad platform of hostility
to Martin Van Buren and will support the nomination."
" The first choice of Maryland," said another, " is well
known.   I came here to support, and did support, that choice
till it was found that there was another name under which
we can carry dismay into the ranks of the oppressors of our
country with perhaps better hope of success."   He moved,
therefore, that the nomination of Harrison be made unani-

* On the first ballot Clay received 103, Harrison 91, and Scott 57 (New York,
New Jersey, and Vermont).   Michigan was divided till the third delegate appeared.
After several ballots Connecticut and Michigan went over to Scott, thus making
the vote Clay 95, Harrison 91, Scott 68.   On the last ballot, New York, Michigan,
and Vermont left Scott and Illinois left Clay and the vote stood Harrison 148,
Clay 90, Scott 16.

mous. The convention and the crowd that filled the galleries shouted a willing response, whereupon the friends of Clay, one by one, rose to express their determination to give to the chosen candidate that support which they had " heretofore felt bound to give to another equally cherished name."

Preston of Kentucky moved for an address to the people, declared the hopes of Kentucky were blighted in the defeat of her favorite son, but assured the convention that no disappointment would rankle in the breast of Henry Clay. " There is," he said, " a letter in possession of the convention which will prove the truth of my statement, and I hope the letter will be read." A great clamor for the reading of the letter brought another delegate from Kentucky to his feet, and in the midst of a profound silence a document which Clay had never expected would be used was laid before the convention. Appeals, Clay wrote, direct and indirect, had been made to him by a Pennsylvania convention and by private citizens urging him to withdraw his name in favor of a distinguished son of Ohio who was the first choice of the opposition in Pennsylvania. Respectable citizens of New York had also addressed him and recommended him to decline in favor of another citizen distinguished alike in the military and in the civil service of the United States. On the other hand private citizens, public meetings, and conventions in various parts of the country had called on him to be the candidate of the opposition. Under these embarrassing circumstances it seemed best to leave to the Harrisburg convention the free selection of a candidate. Should another than himself be chosen, " far from feeling any discontent the nomination " should have his " best wishes and receive " his " cordial support."

More eulogies followed. Delegate after delegate declared that his first choice had been Clay; but that he would support the nomination and, in the words of Wise of Virginia, he was for " Union for the sake of Union." In the midst of this speechmaking the chairman of the committee of three from each State reported that John Tyler was the unanimous choice of the States for Vice-President. The convention confirmed this choice, recommended that the

Whig young men of the several States hold a convention at Baltimore on Washington's Birthday, or at any other time, for the purpose of organization, and then adjourned without day. No platform was adopted; no address to the people was ordered.

The convention having come to an end many delegates with one accord started for Washington. Happening to take the same train, it was found on comparing notes that all—all to a man—were the earnest admirers and steadfast friends of Clay. A meeting was forthwith called, a chairman elected, and a resolution passed to wait on Clay and assure him that his crowning act of self-sacrifice was fully appreciated, that his letter urging the convention to merge all other considerations in that of helping their country and their cause was an everlasting monument to his principles and a justification of all that had ever been said of him by his warmest friends. After reaching Washington and gathering for the purpose of their visit to Clay, it was found that of the twenty-two States which sent delegates to Harrisburg, eighteen were represented in Washington.

The meeting with the great man is described as most affecting. All hearts were moved. A profound solemnity settled over the faces of the delegates and some shed tears, for Harry of the West has " been offered up, not so much by his friends, however, as by himself, a living sacrifice to the great principles of our political faith which forbids man worship "?

The affecting ceremony over, a committee from the Whig members of Congress invited the delegates to a dinner which took place on the night of the following day. There was a speech from Clay, who was astonished to hear of sacrifices. There had been no sacrifice, none whatever! How could it ever have entered the hearts of men to suppose that what the Whigs of the New World were toiling for ever was, or ever could be, a contest for men—for Henry Clay, or William Henry Harrison, or Daniel Webster, or Winfield Scott? There were speeches from Tyler, from Crittenden of Kentucky, and Wise of Virginia, and Bell of Tennessee, and Granger of New York, and Lincoln of Massachusetts, and

happy allusions to " the North Bender," to Harry and to
Harry's-son and Harry's-burg, where those who could not
get Harry had wisely determined to take Harry's-son.*

As the result of the labors of the convention became
known great ratification meetings were held at Philadelphia,
New York, and Poughkeepsie. When the Whig members of
the Kentucky legislature heard the news they met at once
and appointed a committee to address the people, and the
Whig Central Committee called earnestly on the voters to
support Harrison, for the defeat of Clay was keenly felt in
Kentucky. In New Jersey the Whigs of Mercer County
met at Trenton and, in the resolutions then adopted declared that they rejoiced over the nomination of Harrison
as a bright omen for the country, as the morning star of
hope, as the sure forerunner of the return of good government; that their ardent and long-cherished admiration for
that high-souled man, devoted patriot, and preëminent statesman, Henry Clay, was still more elevated by his noble
conduct in espousing the cause of Harrison; and that the
Whigs of New Jersey were impatient for election day when,
at the head of a long array of admiring supporters, they
would lead the Hero of Tippecanoe in triumph to the presidential chair.† The Abolition press was delighted with the
nomination and hailed the defeat of Clay as a new triumph
for the cause.

The *Liberator* regarded it as another sign of the times,
as a signal defeat to slavocracy. Had it not been for the
Abolitionists, Henry Clay would surely have been nominated. Never again would a slaveholder be permitted to
fill the presidential chair. " Praise God! " exclaimed the
Emancipator, " for a great anti-slavery victory. A man of
high talents, of great distinction, of long political service, of
boundless personal popularity has been openly rejected for
the Presidency because of his devotion to slavery. A slaveholder is incapacitated for the Presidency of the United
States! Set up a monument of progress! " " The rejection

* All these proceedings are narrated in the National Intelligencer, December
14, 1839.

† National Intelligencer, January 3. 1840.

of Mr. Clay," said the *Philanthropist,* " and the selection of
General Harrison is to some extent a concession to the spirit
of liberty in the North." " The rejection of Henry Clay,"
said the Oberlin *Evangelist,* " shows that a slaveholder can
never again expect to be President of this free Republic.
For what has been gained, we thank God, and for what is
yet to be gained we trust in the same God." Another journal declared that the Abolitionists of Ohio were in ecstasies
over the defeat of Clay and the nomination of Harrison.
The *Globe,* the administration newspaper, charged Harrison
with being an Abolitionist, and as such, attacked him vigorously. An Ohio newspaper * assured its readers that if
Harrison were elected the twenty-eight millions of surplus
revenue deposited with the States would be recalled and used
to buy " refuse negroes to be set free to overrun our country." Had he not said in a speech that nothing was nearer
his heart than to see the whole surplus revenue appropriated to the cause of emancipation?

To this charge the Whig members of the Virginia legislature made reply. On every question involving political
principle Harrison was, they held, more orthodox than his
competitor. Especially was this true on that all-absorbing
and, to the South, vital, question, Abolition. Surely Harrison, who had lost a high and honorable position because he
opposed the Missouri restriction, and who denied the power
of Congress to meddle with slavery in the States, ought to
be preferred by the South to Van Buren, who was chiefly
instrumental in getting up the restriction and who had
voted to give the negro the same right of suffrage as the
white man in New York.†

The Whigs having failed to provide a platform for their
opponents to attack, the Democratic press fell upon the man,
and in sneers at his poverty and humble occupations as a
farmer and clerk of a court, gave to the Whigs the most
popular of platforms. A correspondent, writing to a Baltimore newspaper, observed that when a friend of Clay heard

---

* Ohio Statesman. The Globe, January 13, 1840.
† The National Intelligencer, January 16, 1840.

of the Harrisburg nomination, he remarked that if Harrison were given a pension of two thousand dollars a year, plenty of hard cider, and a log cabin to live in, he would never trouble anyone about the Presidency.*

Because of this Harrison was promptly dubbed " The Log Cabin and Hard Cider candidate," an old granny, a deserving old gentleman, doubtless, but one his friends should be content to leave in the quiet enjoyment of his fees as clerk of a court in Ohio.† The sneer, Log Cabin, Hard Cider candidate, was just such a campaign cry as the Whigs needed. It was taken up instantly, and in a little while the plain people the country over believed that he really did live in a log cabin, that he was a man who never touched strong liquor, earned his bread by cultivating his farm with his own hands, and was, in fine, a modern Cincinnatus at the plow.

Log Cabin candidate, said the Whigs, is the term of reproach given by the Van Buren party to General Harrison because, after fifty years of patriotic devotion to his country, he has retired to his farm poor and dependent on his daily labor for his daily bread. The pampered officeholders of the Federal Government sneer at the idea of making a poor man President. These scoffers at Republican simplicity point with exultation to the palace of Van Buren, to his liveried servants, his numerous outriders, and ask if a man who has drunk hard cider all his life is fit to occupy the White House.‡ He has lived in a log cabin long enough,

---

* " Give him a barrel of Hard Cider, and settle a pension of $2,000 a year on him, and my word for it, he will sit the remainder of his days in his Log Cabin, by the side of a ' sea-coal ' fire and study moral philosophy."—Baltimore Republican.

" A Proposition. It was proposed, some time since, that Gen. Harrison should be presented with a barrel of Hard Cider, on condition of his retiring from the field as a candidate for the Presidency."—Baltimore Republican.

" Gen. Harrison's poverty has awakened the sympathy of the ladies of this District, and they are now at work getting up a subscription to supply the ' war-worn hero' with a suit of clothes. If you have any old shoes, old boots, old hats, or old stockings, send them on and they will be forwarded to the 'Hero of North Bend.' "—Washington Correspondent, New York Evening Post.

† Utica Observer. National Intelligencer, January 4, 1840.

‡ New York Daily Whig. National Intelligencer, January 14, 1840.

and the people intend on March fourth, 1841, to give him free rent of their great white house in Washington.* Every log cabin beyond the mountains and throughout the mighty West will rush to the contest in support of a gallant soldier and veteran statesman and seat him in the Presidential chair.

" Listen," exclaimed a North Carolina Whig editor, " to the fawning minions of power casting sneers at the venerable hero of Tippecanoe on account of his poverty! Hear them urging it against him that he is a clerk in a county court! He who has fought more and harder battles than any other warrior now living in the United States, who gained more splendid victories than any other American hero now living; who was Governor of the Northwest Territory for fifteen years; who was a delegate, and a Representative in Congress, a Senator of the United States, and a minister to a foreign court, has come out of all these offices poor. He might have been as rich as Jackson or Van Buren." †

At a Harrison and Tyler ratification meeting at Harrisburg a huge transparency was displayed. On one side was Harrison's log cabin; on the second, the battle of the Thames; on the third, the flag of the Republic; and on the fourth, " Democracy, Reform, and one Presidential term." ‡ Such popular meetings in the East were tame when compared with the enthusiastic rallies in the West. When the Indiana Whig State convention was about to assemble at Indianapolis the delegates came with bands of music, flags, banners, and mottoes, and came in such numbers that they formed a procession a mile long.# At another, in the Western Reserve, described as the greatest ever known there, were three thousand men who left their " log cabins " to " cheer on the friends of the log-cabin candidate." There, too, was a procession with banners bearing such inscriptions as " Don't give up the ship "; " The Union of the Whigs for the sake of the Union "; " The Hero of Tippecanoe ";

---

* National Intelligencer, January 10, 1840.
† North Carolina Star. National Intelligencer, January 14, 1840.
‡ Ibid., January 27, 1840.
# National Intelligencer, January 28, 1840.

"The Farmer's President; the People's candidate." *
Twenty-five hundred were counted at the Cleveland rally.
No building could contain the crowd, so "the temple of
nature was used."

Greater still was the attendance at the Ohio Whig convention, at Columbus, on Washington's Birthday.   Travel
at that season of the year was, indeed, difficult.   But neither
snow nor rain, nor roads knee deep with mud could dampen
the zeal of the Whigs.   Twenty thousand, it was claimed,
came from all parts of the State.   Some walked, some rode,
whole delegations arrived in canoes or log cabins or boats,
mounted on wheels and drawn by six or eight horses, and
decorated with banners and mottoes.   On one banner was
the American Cincinnatus with his hand on the plow.   On
another he stood at his cabin door dealing out hard cider
to canal laborers.   A delegation from the Maumee brought,
on wheels, a model of Fort Meigs.   A company of Mad
River trappers came in a log cabin decorated with coon
skins; the men from Cleveland had a square-rigged brig;
a party on foot shouldered corn-shuck brooms; on the roof
of some of the log cabins as they rolled along sat "merry
fellows eating johnnycake, and drinking hard cider and
singing patriotic songs." †   The great procession was on the
second day of the convention.   With eight men marching
abreast, and the cabins, canoes, and boats in line, it was
two miles long.

The West, it was truly said, was aflame.   "There is not
a tree, not a stone in all the West," exclaimed one enthusiastic editor, "that does not own to the Harrison cause.
Women name their children Tippecanoe, North Bend, anything that smacks of Harrison.   We know a drayman who
has called one of his horses Tip and the other Ty, and as he
snaps the whip crys out, 'Go it, Tip! come it, Ty!'   Harrison and Tyler are everywhere.   They are seen in the beams
of the western sun.   They are heard in every breeze that
blows.   'Huzza for Harrison!' say the boys as their sleds

* National Intelligencer, January 5, 1840.
† Ibid., February 28, 1840.

glide down the streets. 'Huzza for Harrison!' shout the urchins as they go home from school. The people are struggling to hold in; they want to vote now." *   "The hens in the West," said a wag, "never lay an egg nowadays but they cackle, 'Tip-tip! Tip-tip! Tyler'!"

"In what grave and important discussion," a Van Buren editor asked, "are the Whig journals engaged? How are they enlightening the public mind and supplying material for that deep and solemn reflection which befits a great people about to choose a ruler? We speak of the divorce of bank and state; and the Whigs reply with a dissertation on the merits of hard cider. We defend the policy of the administration; and the Whigs answer, 'log cabin,' 'big canoes,' 'go it, Tip, come it, Ty.' We urge the reëlection of Van Buren because of his honesty, sagacity, statesmanship, and show the weakness and unfitness of his opponent; and the Whigs answer that Harrison is a poor man and lives in a log cabin. We show that he is not a poor man, that he does not drink hard cider, unless from choice, that his home is not a log cabin, but a fine house, and that as clerk of a court he receives a clear income of six thousand dollars a year in fees; the Whigs reply, 'No matter, the prairies are on fire.'" †

The poverty, the log cabin, the hard cider, the Democrats never wearied of pointing out, were false appeals to sympathy. The man the Whigs pictured as poor really lived in a large and splendid mansion on the banks of the Ohio, in the midst of a princely estate of two thousand acres. That he was mentally unfit to be President was proved, they said, if it needed to be proved, by the way his friends guarded him. When an association in Oswego addressed a letter questioning Harrison as to his political faith, they received a reply signed by three men who called themselves his confidential committee. For General Harrison to answer the many letters received each day was impracticable. The duty of replying had therefore been taken over by the

---

* The Pennsylvanian, February 28, 1840.
† Ibid., March 25, 1840.

committee whose policy it was that General Harrison should make no further declaration of his principles for the public eye.*   Delighted at what it considered a sure sign of imbecility the Democratic press ridiculed the committee as the " sense-bearers," dubbed Harrison " General Mum," and declared that the poor old gentleman had been taken in charge by a committee without the formality of a writ *de lunatico inquirendo.*

Scoffs and jeers, however, went unheeded by the Whigs, or served but to inflame the rising enthusiasm for their candidate. Most wisely did a Democratic journal call on the party to let Harrison and his history alone and " fire away " at what were supposed to be Whig principles.   Everywhere Whig young men were holding meetings for the choice of delegates to their convention, and at these meetings sneers at the herc of Tippecanoe made good campaign material. The East, catching the enthusiasm of the West, was holding Whig festivals with log cabins on wheels, with Whig banners, Whig music, and Whig songs,† and began to put up Tippecanoe log cabins to serve as headquarters for town committees during the campaign,‡ and to organize Tippecanoe clubs to march and sing and work for the election of " Tip " and " Ty."   When the Whig young men of New Jersey met in convention ten thousand men marched in the procession.   From five to ten thousand attended the rally at Winchester, to which a delegation came with a log cabin on wheels and drawn by ten horses.   Smoke issued from its chimney, and within were men in hunting shirts. At St. Clairsville there were ten thousand.   Fifteen hundred came on horseback, and hundreds in wagons.   At Frederick City, Maryland, the usual ten thousand attended and " flags,

---

* The Pennsylvanian, March 27, 1840.

† One of the most popular campaign songs called " Old Tip," and sung to the music of " The Old Oaken Bucket," was written by a young Whig of New York City and read at the Third Ward Whig meeting in March.

‡ " The Whigs of Auburn (N. Y.) are putting up a Tippecanoe Log Cabin. The Tippecanoe boys have gone into the woods to cut the logs.   The building will be 35 × 40 feet, and calculated for a committee room for the friends of the Hero of the Thames and Tippecanoe of the county to meet in."—National Intelligencer, March 21, 1840.

banners, log cabins, bands of music, and smiling women cheered the day."

In the midst of these Whig rejoicings a little band of men, gathered from six States, met at Albany, laid the foundation of a third party, and placed two other men in nomination for the Presidency and Vice-Presidency of the United States. No newspaper mentioned their proceedings, save to comment on them with contempt. Yet the political movement there begun proved to be the most important in our history since the adoption of the Constitution.

That the time had come when the anti-slavery people should break away from both the old parties and put in the field candidates of their own had been the firm belief of certain leaders in New York and Massachusetts for a year past. Hitherto the Abolitionists had acted as a third party, and by throwing their support to one side or the other had defeated this man or elected that, or forced the Whigs to take up anti-slavery candidates. The defeat of Governor Vance of Ohio because he surrendered the Rev. John B. Mahan to the Governor of Kentucky; the election of Luther Bradish, Lieutenant Governor of New York, by a vote greater than was cast for any other Whig on the ticket; the election of William Sprague, Governor of Rhode Island, and the election to Congress of Joshua R. Giddings of the Western Reserve, Seth M. Gates of the Genesee district in New York, and of a member from Massachusetts who died before taking his seat, were but so many signs of growing power. From a party thus giving its support to the least objectionable Whig or Democratic candidate, to a party with its own platform, candidates, and leaders, the transition was easy and sure to come. Indeed, it was a clear perception of this independence that led Clay in his famous anti-slavery speech in February, 1839, to say, " It is because these ultra-Abolitionists have ceased to employ the instruments of reason and persuasion, have made their cause political, and have appealed to the ballot box, that I am induced on this occasion to address you." And it was this denunciation by Clay that brought from Senator Morris of Ohio the retort, " Who shall dare say that an Abolitionist has no right to carry his principles to the ballot box? Let me then proclaim here, from this high arena, to the citizens, not only of my own State, but of the country, to all sects and parties who are entitled to the right of suffrage: To the ballot box."

That the attack of Clay did much to stimulate the independent party movement is not to be doubted. What had hitherto been discussed now took the form of action. A circular sent out from New York suggesting the nomination of an anti-slavery ticket for State officers and members of Congress brought hearty responses. But an attempt to obtain a nomination of candidates for the Presidency and Vice-Presidency by the anti-slavery convention which met at Albany in July and August, 1839, ended in failure. A Monroe County convention at Rochester in September, a convention of fourteen members, was more considerate, and under the influence of Myron Holley adopted resolutions urging Abolitionists to set up a national ticket, appointed a committee to address the public, and requested the anti-slavery convention about to meet in Cleveland to name the candidates for President and Vice-President.

Against this the managers of the Massachusetts Anti-Slavery Society protested vigorously in an address to abolition voters.* They had seen with regret and alarm a growing disposition to persuade Abolitionists to form a distinct political party. Any such action would be ill advised, because it would not unite but would divide Abolitionists, and " a house divided against itself cannot stand "; because it would bring into the abolition ranks a swarm of unprincipled aspirants who, for the sake of the loaves and fishes of office, would resort to the worst artifices to justify their ambition; because it would strip the anti-slavery cause of its disinterested, philanthropic aspect, would be a virtual denial of the power of moral suasion and eternal truth to overcome prejudice; would incline the pulpit to plead less frequently and far less effectively in behalf of the anti-slavery cause; would be a hazardous experiment; would array against anti-slavery

---

* Address to the Anti-Slavery electors of Massachusetts. The Liberator Extra October, 1839.

the whole power of the Whig and Democratic parties, and
bring down upon Abolitionists the charge of inconsistency.
Again and again the Society, by resolution or through its
executive committee, had repudiated the idea of organization
as a political party. Now it was a resolution that Abolitionists ought neither to organize a distinct political party, nor,
as Abolitionists, to attach themselves to any existing party;
now " that we shall deprecate the organization of any Abolition political party "; and again, " that Abolitionists have resolved from the first to act upon slavery politically, not by
organizing a new political party, but by making it the interest of the parties already existing to act upon abolition
principles." To these principles every true friend of emancipation should hold fast and, forgetful of party names,
heedless of party badges, give his vote for no member of the
State or National Legislature who did not favor the immediate abolition of slavery in the District of Columbia and
the Territories.

From Ohio, where the convention was to meet, came a
like protest. " Our object," said a convention of Abolitionists in the Western Reserve, " is not the formation of a distinct political party. We repudiate the name of party."
" Anti-slavery men," said the *Philanthropist*, " are against
slavery everywhere; but an anti-slavery political party can
only be against slavery somewhere, as in the District, or in
the Territories, or against the admission of Florida, the an-
nexation of Texas, or against the interstate slave trade."

When the Cleveland convention met, in October, the
proposition to nominate candidates for the Presidency and
Vice-Presidency, after a long debate was laid on the table,
and the advocates of an independent ticket turned once more
to New York, and by a convention which met at Warsaw in
November secured the nomination of James G. Birney and
Francis J. LeMoyne. Both declined; LeMoyne from mod-
esty; Birney, because the nomination did not come from
a national convention called for the purpose.

This objection was speedily overcome in January, 1840,
by a State convention of New York Abolitionists who issued
a call for a national convention to meet at Albany on April

first, 1840, to take into consideration the formation of a Liberty Party. Six States were then represented and the delegates, convinced that they were pledged not to vote for nor support any man for President or Vice-President who was not in favor of immediate abolition and sure that neither the Whigs nor the Democrats would put up such men, resolved that they owed it to the sacred cause of human rights to nominate such men, and selected Birney and Thomas Earle of Philadelphia as the candidates of the Liberty Party.

Nowhere did this entrance into politics as a third party meet with hearty approval. A Whig journal in Boston was glad the Abolitionists had decided to support their own candidate; they were not wanted as an adjunct to the Whigs. The *National Intelligencer* believed the movement was a Van Buren scheme to draw away votes from the Whigs and lead to their defeat in New York and Massachusetts.

That this bold attempt of Birney, Holley, Elizur Wright, and other old-time leaders to found a political abolition party, if persevered in, would sooner or later split the anti-slavery ranks was certain. But when the annual convention of the American Anti-Slavery Society met at New York a few weeks later, causes of a very different sort rent the Society in twain. The minority, led by Birney, Wright, Stanton, Tappan, and others, formed a new organization which they called The American and Foreign Anti-Slavery Society, and charged the old Society with a pursuit of purposes and objects not contemplated by its founders, foreign to its original aims, not necessary to their attainment, and fatal to success, and specified these foreign issues as the woman question, no political action, and the acceptance of Garrison's no human government views.

The great gathering, the greatest political demonstration which, up to that day, had taken place in the United States, was the Young Men's Whig convention at Baltimore. Every State and the District of Columbia were represented. "Not a district of this great Republic," it was boastfully said, "was without its delegates. Representatives were here from beyond the Mississippi, from the borders of the Great Lakes, from the shores of the Gulf of Mexico. The sons of the Puritans met with the descendants of the Cavaliers; the Western Buckeye was seen side by side with the Palmetto of the South; the dweller on the seashore saluted the hardy mountaineer.".* One hundred thousand people, it was claimed, beheld the great parade of delegates as they marched through the streets to the race grounds where the convention was to meet. All shops were closed; no business was done. Across the streets hung flags, mottoes, portraits of Harrison. Roofs, windows, balconies, and doors were crowded with spectators shouting, cheering, and waving flags and handkerchiefs. The sidewalks " seemed wedged by a solid mass of men."

At the head of the procession marched the Baltimore delegation carrying a banner inscribed with a stanza from the popular Whig song " Old Tip," which well described the scene.† The invited guests came next, and then followed the State delegations bearing silk banners, with mottoes, and devices fitting for the day. Log cabins abounded. One from Pennsylvania was drawn by six horses and adorned with fox skins, buck horns, and implements of frontier husbandry. The latchstring was hanging out; a barrel of hard cider was in the rear, and a gourd near by. A delegation from Alleghany rolled along a ball ten feet in diameter covered with mottoes, inscriptions, apt quotations, and rhymes.

When the race course was reached the procession passed under a triumphal arch, to one side of which stood a log cabin built in true backwoods style. The chimney was of

---

* National Intelligencer, May 7, 1840. Baltimore American, May 5, 1840.

    † " The people are coming from plain and from mountain,
        To join the brave band of the honest and free,
    Which grows as the stream from the leaf-sheltered fountain,
        Spreads broad and more broad till it reaches the sea.
    No strength can restrain it ; no force can retain it,
        Whate'er may resist, it breaks gallantly through,
    And borne by its motion, as a ship on the ocean,
          Speeds on in his glory
          Old Tippecanoe !

    " The iron-armed soldier, the true-hearted soldier,
        The gallant old soldier of Tippecanoe ! "

sticks, the chinks were stuffed with clay, and the latchstring hung out. Not far away was a miniature Fort Meigs, with real guns. Two platforms were provided—one for the invited guests and one for the officers of the convention. Gathering about these stands while the band played and the guns of Fort Meigs fired a salute, the Whig young men beheld before them the great leaders of their party, Webster, Clay, Preston, Crittenden, Cushing, Fillmore, Wise, and listened to speeches till late in the afternoon. Next day the delegates, assembled in Monument Square, were addressed by a score of speakers, and toward nightfall adjourned.

From Baltimore, the Harrison Ball, as it was called, was taken to Philadelphia to be passed on eastward and rolled in Whig parades. Unhappily, as the returning city delegates were marching through the streets of Philadelphia rolling the ball along, it collapsed in the middle of the street to the great delight of the Democrats, who suggested that nothing was needed to complete this campaign of songs, cider, and puffballs but a popular Whig dance after the fashion of a country breakdown.

While the Whigs were crowding about the speakers in Monument Square the delegates to the national Democratic convention assembled in Musical Hall. The meeting had been called and the time and place suggested by the Central Committee of New Hampshire, for the purpose of agreeing on candidates for the Presidency and Vice-Presidency. To select a name for the first place was a matter of no difficulty. So many States had called for Van Buren that it was the undivided wish of the party, the nominating committee told the convention, that he should be the candidate for President. To agree on a name for the second place was not an easy matter. Many of the States which nominated Van Buren had not agreed on any one man for the Vice-Presidency. The committee, therefore, advised that it was inexpedient to make a choice, and suggested that the matter be left with the States. The convention took the advice, presented Van Buren to the people as the Democratic candidate for the Presidency, named nobody for the Vice-Presidency, and adopted a platform of principles. The

Federal Government was declared to be one of limited powers; was denied authority to carry on a general system of internal improvements; to assume directly or indirectly the
debts contracted by the States for internal improvements;
to charter a national bank, protect manufacturers, or interfere with slavery in the States. Divorce of bank and state
and resistance to every attempt to change the naturaliza-
tion laws were asserted to be sound Democratic doctrine.

The labors of the two Baltimore conventions having been
thus happily ended, the Locofocos began to draw compari-
sons. " What a striking contrast," it was said, " is presented
to the people by the proceedings of the two conventions.
The one, casting aside reason as something not likely to answer its purpose, assembled not to show enthusiasm, but to
create it. The other, a dignified, deliberative body, regularly
formed, met quietly and broadly and plainly stated its principles and submits them to the consideration of the people.
The one kept Baltimore in a whirl of excitement for several days with its marchings and counter marchings; its banners, cider barrels, log cabins, badges, songs, and huge balls
rolled along to make the children stare. The other made no
inflammatory appeals, held no parade of unmeaning con-
trivances, resorted to no clatter of barrels and tin cups. The
one uttered not a word in reference to party principles and
offered no reason why Martin Van Buren should be opposed.
The other, shunning all fustian rant, defined the sound max-
ims of political economy and national finance on which the
administration of Van Buren rests.

" The Whig's party has refused to put forth an address
to the people stating its views on the issues of the hour; the
candidate is closely guarded by a committee and is not suffered to speak. Is it not fair to presume, therefore, that
there is something to conceal, and that this something is the
fact that William Henry Harrison is still a member of the
old Federal party of '99—the party that established the
National Bank, opposed the war of 1812, supported a high
tariff for protection and internal improvements at government expense, and now calls for a second assumption of
State debts and has formed an alliance with the Abolition-

ists? This old Federalist has been chosen as the candidate not because of fitness as a statesman, but because of availability as a military chieftain, and a man of the people. The cry of log cabin, hard cider, Cincinnatus at the plow, is raised in order to convey the belief that the one is his habitation, the other his beverage, and that agriculture is his pursuit. Far from suffering the stings of poverty, he lives in a large and commodious house, enjoys the products of a fruitful farm, and the income of a lucrative county office.

"He bears the military title of General; but his reputation as a military man added nothing to the glory of his country and was so doubtful that the Senate of the United States refused him the compliment of a sword. Neither has he been more fortunate in his civil career. He was defeated as a candidate for Governor both in Indiana and Ohio, and in both Indiana and Ohio was in favor of selling poor white men into slavery when unable to pay the costs of suits at law.* Do the farmers, mechanics, laboring men suffer from

---

* In 1807, when Governor of Indiana Territory, Harrison approved an act which provided: "Sec. 30. When any person, or persons, shall, on conviction of any crime, or breach of penal law, be sentenced to pay a fine or fines, with or without costs of prosecution, it shall and may be lawful for the court, before whom such conviction shall be had, to order the Sheriff to sell or hire the person or persons so convicted, to service, to any person or persons who will pay the said fine and costs for such term of time as the court may think reasonable." If the person "so sentenced and hired or sold" ran away, and was captured, he "shall, on conviction before a justice of the peace, be whipped with thirty-nine stripes and shall moreover serve two days for every one so lost."

In 1821, when a member of the Ohio Legislature, Harrison voted for an act for the punishment of certain crimes. One section provided that "when any person shall be imprisoned, either upon execution or otherwise, for non-payment of a fine or costs, or both, it shall be lawful for the Sheriff of the county to sell out such person as a servant to any person within this State, who will pay the whole amount due, for the shortest period of service."

While the Democratic speakers and newspapers were making the most of these acts, the Governor of New Hampshire, in his message to the Legislature, made a recommendation which the Whigs cited with glee. "So fluctuating have been the prices of manufactured articles in the market, that few are disposed to contract for the labor of convicts; perhaps those convicts who are mechanics can be advantageously let for particular branches of business. I would, therefore, suggest the propriety of continuing authority to hire out a part or all the convicts of a suitable term."

the reduction of prices, the scarcity of money, and the difficulty of finding work? If so, let them know that they owe their troubles to the banks and bankers. Are business men embarrassed by the want of specie change to such an extent that they are forced to take the worthless small bills of the States? If so, the banks are the cause, for they have two thirds of the specie locked up in their vaults."

Temperance people were next appealed to and asked what they, as grave and sober citizens, thought of the statement of Mr. Leonard Bacon before the annual temperance convention at New Haven? "There is," said he, "another reason why the temperance cause is retrograding. Within three or four months intemperance has become the badge of a political party. The hard-money humbug was bad enough; but the hard-cider humbug will prove more disastrous to the country. More than ten thousand men will be made drunkards in one year by the hard-cider enthusiasm." Will fathers of families, the Democrats asked, consent to have their sons join Tippecanoe clubs, and march about the streets of our cities dragging barrels of hard cider, sham forts on wheels, canoes, sticks of wood put together like a huge crow's nest and called a log cabin, and shouting like demons let loose from the infernal regions?

That the popularity of the log cabin was much abused admits of no doubt. Rum sellers found it a most profitable resort, and in many towns and cities cabins were fitted up with a bar and all the appliances of a grog shop. Against this decent Whigs protested. One cabin in particular, known as the Broadway Log Cabin, in New York City, excited much indignation. "Let cider barrels," it was said, "be adopted, if need be, as political insignia; but let them be empty. If the Whigs expect to retain in their ranks the true friends of temperance and morals their log cabins must not be converted into rum holes. That which is morally wrong cannot be politically right, and any party which shall thus outrage the consciences of the religious community need not expect its vote."

"Let it never be forgotten," said the Whigs, "that the sentiment for which the log cabin stands is of thrilling interest not merely to the cultivator of the soil, but to every poor man the country over, for the purpose of the Van Buren press when it called General Harrison the Log Cabin candidate was to throw contempt on honest poverty. Deeply do the more candid of the party now regret the sneer; but it is too late. The leaven is at work, the log cabin is woven on handkerchiefs, struck on medals, stamped on buttons, and the eyes of the whole people are turned to it as the symbol of the hardihood, independence, honest toil which have made this nation great."

"The words 'Log Cabin and Hard Cider,'" said the Democrats, "were never uttered as a sneer by any member of the Democratic party. They were uttered by a friend of Mr. Clay when he heard of the nomination of Harrison, were overheard by a correspondent of a Baltimore journal, and were published as reported. No member of the Democratic party had anything to do with the introduction of these celebrated words into the political vocabulary." *

Who originated the phrase, the Whigs cared not. The sentiment it expressed appealed strongly to the people. Scattered over all our country were millions of men and women who still lived in log cabins, or had been born in log cabins, or whose parents had lived in that humble abode. It was the home of the pioneer; it was the symbol of American hardihood, and no sneer could have been more galling than this insult to the early homes of the builders of the nation. In every city, town, and village where twenty Whig voters could be mustered, old men and young formed Tippecanoe clubs and raised log cabins to be true Whig headquarters. They stood on village greens, on vacant lots, on street corners. Beside each cabin was a cider barrel and a gourd; to the wall of each a coon skin was made fast; from each door a latchstring was always hanging out, and before the cabin, from a tall pole, waved a banner on which was painted "Harrison and Reform." Within were benches and a roughly made table heaped with the newspapers, pamphlets, and broadsides that made the literature of the campaign.

* The Globe, September 23, 1840.

Among such were the " Tippecanoe Text Book," the " Log
Cabin Song Book," " Log Cabin Anecdotes," the " Harrison Almanac," and one or two of such stanch campaign
journals as *The Log Cabin Farmer, The Log Cabin Rifle,
The Log Cabin Advocate, The Harrison Eagle, The Harrison Flag, The Harrisonian*, or, best of all, *The Log Cabin*,
which Horace Greeley edited, and which reached a circulation of eighty thousand copies.

Every ardent Whig carried a Tippecanoe handkerchief,
wore a Tippecanoe badge, or a Tippecanoe breast pin, and
hung in some conspicuous place in his home a richly ornamented certificate of membership in a Tippecanoe club, and
knew by heart the popular Tippecanoe songs.*

---

* Some stanzas from a few of the popular songs may serve as specimens :

> " Make way for old Tip, turn out, turn out !
> Make way for old Tip, turn out !
> 'Tis the people's decree,
> Their choice he shall be,
> So Martin Van Buren turn out, turn out !
> So Martin Van Buren turn out ! "

Kinderhook *vs.* Tippecanoe.
Office holders for plaintiff, Clay and Webster for defendant.
The plaintiff charges,

> " That he lives in a cabin built of logs,
> Drinks nothing but hard cider too,
> He plows his own ground, and feeds his own hogs,
> This fellow of Tippecanoe."

Webster and Clay admit all the charges.   The jury give a verdict for Tip
pecanoe whereupon

> " The Martin that made the White House his nest,
> Away with his noisy flock flew
> When he saw, come sweeping on from the West,
> The eagle of Tippecanoe."

> " Oh, know ye the farmer of Tippecanoe ? "
> The gallant old farmer of Tippecanoe ?
> With an arm that is strong and a heart that is true,
> The man of the people is Tippecanoe.
> Away in the West the fair river beside
> That waters North Bend in its beauty and pride,

This enthusiasm the Democrats met with derision, cartoons, attacks on the courage and military fame of Harrison, and the old cry of black cockade Federalism.

"Keep it before the people," said they, "that William Henry Harrison supported the Alien and Sedition laws passed by the Federalist party in the memorable reign of terror; wore the black cockade in 1800, and was one of old John Adams' officeholders for many years. Keep it before the people that he justified the administration of his chief when it sent armed soldiers among the people to stop them putting up Liberty poles, and to cut down those already erected. Keep it before the people that Harrison, in the Senate of Ohio, voted in favor of a law for selling white men into slavery,

---

And shows in its mirror the summer sky blue
Oh, there dwells the farmer of Tippecanoe.
When the clear eastern sky in the morning's light gleams
And the hills of Ohio grow warm in its beams,
When the fresh spring grass is bent down by the dew,
With his plow in the furrow stands Tippecanoe.
Hurrah for the farmer of Tippecanoe,
The honest old farmer of Tippecanoe,
With an arm that is strong and a heart that is true,
The man of the people is Tippecanoe."

"Should brave old soldiers be forgot?"

"What tho' the Hero's hard 'huge paws'
  Were wont to plow and sow?
Does that disgrace our sacred cause?
  Does that degrade him? No!
Whig farmers are our nation's nerve,
  Its bone—its very spine,
They'll never swerve—they did not swerve
  In days of old lang syne.

"No ruffled shirt, no silken hose,
  No airs does Tip display;
But like 'the pith of worth' he goes
  In homespun 'hoddin-grey.'
Upon his board there ne'er appeared
  The costly 'sparkling wine,'
But plain hard cider such as cheered
  In days of old lang syne."

a law under which a poor soldier of the Revolution could be sold to a free negro and led into captivity by his sable master. Keep it before the people that in the Territory of Indiana Harrison approved and signed such a law, to which was added the penalty of thirty-nine lashes if the white slave, male or female, sought liberty in flight and was caught; that he placed the money of the rich man and the liberty of the poor man on a level; that while the man with money could pay his fine and go free, the man without money must forfeit liberty and atone for his misfortune in chains and a dungeon. Keep it before the people that Harrison, as Governor of Indiana, approved and signed a law imposing a property qualification on voters to entitle them to vote; that he would allow the man with a freehold of fifty acres to approach the ballot box, but would keep away the man who had but forty-nine. Keep it before the people that during the last war Harrison resigned his commission in the hottest and thickest of the fight and went home; that the Senate of the United States refused to present him with a medal and a vote of thanks; that New York refused him the freedom of the city; that he is an Abolitionist and secretly in league with them; that he still hangs on to his clerkship; and that he presents the first and, let it be hoped, the last example of an aspirant for the presidential chair standing mute before the people." *

That the Northern Whigs were Abolitionists was openly asserted in an address to the people of the slaveholding States by their Representatives in Congress. " It is not," the Congressmen said, " as members of a political party that we appeal to slaveholders. A crisis has arrived which makes party interests a secondary consideration with Southern men. The time is near when it must be determined not whether the Federal or the Democratic party shall govern the country, but whether in a large part of the Union States shall exist as organized. Some States have abolished slavery; others have not. In those which have abolished slavery vast associations have grown up for the

---

* The Magician, a Van Buren campaign newspaper.

avowed purpose of attacking slavery in the States where it still exists. These associations are powerful in money and in men and control many presses zealous to spread their doctrines and strengthen their organization. The plain duty of every friend of State rights is to ignore them. Separated from the great parties which divide the people, the extravagance of their doctrines would check their increase. Unhappily this course has not been followed. That their aid has been sought and their support secured by Northern Whigs is made clear by the proceedings of Congress, of State legislatures, and of the Whig National Convention. In December, 1836, the House of Representatives having before it the resolutions of Pinckney, every Northern Whig, save four, voted against the second resolution, and every Northern Whig, save one, against the third. During the session of 1837–38 the resolution of Patton was brought to a vote. Fifty-nine Northern Whigs were for and one against it. At the session of 1839–40, on the proposition to amend the rules and insert in them the substance of Patton's resolution, sixty-four Northern Whigs voted nay and one yea. How was it with Northern Democrats? On the second of Pinckney's resolutions there were sixty-seven for and nine against; on Patton's resolution fifty-one Northern Democrats were for and fifteen against; on the motion to amend the rules twenty-seven Northern Democrats voted yea and thirty-eight no, and so did four Southern Whigs. The compact front of the South was broken, and this may justly be considered as the first fruits of the political coalition which brought about the nomination of Harrison.

" How has it been with Whigs in Northern State legislatures? In 1838 the Abolitionists of Maine petitioned the legislature to demand the abolition of slavery in the District of Columbia, and a resolution so instructing the Senators and Representatives of Maine was reported. Every Whig save two voted for it, and every Democrat save seventeen against it, and it was lost. New Hampshire, in 1839, by resolution, denied the right of Congress to meddle with the relation of master and slave. In the only vote taken, by yeas and nays, every nay save one came from a Whig. In

Vermont, in Rhode Island, in Connecticut, the story is the same. New York, under her Whig Governor and legislature, passed ' an act to extend the right of trial by jury,' and intended to prevent the recovery of every Southern slave who may reach the soil of that State. Acting under the same fatal influences the Whig Governor of New York has refused to deliver for trial three men guilty of slave stealing in Virginia. Contrast this with Democratic Pennsylvania. In the Convention of 1838, called to amend her constitution, an attempt was five times made to extend trial by jury to fugitive slaves. Every Whig, save ten or fifteen, was for it, and every Democrat, save two or three, against it.

" Look next at the Democratic State of Ohio. Recall her strong resolutions of 1839; recall her action toward Kentucky. The Abolitionists were busy enticing slaves from such counties in Kentucky as border on the Ohio River, concealing them and sending them to Canada. Kentucky appealed to Ohio to end this evil by the passage of an effective law. A bill relating to fugitives from labor from other States was brought in and passed. In both House and Senate every vote cast against it was given by a Whig. Every Abolitionist and Northern Whig in Congress supports Harrison. He was nominated by the coalition of Whigs and Abolitionists, and the Abolition press hailed his nomination as a triumph. The Southern voter was assured that Northern negroes wore log cabin breast pins and carried log cabin canes, and that in some of the Southern States the very slaves were saying they would all be free when Harrison was elected."

To the charge of Federalism the Whigs replied that Harrison had been three times appointed to office by Madison and three times by Jefferson, and that if it was wrong for Harrison to accept office at the hands of old John Adams, it was equally so for Washington, whom Adams had appointed and commissioned lieutenant-general.[*]

To the question, so often asked with great effect from the stump, " How would you like to see one of your poor neigh-

---

[*] The Globe, August 25, 1840.

bors sold as a servant to a negro?", to the charge that Harrison had approved a law which "exposed the bare backs of women and of children to the lash, and their persons to sale for inability to pay fine and costs for petty offenses," for perhaps "buying a chicken from a servant," or "trotting over a bridge when the law says it must be passed at a walk," the Whigs found it necessary to make an elaborate defense.

Indiana was not a State, they said, when the selling and whipping laws were passed, and had no penitentiary and few jails. The purpose of the laws was punishment, not reform. If a vagabond stole a settler's hog or rode off with his horse, was it not better to sell the rogue to service than burden the Territory with the cost of feeding and keeping him? That a white man could be sold to a negro was false; a law, also approved by Harrison, expressly forbade such a sale.* And were there no Southern States which had on their statute books laws providing for the sale of white men? Was it not law in Maryland that a person unable to pay a fine should remain thirty days in jail, and if during that time security for payment within six months could not be obtained, the sheriff should "sell such person at auction as a servant for a term not exceeding one year?" † Did not this act become a law of the District of Columbia in 1801? Was it not still in force? Did it not follow, therefore, that Martin Van Buren and his Locofoco friends were in favor of selling white men in the District of Columbia? If not, why had Martin Van Buren never asked for its repeal? How was it in Virginia? Why, an act on her statute book ‡ provided that a vagrant may be "hired out for the best wages that can be procured," and if he runs away "he shall be dealt with in the same manner as other runaway servants." Were not gamblers sold into service in Virginia as late as 1810? South Carolina directs that offenders may be sold for not

---

* "No negro, mulatto, or Indian, shall at any time purchase any servant other than of their own complexion, and if any of the persons aforesaid shall, nevertheless, presume to purchase a white servant, such servant shall immediately become free."—Chapter 48, Section 9. Approved September 17, 1807.

† Maryland Laws, Act of 1793, Chapter 57, Section 16.

‡ Act of February 10, 1819, January 1, 1820, R. C., Chapter 239.

more than one year. If they are such hardened rascals that nobody will buy them they may be given not less than ten nor more than thirty-nine stripes. Georgia has a similar law. There, too, vagabonds and idle and disorderly persons may be sold to service; or, if nobody will take them, they may be flogged. Is it not true that in Alabama, vagrants, black and white, male and female, may be hired out, or if nobody will buy their time, may be flogged thirty-nine lashes on the bare back? Does not the law of Louisiana provide that vagrants shall be imprisoned for from six months to three years and that the sheriff may, with the consent of a justice of the peace, bind out such offenders to householders to serve at labor for the terms of their sentences? No white slavery there! In Missouri may they not be hired out for six months at public sale? No white slavery in Missouri! On November 21, 1811, just fourteen days after the battle of Tippecanoe, the legislature of Tennessee enacted that gamblers on conviction should be sent to jail and that the sheriff, or a constable, should " sell as servants all such persons for the term of three months, the said officer giving three days' notice of the time and place of sale? " No white slavery in the South!

And what did the people of Ohio do to the men who, with Harrison, voted for the selling law? The man who brought the bill into the Ohio legislature was sent to the Senate of the United States; a man who, with Harrison, voted for the bill has twice been elected Governor of Ohio, and General Jackson appointed another a surveyor-general of the United States.*

The great Whig document of the campaign, the pamphlet that with Harrison Almanacs, Tippecanoe Text Books, and Tippecanoe Song Books, and lives of Harrison and Tyler, found its way into every log cabin, and was carried in the saddlebag of every Whig speaker on his circuit, was

---

* The Northern Man with Southern Principles, and the Southern Man with American Principles; or a view of the comparative claims of Gen. William H. Harrison and Martin Van Buren, Esq., candidates for the Presidency, to the support of Citizens of the Southern States, 1840, pp. 21–26.

A Complete Refutation of the charges against General Harrison of voting to sell white men for debt, 1840.

a speech of Charles Ogle, in the House of Representatives, on " The Royal Splendor of the President's Palace." * Ogle's description of this palace, " as splendid as that of the Cæsars, and as richly adorned as the proudest Asiatic mansion"; of the garden with its rare plants, shrubs, and parterres in the style of the Royal Gardens in England; of the men, paid with the people's money, to spend their time plucking up, by the roots, burdock and sheep sorrel; of the East Room, and the Blue Elliptical Saloon garnished with gilt mirrors big as a barn door, and with chairs that cost six hundred dollars a set, was read with astonishment at the fireside of many a plain farmer. Hoosiers, Suckers, Wolverines, and Buckeyes were asked what they thought of the democracy of a President who slept on French bedsteads, walked on Royal Wilton carpets, and sat down on French tabourets; who ate his *pâté de foie gras* and *dinde desoussé* from silver plates with forks of gold; who sipped *soupe à la Reine* with gold spoons from a silver tureen, and rode in a gilded maroon coach of British make, all in the style and fashion of those in which the richest nobles of England dashed along St. James Street, London.† In vain did the Democratic press deny these charges. They were believed by the plain people everywhere. Harrison was the humble farmer, the Cincinnatus of the West, living in a log cabin and cultivating his own land with his own hands, and Van Buren the aristocrat living in a palace, using silver plates and gold spoons, and riding in an English coach with a haughty sneer on his countenance.

As the autumn came on Whig enthusiasm rose higher and higher. Half the population quit work to attend con-

---

* Speech of Charles Ogle, April 16, 1840, National Intelligencer, July 25, 1840.
† The Log Cabin Song:
> "Let Van from his coolers of silver drink wine,
>   And lounge on his cushioned settee;
> Our man on his buckeye bench can recline
>   Content with hard cider is he!
> Then a shout for each freeman, a shout for each State,
>   To the plain, honest husbandman true,
> And this be our motto—the motto of Fate,
>   Hurrah! for old Tippecanoe."

ventions, march in procession, go to monster mass-meetings, harvest-homes, and picnics, there to be amused by the famous Whig orators and sing "Tippecanoe and Tyler, too"! With more truth than rhetoric did a Whig speaker say that the fisherman left his nets, the mechanic his tools, and the farmer his plow standing in the furrow, that he might bear his part in the great work of reform. Never had such gatherings of men, and even women, been seen in the land. The anniversary of the battle of Fort Meigs was celebrated in May by a gathering of twenty-five thousand sovereign people on the field of battle. They came on foot, on horseback, by steamboat, in conveyances of every sort, and camped for days on the field. Thousands lodged in tents, which, with their provisions, they had brought with them. Every wagon, every buggy, and there were hundreds of them, every sort of temporary shelter, from the half-faced camp to the log cabin, was filled with lodgers. Ohio, Indiana, Michigan, Kentucky, Pennsylvania, and New York were represented. On the evening before the meeting a sham siege was given by troops stationed within and about the Fort. Next morning Harrison was escorted from Perrysburg to the Fort by an immense crowd on foot, and for an hour spoke in defense of his military reputation.

But the Fort Meigs gathering was a small affair to those held in the autumn. Weeks were spent in preparation. For days before the meeting long lines of covered wagons with provisions and sleeping accommodations blocked the roads. To the great southwestern convention at Nashville, in August, came delegates from fourteen States, bearing banners inscribed with mottoes, pictures of log cabins, and of old Tip. One delegation rolled along a huge ball which had been used in a Zanesville parade. On such occasions every Whig householder in the town where the meeting was held put out of a window or fastened to his roof an American flag, to show that his latchstring was out and lodging free to any visiting Whig. The anniversary of the battle of Lake Erie was the occasion of a monster meeting at Dayton, to which Harrison came attended, from place to place, by an immense escort that grew in numbers as it marched along. At Ur-

bana " acres of people assembled " to greet and welcome him.
" Every avenue and street was full, the fields were full, and
all was joy and curiosity." From Urbana the procession
went on to Dayton, where the " body assembled covered ten
acres by actual measurement." * One hundred thousand are
said to have been present. On the same anniversary a like
jubilee was held at Bunker Hill. " From the day when the
Mayflower first landed our Pilgrim Fathers on the rocky and
inhospitable coast of Plymouth to the present time," said a
Whig journal, in true Whig style, " there never has, either
in peace or in war, been witnessed such a mighty gathering
of freemen as was yesterday displayed in the city." † Sixty
thousand at least, it was claimed, were present. Delegates
from nineteen States, carrying banners, marched through the
streets of Boston, and into Charlestown, and " ascended the
eminence consecrated by the blood of our patriotic fathers,"
where speeches were made by Webster and the Whig orators, and a Declaration of Principles adopted. These principles were a belief in the Constitution, public liberty, free
speech, free press, and popular education. Not a word was
said on the great issues of the day. The anniversary of Mac-
donough's victory on Lake Champlain was celebrated by both
parties on the same day, the Whigs at Keesville and the Democrats at Plattsburg. A convention of Whig young men at
Syracuse afforded an occasion for another procession and
another gathering of sixty thousand men.

With August came the State elections. In the West the
Whigs carried Indiana and elected their Governor by ten
thousand majority. Kentucky followed with a Whig majority of over fifteen thousand. In North Carolina the
Whigs gained a great majority in the legislature, made sure
of two Whig Senators in place of the two Democrats who
had resigned, and elected a Governor by eight thousand majority. Illinois went Democratic. Vermont went Whig,
and sent a solid Whig delegation to Congress. Next came
Maine, where the Whigs elected a Governor, to the delight

---

* Urbana Citizen, September 9, 1840.
† Boston Atlas, September 11, 1840.

of the party everywhere. " The Maine question," it was said, " has now been put and carried. Maine is redeemed. Crow, Chapman, crow! " * and a new stanza was added to " Tippecanoe and Tyler too." †

Six States, Georgia, Maryland, South Carolina, New Jersey, Pennsylvania, and Ohio, were to choose State officers and Congressmen during the first and second weeks of October. Delaware, Maryland, and Georgia, which gave Van Buren majorities at the previous elections, now went Whig, or, in the language of the hour, were redeemed from the yoke of Van Burenism.

In Ohio the Whigs rolled up a majority of seventeen thousand, elected their Governor, a Whig legislature, and twelve of the nineteen members of Congress. In New Jersey, where the broad-seal war raged hotly, the Whigs secured the Council and Assembly by a majority of more than three to one, made sure of a United States Senator and Governor, and carried the Counties of Cumberland and Middlesex, where the trouble which caused the broad-seal war began. Even in Pennsylvania important gains were made.

That Harrison would be elected seemed scarcely possible to doubt, but that the Whigs would actually sweep the country was not really expected by the most ardent Whigs. Electors of President and Vice-President were to be chosen at various dates between the close of October and the last

---

* A Democratic editor in Indianapolis, writing to a friend in a neighboring county before the election, said : " I hear that thirty voters have turned to Harrison in one neighborhood in your county. Write me if it is so and I will come down and address the people on the policy of the administration. Tell Chapman (the Democratic editor in that county) to crow. We have much to crow over." After the election his words " Tell Chapman to Crow " passed into the political vocabulary of the time, and " Crow, Chapman, crow " became a favorite Whig cry.

† " Oh, have you heard the news from Maine, Maine, Maine,
　　All honest and true ?
　For Governor, Kent, and six thousand gain
　　For Tippecanoe and Tyler, too.
　　And with them we'll beat little Van.
　　Van, Van, Van is a used-up man
　　And with them we'll beat little Van."

of November.* But when it was known, on November ninth, that of eleven States heard from, New Hampshire alone had been carried for Van Buren, that Pennsylvania and New York had chosen Whig electors, and that Harrison was sure of one hundred and fifty-three electoral votes, even the Democratic journals conceded that Harrison was elected, and the Whig press burst forth in expressions of wild delight. At last, it was said, the reign of folly, corruption, and misrule is over. What a debt of gratitude do we owe to the Great Disposer of Human Destinies, for the blessing He has vouchsafed to bestow on us. " Blessed be the Lord God who only doeth wondrous things. And blessed be His glorious name forever, and let the whole earth be filled with His glory." †

As the election news came in from the West and the South it was little more than announcements of successive

* State.	Date of Election.	No. of Electors.
Pennsylvania.............	Oct. 30th	30
Ohio....................	Oct. 30th	21
Connecticut..............	Nov. 2d	8
Rhode Island	Nov. 2d	4
Maine...................	Nov. 2d	10
New Hampshire	Nov. 2d	7
Virginia.................	Nov. 2d	23
Missouri.................	Nov. 2d	4
Illinois..................	Nov. 2d	5
Arkansas.................	Nov. 2d	3
Georgia	Nov. 2d	11
Indiana	Nov. 2d	9
Kentucky................	Nov. 2d	15
Michigan	Nov. 2d and 3d	8
New York	Nov. 2d 3d and 4th	42
Louisiana................	Nov. 3d	5
Tennessee	Nov. 3d	15
New Jersey	Nov. 3d and 4th	8
Mississippi...............	Nov. 2d and 3d	4
Massachusetts............	Nov. 9th	14
Maryland................	Nov. 9th	10
Alabama	Nov. 9th	7
Vermont	Nov. 10th	7
Delaware................	Nov. 10th	3
North Carolina	Nov. 11th	11
South Carolina...........	Legislature	11

† National Intelligencer, November 10, 1840.

Whig triumphs. By November eleventh it was known in the East that Michigan and Kentucky were in the Whig column, and by the thirteenth, that Massachusetts, Delaware, and Tennessee should be added to the list. Next came Louisiana and Mississippi. Vermont and North Carolina, and nineteen States, it was said, had pronounced sentence of condemnation on Van Buren. To the Van Buren column, meantime, were added Virginia and Missouri, and the returns stood two hundred and thirty-four electoral votes for Harrison and thirty-four for Van Buren. Alabama, Arkansas, and Illinois were then in doubt, and in South Carolina electors had not been chosen; but each chose Van Buren electors and raised his electoral vote to sixty, and the number of States he carried to seven.

On the second Wednesday in December the electoral colleges met in all the States. In Virginia one Democratic elector voted for James K. Polk for Vice-President; in South Carolina the entire college voted for Littleton W. Tazewell; in the other Van Buren States the votes were cast for Richard M. Johnson for Vice-President.

Stung by defeat the Democratic press from one end of the country to the other now gave vent to its disappointment in an outburst of unseemly rage. " The standard bearer of the Federalist and Abolition party," it was said, " has been elected, if the process by which this has been brought about may be called an election. It was a hollow mockery, a result produced not by the action of the popular will, but in spite of it." *

" For the first time in the history of the Republic the power of money has triumphed over intelligence. Democracy has been beaten by a new description of voters, some having flesh and bones and others mere men of straw. The former raked and scraped from the jails and penitentiaries had been gathered at the log-cabin rendezvous and organized for action. The latter were the pipe layers, the illegal voters, the fraudulent voters trained to perpetuate fraud by voting twice, changing their names and dress, going to different polls, putting in two votes and using every device the ingenuity of

* The Globe, November 9, 1840.

man could devise.* The Bourbons are restored! Let the people, the real betrayed people, prepare for the new reign of terror that is approaching. For the first time since the adoption of the Constitution a Democratic President has been defeated when placed before the people. Painful and mortifying as the reflection is to the mind of every true patriot, discouraging as it must be to the advocates of popular liberty, fatal as it may be to the stability of our Government, we trust in Heaven that the obsequiousness to wealth that has marked the conduct of those who have turned the scale against us will not become habitual with any great portion of the true people. As a lover of freedom and good order, an ardent advocate of the supremacy of sober thought over noise and senseless mummery, we sincerely hope the political buffoonery of 1840 will ever stand, solitary and alone, on the page of history, a damning stain on the brow of Federalism. No more may the world see coons, cabins, and cider usurp the place of principles, nor doggerel verse elicit a shout while reason is passed by with a sneer.† Our contempt is increased for Federal Whiggery and its election paraphernalia. We detest its principles, scorn its treachery, and defy its power. Does it follow that because a majority of the electors have declared against the candidates of the Democratic party, the principles of Federalism are correct? Can success sanctify error or transform wrong into right? injustice into equity, falsehood into truth, special privileges into equality, or aristocracy into Democracy? Far, very far from it. Had we been beaten, in a fair field, by such men as Webster or Clay, by manly argument, we should feel but half the mortification we do at being beaten by such a man as Harrison. And in such a fashion! We have been sung down, lied down, drunk down." ‡

"The contest of 1840," said a Whig journal, " is over. The victory is won. The people are free again. Our Republican institutions are redeemed from the grasp of tyrants. Let the people, the whole people, rejoice." #   " The morn of a real political reformation is at hand. We hail the election

---

* The Globe, November 11, 1840.   † New Era, November 9, 1840.
‡ Wheeling Times.   # Lexington (Virginia) Gazette.

of General Harrison as a most auspicious assurance of the future prosperity and happiness of our country. The sagacity and virtue of the American people are not mere empty names." *   At length we can confidently congratulate the friends of reform, lovers of law and order, supporters of Constitutional Government, on the success of the great cause of civil liberty in this country." †   " The nation is redeemed. The sun has set on Martin Van Buren and risen in all its moral splendor on William Henry Harrison.   The consummation so devoutly to be wished has been gratified." ‡ " The arrogant party which, but a short time since, set itself above all sympathy with the people, declared that the Government was bound only to take care of itself and that the people must take care of themselves, is now a miserable minority." *   " We confidently believe that General Harrison will realize the wishes and expectations of the real Whigs and his true friends; that he will serve but one term, will not remove honest and competent men from office for party reason, will not appoint members of Congress to office, nor permit the patronage of the Government to interfere with the freedom of elections." ▲   " The election is a great triumph of principle over power, of liberty over despotism, of right and justic over wrong and oppression, of prosperity and happiness over fearful and widespread ruin and desolation.   A great people have placed their seal of condemnation upon a band of the most desperate, aspiring, and unprincipled demagogues that ever graced the annals of despotism, a band of bold and reckless innovators calling themselves the democracy of the land, at whose head was Martin Van Buren, a monarchist in principle, a tyrant and a despot in practice." ◊   " It is not to be expected that a victory so important in its results, so signal and complete, should be passed over without public demonstrations of joy.   It is right that we should rejoice; but let us rejoice like men and Christians." ‡

---

* Savannah Republican.   † Bangor Whig.
‡ Providence Journal.   * New Haven Register.
▲ Green River (Kentucky) Gazette.   ◊ Toledo Blade.
                    ‡ Newark Gazette.

" For two years past," said a newspaper which claimed to be neutral, " the most ordinary operations of business have been neglected and President-making has become every citizen's chief concern.   The result being uncertain, some have been afraid to engage in new enterprises, others have retired from business, others have not dared to prosecute their business with the old vigor.   Millions of dollars will now change hands on election bets; millions of days have been taken from useful labor to listen to stump orators, and millions more to build log cabins, erect hickory poles, and march in ridiculous, degrading, mob-creating processions; millions of dollars have been wasted in soul and body destroying intemperance, in paying demagogues for preaching treason and bribing knaves to commit perjury and cast fraudulent votes.   However high the hopes inspired by the election of General Harrison they will prove to be delusive.   A national bank cannot be created; the sub-treasury cannot be repealed; the momentary expansion and speculation which the hope of these measures will create will be quickly followed by contraction, by ruin, and the prostration of the speculators." *

---

* Public Ledger, Philadelphia.

Epilogue

All this, and so much more. . . . Texas. . . . Oregon. . . . The Mormon trek to Utah. . . . Special problems of the time, like the Sub-Treasury Plan, significant in politics, if nowhere else, thick with feeling and confusion. . . . McMaster's empathetic prose reflects the heated arguments, the wild and urgent accusations and rebuttals. . . . He lets the record speak for itself: the volumes begin in the midst of things, and end with nothing decided, with no effort at summary or retrospect. . . . Yet a point of view emerges. . . . America is a land of powerful, and largely uncontrolled energies, governed by Constitutional limitations, but not confined by them. . . . America is always in danger, and its destiny is always in the hands of its broad-based citizenry. . . . It is subject to vagaries, to fads, to illusions, but its instincts are soundly directed toward unity and individual freedom. . . . As he said, in "Political Ideas in the First Half Century":

> When our forefathers threw off their allegiance to Great Britain, and founded the republic of the United States, they announced to the world certain political ideas, all of which they firmly believed, but very few of which they ventured to put in practice. They declared that all men are created equal, and endowed by their creator with the inalienable rights of life, liberty, and the pursuit of happiness; that government is constituted among men for the sole purpose of securing these rights; that it derives its just powers from the consent of the governed; and that, failing to accomplish the high purpose

for which it is established, it becomes the duty of the people to alter or destroy it. Had they attempted to apply these new truths generally, the whole social fabric would have gone to pieces. Happily they were not so applied. They were ideals to be held up and attained to gradually, and the very men whose lips were constantly heard demanding the rights of man, the inalienable rights of man, went on and set up State governments in which these rights were very little regarded. . . .

It could not have been otherwise, McMaster believed. . . . Proper government for actual circumstances had to be devised by pressure and experiment. . . . But McMaster never doubted that the American democratic enterprise grew stronger as well as more expansive. . . . Ahead, were the crises of the 1840's: the Dorr War in Rhode Island, where two governors claimed lawful title to their office, slavery and anti-slavery actions, in and out of law, the acquisition of Texas, over the doubts and protests of New Englanders, whose nightmare was six to eight slave states carved out of that domain, each with two Senators in Washington, war with Mexico, and the national crisis created by passage of the Fugitive Slave Law of 1850. Still further ahead was Kansas, and Dred Scott, and the firing on Fort Sumter. . . . Yet McMaster's faith in the American enterprise never faltered. . . . Whatever his personal views of Indians, and embattled labor, and Negroes, . . . his vast unveiling of American experience forged a weapon for understanding which he placed in the hands of those whom circumstances would present with their own crises of war, and unemployment, insecurity, and unfair administration of law, assassination, and undermined faith, in God, or country, or even humanity. . . . Crises in many cases little different from those which had earlier confronted Americans, but in other cases filled with novelties which would require all their energies, all their resources for solution. . . .